Practices,

profession and

pedagogy in accounting

Essays in honour of Bill Birkett

Edited by Jane Baxter and Chris Poullaos

SYDNEY UNIVERSITY PRESS

Published 2009 by SYDNEY UNIVERSITY PRESS
University of Sydney Library
www.sup.usyd.edu.au

National Library of Australia Cataloguing-in-Publication entry
Title: Practices, profession and pedagogy in accounting : essays
                  in honour of Bill Birkett / editors, Jane Baxter, Chris
                  Poullaos.
ISBN: 9781920899202 (pbk.)
                  9781920899462 (hbk.)
Notes: Includes index.
                  Bibliography.
Subjects: Birkett, Bill.
                  Accounting.
                  Festschriften.
Other Authors/Contributors:
                  Baxter, Jane A.
                  Poullaos, Chris
Dewey Number: 657

Printed in Australia

Contents

Foreword

It is indeed a great honour to be asked to write the foreword to this book of essays dedicated to the memory of the late Professor Bill Birkett.

I first met Bill in the mid-1980s and we struck up an immediate friendship. I was drawn to Bill's great intellect and his restless and relenting desire to push the boundaries of knowledge in management accounting and management thinking generally.

We spent many periods of relaxation debating these issues. It was one such sunny Sunday afternoon that I casually asked Bill what ever happened to Current Cost Accounting. For over two hours we vigorously debated the contribution of management accountants not only to the profitability and survival of businesses but to their strategic direction as well.

In future years, Bill very generously attributed that Sunday afternoon debate as the catalyst for the creation of the Australian Centre for Management Accounting Development (ACMAD). I however suspected that Bill had long held the desire to create such a centre to bring practitioners together to further the advancement of management accounting. This centre became a very successful network which stimulated thinking, research and provided mentoring to many management professionals.

While managing a division at Clyde Industries Limited, as an ACMAD project, Bill assisted my team to implement Activity Based Costing. This revealed striking differences in the cost of a series of manufactured products compared to the Standard Cost system.

The work of ACMAD also demonstrated to me personally the power of a network and as a direct consequence of this experience I became involved and now chair the Industry Advisory Network for the Faculty of Engineering and IT at the University of Technology in Sydney. This network has members including IBM, Oracle, Alcatel-Lucent, Worley Parsons, Leighton Holdings, Resmed, Alstom to name just a few. It has become a leading example of a university/industry linkage just as ACMAD did when Bill pioneered the concept.

Bill, I repeatedly found, had great wisdom and an enormous capacity to absorb information, as in an old saying, "The wisest mind has something yet to learn". I hasten to add that this is not always the case for academics. I often would pass a comment to Bill and then find myself replaying his answer over and over in my mind and wondering why I didn't think of that.

As I read the abstracts of the essays I could not help but think that Bill would have been proud of the authors and their contributions to the profession. In particular it made me realize how much I miss those weekend debates with Bill. I would have loved to have had his views on the causes of the global financial crisis, better corporate governance or more effective performance management systems.

Bill Birkett was an international expert in management accounting. His major work on competency-based standards for professional accountants in Australia and New Zealand is highly regarded and is still used around the world. He made a significant contribution to the accounting profession both in Australia and overseas.

The following essays are indeed a wonderful and appropriate tribute to a great man missed by many.

Mr Bruce Grey FTSE
Former Managing Director
Bishop Technology Group Limited

Notes on contributors

Dr Paul Andon

Paul Andon PhD CA is a senior lecturer at the School of Accounting at the University of New South Wales (UNSW). He has over 10 years of curriculum development and teaching experience in a range of management accounting and introductory financial accounting courses at both undergraduate and postgraduate levels. Currently, Paul teaches and researches primarily in the area of management accounting. In terms of research, he specializes in case-based methods and concentrates on investigating the situated performance (e.g. development, uses and effects) of contemporary management accounting practices. For his PhD, Paul studied the performance of 'Value for Money' appraisals for a Public Private Partnership scheme. His other research interests relate to public governance and accountability, customer profitability and valuation, risk management, and the career development of accounting professionals. Paul has published in internationally refereed journals (including *Management Accounting Research, Australian Accounting Review* and *Pacific Accounting Review*), presented his research at a range of international conferences, and has contributed to books on contemporary management accounting practice. Prior to joining UNSW, Paul was employed at PricewaterhouseCoopers in their Assurance and Business Advisory Services division, specializing in technology, communications and entertainment clients. He is also qualified as a Chartered Accountant.

Maria Barbera

Maria Barbera MCom (Hons) FCPA is now retired but was an active member of the School of Accounting at the UNSW for many years. Maria was a particularly versatile member of staff who taught auditing, financial accounting and management accounting courses. She was also seconded to CPA Australia and worked on a number of applied research projects during this period.

Maria was instrumental to the smooth functioning and success of the Australian Centre for Management Accounting Development (ACMAD), working closely will Bill Birkett and many practitioners in this arena. She played a key role by contributing to various ACMAD monographs and editing many others. The latter years of Maria's career were devoted to the development of competency standards for the internal auditing profession. Maria is still missed by her former colleagues in the School of Accounting who fondly remember her wise counsel, earthiness, youthful vigour and desire to get things done well.

Associate Professor Jane Baxter

Jane Baxter PhD FCPA is Associate Professor of management accounting in the School of Accounting at UNSW. Jane has taught and developed a number of postgraduate and undergraduate courses in this area. She is an active supervisor of research students undertaking field-based studies of a variety of management accounting practices. Jane has published in internationally refereed journals, including *Accounting, Organizations and Society, Journal of Management Accounting Research, Management Accounting Research, Behavioral Research in Accounting, Critical Perspectives on Accounting, Australian Accounting Review, Pacific Accounting Review* and *Qualitative Research in Accounting and Management*. Jane has also contributed to a number of books. She currently holds a large ARC research grant with Wai Fong Chua and Norio Sawabe. Her research interest lies in the area of critiquing and undertaking theoretically-informed management accounting fieldwork, with current projects focusing on management control systems, public-private partnerships and sustainability.

Dr Christina Boedker

Christina has over 12 years of research and industry experience with UK, US and Australian organizations. Prior to entering academia, she held positions as department head in operations and marketing management with US and UK companies. During her time at UNSW, Christina has acted as a lecturer in charge of three postgraduate units: Managing Intangible Resources, Managing Agile Organisations and Financial Accounting. Christina has led research projects on strategy and management control systems, measuring and reporting intangible resources, and innovation, leadership, culture and management with organizations such as Microsoft, the Department of Finance, the NSW Department of Lands, Westpac Banking Corporation, the Department of Education, Employment and Workplace Relations, the Victorian Government, the Business Council of Australia, and others. Christina is the Acting CEO of the Society for Knowledge Economics (SKE) and the author of the Australian Guiding Principles on Extended Performance Management and other policy and industry research papers prepared in collaboration with SKE stakeholders. Since 2005, she has assisted the SKE Board and Corporate Members to bring together industry practitioners, associations, policy makers and others to advance research into better workplace practices. Christina leads the SKE's participation in the World Intellectual Capital Initiative alongside the OECD, EBRC, European Commission, Japanese Ministry of Trade and Industry and others. Christina and the collaborating organizations and universities of the SKE received an Honourable Mention at the 2008 Business and Higher Education Roundtable Awards for Outstanding Achievement in Research and Development Collaboration. In 2006, Christina was awarded the Emerald Literati Network Awards for Excellence for her research on intellectual capital. She also holds the UK Advertising Standards Authority Award; the Mindshift Consulting Group Prize; Saunders Harris' Prize for Outstanding Academic Achievement; the Carlson Companies' Award; MGSM's Award for Competitive Intelligence; and MGSM's Award for Human Resources Management.

Linda Chang

Linda Chang is a lecturer in the School of Accounting, UNSW. She teaches second- and third-year courses in management accounting. Linda is currently enrolled in a PhD program with Professor Ken Trotman and Associate Professor Mandy Cheng as her supervisors, and has published articles in international accounting journals such as *Accounting, Organizations and Society*, and *Management Accounting Research*. Her research interests include studying the impact of management controls on intra- and inter-firm negotiations, management of knowledge and intellectual capital in professional service firms, and organization innovation.

Professor Robert Chenhall

Robert Chenhall is Professor of Accounting and Finance in the Department of Accounting and Finance, Monash University, Clayton, Victoria, Australia. Robert's research has focused mainly on theory-based, empirical studies in management accounting employing organizational and behavioural frameworks. Methods have included survey-based, case-based and experimental approaches. His research has examined conditions in which different types of management control systems are effective and how those systems are implicated in strategic and organizational change. He has published a wide selection of articles in professional and prestigious academic journals and is on the editorial boards of a large number of accounting journals. He has assisted with implementing accounting innovations in a variety of Australian organizations in both private and public sectors.

Professor Wai Fong Chua

Wai Fong Chua is the Senior Associate Dean of the Australian School of Business at UNSW. She has been a Professor at UNSW since 1994 and was Head of the School of Accounting from 2000–2006. She was recruited to UNSW by Professor Bill Birkett. Wai Fong is a Fellow of the Academy of Social Sciences of Australia and holds an honorary doctorate from the University of Jyvaskyla and a PhD and First Class Honours from the University of Sheffield. She teaches and researches primarily in the area of management accounting. Her current research interests include the connections between accounting and strategizing, the management of inter-organizational relationships, management accounting change and the historical professionalization of accounting. She is a member of several editorial boards including *Contemporary Accounting Research, Journal of Management Accounting Research* and *Critical Perspectives on Accounting*. Wai Fong is also an editor on the board of *Accounting, Organizations and Society*.

Professor Frank Clarke

Frank Clarke is Emeritus Professor of Accounting at the University of Newcastle and Honorary Professor of Accounting at the University of Sydney. He has held appointments at the University of Sydney, University of Glasgow,

University of Canterbury, and Lancaster University. He is a past editor and currently a consulting editor of *Abacus*, an author or co-author of nine books and numerous articles in refereed and business journals. He is a frequent presenter at international conferences and contributor to the financial press (with Dean).

Bill Connell

Bill Connell was Chair of the Business Committee of International Federation of Accountants (IFAC) from 2000 to 2006. He was also on the Chartered Institute of Management Accountants (CIMA) Council until 2006 and chaired their Technical and International Committees. He worked for the BOC Group PLC for 40 years and was their worldwide Director of Risk Management. He sponsored the BOC finance management program and mentored the graduates. The program won five awards in the UK. His current interests are strategy and risk and he helps companies implement a Strategic Scorecard.

Dr Rod Coyte

Dr Rodney Coyte of the University of Sydney specializes in research combining strategy and the management of resource development and deployment in organizations. In his PhD he examined how teamwork structure affected organizational resource management and the effectiveness of strategic change. Rod's recent research explores: organizational structure and change factors enhancing situated learning and its effect on intellectual capital development in organizations; the effect of performance-evaluation systems on information-sharing behaviour and strategic alignment; and processes affecting change in management accounting practices. Rod has published on the role of empowered teams, shareholder value measurement techniques and knowledge development processes. He has managed operations as an Information Systems Manager, and conducted strategic and operational planning as a Business Planning Manager with the Mars Corporation. He also has extensive experience in information technology and management consulting to a diverse range of organizations in Australia and South-East Asia.

Professor Graeme Dean

Graeme Dean, Professor of Accounting and formerly Head of Discipline of Accounting at the University of Sydney, has held visiting appointments at several overseas universities including University of Glasgow, University of Frankfurt, Munich University and University of Canterbury. From 1994–2008 he was the sole editor of *Abacus*, the fourth oldest and one of the leading Anglo-American accounting academic journals. He is currently its co-editor. Dean has published several books and over 40 refereed journal articles. He is a frequent presenter at international conferences and contributor to the financial press (with Clarke).

Associate Professor Maria Dyball

Maria Dyball is an Associate Professor in Accounting at Macquarie University in Sydney, Australia. Maria's wide-ranging research interests include the accounting profession, regulation and history. She completed her PhD at the School of Accounting of the UNSW after working in industry as a joint venture and financial analyst, and auditor.

Associate Professor Elaine Evans

Elaine Evans is an Associate Professor in the Department of Accounting and Finance at Macquarie University. She has held academic positions in accounting at the University of Western Sydney and ANU, and in health services accounting at the UNSW. Her current research interests include financial reporting in Australia under International Financial Reporting Standards (IFRS), corporate governance, the interface between academic education and professional training for accountants, the accounting profession in Australia and the integration of graduate attributes into the accounting curriculum.

Professor Michael Gaffikin

Michael Gaffikin is Emeritus Professor of Accounting and Finance at the University of Wollongong, Australia and Adjunct Professor of Accounting at the University of Canterbury, New Zealand. His research interests are accounting theory, the development of accounting thought and alternative methodologies for accounting research and theory, accounting history, financial accounting regulation and Islamic accounting. He has supervised a large number of accounting doctoral candidates and has published widely on accounting theory and history. He serves on the editorial boards of several international accounting journals. Despite being officially retired from full time academic life he continues to teach, research and publish in accounting and to present at international accounting conferences.

Professor Sid Gray

Sidney J. Gray is Professor of International Business and Co-Director of the International Entrepreneurship Research Group in the Faculty of Economics and Business at the University of Sydney. He was formerly a professor at the UNSW, Warwick Business School in England and the University of Glasgow in Scotland. Sid's main teaching and research interests are in the areas of international accounting and corporate transparency, international business strategy and cross-cultural management. In 2006, he was elected a Fellow of the Academy of the Social Sciences in Australia for distinction in accounting research. He is a co-founder and an Associate Editor of *the Journal of International Financial Management and Accounting* (US). From 1992–97 he served as President of the International Association for Accounting Education and Research (IAAER). He also served as a member of the Accounting Standards Committee (ASC) for the UK and Ireland, the peak standard setting body, from 1984–87.

Professor Kim Langfield-Smith

Kim Langfield-Smith is Deputy Dean (Research) and Professor of Management Accounting in the Faculty of Business and Economics at Monash University. She has obtained a Bachelor of Economics from the University of Sydney, Master of Economics from Macquarie University, and a PhD from Monash University, and she is a Fellow of CPA Australia and the Institute of Chartered Accountants in Australia. Her research interests are in management control systems, and include the design and implementation of performance measurement systems; the relationship between management control systems and organizational strategy; and the design of management control systems in inter-firm relationships. She has published in accounting, management and psychology journals and has been awarded research grants from the Australian Research Council and other bodies. Kim is an active member of the accounting profession. She sits on the Education Advisory Committee of CPA Australia and is the nominee of CPA Australia and ICAA on the International Accounting Education Standards Board (IAESB).

Professor Anne Lillis

Anne Lillis is Professor of Management Accounting and Deputy Head of the Department of Accounting and Business Information Systems at the University of Melbourne. Anne researches and teaches in management accounting. Her research interests focus on the design and behavioural influence of performance management and control systems, corporate downsizing and cost management practice. Anne's work is predominantly conducted using field interviews with practicing managers. Anne has both published her work and participated in editorial boards of leading journals. She has held senior roles within the Management Accounting Section of the American Accounting Association. Anne is also Chair of the Management Accounting Advisory Committee and a member of the Education Board of the Institute of Chartered Accountants in Australia.

Dr Rosina Mladenovic

Rosina Mladenovic is a senior lecturer in accounting within the Faculty of Economics and Business at the University of Sydney. Rosina is recognized as an outstanding teacher and in 2006 she was awarded a National Teaching Award (Carrick Citation) for Outstanding Contributions to Student Learning. In 2009 she was awarded both the Faculty and University outstanding teaching awards. Rosina is also an accomplished researcher, receiving four Best Paper awards in the last seven years and has an impressive record of published education research including numerous papers in top accounting education and general higher education journals. Rosina serves on the editorial board of four international journals and is an associate editor of *Accounting Education: An International Journal.* Rosina's research interests include environmental reporting, ethics, curriculum design, assessment, students' learning approaches and students at risk of failure.

Associate Professor Richard Morris

Richard D. Morris is Associate Professor of Accounting at UNSW. His main research interests are in financial accounting, international accounting and corporate transparency, and accounting history. These include the determinants of corporate transparency in Asian countries and the impact of the introduction of IFRS in 2005, for which he and Sid Gray (University of Sydney) have been awarded prestigious ARC Discovery Grants. His work has appeared in many international and professional journals, monographs and book chapters. Richard teaches financial accounting to undergraduate and postgraduate students. He is also an experienced supervisor of undergraduate and postgraduate research theses.

Professor Jan Mouritsen

Jan Mouritsen is Professor of Management Control at the Copenhagen Business School, Denmark. His research focuses on management technologies and management control in various organizational and social contexts. His research is empirical and attempts to develop new ways of understanding the role and effects of controls and financial information in organizations and society. He is interested in translations and interpretations made of (numerical) representations (e.g. as in budgets, financial reports, non-financial indicators and profitability analysis) throughout the contexts they help to illuminate. Other topics of interest include intellectual capital and knowledge management, technology management, operations management, new accounting and management control. Jan Mouritsen is currently an editorial board member of more than 20 academic journals in the area of accounting, operations management, IT and knowledge management, and management generally, and he has published in journals including *Accounting, Organizations and Society*; *Management Accounting Research*; *Accounting, Auditing and Accountability Journal*; and *Critical Perspectives on Accounting*.

Tam Pham

Tam graduated from UNSW in 2002. She completed her CA in May 2005. On graduating from UNSW, she joined Ernst & Young as an auditor in the banking and finance sector for a couple of years. She changed her career path to management accounting and worked for UBS for a period of time. Currently, Tam is a financial accountant at QBE Insurance Group Ltd.

Associate Professor Chris Poullaos

Chris Poullaos is Associate Professor of Accounting at the University of Sydney. His work on the history of the accounting profession in Australia, Britain, Canada, South Africa and the Philippines has appeared in *Accounting, Organizations and Society*; *Abacus*; *Accounting, Auditing & Accountability Journal*; *Critical Perspectives on Accounting*; and several monographs.

Associate Professor Prem Ramburuth

Prem Ramburuth is currently Associate Dean Education in the Australian School of Business, UNSW. She is also Associate Professor of International Business and has researched and taught extensively in the areas of cross-cultural and diversity management in business and higher education. She was Associate Dean Undergraduate Programs, Head of the School of Organisation and Management and Foundation Director of the Education Development Unit in the Australian School of Business, a unit she established to address the diversity of staff and student needs that emerged as a result of the internationalization of Australian higher education. She is the recipient of four teaching awards for her innovations in teaching, including a recent Australian Learning and Teaching Council (ALTC) Citation for outstanding contribution to student learning, a UNSW Vice-Chancellor's Award for Teaching Excellence, the inaugural Pearson ANZAM Management Educator of the Year Award, and National Finalist in the Australian Awards for University Teaching.

Peter Roebuck

Peter Roebuck is an associate head and senior lecturer at the School of Accounting, UNSW. Peter's role encompasses the school's highly successful Co-

op Program through which major Australian companies provide scholarships
and work experience opportunities to a number students. Peter is a chartered
accountant and is actively involved in the Institute of Chartered Accountants
in Australia. In the past he was a member of State Council, a Chairman of the
Accounting/Auditing Panel and a member of the Continuing Education
Committee of ICAA. He is currently a member of the National Careers and
Marketing Committee. He is also Chairman of the Academic Review Committee of the Institute of Internal Auditors – Australia and a member of the
Education Committee of the Institute of Internal Auditors Inc. Peter's teaching interests focus primarily on the area of auditing and assurance and he is
the co-author of a widely used case-study-based teaching resource, *Case
studies in auditing and assurance* (with N Martinov). Peter's research interests
include the audit review process, audit reporting and other assurance services as well as the development of competencies for the internal audit
profession.

Associate Professor David Smith

David Smith is Associate Professor of Management Accounting in the Department of Accounting and Finance, Monash University, Australia. His
current research interests include the social and behavioural implications of
management control system (MCS) design and use, the use of MCS in inter-
organizational relationships (such as outsourcing arrangements and supply
chains), and the use of MCS in non-government organizations.

1

Embodying a life of praxis

Jane Baxter (UNSW) and Chris Poullaos (University of Sydney)

Abstract

This chapter introduces a volume celebrating the manifold contributions of the late Bill Birkett in his various roles as teacher, administrator, researcher, intellectual, thought leader, institution builder and colleague in the academic and professional domains. Engagement between research and practice was a notable feature of his praxis. It is reflected in the chapters that follow. In addition to a succinct account of Bill's career highlighting the distinctiveness of his praxis and research agenda, this chapter provides a brief outline of the contributed chapters.

This volume is presented as a celebration of the intellectual legacies of the late Professor William (Bill) Birkett. Bill was 64 years old when he passed away in August 2004 after a sudden and brief illness. At the time of his death, he was the Executive Dean of the Faculty of Law, Business and Creative Arts at James Cook University (JCU) in Townsville in Northern Queensland, Australia. In this role, Bill devoted his relatively recent 'retirement' to a continuation of the activities that had established and distinguished his long career as a major intellectual figure in the discipline of accounting in Australia: Bill was reforming curricula and programs of studies; Bill was encouraging staff to think rigorously and theoretically about their research; and Bill was central to the institution (re-)building processes of his faculty. In addition, and perhaps even more importantly, Bill had become a source of great personal support, friendship and inspiration for many with whom he worked. Although Bill had worked at JCU for only two years, the sheer pace and visionary nature of his work was such that the impact of his death was felt as acutely within JCU as it was amongst the many colleagues and friends that he had garnered over the previous 40-odd years of his academic career.

Bill commenced his academic career in 1962 as an associate lecturer in accounting at the University of New South Wales (UNSW) in Kensington, Sydney. Bill was attracted to UNSW by the work and interests of the late Professor Bill Stewart who, like Bill, was keen to explore the connections between management studies and the discipline of accounting. Whilst Bill had worked prior to this as an accounting trainee for Australian Iron and Steel Pty Ltd (which is now part of BlueScope Steel), it may be conjectured that this early intellectual sojourn at UNSW had developed and ignited Bill's personal appreciation for both management and accounting, providing an opportunity to reflect on his previous work experiences and his emerging theoretical framing of accounting practices. This curiosity to explore and experiment with the fusion of management and accounting remained with Bill throughout his career (see IFAC 2001), leaving a stamp on his work as a researcher, teacher and member of the accounting profession. The chapter contributed by Bill Connell provides further insight into this in relation to Bill's development of competency standards for management accountants on behalf of the International Federation of Accountants (IFAC). Similarly, the chapter authored by Peter Roebuck and Maria Barbera highlights this fusion of management and accounting in terms of the competency frameworks that Bill and his team engineered for the Institute of Internal Auditors (IIA).

During 1964, Bill returned to his intellectual 'home' at the University of Sydney as a lecturer in accounting. Bill had a strong and enduring affinity with the theoretical and research-based ethos of Sydney University (see Birkett & Walker 1972). He had been awarded a BEcon (Hons) from this university in 1962. During his tenure as a lecturer at Sydney University, he also worked towards, and was admitted to the degree of a Master of Economics (via research in accounting) in 1968. Whilst his thesis for this higher degree focused on accounting and auditing as distinct but related areas of practice (see Birkett 1967), the contents are quite exceptional to a contemporary reader because of the breadth and nature of the literature that informed Bill's typification of accounting and auditing work. There are strong influences from philosophical, sociological and psychological writings – pre-empting debates which did not garner momentum in our discipline for a number of years to come (Chua 1986). This is consistent with a common observation made by those familiar with Bill's particular perspective on accounting research and practice: he was a visionary ahead of his time (see Mladenovic's and Coyte's contributions in this publication). The reflections of Wai Fong Chua in her chapter on the framing of situated practices, which is drawn from a paper that she co-authored with Bill over 20 years ago, illus-trates the prescience of many of his ideas and projects when read in the context of the emerging research agenda in management accounting and organizational studies.

Bill stayed at the University of Sydney for ten years, during which time he rose to the rank of a senior lecturer. This period sharpened his intellectual acuity, drawing him into the exciting academic milieu sustained by the pres-ence of Professor Ray Chambers, the Foundation Chair of Accounting at the University of Sydney. Not only was Chambers developing a formidable repu-tation as a scholar of intellectual renown, but he created a space in which rigorous research was respected and encouraged. The contribution from Michael Gaffikin outlines the legacy of Bill's association with Ray Chambers. Similarly, we are also fortunate to be able to include a chapter jointly au-thored by Graeme Dean and Frank Clarke, who were colleagues of Bill's at Sydney University in those early and heady days of the emergence of ac-counting as a research-based discipline within Australian universities. Likewise, we are pleased to have received the chapter contributed by Sid Gray who was once an honours student working under the supervision of Bill Birkett at this institution. Sid's co-author, Richard Morris, worked with Bill later at UNSW and Tam Pham became a research associate of both Gray and Morris.

It was the next phase of Bill's career, however, as the Foundation Head of the School of Financial and Administrative Studies at Kuring-gai College of Advanced Education (now part of the University of Technology, Sydney) that cemented Bill's reputation as a leader and institution builder in the field of accounting. After assuming this newly created position in 1974, and within a relatively short span of seven years, Bill had overseen the development of a suite of courses and degree programs that were regarded as innovative, pro-vocative and relevant. Bill was also instrumental in hiring a number of young academics with strong research skills and often radical views. Whilst this demonstrated the extent of Bill's academic tolerance and curiosity for differ-ent perspectives and paradigms in accounting and business-related spheres of research, the legacy of Bill's tenure at Kuring-gai College of Advanced Education cannot be underestimated – even today. Many staff recruited by Bill during the 1970s went on to become thought leaders in the fields of accounting, communication, finance, management, health administration, policy and sociology. There are many prominent researchers and academic administrators within Australian universities who entered academe as a result of the tolerance, foresight and intellectual values of Bill Birkett.

In 1982 Bill was appointed a Professor of Accounting at UNSW, a posi-tion that he occupied until his retirement in 2002. Arguably, it was this period of Bill's career that consolidated and highlighted his mature capacities as a teacher, mentor, researcher, administrator, intellectual, thought leader, institution builder and valued colleague. Many of the contributors to this book were fortunate to have benefited from an association with Bill during this time. Whilst Bill's achievements at UNSW are many, there were two main areas of accomplishment that are both particularly significant and relevant to this volume of essays: first, Bill's leadership in the field of man-agement accounting; and second, his support for accounting and business education.

In his capacity as Professor of Accounting, Bill was instrumental in ener-gizing the field of management accounting. In doing so, he exerted his charismatic and compelling energy within academe, as well as within net-works of practitioners and the professional bodies. He did this in various ways, but always as a result of leading by personal example, especially with respect to his work ethic. Despite his personal drive to realize a particular vision for management accounting, Bill extended significant levels on aca-demic support and friendship to others engaged in the revitalization of management accounting practice and research. At a grass-root level, Bill managed the development of a research-based culture within the field of management accounting at UNSW. He supported a variety of forms of management accounting research, ranging from quantitative to qualitative re-search methods, mentoring a range of research projects within the school. However, there was little doubt that Bill held a soft spot and gained immense personal satisfaction from historical forms of (management) accounting research (see Birkett & Walker 1971). Maria Cadiz Dyball, a colleague of Bill's who benefited from his wise counsel at important junctures in her development as a researcher, wrote a chapter for this volume exemplifying the historical curiosity encouraged by Bill within the School of Accounting at UNSW. However, it was the concurrent establishment of the Australian Cen-tre for Management Accounting Development (ACMAD), and Bill's appointment as its Foundation Director in 1990, that enabled Bill's energy and vision for management accounting to be channelled within a much broader and diffuse network of both academics and practitioners. ACMAD became a vehicle for Bill to both refine and communicate his vision for the future of management accounting (see Birkett et al. 1992). This is ably dis-tilled in the chapter by Rodney Coyte that outlines Bill's vision for strategic resource management practices in contemporary organizations. ACMAD also became a way for Bill to encourage field-based research in the area of management accounting (see Barbera et al. 1999). The chapter by Anne Lillis, as well as the chapter by Paul Andon, Jane Baxter and Linda Chang, convey the legacies of the type of organization-based research encouraged by ACMAD.

Bill's increasing involvement in university administration at UNSW, espe-cially in his position as Associate Dean, Development at the Faculty of Commerce and Economics (1993–2002), was characterized by an unflinch-ing commitment to the development of sound educational practices, innovative educational programs and the provision of infrastructure to sup-port student learning and the development of basic business and generic skills. Of central importance to this was Bill's championing and implementa-tion of the Educational Development Unit (EDU), which remains a vital and important part of the Australian School of Business (ASB) at UNSW, provid-ing resources both for staff and ASB's diverse student cohort. Bill's understanding of educational issues reinforced his intellectual capacity, ver-satility, thirst for knowledge and desire to address problems with practical solutions – in addition to the importance that he placed on the student experience at UNSW. Prem Ramburuth, who was an important figure in the day-to-day activities of the EDU when Bill was the Associate Dean, has written a chapter drawing on her research conducted within this context. Bill also supervised two PhD students who investigated educational issues in the field of accounting. These former students, Rosina Mladenovic and Elaine Evans, have both graciously provided chapters which are reflective of Bill's influence on their doctoral and continuing research interests.

Bill was a significant figure at a local level in terms of the Australian institutions where he worked and the web of interactions that he sustained and orchestrated within the profession and amongst professionals. He was also an influential thinker, shaping professional policy and practices on a global scale. In addition to his roles on the editorial boards of *Management Accounting Research* (see Baxter 2004) and *Accounting Education: An International Journal* (see Mladenovic & Poullaos 2005), which focus on the dissemination of quality internationally referred research papers in accounting, Bill was influential on the international stage as a result of his involvement with IFAC. Within Australia, Bill was a Fellow of CPA Australia and a member of several committees of this body, notably the National Task Force on Professional Specialisation. Such activities provided a springboard for his nomination in 1993 as Australia's Technical Advisor to the Financial and Management Accounting Committee (FMAC) of IFAC. It was in this capacity that Bill drafted the International Management Accounting Practice Statement No.1 *Management accounting concepts* (FMAC 1998), as well as the so-called *Study 12* (IFAC 2002), which outlined competency standards for management accountants. This was followed by a series of monographs, referred to previously, articulating a competency framework for internal auditing (see Birkett et al. 1999a, 1999b, 1999c, 1999d). These key documents focused on the global profession, and consolidated and extended the frameworks that Bill initially articulated in the early 1990s through his work for the Australian and New Zealand accounting professions on the development of competency standards in the fields of auditing, external reporting, insolvency and reconstruction, management accounting, taxation, and treasury (see Birkett 1992a, 1992b).

Given Bill's sustained achievements within the field of accounting over a number of years it came as no surprise when CPA Australia inaugurated an annual lecture series in his honour and memory. This is an important event for Bill's family and many former colleagues and friends. These free public lectures have been held as part of CPA Australia's annual congress. Robert Chenhall and Kim Langfield-Smith have both delivered the Birkett Memorial Lecture. Both Chenhall and Langfield-Smith were connected to Bill through the activities of the Victorian division of ACMAD, as well as through their participation in research projects that benefited from ACMAD's connections to a range of leading practitioners and interesting case organizations. The chapters contributed by Rob Chenhall and Kim Langfield-Smith (the latter in conjunction with David Smith) convey the themes of their public lectures – that is, performance management and supply chain management respectively. Jan Mouritsen's chapter, written with Christina Boedker, is also based on the theme of his contribution to this lecture series. Their chapter addresses the area of intellectual capital reporting, an aspect of practice that Bill was quick to bring to the attention of the members of the ACMAD network.

Despite the varying institutional locations and emphases in the work of Bill across his distinguished career, his different roles and projects were united by the way in which these activities embodied a commitment to practice. Bill Birkett's praxis was driven by his strong, unique personal vision of leading edge issues at particular times. (The chapters by Paul Andon, Jane Baxter and Linda Chang, Rob Chenhall, Anne Lillis, Kim Langfield-Smith and David Smith, and Jan Mouritsen and Christina Boedker are reflective of issues that Bill was instrumental in championing within Australian curricula, research and professional dialogues.) His vision linked the domains of practice and research dialectically: change in practice was to be achieved (in part) through research and research would be enriched and challenged by ongoing engagement with shifts in practice. Bill Connell was one practitioner challenged by Bill's theoretical approach while academic colleagues were at times cautioned that the issues they were debating passionately had been rendered obsolete by movement in the field of practice. The academic connection was, however, to reflect the best of what counted as academic rigour notwith-standing major (and probably irreconcilable) ontological, methodological and ideological differences between academic 'tribes'. Such differences could be tolerated, encouraged, bracketed, juxtaposed in a state of creative tension, not only because they might move academia into new territory but also because they might shed new light on practice and for practice. The variety of research perspectives apparent in this volume readily illustrates this point.

At times the academic reflection Bill encouraged and practised might be deep and/or iconoclastic (Michael Gaffikin's and Wai Fong Chua's chapters are written in this spirit). At other times it might take place within the bounds of a particular research tradition. Overall, Bill's preference was work-ing for change in both academic and practice domains from within, by promoting ongoing and simultaneous revitalization of both (Rodney Coyte's chapter is reflective of this aspect of Bill's praxis).

For Bill operating at the edge of both research and practice necessarily involved a historical and global consciousness that might sensitize both researcher and practitioner to the extent and intensity of change and to the factors and directionality that, intuitively, 'had the momentum' on which a vision of the future might fruitfully be based. 'Now' was the contemporary space of action in which that vision might be enacted. The different contri-butions of Graeme Dean and Frank Clarke, Maria Dyball, Elaine Evans, Bill Connell, Tam Pham, Richard Morris and Sid Gray, and Peter Roebuck and Maria Barbera explicitly reflect this side of Bill's thought and praxis. Indeed, Rosina Mladenovic's piece with Bill is, in part, a historical (and methodologi-cal) excursion into the evolution (and possibly diminishing future) of a particular research instrument used in educational research.

Combining the above predilections with the variety of Bill's work roles helps to explain the eclecticism in both his interests and the contributions contained in this volume with respect to the topics covered. If Bill was about to (re-)design a university subject (or sequence of subjects or a whole degree program) then 'of course' he would look at the most recent education re-search. If, as an academic leader, he were managing a team of teachers then the same point would apply. If he were restructuring an academic depart-ment or a faculty then 'naturally' he would examine the literature on organizational design. Prem Ramburuth's contribution is illustrative. She outlines research that Bill sponsored to examine students' experiences which both informed and were informed by his development of faculty infrastructure to support student learning in business education at UNSW. Across these various disciplines and sites of practice he would form a view (not to mention a diagram!) of the big picture and the little one, the relationship between structure and agency, the nexus between the detailed observation and the abstract synthetic constructs, the link between panorama (see Latour 2005, Mouritsen & Boedker in this publication) and practice.

Notwithstanding this capacity for praxis, there is little doubt that Bill was held in high esteem because of his intellectual capacity. Bill was a genuine and talented scholar. Bill's scholarship was distinctive and he developed a unique research identity. Moreover, Bill's research was motivated by a well-articulated sense of its trajectory. His research was neither faddish nor imitative. Bill documented the purposes underscoring his scholarship in an article that he authored for *Management Accounting Research* (Birkett 1998). In this article, he set out explicitly the fundamental research questions that concerned him as a scholar in the field of management accounting. (This was the main focus of his scholarly activity at this stage.) Bill wrote:

- What signification/meaning is invested in a label such as 'management accounting' at different times and in different locales?

- With a label such as 'management accounting' as a frame of reference, what relationships are sustained between facets/forms of practice, work technologies, social institutions and forms of inquiry?

- Can transformative points/periods be distinguished historically in different locales in the overarching set of relationships drawn together under the label 'management accounting'?

- How can, or should one 'read' culturally specific accounts of such relationships or transformations, from relatively global perspectives (e.g. from a European perspective, or from an Anglo-Saxon perspective)? (Birkett 1998, p488).

The above research questions highlight Bill's complex and nuanced appreciation of management accounting. The first research question indicates a desire to explore the different ways in which the signifier 'management accounting' is vested with local significance. The second question outlines a preoccupation with both typifying and untangling the complex and mutually constitutive interplay of highly situated, local management accounting practices and the professional, educational, and research institutions that are sustained by and sustain these practices. As stated in the third question, Bill was also interested in transformations and changes in management accounting work. The final question highlights the important role of typification and generalization in Bill's research (see Baxter & Chua 2006).

Significantly and substantively, Bill's commitment to praxis is evidenced by his examination of these particular research questions. He both researched management accounting practice *and* actively intervened in its realization. Bill's leadership of ACMAD and his involvement with a range of professional bodies (such as CPA Australia, ICAA, ICANZ, FMAC/IFAC, and IIA) were critical to his accomplishment of praxis. Such institutional ties enabled Bill to mobilize a view of management accounting as a form of strategic resource management, which is embedded in a series of global narratives in the form of various competency studies.

The legacy of Bill's life of praxis and the particular foci of his research agenda have sustained a number of traces and legacies that continue to infuse the research activities of his former colleagues, students and professional associates, as well as those who have been drawn into the intellectual spaces sustained by this network of researchers. We are pleased to present 16 essays from those connected to Bill's life and work, whilst providing contemporary insights into his interests in relation to accounting as practices, profession and pedagogy.

Chapter 2, by Bill with Wai Fong Chua, is based on research conducted during the early years of her career. This chapter mounts an argument that it is important to research accounting 'as it is practised'. While we are familiar with calls to examine practices using field-based research methods, they also explore a much less familiar terrain – that of the typification of situated accounting practices. Birkett and Chua propose that an understanding of accounting 'as it practised' involves an articulation and comparison of the 'situations' of practices and their frames, with the latter concept being used to refer to the rules and codes embedded in a situation. Their frame analysis aims to link local accounting practices with institutionalized cognitive and social orders.

Chapter 3 is written by Michael Gaffikin, a former colleague of Bill's at Sydney University. He draws upon the philosophy of Martin Heidegger to urge accounting academics and practitioners to think more deeply about their respective crafts to create a 'being' for the discipline of accounting which distinguishes it from economics, finance and law, frees it from the epistemological imprimatur of the physical sciences, positivism and analytical philosophy and tempers the worldly demands of capital. What is required is an understanding of its essence (of whose interests are to be served and of which societal values are to be articulated, promoted and enacted) rather than (just) a technical debate about the 'things' to be researched and reported.

In chapter 4, Graeme Dean and Frank Clarke acknowledge the influence of Bill's advocacy of a historical approach to contemporary problems on their research; an epistemological position that remained an ongoing link between Bill's thought and the 'Sydney School' inspired by Ray Chambers. They reflect on how and why their own work has had a strong historical bent; illustrating and commenting upon the potentials and pitfalls of historical research on price-level changes, corporate collapses and the functions of accounting.

Chapter 5, authored by Richard Morris, Tam Pham and Sid Gray, examines transparency and corporate governance in Malaysia after the Asian financial crisis of 1997–98 with a view to assessing whether there have been improvements since the crisis and the influential factors involved. Both mandatory compliance and voluntary disclosures have improved since the crisis but are still relatively low. The levels of and changes in disclosure are significantly positively associated with the firm's size. Mandatory compliance is higher for companies that raised debt or equity finance, had more small shareholders and were more diversified. While the engagement of Big Five auditors has expanded since the crisis, transparency does not appear to have been enhanced as a result. While Malaysian firms have adopted more corporate governance mechanisms since the crisis, the results suggest they may be substitutes for and not complements of transparency.

In chapter 6, Maria Cadiz Dyball examines the role of government accounting systems as a formal mode of rationality in the early years of the Philippine tobacco monopoly (1766–99). Accounting played an enabling role *via* an elaborate system of control, surveillance and punishment deployed by the Spanish colonial state to increase its revenues. While the full potential of accounting appears not to have been completely attained, it was complicit in perpetuating a colonial project of domination and extraction of revenues from its colonized peoples.

Chapter 7, penned by Rob Chenhall, focuses on the salient contemporary topic of the development of integrative performance management systems, which are an increasingly vital part of organizational functioning. This chapter contains a comprehensive review of relevant research literature related to this topic area. While the Balanced Scorecard has provided a high profile example of the development of an integrative performance management system that has been the focus of an increasing number of accounting research studies, Chenhall's chapter has a much broader focus. He demonstrates the importance of related studies in the areas of manufacturing, marketing and human resource management to an understanding of this topic. Chenhall also addresses a number of the criticisms of the design and the use of the Balanced Scorecard as an exemplar of an integrated performance management system.

Chapter 8, by Jan Mouritsen and Christina Boedker, focuses on intellectual capital statements, a form of extended performance reporting. From an empirical perspective, Mouritsen and Boedker outline the changing intellectual capital reporting practices of the New South Wales Department of Lands, a government department. This case study provides an interesting insight into the experimentation that accompanies practitioners' attempts to report an organization's human, structural and relational forms of intellectual capital. Mouritsen and Boedker argue that intellectual capital statements enable an important form of visibility with respect to an organization's knowledge resources. While such reporting distances knowledge from its local origins, intellectual capital statements and their narratives also construct a 'panorama of achievement' that facilitates knowledge management.

Chapter 9, written by Kim Langfield-Smith and David Smith, addresses performance measurement systems that aim to enhance the performance of supply chain management. The authors review the nature of supply chain management and stress the importance of managing key processes involved in the horizontal linkages of a supply chain. By way of an example of a Melbourne-based Australian supply chain involved with the production and use of textiles for seating in the automotive industry, the authors demonstrate that performance measurement can lead to improvements across the supply chain. However, this creates significant challenges for management accountants who need to become involved in the design and operation of performance measurement systems that span organizational boundaries.

Chapter 10, written by Anne Lillis, reflects on her personal experiences as a management accounting researcher documenting the impact of accounting performance measurement processes on managerial behaviour. She explores the enduring significance of the 'folly of rewarding A while hoping for B'. To do so, Lillis recounts evidence from three research studies. The first study examines the impact of capital market based performance measures on managerial decision making. She finds that decisions in this instance appear to have been motivated by managerial decisions to avoid accounting losses, rather than the economic drivers of performance. In a second study, Lillis recounts that the organizations found it difficult to pursue customer-oriented strategies when the performance measurement systems emphasized efficiency and productivity measures instead. The third research study examines the Balanced Scorecard and its capacity to reduce dysfunctional behaviours. Lillis concludes that there is a disproportionate emphasis placed on aggregated financial measures in performance evaluation in this context, although managers find disaggregated financial information useful in running a business.

Chapter 11, by Rodney Coyte, outlines how Bill's framing of strategic resource management was a response to the changing and discontinuous environment of the late 1980s. As an approach it was heavily influenced by a resource-based perspective of the firm and represented his attempt to address the perceived loss of relevance of management accounting practices at this time. While Bill's notion of strategic resource management developed and evolved, this framework served to convey Bill's vision for the future of the accounting and finance function as strategically engaged and capable of mobilising a range of tangible and intangible organizational resources to manage value at risk. Bill's approach is amply captured by the diagrams incorporated in Coyte's chapter.

Chapter 12, by Paul Andon, Jane Baxter and Linda Chang, is based on research conducted under the auspices of ACMAD. The chapter describes a case study of an innovative Australian organization that fascinated Bill and which exemplified the challenges embedded in his view of strategic resource management. The authors narrate the ways in which the creative and commercial aspects of organizational functioning informed both the core activities of technology innovation and strategic resource management. Relevant to an understanding of strategic resource management in this organization is the balancing of tensions between short- and long-term perspectives, continuity and change, focus and flexibility, and adequacy and expectations with respect to organizational functioning.

Chapter 13 contains Bill Connell's account of his work with Bill Birkett for IFAC revolving around the development of competency standards for management accounting. Both Bill Connell and Bill Birkett were united by their belief that management accounting theory and practice needed to adapt in response to the changing context of contemporary organizational functioning. In this chapter Connell outlines the background to this competency study and provides illustrative extracts from the competency standards in term of the key roles and competence profile for various levels of management accounting practitioners, stemming from entry-level novice management accountants to expert practitioners. He provides some insight also into the impact of the competence standards on the accounting and finance function of BOC Gases where he worked in the United Kingdom for many years.

Chapter 14 provides Peter Roebuck and Maria Barbera with a platform to outline the scope and impact of their joint work with Bill Birkett, Barry Leithhead and Marian Lower. This team of writers contributed to the development of a 'Common Body of Knowledge' for the IIA by establishing a competency framework for the internal auditing profession. This was an ambitious project that was marked by its international character, drawing on data collected from practitioners in 20 countries. It resulted in the production of five monographs which are summarized in the chapter. These monographs outline the global landscape of internal auditing, global perspectives on internal auditing knowledge, structures and methodologies for assessing competence in internal auditing, best practices in this field and the future of internal auditing.

Chapter 15, contributed by Elaine Evans, examines the interaction of government, higher education institutions and professional accountants' bodies as tertiary education in government-funded institutions became a (if not 'the') major mode of entry into the professional bodies in the period 1944–88. Over this time the professional bodies monitored accounting education in higher education institutions through a system currently referred to as course accreditation. Notwithstanding its ongoing failure as a quality control and quality improvement system for the professional accounting bodies, accreditation had mutual benefits for them and the higher education institutions. The author concludes that despite the evidence that the monitoring system was ineffective, the professional bodies became 'locked in' to accreditation during this period. However, the creation of 'new' or 'alternate' entry pathways over the past year or two, may signal that the professional bodies are reconsidering of the efficacy of accreditation.

Chapter 16, by Rosina Mladenovic and Bill himself, critiques the use of Biggs' Study Process Questionnaire (SPQ) by accounting education researchers. Early users concluded that accounting students are 'surface learners' and that accounting education tends to impede quality learning. Mladenovic and Birkett point out, however, that there is a schism between the theory and measurement of 'deep' and 'surface' learning. Theoretically, 'deep' encompasses and builds upon so-called surface attributes but the SPQ *measures* treat deep and surface cognitive activities as dichotomous. The early interpretation of SPQ measures was not cognizant of this disjunction. More recent SPQ-based research has been more nuanced, but the emergence of alternative research instruments raises the question of whether the SPQ's days are numbered.

In chapter 17, Prem Ramburuth outlines the results of qualitative research, which she conducted on the diverse student body of what was then known as the Faculty of Commerce and Economics at UNSW (now ASB). Ramburuth's particular focus is on international students' experiences and the impact on their 'learning and socio-cultural adaptation'. Ramburuth's account of particular students' responses will resonate with readers involved in business education in Australia – she expresses the cultural adaptations and shock that such students confront and the motivational and expectational factors informing their studies, as well as apparent differences in learning, language and communication. The diverse cohort of students embraced by ASB, and the complex of factors affecting their learning, were instrumental in the establishment of the Educational Development Unit.

It has been our great privilege to work on this volume of essays in honour of the late Professor Bill Birkett. We both received enormous personal and professional support from Bill during his lifetime; we are grateful for the opportunity to have worked with him and to have been exposed to his ideas about accounting practice and research. Similarly, we are pleased that so many others have been prepared to express their respect for Bill through their contributions to this work. We would like to thank each contributing author for their time and commitment. Likewise, we are grateful to Roger Simnett as the Head of the School of Accounting at UNSW for resourcing this project. The support of Susan Murray-Smith and her team at Sydney University Press is also gratefully acknowledged. Lastly, we hope that this book may provide Bill's wife, Phillipa, his children and grandchildren with an appreciation of a facet of Bill's life that was marked by his passion for accounting practice and its relationship to accounting education, research, and its global professional context.

References

Barbera M, Baxter J & Birkett W (1999). *Innovative management accounting*. Kensington: University of New South Wales Press.

Baxter J (2004). Obituary: Professor Bill Birkett (1940–2004), *Management Accounting Research*, 15: 381–82.

Baxter J & Chua WF (2006). A management accountant from Down-Under: the research of Professor Bill Birkett. *Management Accounting Research*, 17: 1–10.

Birkett WP (1967). Accounting and auditing – distinct but related functions. Unpublished Master of Economics thesis, University of Sydney.

Birkett WP & Walker RG (1971). Response of the Australian accounting profession to company failure in the 1960s. *Abacus*, 7: 97–136.

Birkett WP & Walker RG (1972). Professional ideas on research in accounting: Australia, 1930–49. *Abacus*, 45: 35–60.

Birkett WP (1992a). Competency standards for the profession: aspirations and issues. *Charter*, 63(10): 64–65.

Birkett WP (1992b). Competency standards for the profession: competency and education. *Charter*, 63(11): 70–71.

Birkett WP (1998). Management accounting in Europe: a view from Down-Under. *Management Accounting Research*, 9: 486–94.

Birkett WP, Barbera MR, Chua WF, Fatseas VA, Luckett PF & Macmullen JS (1992). *Cost management in small manufacturing enterprises*. Kensington: Australian Centre for Management Accounting Development.

Birkett WP, Barbera MR, Leithhead BS, Lower M & Roebuck PJ (1999a). *Internal auditing knowledge: global perspectives*. Florida: The Institute of Internal Auditors Research Foundation.

Birkett WP, Barbera MR, Leithhead BS, Lower M & Roebuck PJ (1999b). *The future of internal auditing: a Delphi study*. Florida: The Institute of Internal Auditors Research Foundation.

Birkett WP, Barbera MR, Leithhead BS, Lower M & Roebuck PJ (1999c). *Competency: best practices and competent practitioners*. Florida: The Institute of Internal Auditors Research Foundation.

Birkett WP, Barbera MR, Leithhead BS, Lower M & Roebuck PJ (1999d). *Internal auditing: the global landscape*. Florida: The Institute of Internal Auditors Research Foundation.

Chua WF (1986). Radical developments in accounting thought. *The Accounting Review*, 61(4): 601–32.

International Federation of Accountants (Financial and Management Accounting Committee) (1998). *Management accounting concepts (IMAPS1).* New York: IFAC.

International Federation of Accountants (Financial and Management Accounting Committee) (2001). *A profession transforming: from accounting to management (Study 11).* New York: IFAC.

International Federation of Accountants (Financial and Management Accounting Committee) (2002). *Competency profiles for management accounting practice and practitioners (Study 12).* New York: IFAC.

Latour B (2005). *Reassembling the social.* Oxford: Oxford University Press.

Mladenovic R, Poullaos C with Barbera M & Connell W (2005). Obituary – Professor WP (Bill) Birkett (1940–2004). *Accounting Education: an International Journal.* 14: 113–17.

2

Situating management accounting practice

William Birkett and Wai Fong Chua (UNSW)

Abstract

The purpose of this chapter[1] is to redirect management accounting research toward the hitherto neglected field of accounting 'as it is practised', and toward intensive field studies as the most appropriate mode of research. The paper elucidates the concepts of situations (as the venues in which management accounting is practised) and of frames (as types of rules and codes manifested in situations). These notions provide researchers with a way of specifying commonalities in different management accounting situations; they aid conceptualisation of management accounting as a form of practice, rather than as a type of (mis)reified system; and they help address linkages between organization-level variables (culture, power structures, technologies, etc) and individual-level experiences within organizations. The paper calls for future research to use frame analysis in order to probe the cognitive and social orders present in situations, expressing the result in the language of frames – and thus for management accounting practice to be situated, by being framed.

This chapter seeks to identify what is involved in characterizing management accounting as situated practice, as a basis for subsequent empirical study. Both 'situations' – as the venues of interactive practice, and 'frames' – as the structures of situations, will be in focus. Research technologies which are suitable for exploring management accounting as situated practice are identified.

---

1 Originally written January 1988.

It will be argued that situated practice is a relatively neglected domain of management accounting research. Further, suggestions for redirecting management accounting research point towards remedying this neglect, in various ways. As a result, some consideration of the notion of 'situation' is warranted; this is pursued by distinguishing the experiential and structural dimensions of situations, and defining the latter as 'frames'. Research needs to address both of these dimensions, in characterizing management accounting as situated practice.

This chapter deals successively with: the neglect of 'the situation' in management accounting research; suggested redirections in management accounting research; situating management accounting practice; the nature of the structures which frame situated practice; and the theoretical and research implications of the notion of a frame. In essence, the paper can be viewed as an attempt to outline a theoretical apparatus as a guide to further inquiry.

The neglected 'situation' in management accounting research

Levels of analysis

Management accounting research, together with other forms of organizational research, can be categorized in terms of the 'level of analysis' predominantly addressed – the organizational (macro) level or the individual (micro) level (Pfeffer 1982, Birkett 1983). Analysis at the organization level can probe relationships between management accounting systems and variables such as environment, structure, power, controls, technology and culture. At the individual level, analysis can probe the effects of management accounting systems on individual functioning, and vice versa.

Many 'individual level' studies implicitly assume a form of interaction between individuals relative to management accounting systems (e.g. between superior and subordinate, or management accountants and managers) and introduce some situational variables that may frame interaction (participation, leadership style, task ambiguity, feedback form or variety). However, while such variables are important to the analysis (either as attributes of management accounting systems or as intervening variables), notions of interaction and situation are treated unobtrusively and without development.

Other types of management accounting research explicitly explore relationships and interactions between individuals and management accounting systems, in competitive (principal and agent) or cooperative (coalitions and choice) settings. Yet research that elaborates the notion of situated interaction raises other questions as well. Are organization-level variables embedded or embodied in situations, so that interaction is channelled or constrained? Or is situated interaction the mechanism through which forms of order ascribed to the organization level (labelled as structure, power, culture, etc.) are explored, tested, created and eventually objectified (as the conditions bounding further situated interactions)? Can organization-level variables be experienced by individuals in organizations, other than through situated interaction? Indeed, do organization-level variables 'exist' only by being realized in particular situations?

Some observations

Management accounting research tends to be concentrated at the extremes of the organization-individual spectrum between organization-level variables and management accounting systems, and between management accounting systems and individual functioning. The 'linkages' between these levels are poorly described and rarely theorized. So organization-level researchers might characterize management accounting systems in terms of level of sophistication or degree of formalization, whereas individual level researchers might characterize the systems in terms of feedback type, frequency or the degree of goal clarity or difficulty. Again, what relationships exist between the uncertainty inherent in principal and agent negotiations and the types of uncertainty confronting organizations or particular organizational sub-units?

A second observation is that the notion of 'interaction' tends to be relatively unexplored in management accounting research, with interaction being treated as unitary, static and unproblematic. Yet interaction may take different forms (e.g. face-to-face encounters, distance communications), be of varying durations, treat varying matters of substance (e.g. resource allocation, control), generate varying outcomes (e.g. task completion, information generation), and draw on varying capacities of participants (e.g. interest, experience). Invariably interaction is dynamic, and is linked to other forms of interaction. Moreover, it is the mechanism of organizational action and adaptation (Weick 1979).

Thirdly, the nature of the varying situations which surround interactions involving management accounting systems, while being recognized in a piecemeal fashion, remains opaque (in terms of the number, complexity and definiteness of the concepts available for their description) and under-theorized (in terms of the extent of exploration of relations between such concepts as are available). Certainly traces or elements of what might be understood by the situations surrounding interaction have been identified (e.g. task uncertainty, information asymmetry, style of participation, organ-izational precedent and organizational slack). Yet such traces themselves may be poorly grounded (in that the reality experienced by participants in inter-actions is not reflected adequately in a construct), and insufficiently developed for theoretical purposes (can they be amalgamated meaningfully and reasonably completely into a composite picture?).

The neglected situation

Although situated interaction appears to have been somewhat neglected in management accounting research, the notions of situation and interaction are important. They define the conditions under which, and the processes through which, all management accounting practice is manifested and ex-perienced. The notions are important also because they offer a point of linkage between organization-level variables and individual-level variables. Structure, power and culture (organization-level variables) may not be ex-perienced or understood directly by individuals, but only through the 'effects' of these variables on the situations in which experiences are secured.

Redirecting management accounting research

In recent years, commentators have raised a variety of issues relating to the coverage, orientation, quality and contribution of management accounting research; and they have suggested a redirection of research effort, along certain consistent lines. An outline of these commentaries and suggestions follows.

Ontological misdirection

It has been argued that management accounting researchers have failed to study management accounting as 'it is practised', in concrete organizational settings (Johnson & Kaplan 1987). Burchell et al. (1980) and Hopwood (1980) argue similarly that, although the roles which management accounting ought to play in organizations have been documented, little knowledge exists about the roles actually played.

Calls to study accounting 'as is practised' appear to have been associated with attempts to illustrate how management accounting might be described in research. For example, Gambling argues that accounting functions as a set of rituals enabling "the human mind to handle the basic uncertainty of the universe, as the human mind sees it" (Gambling 1985, p4). Meyer (1983) argues that accounting functions at a mythical level, portraying images of an organization as bounded and unified, as rational and directed to clear purposes. According to Hayes (1983) management accounting helps sustain a myth of calculative rationality.

Management accounting also is said to perform a 'symbolic' role and to constitute a 'discursive practice' (Meyer 1983, Cooper 1983, Boland & Pondy 1983). Similarly, Ansari and Bell (1985) argue that like any other control tool, accounting systems "have to perform symbolic, behavioral and resource allocation functions" at once (p31).

Coupled with a focus on the symbolic role of accounting, there are various references to how accounting constructs individual, organizational and social order – as a 'language' (Hayes 1983), a 'craft' (Hopwood 1984), an 'apparatus of power' (Miller & O'Leary 1986), and as a 'mode of economic calculation' (Nahapiet 1986, Hopwood 1984, Berry et al. 1985).

Three points should be made about calls to study accounting as it is practised. First, they tend to reflect different normative biases, ranging from concerns to improve the range of technologies available to practice or resolve presently experienced managerial problems, to the uncovering of patterns of domination and control embodied in extant practice as a basis for social critique.

Second, there is a tendency to reify management accounting in pointing to practice. But any reference to a 'management accounting system' is problematic, for a 'system' is not experienced as such by people. Different participants within an organization will experience only 'slivers of the system'; and they may or may not configure some representation of the whole, perhaps unconsciously. Whose experience is to be tapped, and which configurations are to count? Indeed, can such micro-level experiences be accumulated into a meaningful composite and how? Would any composite constitute the reality of practice, objectified through practice, or simply another form of reified practice?

Third, the concepts drawn on to illustrate how accounting might look 'as it is practised' tend to be ill-defined. Labels such as rituals, symbols and myths are used as though their meanings are self-evident, or are defined only loosely. What forms of language and what set of concepts appropriately convey the experience of management accounting practice – for those involved, and for others?

Investigative methods

The prevalence of gathering management accounting research data via survey, through laboratory experiment, or mathematical modelling has drawn some comment (Kaplan 1984). While these methods of inquiry offer various advantages, they tend to be distanced somewhat from practice, and utilize constructs which are 'once removed' from the situations being studied. For example, a questionnaire purporting to measure a construct labelled 'participative budgeting style' may be presented to subjects in the field as a given, and coded and translated to the point where it is taken to represent or even constitute the phenomenon being studied. Because the reality of the field is at no point injected into the construct, it may be a misleading abstraction from the situations experienced, and an element of a theory that is thus poorly grounded.

Further, such methods tend to miss the thick descriptions, the effects of the unfolding of events, and the sense of time and occasion that can be captured only in the field by such methods as participant observation and case studies. Kaplan (1984), for example, has chastised management accounting researchers for not leaving their offices to "muck around with messy data on relationships". He suggests that management accounting researchers should carry out field-based research – because only through a detailed gathering of 'soft data' can "the innovative accounting practices of successful companies" be carefully documented. In other words, Kaplan seeks to distinguish best or new practice from practice generally by the research methods he advocates.

Paradigm expansion

A number of commentators, following Kuhn (1970) and Burrell and Morgan (1979), have sought to locate management accounting research within one or another methodological paradigm (Cooper 1983, Hopper & Powell 1985, Chua 1986). These efforts inevitably placed most research within a 'functionalist' paradigm. 'Functionalist' research is concerned with understanding how social order is produced and sustained, through the development of empirically based causal generalizations about the patterning of events by disinterested investigators using formalized methods of inquiry.

Against this background it has been suggested that forms of research grouped within an 'interpretive' paradigm might be productive (e.g. Colville 1981, Tomkins & Groves 1983). 'Interpretive' research is concerned with understanding the world as it is subjectively experienced by social participants. Interpretive researchers are concerned with order, but with a symbolic order assumed by individuals or created collectively by individuals in interaction. Research inspired by this alternative paradigm may allow underlying assumptions to be drawn out for debate or reflection, investigators might acquire new skills, and potentially rich and different insights might be generated.

Attempts at shifting the functionalist bias in extant management accounting research directs attention to such phenomena as face-to-face interaction, everyday routines and categories, strips of conversation, or definitions of the self and of situations. They offer a distinctive appreciation of empirical phenomena as a reflexive outcome of people's participation in meaningful activity. They also change the research task to one of detailed analysis of what people do, say, and think in the actual flow of momentary experience.

While such emphases can offer potentially rich insights into the nature of management accounting practice, they also embody a number of problems, of a different order.

First, they have not progressed much beyond the speculative, exhortative stage. There is an invitation to adopt a new worldview which is claimed to offer new insights, but there has been little development of a broad philosophical approach into specific, analytical categories that can act as a practical guide for management accounting researchers.

Second, interpretive research does not fully theorize the social world of action (Willmott 1983, Knorr-Cetina & Cicourel 1981). For example, 'symbolic interactionist' research (a particular variant of interpretive research) has been able to illustrate how meanings, situations and events are continually being defined and negotiated, and that cognitive order is emergent; but it has not been able to show how these processes translate into the orderly patterns of behaviour that are observed. While focusing on meaning and the processes through which meaning emerges, symbolic interactionism has ignored the structures which meaning embodies (Hammersley & Atkinson 1983, Payne et al. 1981, Atkinson & Drew 1979, Silverman 1985).

Third, interpretive research is not uniform in emphasis or focus, and hence a blanket advocacy of interpretive approaches offers little guidance to management accounting researchers about the nature of the research task, the conduct of research, or the alternative philosophical traditions or perspectives that can be utilized in fashioning and interpreting research outcomes.

Empirical studies which have been conducted along interpretive lines in management accounting (e.g. Boland & Pondy 1983, 1986; Covaleski & Dirsmith 1986; Merchant 1985) show signs of these problems: the research task is vaguely organized or variously interpreted; relationships between emergent symbolic orders and existing or emergent social orders (and the rules underlying each form of order) are treated uneasily or with difficulty; and considerable reluctance is evident in locating, containing or immersing research processes or outcomes within particular philosophical perspectives.

The result is an eclectic borrowing of interpretive 'approaches', without a commitment to particular philosophical traditions which inform them. Moreover, the outcomes often reflect an implicit blend of functionalist and interpretive research (Chua 1988).

Redirection

In summary, recent commentaries on management accounting research suggest that it be redirected towards the study of management accounting practice *in situ*, utilizing the experiences and language of organizational participants as the initial point of reference. The focus is to be on the constitution of individual (and collective) experiences through interaction, and the coincidental colouring of interaction by the situations in which it is located.

The commentaries point, then, both to a new domain of research-situated practice and to an alternative mode of research-intensive field studies, which might be located profitably within the traditions of interpretive research. In other words, they point to the 'neglected' field of research identified above, and to ways in which it might be addressed.

A focus on management accounting as situated practice, however, raises a number of key issues. How are the symbolic orders constituted through interaction related to the social orders which constitute the situations surrounding interaction? How is the gap between experience and structure bridged in situated interaction and within organizations? More particularly, what part do situations play in linking the 'macro' and the 'micro' within organizations? How can research move beyond depictions of the uniqueness of situations to at least typifications of situations? And what form should be given to concepts and theories used in research with this focus?

The central question is: if management accounting practice is experienced in and constituted through situations, what structures (or frames) a situation?

Situating practice

De-reifying management accounting

It is commonplace to study management accounting practice as though management accounting systems have a continuous, independent reality, 'possess' known characteristics and have determinable effects on people. Yet literally, management accounting systems cannot be seen, touched or even experienced as such. When the notion of management accounting system is de-reified, it may subsist in little more than repeated behaviour in particular settings, using particular physical objects and certain forms of symbolic and linguistic expression.

'Systems' may be realized only as fragments of repetitive action, and may be given cognitive order only through the loosely coupled understandings of relatively isolated participants. For example, an 'internal control system' (a type of management accounting system) may be experienced as follows: 'A' counts the cash received daily in a particular place and records the receipts in a book with a particular format; 'B' drives to the bank to deposit the money at a particular time, obtaining an appropriate entry in a deposit book with a particular format. 'A' and 'B' may be able to articulate some common understanding of what they do together, and each may have a more or less vague apprehension of how their related activities 'connect' with the activities of others. Similarly, budgeting 'systems' may be realized through the recurring practices (negotiating, cursing, undermining and writing) and disjointed understandings of people located at different points within an organization.

It is convenient to assume a notion of 'system' and then look to the situations and manner in which 'it' might be realized. However, it is possible also to look to that which is constituted in certain types of situation first, and label this 'management accounting' – without invoking the notion of system. In either case, as a point of realization or as a point of constitution, the situation is central to understanding the *practice* of management accounting. What, then, is involved in defining the situation?

Defining the situation

It has been argued by some that 'the situation' is the building block of social life. WI Thomas (1931, p176) states:

> The situation in which the person finds himself is taken as containing the configuration of the factors conditioning the behaviour reaction. Of course, it is not the spatial material situation which is meant, but the situation of social relationships. It involves all the institutions and mores.

According to Thomas, any behaviour, by group or individual, cannot be understood apart from the situation in which it occurs and to which it is a potential adjustment. "Every concrete activity is the solution of a situation." (Thomas 1927, p68).

Further, different participants involved in a situation will have a different train of experience and different perspectives. As a result, they are likely to create different 'definitions' of the situation, and, to the extent that behaviour is a consequence of such definition, they will behave differently (Thomas 1937).

It is important to note that the 'definition of a situation' is a reconstruction from sensory experiences; it involves selecting from immediate perception that which is considered pertinent, in association with memories of other events thought to be relevant (Shibutani 1961, Knorr-Cetina 1981). A person who has just missed a budget deadline may not be unduly worried, knowing from past experience that extensions of two weeks or so are normally granted. What is at issue is whether a situation exists apart from idiosyncratic definitions of it.

There are various responses to this issue. Some adopt the solipsist position that sees 'definitions of the situation' as the only matter of importance. Others, like Goffman (1972), see social situations as 'a reality *sui generis*' warranting analysis 'in their own right'. Knorr-Cetina (1981) and others regard 'interaction in social situations' as the relevant unit of analysis. The emphasis on the 'social' in relation to situations requires that the outcome of action be tied to (a) particular occasions, and (b) other participants. The relevance of individual 'definitions of the situation' is recognized, but attention is shifted to the sharing of interpretive schemes and the construction of joint 'definitions of the situation' through interaction in situations that can be more or less objectively identified.

Researching situations

How are researchers to study 'definitions of the situation' and situations?

Symbolic interactionism offers one approach, aiming to discover how actors' conceptions are organized so as to produce the orderly patterns of behaviour that are observed. Actors' definitions of situations are probed to uncover the orderly, stable and shared symbolic schemes that are presumed to be embodied therein; in turn, these schemes are taken to reflect more encompassing forms of social order, realized in the behaviour of actors (Denzin 1970). Research to date has been able to show how meanings, situations, objects and selves are continually being defined, presented, dramatically enacted and negotiated; and that social order is emergent, with a particular dynamic that is context dependent. At the same time, however, it has tended to emphasize the idiosyncratic nature of situations and the uniqueness of 'definitions of the situation'.

This stress on the idiosyncratic and the unique has resulted in a move away from the general to the particular, towards ever more detailed description. The more or less general concepts that have been generated have always been in danger of being rejected on the grounds that they do not capture the 'fullness and richness' of other situations. Indeed, the assertion that each situation is unique has been devastating for theory construction. Even Blumer's (1969) pioneering attempts at typification have given way to a stress on sensitizing researchers to that which is different or unique in a situation (Hammersley & Atkinson 1983). And so, in practice, symbolic interactionism has made little progress towards a systematic description of the commonality in situations, and associated governing rules and structures.

There are some exceptions to this trend in symbolic interactionist research. For example, consider the work of Mangham (1978) and Weick (1979).

Mangham's 'theory' is built around a dramaturgical model within which the notion of a 'script' forms a fundamental part. Scripts define the roles that a minimum number of actors are expected to assume within the confines of an anticipated sequence of events. When sequences of events happen often enough, scripts come to be embedded in them, forming both the cue and the mechanism for repetition of the sequence. As a result, scripts and 'stylized everyday situations' come to be associated together. For example, there may be classroom scripts, buying-a-ticket scripts or exchanging-greetings scripts. Scripts thus mediate between personal definitions of a situation and a situation, as more or less objective governors of performance. As in drama, scripts are interpreted by actors in constituting together a particular performance. Scripts presumably embody the rules that are governing in a situation.

Mangham conflates the notions of situation and script: a situation is somehow identified and defined through the script that is performed. This approach poses problems both for actors in a situation and for researchers of the situation. Not only has the script to be found, but it has to be identified with the 'right' situation. Identifying the rules (scripts) governing typical situations may convey little of the character of particular situations. There is a presumption that scripts 'exist', and that they are relatively 'inelastic'; yet the peculiarity of situations presumes variability in the scripts governing typical situations.

Mangham's elevation of the notion of script has merit nevertheless. It illustrates a form in which the 'definition of a situation' may be collective, rather than individual. It points to the existence of 'typical situations' as a focus for research, as well as the existence of governing structures. And it is suggestive of the form of these structures – 'rules' that have personal, strategic and situational referents.

Weick focuses on interaction, rather than the situation. His basic unit of analysis is interaction between two people. Within this framework he identifies certain classes of rule (labelled 'recipes') which he believes are sufficient to sustain interaction. These classes of rules are: assembly rules – "rules for building social processes out of behaviors"; and interpretive rules – "rules for forming variables and causal linkages into meaningful structures (later called cause maps) that summarize the recent experience of the people who are organized" (Weick 1979, p3). Weick is reaching for a 'grammar' for organizing:

Organizing is like a grammar in the sense that it is a systematic account of some rules and conventions by which sets of interlocked behaviors are assembled to form social processes that are intelligible to actors. The grammar consists of recipes for getting things done when one person alone can't do them and recipes for interpreting what has been done (pp3, 4).

In reaching for a 'grammar', Weick achieves abstraction. He treats 'organizing', not organizations and not situations. He illustrates his grammar, though he does not locate it even in typical situations. For Weick, interaction and situation are divorced; though he does point to a form of rule that may be used in analysing the structuring of situations.

Some symbolic interactionist researchers at least have seen a need to invoke a notion of the structure of a situation, as well as its peculiarities and cognitive manifestations. Moreover, these structures are depicted in generalized forms (scripts, recipes, rules), rather than being context laden or situation specific. This development is suggestive, for it points to a way in which the typical and the peculiar can be distinguished across situations – via a structural grammar of situations.

Situating management accounting practice

Management accounting can be viewed as a form of practice, rather than as an organizational system. Such practice involves different types of interaction, across a range of situations; and it may generate different interpretations of process and outcome in those who are involved. Further, the situations through which management accounting practice is constituted are structured in particular ways, but are likely to embody general structural forms (e.g. types of rule). Hence, reference could be made to certain *types* of management accounting practice, defined in terms of the structures governing certain situations of practice.

In researching management accounting as situated practice, there is a need to probe both 'definitions of the situation' (individual and collective) and situations. Such research involves two tasks: first, fine description (in characterizing situations, for example); and second, the discovery of underlying structures (cognitive and situational). Prior research appears to offer considerable guidance for the first of these tasks, but less guidance for the second (Denzin 1983). And it prompts the pursuit of a further task – the construction of a grammar for analysing and typifying the structures of situations.

What, then, is the nature of the structures that frame management accounting as situated practice?

Framing situations

The nature of frames

Bateson (1972, p186) sought to clarify what is meant by 'frame' and 'context' (situation) as psychological concepts by exploring two analogies: the 'picture frame' and the 'mathematical set'. Both analogies were found wanting as descriptors of psychological concepts, which were seen to be neither physical nor logical in form. Nevertheless, Bateson was able to derive the following characteristics of psychological frames:

1. They are both *inclusive* and *exclusive* (by including only certain messages or actions within a frame, certain other messages are excluded, and vice versa). In psychological terms exclusion and inclusion are not symmetrically related (as in set theory): the intention is to both direct attention to that within, *and* attention *away* from that which is without.

2. The frame, together with that which is constituted 'within', directs certain forms of intellectual functioning. Understanding will arise from a focus on the mutual relevance of included items, and the ignoring of that which is excluded (think about the elements of the picture, not the wallpaper!); and evaluation of that which is within proceeds by reference to the frame (this is a budget meeting, not a dinner party!).

3. A frame is metacommunicative, in the sense that it provides instruction or assistance in understanding the messages included within the frame.

4. A frame itself may be defined by metacommunicative messages (such as: treat this situation figuratively, or literally, or technically!).

5. A frame distinguishes items of one logical type (those within) from those of another (those without), but its logical form is paradoxical –

it is an element of that which is without, but it is 'different' because of its logical construction as a frame.

From Bateson's analysis it is possible to digest some idea of the *function* of frames, but the logical order, or *structure*, of frames remains unclear.

Researching frames

Further insight into the nature of frames can be gained from those who have researched, or would research the involvement of frames in interaction.

Goffman (1974) takes the notion of situation as his starting point in seeking to uncover the structures that surround situations – "the enumeration of forms and their organization, the exposition of signifying structures and their modes of functioning" (Lane 1970, p37). Goffman claims that all experiences are organized through frames which individuals consciously or unconsciously impose on situations. His research task was to uncover the nature of such frames, through their embodiment in individuals' 'definitions of a situation'.

Some outcomes appear below.

1. Frames are *abstract and generalizable across situations*. A frame is described by certain operative rules which apply across situations (e.g. particular productions might exemplify a common dramatic form).

2. Frames are *stable and routinely realized* through adherence to their conventions (as in the playing of games).

3. Frames are *systematic*. A frame consists of a set number of essential elements, with definite arrangements, always found together as a system. The standard elements cohere and are complete, and together constitute the 'reality' (however dimly apprehended) of the situation entered into.

4. Frames are *permeable*. Frames function as 'membranes' through which broader 'cultures' must penetrate to permeate situations and the consciousness of individuals; such membranes select, transform, and modify that which is passed through.

Goffman's approach to research differs from that of symbolic interactionist researchers through his overt attention to the structures embodied in situations and surrounding interaction. He is interested in the unintentional properties of systems of interaction, in classes of situation, in typifications, in syntax rather than speech, in 'fitting people to frames' (Goffman 1974, pp13, 14). However, the process through which he uncovers typifications is not obvious.

Harre and Secord (1972) sought to systematize and extend Goffman's work methodologically (p150). They take the notion of an act as their primary datum point; the research task is to explain it, through an examination of possible sets of actions which may have produced it. Explanation may proceed via determining either causal mechanisms or governing, socially established rules. In the latter case, unexplained episodes can be investigated by comparison with certain types of paradigmatic episode whose rules are well established. To this end, Harre and Secord provide a limited taxonomy of paradigmatic episodes, identified in terms of the types of rule involved (e.g. rituals, routines, games, entertainments).

Harre and Secord, like Goffman, see advantage in the use of a dramaturlogical analogy in researching situated interaction. An episode is a unique production, uniquely experienced by those involved – but it is also the product of underlying rules which are more or less generalizable.

Frames as rules

The revelation of the nature of frames can be seen as a search for the rules that are operative in a situation. Goffman (implicitly) and Harre and Secord (explicitly) treat 'frames' as rules. For example, Goffman (1974, p10) refers to frames as "principles of organization which govern events – at least social ones – and our subjective involvement in them". Recall also that Weick (1979) drew on the notion of rules as outcomes or constituents of interaction.

The notion of rule is complex, and has received extended philosophical examination (see, for example, Black 1958, Hare 1970, Downie 1971). Distinctions have been made between rules (as directives) and commands (as injunctions), and between regulations (rules laid down by proper authority), customs (observed regularities of conforming behaviour), precepts (as to how behaviour ought to be conducted), mores (kinds of conduct deemed appropriate, and supported by unformalized pressures), and principles (general or universalistic rules). Rules have been seen as: uncertain mixes of manners and morals, constraining or constitutive of practice, explicit or implicit, general or specific, absolute or relative, intensive or shallow, and as definitive or emergent (Emmett 1966, Giddens 1984).

Shwayder (1965) in an extended analysis of the notion of rules as a basis for subsequent analysis of behaviour (including language) concludes:

> community rules are either statutory or non-statutory, restrictions or ena-bling rules, constitutive or non-constitutive for practices ... It is not always an automatic matter to place a given rule in this scheme, partly because kinds of rules are related in various ways (p279).

Shwayder believes that his "scheme will be a serviceable guide to the further analysis of conformative behaviour" (p279). Others would extend the analy-sis, to 'misbehaviour' as well as conformative behaviour (Walker 1977).

The examination of frames as rules, then, shifts attention to the form and functioning of rules; and is likely to require the development of both a lexi-con and a grammar of the latter.

Frames as codes

Frames are seen to carry meaning in situations. Goffman (1974, p7) is quite explicit in treating frames as codes that need to be 'cracked' by participants in a situation. For Goffman, a code is an "unconscious system of categories and rules governing the creation and communication of meaning" (Goffman in Gonos 1977). Recall also that Bateson (1972) distinguished a communicative function of frames, and that Mangham (1978) treated the notion of 'script' (a form of message) analogously to a frame. Bernstein (1973) also sees a close connection between messages, codes and frames, using the notion of frame to refer to the form of the context in which knowledge is transmitted and received.

There is a close connection between codes and rules. Bernstein, for ex-ample, sees a code as a "regulative principle, tacitly acquired; codes select and integrate relevant meanings, forms of their realization and their evoking contexts" (Bernstein in Atkinson 1985, p83). Codes, as regulatory mecha-nisms, exert implicit power through their deep structure. What is taken for granted or assumed, is unlikely to be challenged and is likely to be prevailing (Hudson 1972). Indeed, codes may be defined in terms of rules: codes are "an agreed transformation, or set of unambiguous rules, whereby messages are converted from one representation to another" (Cherry 1980, p339).

Codes, then, may be structured as rules, and may have the force of rules. But they also permit the translation of rules into messages, and subsequent translation of messages into meaning. Codes may be classified in various ways. Bernstein (1981), for example, distinguishes between 'elaborated' and 'restricted' codes; the former is not context dependent (as in language), while the latter is (as in speech). Bailey (1983) proposes that different codes operate at different stages in the life of committees; new committees use simple codes (characterized by assertion and counter assertion), mature committees use sophisticated codes (which permit 'fine-grained analyses'), and senile committees use ritualistic codes. Hall (1959) typifies codes in terms of the behaviour patterns they suggest; 'informal' (select a model and copy it), 'formal' (follow precept), and 'technical' (routines are spelled out). And in semiotic theory codes are subdivided (Morris 1938) into syntactics (relating signs to signs), semantics (relating signs and referents), and pragmatics (relating signs and their meanings to specific users).

It is important to recognize that information is conveyed other than through the form or content of discourse present in a situation. Action, settings and the non-verbal behaviour of agents may all convey information. For example, Hall (1959), in exploring the 'silent language' that governs and sustains communication and action in different cultures, demonstrated that 'time talks', that space is a message system, and that a culture embodies a peculiar vocabulary. Similarly Peters (1980) has argued that management systems (or processes) not only convey, but constitute an organization language. "Systems are the language that directs attention"; as 'unobtrusive indicators' they symbolize "how things really work around here". Indeed, the medium is the message (Burke 1966, McLuhan 1973).

It follows that messages will be experienced as complexes in a situation, and warrant complex decoding. Morris (1946, p15), for example, has observed that

the fact that behaviour takes place within a supporting environment implies that the sign alone does not cause the response evoked, since the sign is merely one condition for a response-sequence in the given situation in which it is a sign.

The various messages conveyed through different media need not be commensurate, nor unambiguous, nor even interpretable (to the extent that a multiplicity of codes is involved). Yet together, somehow, the messages convey more than specific pieces of information; they convey information about the nature of the structures surrounding situations, about the particular frame that is operative in a situation.

The problem of the commensurability of messages should be highlighted. Boulding (1961) has referred to 'logical consistency' and 'aesthetic quality' as possible relations between the messages embodied in a frame. Harre and Secord (1972) refer to 'style' in composing messages and actions. Similarly, Hall (1959) argues that "the rule of congruence, or style in the broadest sense, pervades ... all kinds of communication" (p127). Burke (1966, p3) refers to a 'scene-act ratio' in dramatic situations: "it is a principle of drama that the nature of acts and agents should be consistent with the nature of the scene". And Edelman (1967, p110) has argued that, in political situations, "acts must be compatible with settings physically expressive of particular *political* forms, legitimations or postures".

The examination of frames in this way, then, shifts attention to the form and functioning of codes; and so it is likely to require the development of code typologies, as a condition for dissecting or composing the information conveyed by the quite different types of messages carried in frames.

Frame components

Boulding (1961), for example, in exploring relationships between a person's 'image' of the world (another name for 'definition of the situation') and behaviour, partitions the image into components that deal with: space, time, personal relations, the natural world, a world of subtle intuitions and emotions, and relations between the other components ('logical consistency' or 'aesthetic quality'). Shwayder (1965), in focusing on individual action, identifies four essential 'elements' of acts: the agent, the occasion, movement, and belief that conditions for the success of an act are satisfied. He holds that an act 'exists' only when these four elements are present together. Similar categories have been developed by those who focus on interaction (Duncan 1962, Burke 1969): the act (the concerted conduct of two or more individuals, directed towards some social goal or object), the scene (the spatial and temporal framework of action), the agent (individuals taking roles), purposes, and discourse (the forms of communication employed by agents).

Drawing from these types of analysis, the following components of frames are proposed:

1. *Action sequences* – a stream of actual or contemplated happenings, involving human agents, and embodying some 'principle of unity' (such as, the definiteness of the acts to be performed in composing the action sequence, or the outcomes intended by the acts embodied in the action sequence). Action sequences, as such, convey information and exemplify particular rules. And so they affect both the constitution of meaning and the constitution of action.

2. *Agents* – the persons or roles involved in a situation.

3. *Setting* – the 'context' in which action sequences are operative. For example: work or leisure; legal, political or economic; inter-personal or arms length; superior or subordinate; committees; encounters or episodes. Settings may have physical, spatial and temporal dimensions. Settings, then, function as law does, by creating a 'space' in which to act; by defining 'qualities' of action sequences, though not their contents or direction. Again, settings function as a scene might in a drama, at once locating and limiting action (where are budget meetings typically held?).

4. *Discourse* – a form of action which has communicative intent. Discourse, like action sequences, proceeds according to rule. Unlike action sequences, however, the outcomes are defined as the generation of meaning.

5. *Prototypes* – the simple or complex forms of thought or action 'available' to situated practice. Prototypes may consist of customary or exemplar forms of intellectual functioning or of composing interaction. Prototypes may be embodied in: a normative domain (e.g. rules requiring rationality in analysis and legality in action); an interper-

sonal domain (e.g. rules governing participation in budgeting, or hierarchical precedence in decision making); a resource management domain (e.g. the financial models to be used in budgeting, the procedures to be used in project management); or an interpretive domain (e.g. is lay or technical language used?).

6. *Congruence* – refers to the form of relationship established in composing a situation between agents, action sequences, settings, discourse, and the prototypes embodied in each of these. It embodies information about actual, potential or desired relations between other frame components. Not all situations may be framed congruently. Notions of congruence are socially and historically bounded; they are a product of time and circumstance.

Framing situations

It is possible now to be more definite about the nature of the structures that surround situated interaction. These structures have been labelled 'frames'.

A number of attributes of frames have been identified. They serve particular *functions* – partitioning realms of discourse, directing attention and judgment, and containing action. And they have a particular *structural* order – abstractness, generalizability across situations, stability, system and permeability. Together these attributes permit a clear distinction between situations and frames. Situations are concrete and peculiar, even unique – at least in principle. Frames are trans-situational and recurring at least in principle.

Given these attributes, the paradox identified by Bateson (1972) can be reconsidered. Bateson observed that a frame distinguishes items of one logical type (those within – the 'definition of a situation') from another (those without). A frame is a *particular* logical form of that which is without, distinguished by the attributes listed.

Frames consist of rules and codes. Particular *types* of rules (e.g. regulations, customs, precepts, mores, enabling, restrictive, constitutive, principles) and particular *types* of codes (e.g. elaborated, restrictive, syntactical, semantic, pragmatic, technical, sophisticated) have been identified. Within frames, codes serve a dual function: they are the mechanism for accessing rules, and they permit the carriage of information.

Frames may be subcategorized into separate but related components – action sequences, agents, settings, discourse, prototypes, and congruence. Each of these components is implicated in every situation, in principle at least. Singly and together these components embody the rules and codes which are necessary for the constitution of situations. It should be noted, however, that while situations may be probed through frame components, they are likely to be understood only through frames as a composite (recall the attribute of 'system'). Frame components serve analytical purposes, but it is frames that are governing and enabling in situations.

Frames permit the development of typifications, a form of middle ground between social generalizations and the particularity of situations (through their attributes of abstractness, generalizability and stability). Recall that Goffman's (1974, p14) project was to uncover, not 'facts' but 'typifications'; and that Harre and Secord (1972) sought to characterize enigmatic episodes in terms of certain typical, paradigmatic episodes. Typifications stress the commonality of situations over the differences; and they can be identified and described in terms of frames. The phrase 'typical situation', then, denotes that common rules and codes are operative in a certain range of situations.

Frames are 'micro-structures', surrounding situations. They also partition situations from others and from 'broader' social milieux; but they are permeable also. Together these attributes permit their depiction as 'membranes' that filter interchanges between situations and that which is without. To follow the metaphor, the 'macro-world' can be envisaged as entering situations after being reconstituted within relevant frames, and situations can be envisioned as constituting the macro-world through being framed. The 'macro-world' may be configured in various ways: for example, as organizational cultures, power structures, or technologies; or as interpretive, allocative, authoritative, or normative repertoires in the social world, potentially available to situated interaction (Giddens 1976, 1979).

Framing management accounting situations

The investigation of management accounting as situated practice can be informed by the notions of situation and frame developed above. The situations of practice and the experiences of individuals therein are to be studied, but with the intention of uncovering the structures embodied in situations – in the form of frames. The aim of research is to identify the implicit rules and codes that structure interaction in management accounting situations (Gilbert & Mulkay 1984, Knorr-Cetina 1981).

The approach taken to research is adjusted accordingly. Instead of asking only the question – 'how can a definitive version of action be extracted from the actor's variable discourse', an additional question needs to be asked – 'how are the actors' accounts of action and beliefs socially generated?' People do interpret the world around them and act on their often implicit interpretations. However, studying such interpretations is unlikely to be sufficient for identifying the micro-structures that frame interaction. And so, following Goffman (1974) and Harre and Secord (1972), an attempt is to be made to provide close descriptions of the frames surrounding management accounting situations, as one way of explicating those situations.

Frame analysis also permits limited generalization. Typical situations can be identified in terms of common (at least, similar) rules and codes. Hence, the injunction to describe management accounting as situated practice, involves reaching for typifications through the conjoint exploration of situations (in which 'management accounting' is implicated in some way) and frames (the rules and codes that are operative).

Finally, it should be noted that research needs to proceed on two fronts: the empirical mapping of management accounting situations in terms of frames; and the elaboration of the structural grammar (rules and codes) through which frames are formed. In this way, typifications of practice and frame typologies can be joined in explicating management accounting as situated practice.

Conclusions

Two central themes have been sustained in this paper: first, the elucidation of the nature of situations as the venues in which management accounting is practised; and second, the elucidation of ways in which research into management accounting as situated practice could proceed. Pursuit of the first theme resulted in the definition of 'frame' as a structural form applicable to all situations; and pursuit of the second resulted in an outline of 'frame analysis' as a mode of research which blended interactionist and structuralist perspectives (following Mangham 1978, Weick 1979, Goffman 1969, 1974 and Harre & Secord 1972, for example).

These themes expressed twin concerns. First, the recognition that situated practice was a relatively neglected domain of management accounting research (in the sense of being treated incidentally, implicitly or partially), which warranted consideration; attention needed to be directed to both sense-making in, and the structures of, situations. Second, the recognition, by some at least, that this domain could be addressed advantageously by research designs which involved immersion in the field rather than 'abstracted variable analysis' (Blumer 1956), and perhaps by drawing on interpretive research traditions. Interpretive approaches to research were seen to be useful in generating insights about the construction of cognitive (symbolic) order in situations, through interaction: however, they offered less understanding about ways in which various forms of social order infuse situations and cognitive functioning.

The notion of 'frame' (as types of rules and codes manifested in situations through various frame components) offers certain insights and benefits. First, it provides a way of specifying commonalities in different management accounting situations, a way of typifying and comparing situations. Second, it permits the complete specification of a situation, through frame components that are systematically related; as a corollary, that which is 'missing' from the specification of a situation can be identified (e.g. attention might be focused on characteristics of agents and ignore the other frame components). Third, it provides a way of conceptualizing management accounting as a form of practice, rather than as a type of system; as a corollary, management accounting can be reinterpreted as a form of action that generates information, rather than being understood as a type of information that generates action. Fourth, situations, as framed, may be seen as supplying not only a context for management accounting practice, but also a text about such practice. Fifth, the notion of frame provides an avenue for explicating, or at least addressing, 'links' between macro and micro phenomena in organizations generally, and between different manifestations or expressions of management accounting particularly. And, finally, the notion of frame might be fruitfully introduced into more pervasive arguments about the makeup of the social world, and ways in which it might be understood.

The notion of frame also suggests a range of research initiatives. First, the development of detailed descriptions of management accounting practice in a range of situations, viewed through a different lens. Second, the 'translation' of the product of previous interactionist research in management accounting into the language of frames. Third, the 'recovery' of the fragments of prior research findings about management accounting situations generated through 'variable analysis', and their translation into the language of frames (e.g. 'task uncertainty', a term used in variable analysis, might be translated as an incapacity to access the rules or codes relating to action sequences); this exercise might result in the clarification and situational grounding of such conceptual fragments as a basis for further variable analysis, as well as enhanced understanding of management accounting as situated practice. Fourth, research may also examine , in the language of frames, certain notions that are beginning to surface as research tools in management accounting (e.g. myth, ritual, symbol, language). Fifth, the typification of management accounting practice across situations. And, finally, the development of the grammar of frames, as a lexicon of rules and codes.

The investigation of management accounting as a form of organizational practice requires the abandonment of reified constructs and associated research technologies. Instead management accounting practice is to be addressed directly, in the various situations in which it emerges – using appropriate research technologies. Frame analysis is one such technology, in that it probes the cognitive and social orders present in situations, expressing the result in the language of frames. Hence, management accounting practice can be situated by being framed.

References

Abdel-Khalik A & Ajinka BB (1979). *Empirical research in accounting: a methodological viewpoint.* Florida: American Accounting Association.

S

Ansari SL & Bell J (1985). Accounting, control and culture – an explanation. Unpublished working paper.
Argyris C (1952). *The impact of budgets on people*. USA: Controllership Foundation.
Atkinson JM & Drew P (1979). *Order in court*. London: Macmillan.
Atkinson P (1985). *Language, structure and reproduction*. London: Methuen.
Bailey FG (1983). *The tactical uses of passion*. Ithaca: Cornell University Press.
Baiman S (1982). Agency research in managerial accounting: a survey. *Journal of Accounting Literature*, 1: 154–213.
Bateson G (1972). *Steps to an ecology of mind*. London: Intertext Books.
Bernstein B (1973). On the classification and framing of educational knowledge. In R Brown (Ed), *Knowledge, education and cultural change*. London: Tavistock.
Bernstein B (1981). Codes, modalities and the process of cultural reproduction – a model. *Language and Society*, 3: 327–63.
Berry AJ, Capps T, Cooper D, Ferguson P, Hopper T & Lowe EA (1985). Management control in an area of the NCB: rationales of accounting practices in a public enterprise. *Accounting, Organizations and Society*, 10(1): 3–28.
Bhaskar R (1979). *The possibility of naturalism*. Hassocks: Harvester Press.
Bhaskar R (1986). *Scientific realism and human emancipation*. London: Verso.
Birkett WP (1983). Management accounting: theory in practice. In MJR Gaffikin (Ed), *Contemporary accounting thought*. Sydney: Prentice-Hall.
Black M (1958). Notes on the meaning of 'rule'. *Theoria*, 24(3): 137–203.
Blumer H (1956). Sociological analysis and the 'variable'. *American Sociological Review*, 21(6): 683–90.
Blumer H (1969). *Symbolic interactionism: perspective and method*. Englewood Cliffs, NJ: Prentice-Hall.

Boland RJ & Pondy LR (1983). Accounting in organizations: a union of natural and rational perspectives. *Accounting, Organizations and Society*, 8(2–3): 223–34.

Boland RJ & Pondy LR (1986). The micro dynamics of a budget cutting process: modes, models and structure. *Accounting, Organizations and Society*, 11(4–5): 403–22.

Bottomore T & Nisbet R (1978). Structuralism. In T Bottomore & R Nisbet (Eds). *A history of sociological analysis*. London: Heinemann.

Boulding K (1961). *The image*. Ann Arbor: University of Michigan.

Brownell P (1981). Participation in budgeting, locus of control and organizational effectiveness. *The Accounting Review*, 56(4): 844–60.

Bruns WJ & Waterhouse JH (1975). Budgetary control and organization structure. *Journal of Accounting Research*, 13(2): 177–203.

Brunsson N (1982). The irrationality of action and action rationality: decisions, ideologies and organizational actions. *Journal of Management Studies*, 19(1): 29–44.

Burchell S, Chubb C, Hopwood A, Hughes J & Nahapiet J (1980). The roles of accounting in organizations and society. *Accounting, Organizations and Society*, 5(1): 5–27.

Burke K (1966). *Language as symbolic action*. Berkeley: University of California.

Burke K (1969). *A grammar of motives*. Berkeley: University of California.

Burrell G & Morgan G (1979). *Sociological paradigms and organizational analysis: elements of the sociology of corporate life*. London: Heinemann Educational Books Ltd.

Cherry C (1978). *On human communication*. Cambridge: MIT Press.

Chua WF (1986). Radical developments in accounting thought. *The Accounting Review*, 61(4): 601–32.

Chua WF (1988). Interpretive sociology and management accounting research: a critical review. *Accountability, Accounting and Auditing*, 1(2): 59–79.

Cicourel AV (1981). Notes on the integration of micro- and macro-levels of analysis. In KD Knorr-Cetina & AV Cicourel (Eds), *Advances in social theory and methodology*. Boston, MA: Routledge & Kegan Paul.

Collins R (1981). On the microfoundations of macrosociology. *American Journal of Sociology*, 86(5): 984–1014.

Colville I (1981). Reconstructing 'behavioural accounting'. *Accounting, Organizations and Society*, 6(2): 119–32.

Cook DM (1967). The effect of frequency of feedback on attitudes and performance. Empirical research in accounting: selected studies. Supplement to *Journal of Accounting Research*, 5.

Cooper DJ (1983). Tidiness, muddle and things: commonalities and divergencies in two approaches to management accounting research. *Accounting, Organizations and Society*, 8(2–3): 269–86.

Covaleski MA & Dirsmith MW (1986). The budgetary process of power and politics. *Accounting, Organizations and Society*, 11(3): 193–214.

Cyert RM & March JG (1963). *A behavioral theory of the firm*, Englewood Cliffs, NJ: Prentice Hall.

Demski JS & Feltham G (1978). Economic incentives in budgetary control systems. *The Accounting Review*, 53(2): 336–59.

Denzin NK (1970). *The research act*. Chicago: Aldine.

Denzin NK (1983). Interpretive interactionism. In G Morgan (Ed), *Beyond method: strategies for social research*. Thousand Oaks, CA: Sage.

Deutscher I (1973). *What we say/what we do*. Foresman, Illinois: Scott.

Downie RS (1971). *Roles and values*. London: Methuen.

Duncan HD (1961). *Communication and social order*. New York: Bedminster Press.

Edelman M (1964). *The symbolic uses of politics*. Urbana: University of Illinois.

Emmett D (1966). *Rules, roles and relations*. New York: Macmillan.

Ferris KR (1977). A test of the expectancy theory of motivation in an accounting environment. *The Accounting Review*, 52(3): 605–15.

Gambling T (1985). Accounting for rituals. Unpublished working paper, Portsmouth Polytechnic, October.

Garfinkel H (1967). *Studies in ethnomethodology*, NJ: Prentice Hall.

Giddens A (1976). *New rules of sociological method*. London: Hutchinson.

Giddens A (1979). *Central problems in social theory*. London: Macmillan.

Giddens A (1981). Agency, institutions and time-space analysis. In KD Knorr-Cetina & AV Cicourel (Eds), *Advances in social theory and methodology*. Boston, MA: Routledge & Kegan Paul.

Giddens A (1984). *The constitution of society*. Cambridge: Polity Press.

Gilbert GN & Mulkay M (1984). *Opening Pandora's box: a sociological analysis of scientists' discourse*. London: Cambridge University Press.

Goffman E (1969). *Strategic interaction*. Philadelphia: University of Pennsylvania Press.

Goffman E (1972). The neglected situation. In PP Gididi (Ed), *Language and social context*. Middlesex: Penguin Books Ltd.

Goffman E (1974). *Frame analysis*. Cambridge: Harvard University Press.

Gonos G (1977). 'Situation' versus 'frame': the 'interactionist' and 'structuralist' analyses of everyday life. *American Sociological Review*, 42(6): 854–67.

Gordon LA & Miller D (1976). A contingency framework for the design of accounting information systems. *Accounting, Organizations and Society*, 1(1): 59–69.

Govindarajan V (1984). Appropriateness of accounting data in performance evaluation: an empirical examination of environmental uncertainty as an intervening variable. *Accounting, Organizations and Society*, 9(2): 125–35.

Hagg I & Hedland G (1979). 'Case studies' in accounting research. *Accounting, Organizations and Society*, 4(1–2): 135–143.

Haka, SF (1987), 'Capital budgeting techniques and firm specific contingencies: a correlation analysis', *Accounting, Organizations and Society*, 12(1): 31–48.

Hall ET (1959). *The silent language*. New York: Doubleday.

Habermas J (1978). *Knowledge and human interests*. London: Heinemann.

Hammersley M & Atkinson P (1983). *Ethnography: principles in practice*. London: Tavistock Publications.

Hare RM (1964). *The language of morals*. Oxford, London.

Harre R (1981). Philosophical aspects of the micro-macro problem. In KD Knorr-Cetina & AV Cicourel (Eds), *Advances in social theory and methodology*. Boston, MA: Routledge & Kegan Paul.

Harre R & Secord P (1972). *The explanation of social behaviour*. Oxford: Blackwell.

Harre R (1986). *Varieties of realism*. Oxford: Blackwell.

Hayes DC (1983). Accounting for accounting: a story about managerial accounting. *Accounting, Organizations and Society*, 8(2–3): 241–49.

Hayes DC (1977). The contingency theory of managerial accounting. *The Accounting Review*, 52(1): 22–39.

Hirst MK (1981). Accounting information and the evaluation of subordinate performance: a situational approach. *The Accounting Review*, 56(4): 771–84.

Hofstede G (1985). The ritual nature of accounting systems. Paper prepared for the EIASM workshop on accounting and culture, Amsterdam, June.

Hofstede G (1968). *The game of budget control*. London: Tavistock.

Hopper T & Powell A (1985). Making sense of research into the organizational and social aspects of management accounting: a review of its underlying assumptions. *Journal of Management Studies*, 22(5): 429–65.

Hopwood AG (1972). An empirical study of the role of accounting data in performance evaluation. Empirical research in accounting: selected studies. Supplement to *Journal of Accounting Research*, 10.

Hopwood AG (1980). Discussion of 'some inner contradictions in management information systems' and 'behavioral implications of planning and control systems'. In HP Holzer (Ed), *Management accounting 1980*. Champaign: Department of Accountancy, University of Illinois at Urbana.

Hopwood AG (1984). The archaeology of accounting systems. Paper presented at *The Roles of Accounting in Organizations and Society Conference*, University of Wisconsin, July.

Hudson L (1972). *The cult of the fact*. London: Harper and Row.

Jensen MC & Meckling WH (1976). Theory of the firm: managerial be-
havior, agency costs and ownership structure. *Journal of Financial
Economics*, 3: 305–60.
Johnson HT & Kaplan RS (1987). *Relevance lost: the rise and fall of man-
agement accounting*. MA: Harvard.
Kaplan RS (1984). The evolution of management accounting. *The Accounting Review*, 59(3): 390–418.
Kenis I (1979). Effects of budgetary goal characteristics on managerial
attitudes and performance. *The Accounting Review*, 54(4): 707–21.
Knorr-Cetina KD & Cicourel AV (1981). *Advances in social theory and
methodology: toward an integration of micro- and macro-sociologies*.
Boston, MA: Routledge & Kegan Paul.
Knorr-Cetina KD (1981). 'Introduction': The micro-sociological challenge
of macro-sociology: towards a reconstruction of social theory and
methodology. In KD Knorr-Cetina & AV Cicourel (Eds), *Advances in
social theory and methodology*. Boston, MA: Routledge & Kegan Paul.
Knorr-Cetina KD (1981). *The manufacture of knowledge: an essay on the
constructivist and contextual nature of science*. Oxford: Pergamon Press.
Kuhn TS (1970). *The structure of scientific revolutions*, 2nd edn. Chicago:
University of Chicago Press.
Lane M (Ed) (1970). *Introduction to structuralism*. New York: Basic Books.
Larker DF (1981). The perceived importance of selected information
characteristics for strategic capital budgeting decisions. *The Accounting
Review*, 56(3): 519–38.
Lindblom CE (1959). The science of muddling through. *Public admini-
stration review*, 19(2): 79–88.
Lowe EA & Shaw RW (1968). An analysis of managerial biasing: evidence
from a company's budgeting process. *Journal of Management Studies*,
5(3): 304–15.
Mangham IL (1978). *Interactions and interventions in organizations*.
Chichester: John Wiley & Sons.
March JG & Olsen JP (1976). *Ambiguity and choice in organizations*, Ber-
gen, Norway: Universitetsforlaget.

McLuhan M (1973). *The medium is the message*. Phoenix, New York.

Merchant KA (1981). The design of the corporate budgeting system: influences on managerial behavior and performance. *The Accounting Review*, 56(4): 813–29.

Merchant KA (1985). Organizational controls and discretionary program decision making: a field study. *Accounting, Organizations and Society*, 10(1): 67–85.

Meyer JW (1983). On the celebration of rationality: some comments on Boland and Pondy. *Accounting, Organizations and Society*, 8(2–3): 235–40.

Miller P & O'Leary T (1987). Accounting and the construction of the governable person. *Accounting, Organizations and Society*, 12: 235–65.

Morris CW (1938). *Foundations of the theory of signs*. Chicago: University of Chicago.

Morris CW (1946). *Signs, language and behavior*. New York: Prentice-Hall.

Nahapiet J (1984). The rhetoric and reality of an accounting for change: a study of resource allocation. Paper presented at *Conference on Organizational Symbolism and Corporate Culture*, Lund, Sweden, June.

Outhwaite W (1987). *New philosophies of social science*. London: Macmillan.

Payne G, Dingwall R, Payne J & Carter M (1981). *Sociology and social research*. London: Routledge and Kegan Paul.

Peters TJ (1980). Management systems: the language of organizational character and competence. *Organizational Dynamics*, Summer: 3–26.

Pfeffer J (1982). *Organizations and organization theory*. London: Pitman Books.

Pondy LR & Birnberg JG (1969). An experimental study of the allocation of financial resources within small, hierarchical task groups. *Administrative Science Quarterly*, 14(2): 192–201.

Rockness HQ (1977). Expectancy theory in a budgetary setting: an experimental examination. *The Accounting Review*, 52(4): 893–903.

Ronen J & Livingstone JL (1975). An expectancy theory approach to the motivational impacts of budgets. *The Accounting Review*, 50(4): 671–85.

Samuelson L (1986). Discrepancies between the roles of budgeting. *Accounting, Organizations and Society*, 11(1): 35–45.

Shibutani T (1961). *Society and personality: an interactionist approach to social psychology*. Englewood Cliffs, NJ: Prentice-Hall.

Shwayder DS (1965). *The stratification of behaviour*. New York: Routledge.

Silverman D (1985). *Qualitative Methodology and Sociology*. Aldershot, Hants: Gower.

Strauss A, Schatzman L, Bucher R, Ehrlich D & Satshin M (1963). The hospital and its negotiated order. In E Freidson (Ed), *The hospital in modern society*. Chicago: Free Press of Glencoe.

Thomas WI (1931). The relation of research to the social process. In WFG Swann et al. (Eds), *Essays on research in the social sciences*. Washington: The Brookings Institute.

Thomas WI (1937). *Primitive behavior*. New York: McGraw-Hill.

Thomas WI & Znaniecki F (1927). *The Polish peasant in Europe and America*, 1, 2nd edn. New York: Alfred A. Knopf.

Tomkins C & Groves R (1983). The everyday accountant and researching his reality. *Accounting, Organizations and Society*, 8(4): 361–74.

Walker N (1977). *Behaviour and misbehaviour: explanations and nonexplanations*. Oxford: Blackwell.

Weick KE (1979). *The social psychology of organizing*, 2nd edn. MA: Addison-Wesley Reading.

Willmott HC (1983). Paradigms for accounting research: critical reflections on Tomkins and Groves: 'The everyday accountant and researching his reality'. *Accounting, Organizations and Society*, 8(4): 389–405.

Zimmerman JL (1979). The costs and benefits of cost allocations. *The Accounting Review*, 54(3): 504–21.

Prologue

In accounting, we are increasingly interested in researching practice at a micro-organization level. The 'practice turn' or 'practice theory' is presenting challenges to contemporary researchers (see Ahrens & Chapman 2007; Schatzki et al. 2001; Chua 2007). Whether one draws upon the actor-network-theory of Latour (1987, 2005) and his colleagues or on Bourdieu's (1977, 1990, 1998, 2000) notion of 'logics of practice', or focuses on Nelson and Winter's (2002) notion of routines, there is renewed interest on practice. As a result, this paper, which was primarily written by Bill Birkett over 20 years ago, continues to resonate with contemporary research agendas. We argued then that accounting needed to be studied as 'situated' practice; that is, as practices that were framed by particular rules of action. Accounting was located 'within' frames or definitions of situations, within rules of action considered legitimate and possible, within times and spaces that were constituted by and reproduced the historicized action rules of the past, and influenced by visions of rules for the future. In addition, this paper typifies Bill's characteristic focus on careful theoretical delineation of the ideas and frameworks that we were seeking to employ. I hope that this paper will offer a re-engagement with Goffman's (1974) work and provide concepts that will enable today's researchers to study management accounting as situated practices.

References

Ahrens T & Chapman C (2007). Management accounting as practice. *Accounting, Organizations and Society*, 32: 1–27.

Bourdieu P (1977). *Outline of a theory of practice*, (trans by R Nice). Cambridge: Cambridge University Press.

Bourdieu P (1990). *The logic of practice*, (trans by R Nice). Cambridge: Polity Press.

Bourdieu P (1998). *Practical reason*. Cambridge: Polity Press.

Bourdieu P (2000). *Pascalian meditations*, (trans by R Nice). Cambridge: Polity Press.

Chua WF (2007). Accounting, measuring, reporting and strategizing – re-using verbs: a review essay. *Accounting, Organizations and Society*, 32: 487–94.

Goffman E (1974). *Frame analysis: an essay on the organization of experience*. Boston, MA: Northeastern University Press.

Latour B (1987). *Science in action*. Cambridge, MA: Harvard University Press.

Latour B (2005). *Reassembling the social*. Oxford: Oxford University Press.

Nelson R & Winter S (2002). Evolutionary theorizing in economics. *Journal of Economic Perspectives*, 16(2): 23–46.

Schatzki T, Knorr-Cetina K & von Savigny E (2001). *The practice turn in contemporary theory*. London: Routledge.

3

Being in accounting for a time

Michael Gaffikin (University of Wollongong)

Abstract

Consistent with Bill Birkett's predilection for confronting orthodoxy and dogma this chapter reflects on the work of Martin Heidegger and its implications for accounting. For most of his working life Heidegger was absorbed with the problem of 'being' – the essence of existence – something which, he argued, Western philosophers, since Aristotle, had ignored, being more concerned with understanding and explaining 'things' – independent entities. By trying to understand being he believed that we could get a greater understanding of knowledge of the world and our place in it. It is suggested in this paper that, like other 'disciplines', accounting has ignored this essential self-reflection which has resulted in its dependence on intellectual activities in other, related but separate, disciplines leaving accounting in an intellectual vacuum. This has resulted from the domination in Anglophone societies of modernist preconceptions and analytical philosophy as distinct from a more phenomenological hermeneutic orientation which would seem more suited to understanding in the human and social sciences.

I find it useful to think that there are four major periods in Bill Birkett's academic and professional life:

1. Early academic career (at the University of Sydney)
2. Working towards creating a 'school' of thought and teaching (at Ku-ring-gai CAE)
3. Consolidating an established school of accounting (early period at UNSW)

4. 'Senior' academic and professional years (also at UNSW but working closely with professional accounting bodies).

Those who worked more closely with and knew him better may think this a little simplistic as Bill was a tireless worker and always had many projects on hand. He was constantly seeking to extend his understanding of what was important for designing and implementing an appropriate education for professionals. I first met him at the end of what I have labelled the first period. We had very many discussions on what he was attempting to do and how he thought he should go about it. To me it was an intellectually stimulating experience to be in discussions with someone who was a deep and broad thinker, and who seemed really concerned with establishing an innovative and professionally and socially responsible basis for educating accountants. To him it was important to draw from many intellectual sources and not be content to merely extend the fairly conservative conventional extant accounting programs.

Most people would know of Bill through his work in management accounting and accounting education. His interests and concerns, however, extended beyond these areas into other matters including what we might like to refer to as those relating to accounting theory. Like the scholar he was, he was familiar with Aristotle's claim that practice is that which proceeds from theory. Therefore, if we were to build a meaningful accounting education, it was necessary to be aware of the theoretical underpinnings of what we would claim to be appropriate professional practice.

In his early academic period he worked with, amongst others, Ray Chambers who not only required high standards of intellectual rigour from his colleagues but who was developing his theory of continuously contemporary accounting (CoCoA). Part of Ray's *modus operandi* was to sound out his ideas on his colleagues and often vigorous debates, discussions and arguments ensued and went into the early hours of the morning. Bill was a very active participant; one for whom Ray had considerable respect. Unlike some others, however, Bill was not content to simply follow and parrot Ray's ideas but wanted to find his own intellectual path. Nevertheless, he did persist with Ray's demand for high intellectual standards although it was manifest in a slightly different way.

To Bill, as I understood, it was necessary to move beyond the rigid for-malism of conventional modernist – scientific, positivist, hypothetico-deductivism or whatever they are called – methodologies in our search for some sort of conceptual foundation for our practice. I am not for one minute suggesting he subscribed to any *one* of the emerging alternative approaches to accounting theorizing but he believed it important to go beyond the nar-row conventions within which accounting thought had been framed. What, I believe was important to him was to recognize accounting as a socially con-structed system of information generation that would most benefit sound business practices. Consequently, it was important that we did not stop with generally accepted economic and legal theories when searching for the basis for the development of accounting. Rather, it is important that we also con-sider theories developed in political, social, organizational, behavioural, historical and other disciples and how they could assist our understanding of the needs of our own discipline. In this respect, I had found in Bill someone with whom I agreed totally; in *how* we went about this, however, we may have had very different ideas.

The search for a theory

A great deal of the accounting thought in the 20th century involved a search for a (general) theory of accounting and it took many forms – generally accepted accounting principles, accounting standards, theoretical exposi-tions, extensions of 'theories' in economics and finance, research frameworks and other conceptions. They have mostly all been extensively discussed in the literature and are generally well known. No-one of these so-called theo-ries has been fully accepted by the accounting community and none has greatly influenced accounting practice which continues to be based on *ad hoc*-ery and political and ideological whim. A consequence of this 'failure of theory' is that financial accounting practice is increasingly being shaped by regulation so any theoretical discussion inevitably involves questioning the conceptual basis of such regulation. Lest some think this statement is naive it should quickly be pointed out that the question of regulation is highly com-plex and its 'success' (or lack of) has varied greatly over time and place; here too political and ideological whim plays an important role. The debates over the need for regulation have been long and varied, and opinions have ranged from those who believe in the efficacy of markets and who have argued that regulation is not necessary as market forces will operate to best serve society and optimize the allocation of resources, to those who argue that this over-states the capacity of markets and feel that regulation is necessary to ensure the equitable distribution of society's resources and even the operation of the market itself. Recently, to some – the naive and the hard-lined neoclassical economic ideologues (there is probably a fair degree of overlap in these groups) – the suggestion that there is a need for regulatory intervention as a cure for the recent global financial crisis signals the end of capitalism. How-ever, as Sen (2009)[1] has so clearly pointed out, this view is clearly mistaken. The capitalism that all affluent (mostly Western) societies have enjoyed has "for quite some time now, depended partly on transactions and other pay-ments that occur largely outside markets" (Sen 2009, p2). Thus, "the market economy has depended for its own working not only on maximizing profits but also many other activities" (p2) beyond the activities of markets alone. And, he argues, the "most immediate failure of the market mechanism lies in the things that the market leaves *undone*" (p3, emphasis in original).

Sen demonstrates his arguments by drawing on the work of Adam Smith, much of which has been conveniently ignored by many neoclassical econo-mists who have vehemently argued against any market intervention. To Smith an economy can operate effectively only on the basis of trust among different parties. But:

> The moral and legal obligation and responsibilities associated with transac-tions have in recent years become much harder to trace, thanks to the rapid development of secondary markets involving derivatives and other financial instruments. A subprime lender who misleads a borrower into taking unwise risks can now pass off the financial assets to third parties – who are remote from the original transaction. Accountability has been badly undermined,

---

1 I am grateful to Paul Williams for having drawn my attention to this article.

and the need for supervision and regulation has become much stronger (Sen 2009, p3).

It should be stressed that Sen is not opposed to markets. Rather he is opposed to 'today's prejudices' (in favour of the pure market mechanism) which, he argues, "certainly need to be carefully investigated" and "partly rejected" (Sen 2000, p113).

The majority of mainstream accountants have seen themselves as the handmaidens of capitalism, providing information to facilitate optimal economic decision making. In the last 50 or more years many accounting academics have been seduced by the rhetoric of the neoclassical economists and have attempted to provide accounting theoretical explanations based on what was claimed to be scientific neoclassical economic theory. Consequently, if such economic theory has failed it removes any justification for the accounting theoretical explanations made by the mainstream accountants. Casual observation of the current accounting academic literature suggests that accounting researchers have yet to take their heads out of the sand to notice that the 'air' they presumed to have remained unchanged has soured somewhat.

The context of and the arguments for and against regulation in accounting are well discussed in Gaffikin (2008, chapter 4). The issues discussed still hold but the matter of economic regulation in Western economies has become more acute as governments implement interventionist policies as they try to ease the current economic downturn precipitated by the global financial crisis.

Sen has argued that the "present economic crisis is partly generated by a huge overestimation of the wisdom of market processes" (2009, p4). While many governments have turned to Keynesian economics as the basis for their actions they have ignored that it is very much an aggregate analysis. In so doing they have overlooked the work of Pigou whose work was more concerned with economic psychology than that of Keynes. There are 'psychological causes' that play an important role in economic downturns. Business confidence is crucial to the success of economic policies and in these troubled times we are witnessing a steep decline in this. Thus, we need to be concerned with what are often referred to as behavioural issues – we have to extend our vision to include considering the fundamental essences of economic actions.

The behaviour of handmaidens

Accountants have for some time insisted they are value neutral facilitators of informed economic decision making. However, to hold to such a position is rather naive and, as most people are aware, there have been many instances recently (for example corporate scandals) that have clearly indicated that it is simply incorrect. Nevertheless, many accounting teachers continue to attempt to instil this in the minds of their students and there are many practitioners who use it as a defence of their sometimes seemingly inappropriate actions; it shapes many of the activities of various arms of the discipline.

Generally, as practised, accounting has served and continues to serve the interests of particular interests in economic and business affairs. This is by no means a novel observation and there has, over the last 50 years, been quite a bit of research demonstrating it. In the way it has 'defined' itself accounting serves as the bulwark of capitalism and supports those that practise it as the handmaidens. Generally speaking, accountants have avoided meaningful self-reflection. By far the majority of accounting researchers proceed without questioning the very essential features and assumptions of their discipline. Similarly, most practitioners are content to operate on the basis of the fundamental assumptions of past practices despite the fact that some of these have contributed to financial and social crises. Despite the fact that there are probably many very intelligent people operating in both accounting research and practice there is a general avoidance of meaningful intellectual practices. What, however, does this mean: what is an intellectual and what counts as meaningful?

Generally, intellectuals may be described as persons, typically well-educated, who engage their intellect in work which they believe to be of cultural importance.[2] Specifically, intellectuals would be those associated

2 Jary D & Jary J (1991). *Collins dictionary of sociology*. Glasgow: HarperCollins.

with the propagation and advancement of knowledge as well as the articulation of the values of society. In the context of accounting Sikka, Wilmott and Puxty have interpreted the intellectual's role "as being to engage more directly with the values of fairness, justice, greater democratic participation, openness and accountability?" (1995, p114). They quote the well-known post-colonial theorist Edward Said who argues that an intellectual is someone "whose place it is 'to confront orthodoxy and dogma' and to 'represent all those people and issues that are routinely forgotten or swept under the rug' but without claiming that such challenges are themselves value-free" (p115).

A characteristic of an intellectual is the capacity for independent inquiry and reflection. On this score accountants would not fare well as they have constantly relied heavily on ideas developed in other disciplines especially economics, finance and law but many others as well. This in itself is not inappropriate but in doing so they have specifically sought to support particular interests often in contradiction of their claimed objectives. For example, most financial accounting research in the last half century has been consciously designed to promote the material interests of a small section of users of financial accounting reports by addressing questions such as what accounting method choices lead to maximizing the interests of those parties?

There is a general suspicion of, even antipathy towards, intellectualism in the Anglo-American (Anglophone) world so accounting is not alone in eschewing matters seen to be removed from the everyday world of practical affairs; from the world deemed to belong to those who inhabit the lofty matters of the mind. This anti-intellectualism has manifest in many ways. It may even be possible to claim, somewhat ironically, that it contributed to the development that came to dominate Anglo-American (or should that be Anglo-Austrian?) philosophical thought for most of the 20th century (especially the first half but strongly influenced debates in the second half) – analytic philosophy. This can be inferred from the title (and more) of a paper by one of its progenitors – Moore's 'A defence of common sense' (1925).[3]

---

3 However, Moore being such a significant figure in 20th-century British philosophy, it is probably more reasonable to claim that it redefined intellectualism. Nevertheless, it repre-

Some time ago Lowe and Tinker (1977) suggested that "our subject (accounting) is so immature as to presently be without a true intellectual faculty"; that there is "an absence of an intellectual structure with which to frame problems and policy" (p275). In light of the discussion above it would appear that because of the attitudes of those involved in the practice of accounting it cannot be considered to be an intellectual activity. There is little evidence of concern for the values of fairness, justice, greater democratic participation, openness and accountability and virtually no attempts have been made 'to confront orthodoxy and dogma' – quite the reverse! Conventionally, the end result of financial accounting has not been the presentation of 'meaningful' financial reports (including general purpose financial statements) in the sense of pursuing the aims of intellectual activity just alluded to. Rather, financial reports have been designed to serve dominant economic interests. This, of course, is not a novel observation but it does draw attention to the narrow attitudes that dominate the practice of a discipline that claims to be a profession, a defining characteristic of which includes service in the public interest.

Other arms of the discipline are as 'unintellectual' as financial accounting. Although some may try to argue otherwise, management accounting has in the most part been concerned with control measures and has relied on outdated theories (e.g. Taylorism) often rejected (or claimed to be) by other (management) disciplines; or trendy and fashionable whims (e.g. lean accounting and resource consumption accounting). However, in the main it has been seen as a tool of management and (by definition) has obviously sought to serve such interests. It has done this through the preparation of technical reports. The dire state of the auditing industry has been discussed in many places (e.g. Sikka 2008b). Issues include the lack of precise definition of the role and responsibilities of the auditor and the level of independence required of those who serve as both advisors and auditors to the same organizations. The public perception of how effectively auditors

---

sents the general antipathy towards a traditional (say Kantian) mode of intellectual activity in favour of an allegedly more down-to-earth approach.

fulfil their 'duties' is not very high as the number of cases brought and the amounts of litigation outstanding against auditors clearly indicate. Policy-makers are constantly dismayed at the involvement of accountants in the tax avoidance/evasion industry (e.g. Sikka 2008a).

There are probably very many honest and conscientious accountants but overall the discipline fails miserably to meet the standards society expects of a profession. There are many who see accountants (generally) as being com-plicit with – if not deliberately then through incompetence or insouciance – the perpetrators of the many financial scandals and disasters designed to defraud or at least disadvantage individuals and societies generally. If those in the discipline are genuine in wanting to put accounting on a more de-pendable and societally responsible footing then there are serious matters that need attention.

Being

One of the last movies of the late great British actor-comedian Peter Sellers was entitled *Being there* (based on a novel by Jerzy Kosinski). In the film Sellers plays the role of a simple, homely gardener, named Chance, who chances to be taken in by a wealthy businessman and ends up as an advisor to not only the businessman but also the president of the US. Although he talks simply about the only thing he has knowledge of – gardening – his words are taken as metaphors with great depth of meaning. They even mis-take his name and call him Chauncey Gardiner. The title of the movie is the direct English translation of the German term *dasein* a concept that absorbed the attention of the philosopher Martin Heidegger throughout his life and work. Although the film is a 'comedy' there are serious undertones – Sellers' character is created by his *being there (dasein)*.[4] What does this mean? The philosophy of Heidegger is notoriously difficult and even simple introduc-tory books (e.g. Inwood 1997) require careful reading. He and his work are

---

4 There are difficulties in the use of the term *dasein* as 'being there' and there are various publishing conventions. I have used the English *being* most of the time rather than *dasein* and have shown it in italics. Some publications show it as Being, employing the capital letter.

highly contentious. Not only has he been considered by some to be the most important philosopher of the 20th century (and perhaps more), he also has many opponents who claim his work is impenetrable and obscurantist. So, why bother? There are many reasons for turning to Heidegger's work, which include, first, that he greatly influenced several other philosophers used by many accounting researchers to inform their own work. Thus, some recourse to the 'source' is useful and interesting in furthering our understanding. Secondly, there is intrinsic worth in examining his work for what it offers comprehension of notions employed in any theoretical understanding of accounting. Thirdly, he offers a refreshing antidote to the technical, sterile analytic philosophy that has dominated Anglophone philosophy over the past 100 years and still impacts on methodological discussions in the social sciences including accounting.

His concern for questioning *being* was vitally important because to him

> what was at stake was nothing less than Western thought as it had been known – not only its philosophy, but its natural sciences, its human sciences, its everyday discourses (Collins & Selina 2007, p7).

Heidegger is concerned with *being* and not beings. To him Western philosophy had concerned itself with beings, that is, in the history of Western philosophy, attention was directed to entities and their defining characteristics, and philosophers had overlooked *being* – the very existence of the entities (not their properties or substance). In the movie, Gardiner (Sellers) achieves his 'fame' by just being there – his presence/existence – he makes no deliberative actions and although a work of entertainment, the film cleverly presents an effective 'interpretation' of the thrust of Heidegger's work (see, for example, Heidegger 1973a) – what he considered the proper concern of philosophy. However, too much should not be read into this in respect of Gardiner and while he does have some of the elements of Heidegger's notion of *being*, it is much more complex than illustrated in Sellers' character. Nevertheless, he does represent what Heidegger termed being-in-the-world and there are relations to other entities (ready-to-hand) which comprise a network of entities which permits a core 'understanding' fundamental to being-in-the-world (Heidegger 1973a, pp32–35; 1978, pp53–58). Such 'understanding' as well as 'disposition' to being have been ignored or overlooked by modernist theorists (scientists, philosophers etc) who have been more concerned with defining and measuring (the result of) existence.

For a time

Being-in-the-world necessarily means being with others: *being* involves not only 'I am' but 'with them'. Sellers' character was not independent but was really taken over by the others (them) and he became the embodiment of how 'they' envisaged him. This has the consequence of our being not entirely in control of our own being – we (*being*) are (is) subject to the forces of society or what some have perceived as the mass culture of our contemporary society. To Heidegger this identification of societal conditions ('publicness') led to mediocrity ('averageness') or what some of us might recognize from our academic perspectives as 'dumbing down' or, from a sociological perspective, conforming to capitalist commodification. This is Heidegger's notion of 'fallenness' (Heidegger 1973a, pp210, 219–24) – the lack of self-control of *being*.

Fallenness in turn involves his notion of 'thrownness' (Heidegger 1973a, pp219–24) – being in a world not of *being*'s choosing, circumstances into which it is thrown – thus restricting projected possibilities. That is, that which *being* projects forward as its possibilities given its skills, knowledge and risks involved. We determine who we are by what we believe we will be or want to be in some future time – we project.

Fallenness is current – dealing with concerns as they arise in the present. On the other hand thrownness concerns what *has* occurred, that is, the past. Projections obviously concern the future: what are the expectations of *being* in respect of future possibilities. We are always 'on the way' from what we are or have been to what we will be. Thus *being* exists in all temporalities – it involves being in time[5] (at least until our death) and is uniquely and fully historical. Hence the title of Heidegger's major work, *Being and time*.

Heidegger's philosophical aim is radically different to conventional modernist thinking. He was concerned with the question of being – existence itself. He felt that Western philosophy had been sidetracked since Plato into looking for properties of beings as things which, subsequent to Enlightenment times (Descartes etc.), view things as objects of domination and consumption. He criticized the "subject-object paradigm of Enlightenment rationality for reducing the unencompassable power and upsurge of *physis* to an 'object' over which the human subject held juridical authority" (Caputo 1998, p229). It rages around us today "in the unleashed fury of the will to power, of the technological domination of the earth" (p230).[6] Thus, there is in modernist thinking an obsession for measuring 'things' (i.e. attributes of things) which is inevitably superficial and precludes our deeper understanding of essences. Also, it privileges certain entities and leads to misguided attempts to determine theories of everything to account for why things are as they are.

Heidegger's *Being and time* was the work that greatly enhanced his reputation as a foremost philosopher. First published in 1927 it dominated his life's work – the themes therein are central to all his work. Unfortunately in the early 1930s he became involved with politics and was for a while a member of the Nazi party which has discredited him with many groups. This has been defended by many (and not helped by him!) who believe it an aberration and that his work transcends the unfortunate foray into politics. *Being and time* was to be the first part of a major project that was never completed. However, in his later work (1940s on – 'late' Heidegger) he developed some of the themes that were probably to be part of that large project. He refines

---

5 This is complicated as Heidegger would probably claim that *being* does not exist within time but is time itself. However, given his association of *being* with time it is accepted as being historical.

6 Cf Heidegger's 'Letter on humanism' (in Heidegger 1978, pp189–242) and his 'Metaphysics as history of being' (in Heidegger 1973b, pp1–54).

some of his earlier ideas and extends them into other areas as well as criticizing or revitalizing some of his earlier positions. His concern with the essence of existence, meaning, thinking and knowledge remain as dominant themes as does the search for the meaning of truth. However, hermeneutics and language become primary concerns. The terms existentialist, phenomenologist and hermeneutist (amongst others) have been used to describe Heidegger. While there are definite elements of these 'positions' in his work none fully describes him. He in turn has exerted enormous influence on several of those working in these 'movements' as well as many others.

Caputo has claimed that "The 'aftermath' of Heidegger is immense, both inside and outside philosophy" (1998, p231). He suggests that "the two most important continuations of his thought are to be found in the philosophical hermeneutics of Hans-Georg Gadamer and in Jacques Derrida's notion of 'deconstruction'" (p231). But many other philosophers have 'continued' his ideas, including Sartre, Merleau-Ponty, Lacan, Deleuze, Levinas and Ricœur to name a few. Rorty has taken issue with him on many aspects of his work but argues that he is essentially a pragmatist (Rorty 1991). Spanos (2009) has claimed he exerted a strong influence on Foucault and was critical to the development of many of the ideas in poststructuralist thought. It should be stressed, however, that the strongest influence of Heidegger on most of these philosophers was not primarily his notion of *dasein* but rather his solutions to many of the questions philosophers were tackling as he tried to redraw the map of philosophy. It should also be stressed that his influence was not solely in philosophy but many other fields of thinking such as race and gender (e.g. Hannah Arendt), theology, ecology (e.g. the work of Arne Naess), history, language, ethics (Levinas), art and poetry and the social sciences.

Despite his seemingly obscure and esoteric concepts and his abstruse language, Heidegger was concerned with practical affairs – *being* in the everyday world. This is why Rorty concludes that despite making "heavy (and sometimes unnecessary) work" in developing his argument "Heidegger and pragmatism belong together" (1991, p11).

In accounting?

It does not require much of a stretch of the imagination to see accounting as a Chauncey Gardiner, its being in fallenness and thrownness. It exists with little self control over its own being. It has existed as the handmaiden of the economic/business hegemony and its projected possibilities are limited to continuing as it has been – at the whim of those with economic/business (political) power. Consequently, if there is a current crisis in economic thinking, as Sen has argued, then there is a crisis too in accounting. Also, as claimed above, it has adopted, often aggressively, an anti-intellectual attitude. It seems devoid of any interest in self-reflection. Therefore, it is unlikely that, in accounting, there will be the reassessment of capitalism for which Sen was arguing. There are signs (in journals) that it is 'business as usual' in mainstream accounting research circles. The belief in the omnipotence of the market persists despite the evidence that it has failed catastrophically.

Many years ago Watts and Zimmerman suggested that "*not only is there no generally accepted accounting theory to justify accounting standards, there never will be one*" (1970, p305, emphasis in original). To date they have been proved right (but for the wrong reasons!). As suggested earlier, in the absence of any satisfactory theorizing in accounting regulation has assumed considerable significance. Nevertheless, as implied by Watts and Zimmerman, successful regulation needs some sound theoretical grounding. Consequently, theorizing is still important. The fact that all professional and regulatory bodies have sought and are still seeking some sort of conceptual framework on which to structure their regulation bears this out, so we have travelled 'the full circle' (a Catch-22?).

The two major regulatory bodies in the world today are the International Accounting Standards Board (IASB) and the US Financial Accounting Standards Board (FASB). Popular opinion suggests that there has been a power struggle between these two bodies on the most appropriate manner in which effective regulation should be established. Again, popularly these are referred to as whether the regulation should be 'principles based' (IASB) or 'rules based' (FASB). The distinction has been well aired and most people are aware of it. If regulation needs theoretical backing then there are obviously implications for what passes as theory. However, as obvious as this is it has escaped the attention of many people in the accounting industry. It seems inconceivable that anyone could argue for a rules-based theory yet this seems to have strong support in the US. For example, anyone who subscribes to the internet ACEM list (primarily academic accountants) will have noted the strong majority support for the FASB approach, mostly from the US-based academics. The arguments are simplistic and seem to be based on fear of having to *think* conceptually rather than have actions dictated – probably based on a lack of confidence in the capacity of accountants to think. If this list is representative of the bulk of accounting academics in the US then they have every reason for this lack of confidence. On a more sophisticated level there has been considerable research undertaken primarily by academics in the US on determining a conceptual basis for regulation. Unfortunately, this research has mostly been that, with contested methodological bases and narrow focus. In addition there has been the lack of enthusiasm for research (alluded to above) by the practitioner arms of the discipline.

The IASB has put its faith in its incomplete *Framework for the preparation and presentation of financial statements* to provide the basis for determining what would constitute a conceptual response to signalling appropriate regulations and practices. It is claimed that rather than have actions dictated (rules), practitioners must 'reason out' on the basis of a conceptual understanding, what is the most appropriate action. This, of course, would seem to be the most appropriate basis for a 'real' professional to proceed. But, can the 'real' professional be expected to have a conceptual understanding? Given the current economic state of the world and the role played by those with supposed financial expertise there seems to be ample evidence that the conceptual understanding is at least defective or at the most missing altogether.

The debate over the basis for standard setting is well known to most people. It is introduced here to suggest it is a symptom of a lack of accounting's willingness to reflect on its *own* existence. This is not mere pretension but is important if accounting is to exist as a socially meaningful entity. Over time, accounting has made claims to be concerned with truth, fairness and representation. However, such notions have been approached rather superficially and this may be acceptable if accounting is taken to be an enterprise for simple calculable technical reproduction in which case it will simply *be*; like Chauncey Gardiner. It seems that as long as the fees have kept rolling in this has suited many people. But where does this leave those with grander claims for involvement – academics? regulators? policy makers? Do they continue with the self-delusion that they are doing something socially meaningful? In Heideggerian terms a lack of awareness of one's own existence (thus the need for self-reflection) leads one to simply merge with the masses (the others). Accounting could simply become a part of other disciplines – say, (business) economics or finance – and accounting does not exist. (This all sounds vaguely familiar!)

Politics and science

Any 'favourable' discussion of Heidegger's work is fraught with danger. Although regarded as one of the foremost thinkers of the 20th century, such discussion raises some strong passions, part of which relates to his active membership of the Nazi party for 10 months in the years 1933–34. Some, like the critical theorist Adorno, dismiss his work as "fascist right down to its innermost components" (quoted in Bernstein 1992, p81). Others like Hannah Arendt and Richard Rorty are more 'forgiving' – on intellectual grounds (see Bernstein 1992, pp79–81). There is a wide spectrum of opinions but we can follow Rorty's advice and read his work with "curiosity, and open mind" (quoted in Bernstein 1992, p82).

A second 'danger', and more important for the purpose of this paper, is his antagonistic opposition to the central tenets of analytic philosophy especially as found and maintained in its most outspoken supporters – the logical positivists. Crucial here is the belief that the only worthwhile and reliable knowledge was scientific knowledge. In challenging the bases of the logical positivist program Heidegger 'influenced' the thinking of many later philosophers (as stated above). However, the dogmatism, the arrogance, intolerance and the narrowness of the logical positivists seem to have been reflected in the positions adopted by advocates of what has been called the mainstream accounting research community as, for example, demonstrated in the collection of papers in Tinker and Puxty's *Policing accounting knowledge* (1995) and a paper by Macintosh (2004).

The sort of criticism of logical positivism – and probably analytic philosophy generally – that Heidegger's work suggests would include, first, that the logical reform of language – the objectification of language through the application of severe rules of logic – removes it from the everyday world of experience of language users.[7] Secondly, such formalisation of language makes it a technical instrument and reduces philosophy to technology. And, thirdly, 'redefining' some parts of language is inconsistent with the claims of logical positivism and represents 'double standards'. It is interesting that very similar criticisms could be levelled at mainstream accounting research over the past 40 years. It has resulted in removing many research findings from the comprehension of many practitioners and probably led to reinforcing practitioner anti-intellectual prejudices. It has also made regulators wary of the potential of accounting research aiding policy formulation. A consequence seems to be that regulators, for any theoretical considerations, have reverted to more traditional approaches to accounting 'theorizing' as is evident in the various conceptual framework projects. Even many academics seem to feel more secure with this sort of theory nostalgia. For example, the self-styled Sydney School has been content to regurgitate the wisdom of their mentor rather than continue to develop it. This, together with the narrow methodological stance dictated by the US business schools has resulted in very little agreement over any proposed accounting 'theory'. Thus, with both regulators and many academics loathe to reflect on their discipline and seek out alternative, possibly fruitful, avenues it is little wonder there have been no intellectual advances in accounting thought. Accounting has fallen into what Heidegger saw as the limitless domination of modern technology. Of course accounting is technical but it must also be more if it is to uncover truths – this involves 'thinking'.

---

7 Interestingly this seems to conflict with the aim of Russell and Moore in their advocacy of ordinary language.

Thinking about thinking

Most people would agree that in accounting we have had and still have many good thinkers. When considering the past, I immediately think of names like Ray Chambers and Carl Devine but there are many more that should also come to mind. I would certainly include Bill Birkett in any roll call of accounting thinkers. Today, in accounting, we probably have even more very thoughtful people than any period in the past (as a function of size at least). What does all this mean? Heidegger says that

> only when we are so inclined towards what in itself is to be thought about, only then are we capable of thinking … In order to be capable of thinking, we need to learn it (1978b, p346).

He is not trying to be offensive: he is concerned with the processes by which we determine what speaks for a matter – whatever is regarded as essential – that which is thought-provoking. It is confounding and we (including him) need to learn how to think. This involves radically unlearning what thinking has traditionally been – "we can learn only if we unlearn at the same time" (p350). It is also necessary to avoid prejudice which necessitates being ready and willing to listen.

Thinking can be considered on two levels. Traditionally we associate it with problem solving, calculating, planning, and figuring and so on. It is what we do before we act. On another level we need to consider what 'calls on' us to think. It is not so much the problem but the way it poses itself. A financial accountant should not merely prepare a financial report on the basis of the form that reports usually take, but she or he must consider the very essence of what the report represents; why and what is the report rather than merely how. In fact these are the sort of matters that seemed to preoccupy Chambers in his early work but later he seemed to revert to 'form'. It could even be argued this (the essence) was the initial impetus for the search for accepted accounting principles in the early 1930s but which certainly did not last long once the process started.

Paths to theory?

This paper started with the claim that Bill Birkett and I found common ground in the belief that the methods of the natural sciences could (and should) not provide the methodological basis for attempting to develop an accounting theory. In this belief we were far from alone. My search for authoritative support for this position has led me back to the work of Martin Heidegger who has influenced or been relied on by many later philosophers. The rejection of scientism is shared by many philosophers including non-Heideggerians. Jurgens Habermas, renowned critical theorist, is equally opposed to identifying knowledge with science. To him, positivism and scientism disavow any notion of critical reflection and are overall far too constraining, and certainly deny any self-reflection. To Heidegger this was because of the Cartesian separation of *being* from beings discussed above. Empiricism necessitated direct sensory perception such that observation and experimentation were the only paths to knowledge. Positivism extended – or rather restricted – the search for knowledge to scientific method and all that that implies. To suggest that there are recipes by which effective theory can be developed would be to contradict the thrust of what Heidegger was arguing. What the above has attempted to show is that he felt that Western philosophy (ontology), since Aristotle, has erred in promoting the tyranny of substance. That is, the concern of knowledge is to explain things in themselves and which can be separated from other things (substances) so we seek out attributes (of these substances). So, in accounting we concentrate on measurement – we measure the attributes of 'things'. We do not consider why these 'things' are but that is the concern of Heidegger. One can only speculate on the effect a change of emphasis would have on accounting. If we looked to see why the 'things' exist we might approach our practice differently. This is not a simplistic functionalist argument but one which suggests consideration of the essences. This is easier to comprehend if we seek the 'essence' of *accounting* and not the *objects* of accounting – the 'things'. This then would entail greater self-reflection and examination of why we account.

The above has only been a brief (speculative) introduction to the ideas of Heidegger which are seen, as indicated, as an antidote to the overbearing influence of analytical philosophy on Western thought: what Spanos (2009, p29) has referred to as ontological and epistemological imperialism. It turns analysis of knowledge away from epistemology to ontology. This influence, it could be argued, has been a cause of many of the problems the world now faces – economic, ecological and social. Thus, alternative ways of thinking need to be sought. This introduction has not discussed many other aspects and implications of Heidegger's work, the influence of which is evident in the work of many other philosophers and in accounting scholarship. Paramount amongst these other aspects is his influence in the development of philosophical hermeneutics by Hans-Georg Gadamer. Gadamer was opposed to the excessive claims of the Enlightenment, in the "dominance of the model of the natural and mathematical sciences in reflection about human affairs"; against the "progressive scientization, and its demands for certitude and perfectibility" (Schmidt 1998, p436). To him the medium in which effective life is transmitted is language.

Paul Ricœur was also concerned with hermeneutics but perhaps less directly influenced by the ideas of Heidegger. Nevertheless, there was a common concern with issues of language. Accounting scholars, such as Arrington (1986), have employed the work of both Gadamer and Ricœur .

Derrida was also concerned with language and was greatly influenced by, and critical of Heidegger. His deconstruction was more concerned with an interpretation of language for greater social awareness. His work, too, has been employed in accounting, for example by Arrington and Francis (1989). Levinas shared some of Derrida's concerns and is regarded as Heidegger's "most famous and relentless critic" (Caputo 1998, p232). Nevertheless, Levinas is regarded as someone on whom Heidegger had an influence and he has made it "impossible to discuss Heidegger today without wrestling with the question of ethics" (Caputo 1998, p232). In accounting, Shearer (2002) has drawn on the work of Levinas.

Spanos argued there is a very strong link between Foucault and Heidegger. He quoted Foucault's statement that "For me Heidegger has always been the essential philosopher ... My entire philosophical development was determined by my reading of Heidegger" (2009, p44). There are many accounting studies which have employed various aspects of Foucault's work.

While these studies address different questions, they share the rejection of positivist approaches to resolving the many problems faced by accounting.

Being in time

There are many other scholars, 'thinkers', 'theorists' and contributors to the question of knowledge that have felt some influence of Heidegger's work; some have influenced accounting researchers. It may well be an indulgence to attempt to draw a link between accounting and Heidegger's ideas, concerns and solutions. However, it was done here because of the intellectual barrenness that marks attempts to determine some sort of conceptual understanding or theoretical basis for the discipline of accounting. The major reason for this is that accounting has failed to reflect on being an independent discipline. Rather, it has been content to see its existence in terms of an extension of economics, finance, law and some other disciplines. However, the self-reflection and debates in those disciplines, such as those discussed at the start of this paper are ignored. It has existed as a reflection of dominant and powerful economic interests and in doing so has failed in its professional responsibility to fully serve the interests of the societies in which it has been allowed to operate.

However, there have been voices of dissent – those who have been out of step with the mainstream and who have tried to achieve genuine improvement and a greater awareness of the roles accounting should play. I believe Bill Birkett was one of these people. I am very pleased to have been asked to contribute to a work devoted to the memory someone who worked so tirelessly to improve the intellectual base of this discipline.

References

Arrington CE (1986). The rhetoric of inquiry and accounting research. Working paper, (pp86–102), University of Iowa.

Arrington CE & Francis JR (1989). Letting the chat out of the bag: deconstruction, privilege and accounting research. *Accounting, Organizations and Society*, 14: 1–28.

Bernstein RJ (1992). *The new constellation – the ethical-political horizons of modernity/postmodernity.* Cambridge, MA: MIT Press.

Caputo, JD (1998). Heidegger. In S Critchley & WR Schroeder (Eds), *A companion to Continental philosophy,* (pp362–69). Oxford: Blackwell.

Collins J & Selina H (2007). *Introducing Heidegger.* Cambridge: Icon Books.

Gaffikin MJR (2008). *Accounting theory, research regulation and accounting practice.* Sydney: Pearson Education Australia.

Heidegger M (1973a). *Being and time,* (trans by J Macquarrie & E Robinson). Oxford: Blackwell.

Heidegger M (1973b). *The end of philosophy,* (trans by J Stambaugh). London: Harper & Row Inc.

Heidegger M (1978a). *Basic writings from 'Being and time' (1927) to 'The task of thinking' (1964).* D Farrell Krell (Ed). London: Routledge & Kegan Paul.

Heidegger M (1978b). What calls for thinking, (trans by FD Wieck & J Glenn Gray). In Heidegger (1978a), (pp345–67).

Inwood M (1997). *Heidegger: a very short introduction.* Oxford: Oxford University Press.

Lowe EA & Tinker AM (1977). Siting the accounting problematic: towards an intellectual emancipation of accounting. *Journal of Business Finance and Accounting,* 4: 263–76.

Macintosh, NB (2004). A ghostly CAR ride. *Critical Perspectives on Accounting,* 15: 675–95.

Moore GE (1925). A defence of common sense. In Moore GE (1959), *Philosophical papers.* London: George Allen and Unwin.

Rorty R (1991). *Essays on Heidegger and others.* Cambridge: Cambridge University Press.

Schmidt DJ (1998). Gadamer. In Critchley S & Schroeder WR (Eds), *A companion to continental philosophy,* (pp433–42). Oxford: Blackwell,.

Sen A (2000). *Development as freedom.* New York: Anchor Books.

Sen A (2009). Capitalism beyond the crisis. *The New York Review of Books,* 56(5).

Shearer T (2002). Ethics and accountability: from the for-itself to the for-the-other. *Accounting, Organizations and Society,* 27(6): 541–74.

Sikka P (2008a). Accounting firms can't help on tax. [Online]. Available at www.guardian.co.uk/commentisfree/2008/aug/01/regulators.economy.

Sikka P (2008b). The auditors have failed. *The Guardian,* 7 October 2008.

Sikka P, Wilmott H & Puxty T (1995). The mountains are still there: accounting academics and the bearings of intellectuals. *Accounting, Auditing and Accountability Journal,* 3: 113–40.

Spanos WV (2009). *The legacy of Edward W Said.* Urbana: University of Illinois Press.

Tinker T & Puxty T (1995). *Policing accounting knowledge – the market for excuses affair.* Princeton: Marcus Wiener Publishers.

Watts RL & Zimmerman JL (1970). The demand for and the supply of accounting theories: the market for excuses. *The Accounting Review,* 54(2): 273–305.

4

History's role in resolving accounting's dilemmas

Graeme Dean and Frank Clarke (University of Sydney)

Abstract

This paper examines matters of history and causality, issues of concern to Bill Birkett. It briefly considers the potential for history to provide insights into the current global financial crisis. It provides a brief background to accounting research in the history paradigm generally, illustrating its capacity to inform current debates by reflecting on the authors' research into: (i) price and price level debates in the private sector in the mid-1960s through to the early 1980s, and then in the public sector in the late 1980s and 1990s; (ii) corporate law reforms following corporate distress in extended boom and subsequent bust periods, such as *unexpected* corporate collapses and major takeover plays; and finally, (iii) more recent works seeking insights into historical treatises on the function of accounting – (a) by re-examining through the lens of early double-entry bookkeeping manuals the role of double-entry bookkeeping from the 16th to 18th centuries, and (b) by examining previously unpublished correspondence of several 'golden age' accounting scholars. The public policy implications relating to (iii) provide input to modern debates about the functions of accounting – decision making and accountability and related accounting measurement issues. These provide a contextual framework on what has otherwise frequently been based on multiple observations quarantined from an understanding of their underpinnings – their valuable heritage and their baggage.

Here, some thoughts about accounting history are provided in honour of our 'Sydney School of Accounting' colleague Bill Birkett.[1] This is most apt as Bill, like our other colleagues at the time, owed a debt of gratitude to our common mentor, Ray Chambers, whose penchant for recourse to history to better understand the present is well captured in one of his magna opera, *An accounting thesaurus: 500 years of accounting*.

Historical analysis in accounting is much the same as in other areas of social science. Accounting history has its conventional mainstream (such as the works of Previts, Edwards, Napier, Gary and Lee Parker, Tyson, Fleischmann, Boyns, Funnell, Dale and Tonya Flescher), as well as the works of more critical theorists (such as Merino, Bryer, Tinker, Cooper, and Sikka, to name a few) who also examine historical events affecting the discipline. Data on the subject matter pursued, and on the methods employed, in historical inquiries in accounting reveal substantial variety, including: biography, institutional, development of thought, general, critical history, taxonomic and bibliographical databases and historiography. For an example, Goodman and Kruger (1988, p316) define historiography as a "body of techniques, theories and principles associated with historical research", indeed a mode of addressing data and data sources, asking questions and building theories based on evidence; while *methods* employed in pursuing accounting history include: the cliometric, counterfactual and empirical. It is often claimed that affecting policy through the products of historical inquiries is difficult, but probably no more so than for other forms of academic inquiries.

It is in this context that Bill Birkett demonstrated his academic wares; how he showed his colleagues, in particular to us, the prospect of drawing connections between what otherwise might appear unrelated, invariably dated, events (see Birkett & Walker 1971, 1972; Birkett & Chua 1988). Thinking of his example set us examining why we have been so retrospective in our

---

1 Reference to the Ray Chambers-inspired 'Sydney School of Accounting' first appeared in the accounting literature in Wells (1976) and again in the AAA's *Statement of accounting theory and theory acceptance* (1977).

own enquiries into various aspects of accounting. Accordingly, we acknowledge his influence and try below to illustrate his 'visible' hand.

Unquestionably, reflection on past events provides insights; sometimes *sobering* insofar as they enlighten regarding the possible consequences of the event in focus being perhaps more serious than first thought; sometimes *relieving* insofar as they reveal less serious outcomes than feared. Frequently on that journey previous successful and unsuccessful solutions are exposed. No doubt that experience feeds the idea that historical research is a learning experience.

Much of what is recounted (in settings 1–3 below) is influenced by Birkett's and Chambers' encouragement to draw systematically on commercial evidence (much of it historical) to test accepted ideas about accounting, to *test* conventional wisdoms – the dogma that had characterized accounting for decades – against today's observable commercial world. By examining varied historical documents, manuals and letters, much of our work seeks to mitigate the types of concerns raised by critics, such as in Taleb's *The black swan* (2007), that historical work engages in a mission impossible, akin to 'unscrambling an egg'. In this way, one might seek to provide evidence to satisfy Napier's (2002) concerns that historians need to be careful to only make 'justified statements' on the 'evidence' they are drawing upon. Such rigour was a feature of the historical and theoretical works of Ray Chambers and many other 'golden age' theorists. It likewise remains in the works of many contemporary historians, like: Bryer (2000a, 2000b), Chiapello (2007) and Mattessich (2007).

It is not surprising to us that in the current global financial crisis (GFC) there have been appeals to history, particularly to the events leading up to the 1930s Great Depression and on the solutions to it presented in President Roosevelt's New Deal. Indeed, a possible upside of the GFC is how it has created a setting in which past literature has resurfaced and new literature has emerged examining the circumstances of past events. For example, the 'Panic of 1907' in the US (Bruner & Carr 2007), the origins of the Great Depression and Roosevelt's New Deal solution are analyzed in Powell's (2003) *FDR's folly* and a more recently in Parker's (2008) *The great crash*. Plus there's an analysis of their current counterparts in Ritholtz's (2009) *Bailout nation*, and a review of mortgage business in the US through the Savings and Loans debacle of the 1980s to the sub-primes of the 2000s in Muolo and Padilla's (2008) *Chain of blame*. Past and present bubbles are considered in Baker's (2009) *Plunder and blunder: the rise and fall of the bubble economy*, and they go back to Pecora's (1939) examination of 'banks behaving badly' in his *Wall Street under oath*. These and their likes have played an important part in the debate regarding both the causes of the past and present crises and the remedies applied by past and present national governments.[2] Reflection on how that has been pursued is instructive. Underpinning complaints that market participants and regulators have not learned much from history is the pervading idea that the function of history is to provide a template for the resolution of contemporary problems. Not perhaps so much because of perceived commonalities between the past and the present, as by virtue of the illustration in history of how things might be better thought through and resolutions found.

This focus indicates that as much as wanting the past to provide guides as to what to do in the present, examining the history of what are perceived to be similar events serves to expand our understanding of how the intermingling of events blurs both their likely causes and their possible solutions. It also serves to give us now a window on the excitement and confusions of that moment, on the complications long forgotten. That is, history provides a unique opportunity to *experience* what we are otherwise denied. In that respect historical enquiry is a privilege. For, whereas reconstructing the past is possible for us, our present would have been, at best extremely difficult for those preceding us to predict. We recall Bill Birkett suggesting something like that during one of his many moments explaining his understanding of human behaviour. In this setting, historical enquiry becomes a motivating force in that it allows recall anew of matters that we had not thought about for a

---

2 Whilst there are many references one could cite, Paul Krugman's *Return to depression economics and the crisis of 2008* (2008) and George Cooper's *The origin of financial crises* (2008) will suffice.

long time and exposes us to facets of those events that we never knew of before.

Historical enquiry thus facilitates the gaining of insight into the business environment of the 1920s – it forces us to imagine the rampant investment-trust driven stock-jobbing environment of the time, fuelling the path to the momentous 1929 Great Crash (Galbraith 1967) and the 1930s Great Depression. We are thrown into the bewilderment of the crash of Carlo Ponzi's money-making arbitraging with International Reply Coupons (Zuchoff 2006); Kreuger's infamous international match conglomerate's rise and fall (Sparling 1932, Shaplen 1960, Partnoy 2009), the crash of Samuel Insull's utility empire (McDonald 1962, Wasik 2006), President Hoover's belligerent attitude to commercial behaviour, Roosevelt's promise to invoke legislation – the Securities and the Securities Exchange Acts – to drive his New Deal remedies to inject 'truth in securities', creation of the Securities and Exchange Commission, Ferdinand Pecora's witch hunt on American bankers and his hounding, eventually into jail, of New York Stock exchange chief Richard Whitney, and the creation of Fannie Mae in 1938. Here, studying history truly takes on its learning mantle.

History and causality

Debate over historical causation has a long pedigree. It may be that the above brief discussion of enquiry into matters like the GFC will provide a window to explain what has gone awry in the present climate by reconstructing what went wrong 75 years ago. The idea, no doubt, is that whatever was the cause then might be similar to the cause now.

Accounting provides an ideal laboratory setting to consider history and causality issues. We can, for example, research and faithfully report when 'double entry' was first used, according to the available evidence; we can partially reconstruct the patterns of accounting practices 400 years ago by analysing the timing of variations in methods employed in the early Italian ledgers; and we can form opinions as to when the practice of allocating common costs in particular ways seems to have emerged and when transfer pricing became a common practice. We show later in setting 3 that we can identify whether a decision-making or accountability function underpinned double-entry bookkeeping treatises around the time and after the Renaissance. The details of those events and of others like them are an important element in obtaining an overall perspective of the development of accounting *practices* in general and of those noted in particular. But, changes in ideas precede deliberate changes in practice. If we are interested in the development of ideas, then the chronology of practices is a useful device for signalling approximately when changes in ideas may have occurred.

Ideas are products of the settings in which they arise. When ideas have become firmly entrenched in the literature of a discipline, a mere chronology is insufficient to explain their persistence. Descriptions of the contexts in which the ideas first arose, and of those into which they subsequently have been transported, are essential for that task also. For, if the contexts are different and the differences have not been detected, the propriety of any continued acceptance of them may properly be questioned.[3]

In seeking to better understand how 'fair value' ideas had 'drifted' into accounting thought and practice in the early part of the 20th century, it was noted (Clarke 1980) that "*the* cause of an event is likely to be impossible to detect amongst the agglomeration of occurrences about the same time" (emphasis added); 'the fetish of the single cause', or of a cause *par excellence*, to Black (1954) was 'a value judgment' and an 'impediment' for history (pp193–94). If the 'real cause' of a historical event was asked for, Walsh (1951) explained, "the proper answer would be that there was no cause over and above the several causes given" (p197). At best, only numerous other events that may have contributed collectively to the one being examined can be identified'. Clarke further observed:

---

3 One of Bill Birkett's Sydney School colleagues Wells (1978) identified such an instance in relation to the allocation of overhead costs. Arguably this 'sliding' from one context to another provoked Ray Chambers' attack on Historical Cost accounting, and Bill Birkett's determination to change the way in which accounting was taught and practised – one of Bill's more significant achievements. His reports on competencies for IFAC and the IIA discussed in chapters 13 (by Bill Connell) and 14 (by Peter Roebuck and Maria Barbera) of this book bear this out.

Generally, the overall pattern of antecedent events can only be regarded as accidental. Some antecedents may be planned and occur according to the plan, so may the sequence of them ... [but] 'To the purist historian nothing is accidental' (Walsh, p191), there is some cause for every occurrence. 'Accident' has been used in discussions of the philosophy of history to describe events which 'represent a sequence of cause and effect interrupting ... clashing with – the sequence with which the historian is primarily concerned (Carr 1964, p99).

Nevertheless, so-called accidents such as the shape of Cleopatra's nose, which is reputed to have infatuated Antony, the monkey bite that led to King Alexander's death, and the premature death of Lenin at 54, did influence the course of subsequent events and "it is futile to spirit them away, or to pretend that in some way or other they had no effect" (Carr 1964, p103). The meaning given to 'accidents' here does not conflict with the one just noted. *Accident* is used here to describe the *combination* of elements implicated in particular events, their *pattern* and not the events themselves. It applies also to the patterns which created settings conducive to the development and the entrenchment of particular ideas in the accounting literature.

Curiously, at a time when the Great Depression events outlined above were occurring, Oakeshott (1933) observed that history should give "a complete account of change ... in history, *pour saviour les choses, il fait saviour le detail*" (p143), thereby restricting history to a narration of the facts. Later, in contrast, Melden (1952) asserted the opposite view that history written as "a mere catalogue arranged in chronological order ... would explain nothing because it included everything" (p24).

There is no need to engage in that dispute, except to observe that for the purpose of the following commentary, it serves us well to bear both in mind. For in relation to the Great Depression and the measures taken to root out its causes and those contributing to them, both have their place. Knowledge of the facts, their time and place is critical to understanding the vagaries of the time, their similarities and dissimilarities with those of the present. Discriminating those that are the more important and the anecdotal insights into the Ponzi's, Insull's, Kreuger's, Pecora's actions and Roosevelt's almost legendary willingness to jump at solutions, colours, but also informs our appreciation of what we should look for in understanding the present.

Fair-value accounting and the GFC

Consider the recurring examinations of accounting's role in economic boom and busts during the past 75 years. Most recently this has re-emerged in the context of 'fair-value accounting' being perceived as *the*, or *a*, major culprit in the current credit crisis, with its associated *unexpected* collapses and bailouts of financial institutions worldwide. Many financial press articles have suggested a line of argument similar to that in the following extract from Sarah Johnson, 'New tips for testing fair value amid turmoil':

> Another standard setter has entered the fray to try helping accountants and auditors deal with fair values during the credit crisis. The guidance from the IASB – is the latest in a rush of advice geared to dealing with the intricacies of marking assets to market. And it comes as critics increasingly are calling fair-value [accounting] a major culprit behind the current financial turmoil.[4]

Contiguously, several in the financial sector have engaged in special pleading, suggesting that such fair-value prescriptions are not what is required – rather they proposed that fair-value accounting be suspended – and for the US banks it was. It is as if 'fair-value accounting' was a recent device arising in a uniquely contemporary setting. The debate that is emerging lacks input from those who have studied similar crises and accounting's role over the last 75 years. But, the post-World War I hyper-inflation leading to the 1929 crash, the 1930s, the 1965–67 conglomerate boom/bust, Australia's 1967–70 mining boom and bust, the post-1980s savings and loans crisis period, and the UK's 1970s secondary banking property-related crisis were analogous economic settings; as also was the 1990s Japanese banking crisis with its associated 'lost decade' of economic growth.

---

4 7 October 2008, from CFO.com. Many references to accounting being the 'cause of the present GFC' appeared in the financial press in November 2008 through April 2009 (see FCAG 2009).

To consider the merits of whatever accounting system is under scrutiny in the above episodes requires a historical perspective.

Another focus is instructive. In the aftermath of the current sub-prime GFC, monographs are appearing providing prescriptions of how to ensure such a crisis does not return. For example, leading economist Robert J. Shiller (of *Irrational exuberance* [1999] fame) was one of the first, with his book *The subprime solution: how today's global financial crisis happened and what to do about it* (2008). Chapter six, 'The promise of financial democracy' canvasses six reforms to improve what he describes as the 'Information Infrastructure'.

- Providing comprehensive financial advice
- Establishing a consumer-oriented governmental financial watchdog
- Adopting default conventions that work well for most individuals
- Improving the disclosure of information for financial securities
- Creating large national databases of fine-grained information pertaining to individuals' (entities') economic situations (like the SEC's XBRL database just on-line)
- Creating a new system of economic units of measure i.e. an inflation-adjusted currency like the 1967 Chilean inflation-adjusted unit, *Unidad de fomento*.

Here, we might well ignore the first four, arguably, motherhood statements without a detailed enquiry into the funding and monitoring mechanisms involved. From concentrating on the latter two propositions that directly relate to accounting, it is clear that to be able to assess properly such policy prescriptions one needs a detailed knowledge of the history of accounting's role in (i) prior periods of *unexpected* corporate collapses and (ii) previous price-level adjusted proposals.

Specific settings using accounting history by the authors

Below, our inquiries are premised on a belief that historical enquiry would better inform current public policy debates on matters of accounting theory, in three areas in particular: (i) injecting accounts with the effects of price and price level changes in the private sector in the 1970s and 1980s and then in the public sector in the late 1980s and 1990s; (ii) corporate law reforms following corporate dilemmas such as *unexpected* corporate collapses and major takeover plays after extended boom periods; and (iii) seeking evidence from several sources about what are the functions of accounting – decision making and accountability combined. This has entailed two types of studies: (a) those examining historical evidence from the old bookkeeping manuals on the emergence of double-entry bookkeeping; and (b) those analysing material contained in the newly developed *R.J. Chambers Archive* within the archives unit of the University of Sydney.[5] Specifically that work explores Chambers and others' correspondence covering the formative 1950s and 1960s so-called golden age of normative research.

Setting 1: the hyperinflation/accounting translation projects – implications for present fair-value accounting debates

Private sector exercises

During the 1960s the problems of accounting for price and price-level changes emerged in the context of the rampant inflation at the time. *Inflation* was the focus. But the episode refocused attention on matters that had first arisen as a specific accounting focus during the German hyperinflation and similar major spikes in price levels in many European countries following World War I. Researchers sought a better understanding of the factors that had influenced the 1920s European business economists' accounting proposals in the light of the economic vicissitudes of the 1921–23 hyperinflation, and the re-emergence of many of those proposals in the Anglo-American inflation accounting literature during the late 1960s through to the mid-1980s. In a peculiar coincidence it brought leading scholars into contact and placed them on similar paths of enquiry. Richard Mattessich (1982, 1984), for example, was exploring a similar territory. Thus, whereas it emerged as a

---

5 See at chamberslibrary.econ.usyd.edu.au. For a summary of the Archive see Dean et al. (2006).

consequence, not as a deliberate primary path of enquiry, accounting measurement emerged as a contiguous development.

The aim was to provide public policy inputs into lengthy private and later public (see below) sector debates on the accounting for price and price-level changes during the 1970s and 1980s. Inflation peaked in Anglo-American countries in the mid-1970s at around 25%. Of course some countries experienced much higher levels (Israel, Brazil, Mexico, etc.). More generally, the historical inquiries were to glean a better understanding of the antecedents of alternative systems of accounting, particularly indexed historical cost accounting and current value accounting. This entailed numerous lengthy translation exercises coupled to analyses of those translations of the early 1920s German and Dutch accounting literature. Specifically, original works of the leading German and Dutch authorities, Fritz Schmidt and Theodor Limperg, were examined. Many of those works had their first exposure in the Anglo-American accounting literature.[6] Such enquiry entailed the resurrection of the musings of earlier scholars, generally long-forgotten, exiled from the contemporary accounting literature. Schmidt and Limperg re-emerged as leading protagonists regarding accounting for price level changes.[7]

Research into public sector performance measures

A related program of historical inquiry occurred in the latter part of the 1990s through research into public sector accounting, especially examining the efficacy of Public Trading Enterprises' financial performance indicators, infrastructure asset valuation practices, and accounting developments for local governments in NSW. This was undertaken jointly by Clarke and Dean with Bob Walker. Several journal articles resulted (1999a, 2000a and 2000b) and an Australian Research Council Large Grant was awarded (Walker, Jones, Dean and Edwards) in 2003, producing further publications, such as Walker, Dean and Edwards (2004) and Walker and Jones (2007).

---

6 See Clarke 1976, 1982, 1984, 1988; Dean & Clarke 1986; Clarke & Dean 1989, 1990; Clarke, Dean & Graves 1990, 1995; and Graves, Clarke & Dean 1989.

7 See Clarke & Dean 1992 and a chapter on the leading 1920s German *Betriebswirtschaftslehre* theorist, Fritz Schmidt in Dick Edwards' *Twentieth century accounting thinkers*, 1994.

Policy implications

A major policy conclusion of our work in this area is the way in which material was transported, 'drifted', over time from one setting to another – in the 1920s from the utility rate-base setting context to the accounting by non-utility public companies, later in the 1970s from the private sector company setting to the public setting of *accounting for inflation*, and more recently to the accounting for financial assets held according to *intended* disposal criteria. Frequently this has been without due consideration of the idiosyncrasies of each setting, nor with reference to the detailed debate on the matter that has preceded each episode. The inappropriateness of assuming a 'one-size-fits-all' solution to the price and price-level problem was the outcome. It is not that such an approach is not a possible solution, but it has to be properly argued not assumed.

Setting 2: how corporate failures fuelled examination of the accounting for corporate groups

The cross-disciplinary nature of this program area is evident in several articles in respected refereed law journals, *Australian Business Law Review, Company & Securities Law Journal* and *Australian Journal of Corporate Law* as well as in many accounting journals (see references). Importantly these articles have been cited in both accounting and law journal articles.

The program had two limbs. The first considered the revealed accounting practices of (often *unexpected)* failed companies (as evidenced from inspectors' reports and other autoptic sources) which have provided a control against which the earlier reported practices are then compared. Numerous anomalies were identified in the areas of management, accounting and auditing, and the regulation of corporate conduct. Analysing these anomalies unearthed recommendations for policy change. The study of anomalies has been a lifelong endeavour of the authors and a characteristic feature of the 'Sydney School' (Chambers 1973b).

For us, it underpinned several article-length publications in the accounting and legal literatures like Clarke and Dean (1992, 1997), culminating in two research books – *Corporate collapse: accounting, regulatory and ethical failure* (1997, substantially revised and republished with changed sub-title in 2003, then translated and published in Chinese in 2006) and *Indecent disclosure: gilding the corporate lily* which was published in 2007. It is to be noted here that Bill Birkett and Bob Walker had previously pursued similar matters

in their analyses of corporate failures. It was a 'Sydney focus' in the 1970s –
Birkett and Walker (1971) and Chambers (1973a). Our books (1997, 2003,
2007) drew on their example and followed in that tradition. There we augmented those earlier exercises, suggesting that creative accounting was
equally likely to be the consequence of complying with the Accounting Standards as deviating from them, that the financials of most companies that had
not failed were thus equally misleading as those that had, that arranging
corporate affairs through groups and the *consolidation* mode of accounting
for those groups were grossly misleading, and thus that auditors faced an
impossible task – they are on 'a hiding to nothing'. Recent revelations in the
aftermath of the sub-prime mortgage credit crisis associated with *unexpected
collapses*, bailouts and government guarantees of financial institutions, attest
to that.

Policy implications

Research into *unexpected* corporate collapse over five decades revealed accounting
to be an ineffective instrumentation. The features of those failures – the frequently
excessive gearing, inadequate disclosure of assets' market worths, and when pressured the resort to *feral* accounting, has justified their being considered recurrent
events, almost invariably entailing manipulations of interrelated companies comprising so-called *corporate groups*. They are not *one-offs*. Their characteristics are
indicative of a seriously fractured reporting system, desperately in need of reform.
Reform, not necessarily to eliminate deliberate misleading reporting, but to avoid being misleading, notwithstanding the best of intentions. For a common experience of
many of those that failed is that their misleading financials were as much the result of
complying with the standards as of deviating from them. This work argued the need
for a new group accounting system – one that highlights the interconnectedness of
the complex groups dominating commercial activities. A related outcome is recognition that accounting is truly auditing's devil. For auditing to be an effective quality
control mechanism, accounting, as currently prescribed, needs to be reformed. We
have advocated the need for accounting measures to 'tell-it-as-it-is', using a form of
mark-to-market accounting, something of critical importance at present. The most recent output in this area are chapters 7–9 of *Indecent disclosure: gilding the corporate
lily* (2007).

The second limb of this program area is a sub-branch of the analysis of failed
companies – administering corporate group liquidations where cross debts
are in focus. It has spawned a series of articles and working papers, involving

joint explorations with University of Sydney colleagues of Bill Birkett (Luckett & Dean 1983, Dean & Luckett 1983) and (Dean, Houghton & Luckett 1999). Initial forays covered the legal and accounting issues, and more recently the econometric issues involved with interrelated debts and corporate group liquidations. Resulting papers have aroused the interest of legal and operations research (OR) scholars and practitioners as evident in the citing in: (i) a leading Australian practitioner text on liquidations and receiverships by McPherson (1985), (ii) the 1995 and subsequent (most recently the 2007) editions of the leading company law text in Australia, Ford and Austin's *Principles of company law*; (iii) numerous legal articles on corporate groups and the law in the 1990s; and (iv) as the basis of invitations to Clarke and Dean to make submissions to legal and parliamentary inquiries like CASAC's late-1990s analysis of Australia's corporate groups (see CASAC 2000), the South African Company Law Reforms in the late 1990s; our appearances before the Joint Committee of Public Accounts and Audit in July 2002, before Justice Neville Owens' HIH Royal Commission in November 2002 and the Federal Parliament's Joint Committee on Corporations and Financial Services in 2004 and 2005.

This line of research had previously resulted in a request by one of Australia's leading legal firms, Minter Ellison, seeking advice (from Dean and Luckett) in the early 1990s regarding litigation in a major corporate law case, *Westmex Operations Pty Ltd (in liq.) v. Westmex Ltd (in liq.) and Ors*, before the New South Wales Supreme Court. This request was specifically based on earlier hypothetical analytical works by Dean and Luckett (1983, 1984) related to implications in liquidation when a Deed of Cross Guarantee is in place within a corporate group of companies. The case involving the Westmex Limited corporate group led to reconsideration of the suitability of the 1983–84 liquidation model with a reformulation culminating in an article in the leading international OR journal, the British *Journal of the Operational Research Society* (Houghton, Dean & Luckett 1999). It was also a progenitor of funding for a successful 2000–03 ARC Large Grant Application, which resulted in several accounting and law articles.

Policy implications

Research into the administration of corporate groups subject to ASIC-administered Deed reveals many issues. The analytical modelling work suggests that a mathematical benchmark for creditors in liquidation is feasible and workable. The other main finding is the lack of evidence to support the view that the ASIC class order deed of cross guarantee (unique to Australian commerce) has proven a net benefit to society. And there is compelling evidence that creditors generally have not benefited. The most recent output in this area is reflected in chapter 8 of *Indecent disclosure: gilding the corporate lily* (2007) and the article 'Solvency solecisms ...' in *Australian Accounting Review* (with Margret, April, 2008). As well there is a working paper by van der Laan and Dean (2009) which is drawn from her PhD thesis.

Setting 3: how historical insights invited a rethink on the function of accounting and the related accounting measurement questions

This entails two avenues of enquiry: (a) examining the role of double-entry bookkeeping from the 16th to 18th centuries, and (b) examining previously unpublished correspondence of several 'golden age' academics on measurement issues in accounting. The explorations reveal historical-based input to modern debates about the functions of accounting – viz, decision making and accountability and related policy implications.

Re-examining the role of double-entry bookkeeping from the 16th to 18th centuries

The part played by double-entry bookkeeping (DEB) in the rise of capitalism in western Europe has been the subject of academic attention and debate for more than a century. Our interest in this topic was aroused by sources of relevant comment concerning early uses of DEB identified in Chambers' *An accounting thesaurus* (1995). These sources, augmented by a systematic search of surviving treatises on DEB published in Britain between 1547–1799, comprise extended evidence that enable us to make '*justified* statements' (Napier 2002, p136) in support of the notion that writers encouraged a capitalist mentality among the rising merchant class. They did this by communicating to the merchant the potential of DEB for presenting economic events in a financial form that enabled a merchant to evaluate the amount and profitability of business investments and provided data on which to base decisions designed to enhance the "value and condition of his estate" (Stephens 1735, p4). Further, based on the known occupations of these writers and drawing on knowledge of the operation of an international trading enterprise, the Hudson's Bay Company, we speculate that DEB might have played a part in helping owners manage their affairs during the major economic and social developments that are known to have occurred in Britain and Western society more generally between the 16th and 18th centuries (Edwards, Dean & Clarke 2009).

Policy implications

Current standards setters are revisiting efforts at developing a conceptual framework (CF) of accounting – they are grappling with matters that first require a specification of the functions of accounting. This problem has been evident for centuries, with still no acceptance that accounting has contiguous multiple functions to be satisfied. Further, there are implications for accounting history researchers. Revisiting the evidence underpinning debate over whether DEB was inextricably connected with the development of capitalism in England and western Europe illustrates the need in historical accounting research to question the conventional (accepted) wisdom that DEB was more directed to addressing accountability than decision making matters, in this case through the interpretation of the evidence upon which that wisdom is derived.

Examination of previously unpublished correspondence of several golden-age academics on measurement in accounting

Historical research (Dean & Clarke 2009) also has provided insights into the development of ideas by the scholarly community. Scholars interact synergistically to produce novel outputs; rarely perhaps is an idea forged without active or passive collaboration. Through analysis of primarily hitherto unexamined archival correspondence between Ray Chambers and (primarily) Ernest Weinwurm from 1955 to 1964, insights were gained into some unresolved fundamental accounting issues about the function of accounting and the related measurement questions. Those issues remain at the forefront of present day IASB and FASB deliberations seeking a CF for accounting. Ernest Weinwurm, former professor of accounting at De Paul University and The Institute of Management Science (TIMS) foundation member, is shown to have been an "unknown accounting academic soldier" in the wider academic community, by facilitating the exposure of the antipodean Ray Chambers' ideas on the function of accounting and measurement, to a wider US audience. Eventually those ideas would penetrate the deliberations of the American Accounting Association, the AICPA and TIMS organizations. By identifying the circumstances of Chambers' ideas gaining a foothold in the US accounting literature in the early 1960s, we gain insights into a vital episode in the development of accounting thought. The subtle influences Weinwurm had on Chambers' thinking are chronicled, especially those ensuring that measurement would be a main foundation of his reforms, eventually coalescing into his continuously contemporary accounting (*Co-CoA*). The importance for current standards setters is an acceptance of the need to develop a technically sound measurement approach as part of its conceptual framework deliberations.

Policy implications

After 30 years of deliberations by the major international standards setting bodies, the IASB and FASB, they still seek to resolve the function of accounting and the related measurement issues. They have set themselves a five-year time horizon (from 2007) to provide the answer. We have demonstrated in this work that one possible path would be to examine more closely the debates of the 1950s and 1960s on measurement (published and unpublished) for guidance. Returning to Chambers 1955 'Blueprint' we show that "accounting is both a means of measurement and a system of communications; both should therefore contribute to its concepts". It is relevant to internal and external uses. This view was fundamental to the alliance formed by Chambers, Weinwurm and others in the 1960s. The implications for today's standards setters are clearly evident. There is a need for the simultaneous consideration of these functions of accounting, with internal and external uses of accounts equally weighted. Failure to do so will result in another opportunity lost. The latest CF exercise will be destined to become another example of Sterling's 'recycling of ideas' – without 'resolving problems' (1975, 1979).

Conclusion

In this brief overview we have tried to illustrate Bill Birkett's influence on us (and by implication those who likewise influenced him) by outlining some of our historical analyses across several settings with the use of a variety of historical sources. In all cases the focus has been on searching through a historical lens for ways to improve accounting thought and practice. Identifying practices and thought that are deficient is the first step in that process –

truly a Birkett-inspired endeavour. This was an overarching element of re-search undertaken by his Sydney School of Accounting colleagues. In that, Bill Birkett played an integral part. It underpinned his teaching and engagement with the accounting profession throughout his career. As we reflect on our time with Bill, his penchant for 'wide' reading, his capacity to see the wood despite the trees, his interest in anomalies and similarities, we realize how his influence remains with us.

References

AAA, (1977). *Statement of theory and theory acceptance* (SATTA). American Accounting Association.

Baker D (2009). *Plunder and blunder: the rise and fall of the bubble economy*. Sausalito, CA: PoliPointPress.

Birkett WP & Chua WF (1988). The institutionalization of management accounting, 1950–1985. *Proceedings of the Fifth World Conference of Accounting*, August.

Birkett WP & Walker RG (1971). Response of the Australian accounting profession to company failures in the 1960s. *Abacus*, 7(2): 97–136.

Birkett WP & Walker RG (1972). Professional ideas on research in accounting: Australia, 1930–49. *Abacus*, 8(1): 35–60.

Black M (1954). *The historian's craft*, (trans by P Putnam). Manchester: Manchester University Press.

Bradbury M, Dean G & Clarke F (2009). Incentives for corporate group financing. Forthcoming, *Abacus*, 45(4).

Bruner RF & Carr SD (2007). *The panic of 2007: lessons learned from the market's perfect storm*. New York: John Wiley & Sons.

Bryer R (2000a). The history of accounting and the transition to capitalism in England. Part one: Theory. *Accounting, Organizations and Society*, 25(2): 131–62.

Bryer R (2000b). The history of accounting and the transition to capitalism in England. Part two: Evidence. *Accounting, Organizations and Society*, 25(4–5): 327–81.

Carr EH (1964). *What is history?* Harmondsworth: Penguin.

Chambers RJ (1995). *An accounting thesaurus: 500 years of accounting*. New York: Pergamon.

Chambers RJ (1973a). *Securities and obscurities: a case for reform of the law of company accounts*. England: Gower Press.

Chambers RJ (1973b). Observation as a method of inquiry – the background of *Securities and obscurities*. *Abacus*, 19(2):156–75.

Chiapello E (2007). Accounting and birth of the notion of capitalism. *Critical Perspectives on Accounting*, 18(6): 263–96.

Clarke F (1982). *The tangled web of price variation accounting*. New York: Garland Publishing. Revision of PhD dissertation (1982). *Accounting and the price variation problem: an examination of the development of the ideas underlying the inflation accounting prescriptions issued by the professional accountancy bodies in Australia, Canada, New Zealand, South Africa, the United Kingdom and the United States to 1980*. University of Sydney.

Clarke F (1980). Inflation accounting and the accidents of history. *Abacus*, 16(2): 79–99.

Clarke F (1976). A closer look at Sweeney's stabilized accounting proposals. *Accounting and Business Research*, Autumn: 264–75.

Clarke F (1996). A treasury of accounting thought: R. J. Chambers' '*An accounting thesaurus: 500 years of accounting*'. *Abacus*, 32(1): 111–17.

Clarke F (1988). Accountants' use and abuse of Hicks: the power of literature citation in the development of ideas. *Economia Aziendale*, 3: 409–30.

Clarke F & Dean G (1992). Chaos in the counting house: accounting under scrutiny. *Australian Journal of Corporate Law*, 2(2): 177–201.

Clarke F & Dean G (1989). Conjectures on the European influences on Sweeney's stabilized accounting. *Accounting and Business Research*, Autumn: 291–304.

Clarke F & Dean G (2007). *Indecent disclosure: gilding the corporate lily*. Melbourne: Cambridge University Press.

Clarke F & Dean G (1990). *Limperg and Schmidt: bedrijfseconomie or betriebswirtschaft?* New York: Garland Publishing.

Clarke F & Dean G (1997). Creative accounting, compliance and financial commonsense. *Australian Journal of Corporate Law*, August: 366–86.

Clarke F & Dean G (2009). Ray Chambers and Ernest Weinwurm – scholars in unison: a nurturing of mutual convictions on measurement in accounting. Working paper, April.

Clarke F & Dean G (1993). The law and accounting: the separate legal entity principle and consolidation accounting. *Australian Business Law Review*, August: 246–69.

Clarke F & Dean G (1992). The views of Limperg and Schmidt discovering patterns and identifying differences from a chaotic literature: pattern, chaos and order. *International Journal of Accounting and Education*, 27: 287–309.

Clarke F, Dean G & Graves F (1995). The development of Walter Mahlberg's inflation accounting theory in the light of contemporary critiques by Schmalenbach and Schmidt. In SP Garner & A Tsuji (Eds), *Studies in accounting history*. Westport, CT: Greenwood Publishing Group.

Clarke F, Dean G & Graves F (1990). *Replacement costs for cost accumulation and pricing: accounting reform in post World War I Germany*. New York: Garland Publishing.

Clarke F & Dean G (1989). Graves on Mahlberg: Whither Sweeney and Schmidt's 'Tageswirtbilanz'. *The Accounting Historians Journal*, Summer: 101–09.

Clarke F, Dean G & Oliver K (2003). *Corporate collapse: accounting, regulatory and ethical failure*, 2nd edn. Melbourne: Cambridge University Press. Chinese translation (2006), foreword by Dawaei Xi, Head of Shanghai National Accounting Institute. Shanghai Republic Publishing House with Cambridge University Press.

Clarke F, Dean G & Oliver K (1997). *Corporate collapse: regulatory, accounting and ethical failure*. Cambridge: Cambridge University Press.

Clarke F, Dean G & Margret J (2008). Solvency solecisms: corporate officers' problematic perceptions. *Australian Accounting Review*, 18(1): 71–80.

Cooper G (2008). *The origins of financial crises*. New York: Vintage.

Dean G & Luckett P (1983). A conceptual approach to the problem of incorporating the phenomenon of debt interdependencies upon liquidation. *Accounting and Finance*, 23(2): 31–50.

Dean G, Clarke F & Wolnizer P (2006). The R. J. Chambers Collection – an archivist's revelations of 20th century accounting thought and practice. *Accounting Historians Journal*, June, 2006, pp145–166.

Dean G & Clarke F (1986). Schmidt's 'Betriebswirtschaft' theory. *Abacus*, 22(2): 65–102.

Dean G & Clarke F (2005). Corporate officers' views on cross guarantees and other proposals to lift the corporate veil. *Company & Securities Law Journal*, 23: 299–321.

Edwards RJ (1994). *Twentieth century accounting thinkers*. London: Routledge.

Edwards RJ, Clarke F & Dean G (2009). Merchants' accounts, performance assessment and decision making in mercantilist Britain. *Accounting, Organizations and Society*, 34(5): 551–70.

Financial Crisis Advisory Group (FCAG) (2009). *Financial Crisis Advisory Group Report*. 28 July, FCAG.

Ford A & Austin R (2007). *Principles of company law*. Sydney: Butterworths.

Galbraith JK (1967). *The great crash*. Harmondsworth: Penguin.

Goodman RS & Kruger EJ (1988). Data dredging or legitimate research method? Historiography and its potential for management research. *Academy of Management Review*, 13(2): 315–25.

Graves F, Clarke F & Dean G (1989). *Schmalenbach's dynamic accounting*. New York: Garland Publishing.

Houghton E, Dean G & Luckett P (1999). Insolvent corporate groups with cross guarantees: a forensic-LP case study in liquidation. *Journal of the Operational Research Society*, 50: 480–96.

Krugman P (2008). *Return of depression economics and the crisis of 2008*. New York: Penguin.

Luckett P & Dean G (1983). Cross debts: notional calculations in liquidation. *Australian Business Law Review*, 11: 69–74.

Lee T, Clarke F & Dean G (2008). Scandals. In S Walker & RJ Edwards, *Compendium on accounting*, (pp408–29). New York: Routledge.

Lee T, Clarke F & Dean G (2008). The dominant manager and the reasonably careful and cautious auditor. *Critical Perspectives on Accounting*, 19(5): 677–711.

Mattessich R (1982). On the evolution of inflation accounting: with a comparison of seven major models. *Economia Aziendale*, 1(3).

Mattessich R (1984). Fritz Schmidt (1982–1950) and his pioneering work of current value accounting in comparison to Edwards and Bell's theory. *Proceedings of the Fourth International Congress of Accounting Historians*, Pisa: Editrice.

Mattessich R (2007). *Two hundred years of accounting*. New York: Routledge.

McDonald F (1962). *Insull*. Chicago: University of Chicago Press.

McPherson L (1985). *Liquidations and receiverships*. Law Book Company.

Melden AI (1952). Historical objectivity, a 'noble dream'. *Journal of General Education*, 7(1).

Michaelson A (2009). *The foreclosure of America*. USA: Penguin.

Muolo P & Padilla M (2008). *Chain of blame*. New York: John Wiley & Sons.

Napier C (2002). The historian as auditor: facts, judgment and evidence. *Accounting Historians Journal*, 29(2): 131–55.

Oakeshott M (1933). *Experience and its modes*. Cambridge: Cambridge University Press.

Parker S (2008). *The great crash: how the stock market crash of 1929 plunged the world into depression*. London: Piatkus.

Partnoy F (2009). *Ivar Kreuger: the financial genius behind a century of Wall Street scandals*. New York: PublicAffairs.

Pecora F (1939). *Wall Street under oath: the story of our modern money changers*. New York: Simon and Schuster

Powell J (2003). *FDR's folly*. New York: Crown Forum.

Previts GJ, Parker L & Coffman E (1990). Accounting history: definition and relevance. *Abacus*, 26(1): 1–16.

Previts GJ, Parker L & Coffman E (1990). An accounting historiography: subject matter and methodology. *Abacus*, 26(2): 136–58.

Ritholtz B (2009). *Bailout nation*, New York: John Wiley & Sons.

Shaplen R (1960). *Kreuger: genius and swindler*. New York: Knopf.

Shiller R (1999). *Irrational exuberance*. NJ: Princeton University Press.

Shiller R (2008). *The subprime solution: how today's global financial crisis happened and what to do about it*. NJ: Princeton University Press.

Sparling E (1932). *Kreuger's billion dollar bubble*. New York: Greenberg.

Stephens H (1735). *Italian book-keeping reduced to an art*. London: W Mears.

Sterling R (1975). Relevant financial reporting in an age of price changes. *Journal of Accountancy*, February: 42–51.

Sterling R (1979). *Toward a science of accounting*. Houston: Scholars Book.

Taleb NN (2007). *The black swan: the impact of highly improbable*. New York: Penguin.

Van der Laan S & Dean G (2009). Corporate groups in Australia: state of play. Working paper, May.

Walker R & Jones S (2006). An alternative approach to identifying councils at risk. *Economic Papers*, 25(4): 347–57.

Walker R, Clarke F & Dean G (2000). Options for infrastructure reporting, *Abacus*, June:123–59.

Walker R, Dean G & Clarke F (1999). Reporting on the state of infrastructure by local government. *Accounting, Auditing and Accountability Journal*, 5(4): 441–58.

Walker R, Dean G & Clarke F (2000). Use of CCA in the public sector: lessons from Australia's experience with public utilities. *Finance, Accountability & Management*, 16(1):1–32.

Walker R, Dean G & Edwards P (2004). Infrastructure reporting uses and attitudes of preparers and potential users. *Finance, Accountability & Management*, 20(4): 351–76.

Walsh WH (1951). *An introduction to the philosophy of history*. London: Hutchison of London.

Wasik J (2006). *The merchant of power*. London: Palgrave Macmillan.

Wells MC (1976). A revolution in accounting thought. *The Accounting Review*, 51(3): 471–82.

Wells MC (1978). *Accounting for common costs.* Centre for International Education and Research in Accounting, Monograph 10.

Zuckoff M (2006). *Ponzi's scheme: the true story of a financial legend.* New York: Random House.

5

Transparency and corporate governance in Malaysia: before and after the Asian financial crisis

Richard Morris (UNSW), Tam Pham (UNSW) and Sid Gray (University of Sydney)

Abstract

Motivated by the Asian financial crisis of 1997–98, this study examines transparency and corporate governance in Malaysia, one of the worst affected countries, with a view to assessing the extent to which there have been improvements since the crisis and the influential factors involved. Our analysis of Malaysian listed companies in 1996 and 2001, i.e. before and after the crisis, reveals that both mandatory compliance and voluntary disclosures have improved since the crisis, but are still relatively low. The levels of and changes in disclosure are significantly positively associated with firm size. Mandatory compliance is higher for companies that raised debt or equity finance, had more small shareholders, and were more diversified. Voluntary disclosure is higher among more profitable companies but only in 2001. While Malaysian firms have adopted more corporate governance mechanisms since the crisis, our results suggest they may be substitutes for and not complements of transparency.

This chapter examines corporate financial reporting transparency in Malaysia before and after the Asian financial crisis of 1997–98. Transparency is measured in terms of compliance with Malaysian accounting standards (MASBs) as well as voluntary adoption of items in International Accounting Standards (IASs) and US Generally Accepted Accounting Principles (GAAP) covering a range of financial reporting issues. An early paper by Haniffa and Cooke (2002) investigated whether voluntary disclosure levels of Malaysian companies in 1995 were associated with corporate governance and cultural variables. The present study updates and extends Haniffa and Cooke (2002) by examining the determinants of both mandatory and voluntary disclosure by Malaysian companies before and after the Asian financial crisis.

Much happened in Malaysia after 1995. The Asian financial crisis of 1997–98 hit the country particularly hard. In all affected countries, poor levels of financial reporting transparency were an alleged cause of the crisis. Given that all such countries have endeavoured to improve accounting standards and standards of corporate governance, an increase in financial reporting transparency after the crisis would be expected. This paper investigates the extent to which Malaysian companies complied with MASBs and voluntarily adopted IASs or US GAAP before and after the Asian financial crisis. Also investigated is whether certain corporate governance factors are associated with transparency before and after the crisis

This chapter starts with background information on the Asian financial crisis and its impact on Malaysia. Next, the development of the hypotheses is discussed. The research methods, including data collection and sample selection, are then described. The results and findings are presented and finally the study's limitations and conclusions are discussed.

The Asian financial crisis and its impact on Malaysia

The Asian financial crisis began on 2 July 1997 when the Bank of Thailand abandoned pegging the *baht* against the US dollar. This triggered a wave of investor panic, currency collapses, stock market falls and property market slumps which quickly spread to neighbouring East Asian countries. The crisis reached Malaysia on 14 July 1997 when the Bank Negara Malaysia gave up its defence of the *ringgit* against the US dollar. The worst hit countries in the region were Thailand, Indonesia, Malaysia, South Korea and the Philippines.

The alleged causes of the crisis fall into two groups: the financial panic/ contagion view and the fundamentalist view (ADB 1999). In the financial panic/contagion view, most East Asian economies pre-crisis were basically sound – or at least not so unsound as to warrant the severity of the downturn that occurred. The crisis was spread through the region by a wave of international investor panic or 'herd behaviour' (Radelet & Sachs 1998). In the fundamentalist view, East Asian countries pre-crisis had endemic macroeconomic structural and policy weaknesses that left them unusually vulnerable to a loss of investor confidence (Poon 1999).

One of these weaknesses, of relevance to this study, was deficient corporate governance in East Asian countries. Dr S Mahbob, head of the National Economic Action Council Secretariat in Malaysia, stated that:

> The Asian financial crisis undeniably brought to the fore the issue of weak corporate governance. In fact, weaknesses in corporate governance were identified as among some of the factors contributing to the collapse of the equity markets, as well as the decline in investors' confidence in the region. (Mahbob, Forum Professional Muda Malaysia, 2000).

The crisis also created an environment where outside investors were vulnerable to expropriation by insiders (Francis et al. 2003). Outside investors therefore became sensitive to firms' corporate governance structures, which they may have previously ignored (Rajan & Zingales 2002).

Malaysia had many of the weaknesses described by the fundamentalist view. During the 1990s Malaysia had the largest debt and equity markets of ASEAN countries. A pegged exchange rate (against the US dollar) and free capital inflows led to a high level of foreign debt among Malaysian firms (Capulong et al. 2000). Excessive foreign borrowing on the part of Malaysian banks and corporations in the years leading up to the crisis fuelled investor panic and accelerated the Asian crisis. In addition, poor corporate governance and risk management on the part of Malaysian firms meant that many of them became insolvent when the Asian currencies were devalued (Poon 1999).

Malaysia is unique because of the long-term racial tension between the ethnic Malays and the minority Chinese. It is also unique in that Dr Mahathir, the Malaysian Prime Minister, rejected the International Monetary Fund (IMF) rescue package because of the conditions attached to it. These included: ending the discriminatory practices against minority Chinese and financial restructuring proposed by the IMF that would result in greater foreign ownership of many bumiputra (i.e. Malay-owned) companies. Dr Mahathir took alternative steps to stabilize the economy such as cutting interest rates, raising foreign debt from neighbouring Asian countries, re-pegging the *ringgit* against the US dollar in September 1998, restricting the trading of Malaysian stocks outside Malaysia, introducing a punitive tax for holding Malaysian stocks less than one year and making unofficial trading of the *ringgit* an illegal activity (Poon 1999).

Like other East Asian countries, Malaysia is in a recovery phase. Although the Malaysian equity market has been stable since mid-1998, desired government reforms included improvements in corporate governance and transparency, strengthening the enforcement of investor protection laws, corporate and debt restructuring and greater resource allocation to develop the Malaysian financial and equity markets (Capulong et al. 2000).

Development of hypotheses

Corporate governance and transparency before and after the Asian crisis

Previous studies indicate that investors value more highly firms in countries with legal environments conducive to more transparent disclosure (Francis et al. 2003). Johnson et al. (2000) found that the countries most affected by the Asian financial crisis had weak corporate governance systems. Poor corporate governance and weak investor protection laws in Malaysia made it vulnerable to a sudden loss of investor confidence (Johnson et al. 2000). Malaysia responded to the effects of the Asian financial crisis by increasing the number of accounting standards issued and by improving its corporate governance guidelines. This is consistent with the suggestion of La Porta et al. (2000) and Francis et al. (2003) that countries with weak investor protection laws are more likely to make accounting changes in the short-term than to undertake fundamental legal reform of investor protection laws. This is because regulators would be facing strong resistance to change by parties that benefit from weak investor protection laws (La Porta et al. 2000).

As at November 2002, the Malaysian Accounting Standards Board had issued 30 new accounting standards since its establishment in 1997. These standards covered more accounting issues than before the crisis and required greater disclosure by firms. Accordingly, by complying with the new accounting standards and corporate governance regulations, it is reasonable to expect that the disclosures of Malaysian firms will have become more transparent after the Asian financial crisis than before.

Gelb and Zarowin (2002) have examined the association between level of disclosure and the informativeness of stock prices. They found support for their hypothesis that high disclosure is more likely to have a positive association with current returns and future earnings. Furthermore, greater disclosure can reduce estimation risk and increase analyst following (Barry & Brown 1985, Coles & Loewenstein 1988, Handa & Linn 1993, Coles, Loewenstein & Suay 1995, Lang & Lundholm 1996). It follows that an increase in the transparency of a firm would restore the confidence of both domestic and foreign investors. This would give Malaysian firms greater access to other sources of funding including foreign equity. Consequently, it is hypothesized that disclosure by Malaysian firms will have become more transparent following the Asian financial crisis in order to restore investor confidence.

Hypothesis 1 (H1): Disclosure in the annual reports of Malaysian firms will be relatively more transparent after the Asian financial crisis than before the crisis.

The Asian financial crisis resulted in greater scrutiny of the operations and disclosures of East Asian countries and their firms by the IMF, the World Bank and international and domestic investors. Malaysia introduced a Code of Corporate Governance for individual companies in 2000. Therefore, a positive association between firm-level corporate governance mechanisms and transparency might be expected. In saying this, it is assumed that corporate governance mechanisms are complements rather than substitutes. Given the seriousness of the financial crisis of 1997, and evidence of complementarity from studies in other countries,[1] such an assumption seems warranted. Accordingly, we hypothesize that:

Hypothesis 2 (H2): The greater the adoption of firm-level corporate governance measures the higher will be the transparency of financial reports.

Ownership concentration and family control

La Porta et al. (1998), Claessens et al. (2000), Backman (2001), Ang and Ciccone (2002) and Ball et al. (2003) have found that the ownership structure of East Asian countries is highly concentrated, with family ownership dominating. In the early 1990s, the total market capitalization of the top 500 listed firms in Asia controlled by overseas Chinese family groups was greater than $400 billion, of which $155 billion was in Hong Kong, $55 billion in Malaysia, $42 billion in Singapore, and $35 billion in Thailand (Ball et al. 2003). This type of ownership structure may arise due to weaknesses in countries' investor protection laws (La Porta et al. 1998, Ang & Ciccone 2002). Shleifer and Vishny (1997) and Claessens et al. (2000) posit that the primary agency problem in countries with weak investor protection laws is between insider and outsider shareholders, rather than between managers and owners, where family insiders are concerned to retain control of their businesses.

Claessens et al. (2000) found that in all East Asian countries, including Malaysia, control by insider shareholders is enhanced through pyramid structures and cross-holdings among firms. They also found that 60% of firms that are not widely held have board members who are related to the controlling shareholder. Fan and Wong (2001) posit that in East Asian firms it is difficult to challenge the dealings of the controlling owner(s) with internal and external control systems. This is because the board of directors, particularly independent directors, and the take-over markets appear to be ineffective. In this way, firms with a significant controlling shareholder and/or a family-controlled board are likely to have greater incentives to

---

1 For example, Ho and Wong (2001) report a positive association between voluntary disclosure by Hong Kong companies and their proportions of independent nonexecutive directors and the existence of audit committees.

expropriate wealth from minority shareholders and to be less transparent. This conjecture is consistent with Francis et al. (2002) who argue that less outsider ownership results in more information asymmetry between insider and outsider shareholders. Conversely, firms with a greater number of small shareholders (i.e. greater shareholder dispersion) are likely to be more transparent because of greater demand for more disclosure on the part of outsider shareholders. Similarly, where a company has substantial institutional shareholders, there will be greater demand for more disclosure as these large external shareholders attempt to monitor their investments. Thus the following hypotheses will be tested:

> Hypothesis 3a (H3a): Firms with a greater proportion of insider (family or management) ownership relative to outsider ownership will be less transparent than firms with a greater proportion of outsider ownership.

> Hypothesis 3b (H3b): Firms with a greater dispersion of shareholders will be more transparent than firms with lesser dispersion of shareholders.

> Hypothesis 3c (H3c): Firms with a greater number of institutional shareholders will be more transparent than firms with fewer institutional shareholders.

Auditor type

The role of auditing is to add credibility to a firm's financial reporting by constraining any opportunistic behaviour on the part of the management (Hung 2000, Reynolds & Francis 2000). Choi and Wong (2002), Fan and Wong (2001), and Francis et al. (2003) present evidence that quality auditing, particularly that done by Big Five auditors, may act as a substitute for weak corporate governance. Fan and Wong (2001) also find that firms with large agency problems are more likely to hire a Big Five auditor. Consistent with US studies, Fan and Wong (2001) find that Hong Kong and Singaporean Big Five auditors tend to charge clients who have greater agency problems a higher audit fee and set a lower audit qualification threshold. They therefore concluded that auditors do play a monitoring role and do alleviate agency conflicts in East Asia. Surprisingly, the monitoring role of the auditors does not hold for their Malaysian sample. They found that from 1994 to 1996, the Malaysian Big Five auditors gave a *discount* if the client's controlling shareholder possessed effective control and there was a large divergence between control and ownership. They attribute the opposite effect found for the Malaysian sample to the fact that the Malaysian audit market is subject to fee regulation, which may result in a different fee structure to that of other East Asian countries.

In the wake of the Asian Crisis, the Big Five have changed their audit approach to a risk-based approach. This involves continuously identifying a client's business risks and continually assessing the client's ability to control for these risks. For example, Ernst & Young introduced its 'Audit Innovation' to Asia and KPMG introduced its 'Business Management Process' (Backman 2001). Thus one would expect that Big Five auditors provide higher quality auditing and that firms engaging a Big Five auditor are more transparent. Further, Morris et al. (2004) found a positive association between auditor type and the transparency level of Indonesian firms. We will therefore test the following hypothesis:

Hypothesis 4 (H4): Disclosure by firms that engage a Big Five auditor will be more transparent than firms with a non-Big Five auditor.

Transparency and leverage

The literature on voluntary disclosure shows that greater disclosure also creates other benefits. These benefits include a lower cost of capital (e.g. Botosan 1997, Botosan & Plumlee 2002) and a lower bid-ask spread (e.g. Welker 1995, Healy et al. 1999). Consistent with Healy et al. (1999), Leuz and Verrecchia (2000) conducted a study on German firms and found that higher disclosure not only results in a lower bid-ask spread but also leads to higher trading volume.

Previous studies suggest that in Asian firms in general, and in Malaysian firms in particular, family ownership tends to predominate (Ball et al. 2003). Ball et al. (2003) argue that these family-owned businesses tend to prefer financing by internal funds, through an internal market, and bank loans rather than by public equity and debt. In addition, Asian firms tend to form contracts based on personal networking. Rajan and Zingales (2002) argue that relationship-based systems work in an environment in which contracts are poorly enforced and capital is scarce. As a result, the price system and the signals it provides may be suppressed. Thus one may argue that the benefits of a lower bid-ask spread for public debt, achieved through greater disclosure, may be limited for Asian firms. Even if this is the case, the Asian financial crisis has prompted further regulation of the banking system in Malaysia and in East Asian countries generally. Banks are now faced with greater scrutiny of their operations and risk exposures. It follows that banks would prefer more transparent borrowers, or they will impose a higher cost of debt to compensate for the higher level of risk. High leverage firms would therefore benefit from a lower cost of debt through greater transparency. The following hypothesis will therefore be tested for our Malaysian sample:

> Hypothesis 5: Firms with higher leverage will be more transparent than firms with lower leverage.

Transparency and firm size

Firm size is the factor most consistently reported as significant in studies of firms' disclosure policies; large firms disclose more information than small firms (Gray et al. 1995). They thus will have more transparent annual reports. From agency theory, the potential benefits of negotiating the extent of disclosure would also increase with firm size. In disclosing more, larger firms might face smaller competitive losses than would smaller firms. Providing more information also incurs information production costs, and larger firms are more able to afford the extra costs. Furthermore, the skills required in collecting and disclosing extra information may be more available in larger firms. Larger firms might also be more likely to list on overseas stock exchanges, particularly US stock exchanges, and thus be required to provide additional information. Finally, larger firms by virtue of their size may simply have *more* to disclose. Accordingly, we hypothesize that:

> Hypothesis 6 (H6): The greater the size of Malaysian firms, the higher will be the transparency of their financial reports.

Cultural variables

Based on Gray's (1988) model about the influence of culture on accounting, and that model's antecedents in Hofstede (1980), Haniffa and Cooke (2002) argued that the ethnic mix of Malays and Chinese on corporate boards and the ethnicity of Malaysian companies' chief executive officers would be associated with voluntary disclosure levels. Specifically, companies with a higher proportion of ethnic Malays on the board of directors and/or with an ethnic Malay chief executive officer will disclose less than companies where ethnic Chinese predominated. They found some limited support for their hypotheses. We will therefore test their hypotheses on our data:

> Hypothesis 7a (H7a): The greater the proportion of ethnic Malays on the boards of Malaysian firms, the lower will be the transparency of their financial reports.

> Hypothesis 7b (H7b): Companies with ethnic Malays as chief executive officers will have lower transparency in their financial reports than companies with ethnic Chinese chief executive officers.

Profitability

Given the scope for opportunistic earnings management practices available to some companies, those companies which are genuinely profitable, would wish the market to find their profit reports credible. Consistent with signalling theory (Morris 1987), genuinely profitable companies are likely to increase their disclosures so that the share market can better judge the credibility of their profit numbers. Therefore, the following hypothesis will be tested:

> Hypothesis 8 (H8): Companies which are more profitable will have higher transparency in their financial reports

Raising finance

Previous studies (Healy & Palepu 2001, pp420–21) have found that companies approaching the debt or equity markets will increase their disclosures in order to reduce the costs of equity and debt financing. Therefore the following hypothesis will be tested:

> Hypothesis 9: Companies which have raised equity or debt finance in the current year will have more transparent financial statements than companies which did not.

Corporate complexity

Corporate complexity was included as a control variable. Complexity can occur through corporate diversification. Rather than diversifying horizontally or vertically, East Asian conglomerates tend to expand by acquiring many small companies that are unrelated to their core operations (Backman 2001). Some examples of Malaysian conglomerates are the Hong Leong Group, controlled by Quek Leng Chan, with interests spanning banking, finance, hotels, property and media. The Malaysian Resources Group is another conglomerate operating in infrastructure development, engineering, power generation, property and media (Backman 2001). Such diversification, due to the resulting corporate complexity, may impede corporate governance (Mitton 2002). Corporate complexity can also increase through cross-holdings, where individual companies within a group take equity stakes in each other (Backman 2001).

Lins and Servaes (2002) argue that corporate complexity provides incentives for the controlling shareholders to pursue their own objectives. Another significant implication of corporate complexity is the difficulty it creates for consolidating results. It is even difficult for stock analysts and auditors to analyze the overall performance of a particular group because holding companies in Asia are almost never listed. Usually only the subsidiary(ies) is (are) listed. Backman (2001) argues that one possible reason for this is that by listing on the stock exchange, the holding company itself would then have to be consolidated in the group, as part of the listing requirements. Mitton (2002) found that highly diversified firms were the worst stock performers during the Asian financial crisis. This finding is consistent with that of Claessens et al. (1999) and Lins and Servaes (2002) who also found a diversification discount for East Asian firms.

On the other hand, firm complexity may also mean that the company has a lot to tell about itself because its operations are so diverse, so it will disclose more. Morris et al. (2004) found that complexity, as measured by the number of business segments a firm had was positively related to transparency among Indonesian firms. Therefore, we are unable to say whether firm complexity will be positively or negatively related to transparency in Malaysia. Accordingly we include it as a control variable.

Industry effect

As in disclosure studies in some other countries, Haniffa and Cooke (2002) argued that the level of voluntary disclosure in Malaysia would vary with industry. They found such an effect. *A priori*, it is impossible to predict which industries will disclose more than others. Accordingly we include industry in the study, but as a control variable.[2]

Research methodology

Measuring transparency

Transparency has been defined as: "a process by which information about existing conditions, decisions and actions is made accessible, visible and understandable".[3] However, while transparency is an intuitively appealing concept, there is little consensus about its measurement. For example, transparency has previously been measured broadly and narrowly: broadly as a combination of factors including adoption of international accounting standards, and narrowly as timeliness in incorporating economic income, particularly negative economic income or bad news, into accounting profit (Ball et al. 2003).[4]

---

2 Haniffa and Cooke (2002) tested 27 hypotheses, but found support for less than half of them. The present study covers most hypotheses of Haniffa and Cooke (2002) for which they found empirical support. We have changed some of their measures in light of recent literature on corporate governance and accounting.

3 Willard 1998, p.v. Other definitions of transparency exist. For example, Vishwanath and Kaufmann (2001, p41) define transparency as "the increased flow of timely and reliable economic, social, and political information about investors' use of loans; the creditworthiness of borrowers; government's provision of public services, such as education, public health, and infrastructure; monetary and fiscal policy; and the activities of international institutions." They identify four characteristics of transparency, namely information accessibility, relevance, quality, and reliability.

4 Ball, Robin and Wu (2003) adopt this interpretation because they argue that information quality is determined in large part by the underlying economic and political factors influ-

In the Malaysian setting, it seems clear that any measure of financial reporting transparency should include the extent to which Malaysian companies comply with the MASBs. Compliance with MASBs is considered a necessary but not sufficient component of transparency.

Companies may also wish to voluntarily disclose information not required by the MASBs. Although the scope for voluntary disclosure is broad, credible guidance on what to disclose voluntarily are the benchmarks provided by IASs and US GAAP to the extent not already covered by the MASBs. Although MASBs are re-badged IASs, at any time they lag behind the then latest IASs; and US GAAP is not mandatory in Malaysia.

As a result, we measured transparency, in a manner similar to Gray et al. (1995), via a series of indexes based on (a) MASBs and (b) IASs and US GAAP. Our approach extends previous attempts to measure transparency by Rahman (1998) and is consistent with suggestions by Ho and Wong (2001) and Capulong et al. (2000, p.10). The transparency indexes are comprised of disclosure items from MASBs, IASs and US GAAP in relation to seven major areas of accounting: consolidation, business combinations, goodwill, segment reporting, related party disclosures, foreign exchange, and financial instruments (table 1). Arguably the seven selected areas are most likely to be sources of unexpected bad news during times of macroeconomic crisis. They are thus areas in which poor accounting and disclosure practices are likely to have the greatest impact. The seven areas include those selected by Rahman (1998) in his examination of disclosure quality among East Asian firms.

---

encing managers' and auditors' incentives, and not only by accounting standards. They argue that in countries with more market-oriented information, debt is more likely to be issued to parties that do not hold private information. In this market-oriented environment, enforcement of dividend and debt covenants from public agreements create greater demand for timely information. In the more market-oriented countries, stockholders and analysts play a larger economic role in monitoring company management. Timely incorporation of economic income into accounting income would increase the effectiveness of this monitoring role.

Table 1: Accounting standards included in transparency indices.

	Malaysian Accounting Standards (Masbs)		International Accounting Standards (IASs)	US GAAP
	Prior to 1996	2001		
Segment Reporting	IAS 14 (SI 14) – Reporting Financial Information by Segment 1987	MASB 22 (2001) – Segment Reporting	14 (1997 revised)	SFAS 131 (1997), SFAS 14
Foreign Exchange	IAS 21 (1985) – Accounting for the Effects of Changes in Foreign Exchange Rates	MASB 6 (1999) – The Effect of Changes in Foreign Exchange Rate	21	SFAS 52
Related Party Disclosure	N/A	MASB 8 (2000) – Related Party Disclosures	24	SFAS 57
Consolidation	IAS 27 (1990) – Consolidated Financial Statements and Accounting for Investments in Subsidiaries	MASB 11 (2000) – Consolidated Financial Statements and Investments in Subsidiaries	27	ARB 51, SFAS 94
	MAS 2 (1989) – Accounting for Acquisition and Mergers	MASB 21 (2001) – Business Combinations	IAS 22 (1999 revised)	APB 16, SFAS 141 (2001– superseded APB 16)
	MAS 6 (1997) Accounting for Goodwill	MASB ED 28 – Goodwill		

	Malaysian Accounting Standards (MASBs)		International Accounting Standards (IASs)	US GAAP
	Prior to 1996	2001		
Accounting for Associates	IAS 28 (1994) – Accounting for Investments in Associates	MASB 12 (2000) – Investments in Associates	28 (1998 revised)	APB 18
Joint Ventures	IAS 31 (1993) – Financial Reporting of Interests in Joint Ventures	MASB 16 (2000) – Financial Reporting of Interests in Joint Ventures	31, 31 (1998 revised)	APB 18
Financial Instruments	N/A. The only standard on Financial Instruments available prior to 1996 is IAS 32 (1995). The MAS was yet to adopt this standard in 1996. Accordingly, Malaysian companies may voluntarily disclose information in relation to financial instruments	MASB 24 (2001) – Financial Instruments: Disclosure and Presentation	32 (1998 revised), 39 (1998)	SFAS 119 (1994), 133 (1998) – superseded SFAS 199, 137 (1999), 138 (2000)
		Currently Reviewing IAS 39 (1998) – Financial Instruments: Recognition and measurement		

In the transparency measure used, each company's disclosures were coded '1' if the item was disclosed, and '0' if not disclosed. A transparency score was obtained by adding up all scores of 1 and dividing by the maximum possible score. Thus for company *i* the transparency score would be:

$$TRANSP_i = \frac{\sum_k \sum_j a_{jk}}{TOTM}$$

where:

a_{jk} is company *i*'s score on the jth item in the kth accounting standard.

TOTM is the maximum possible score across all standards.

A difficulty arose in handling items thought to be 'not applicable' for a particular company. If undisclosed items were genuinely 'not applicable', coding them as zeros would bias that company's transparency score downwards. For example, if a company actually had no joint ventures the company would still be assigned zeros for all joint venture items in the index even though they were irrelevant. If a particular firm has 31 '1s', 40 '0s', and 10 items which seem to be 'non-applicable', then assigning zeros to the non-applicable items would mean that the transparency score would be 31/81 = 0.3827. The alternative is to subtract 'not applicable' items from TOTM, in which case the transparency score would be 31/(81–10) = 0.4366.

However, the accuracy of adjusting TOTM for 'not applicable' items depends on the overall quality of annual report disclosures. As mentioned, South-East Asian countries allegedly had poor annual reporting transparency before the crisis. Therefore, *a priori* the probability of being able to tell whether an undisclosed item was genuinely 'not applicable' seemed to be low and thus the probability of coding error high. On balance, it was considered more prudent to code all undisclosed items as zeros. The strategy has three advantages. First, it eliminates judgement errors by the researcher (although, of course, the resulting transparency measure is biased downwards). Second, if an improvement in transparency is found, we can be confident that the improvement in transparency is not driven by coding factors. Third, as discussed later in the section on robustness checks, the strategy gave better fitting statistical models than one in which 'not applicable' items were deducted from TOTM.

TRANSP1 measures disclosures required by MASBs as at 2001. TRANSP2 contains disclosure items that were required by MASs in 1996 and that continued to be required by MASBs in 2001. By holding the accounting standards constant between 1996 and 2001, TRANSP2 permits an assessment of any change in compliance with national accounting standards that is not attributable to an improvement in the accounting standards themselves. If there is any improvement in disclosure compliance in TRANSP2, it could be attributed to the improvement of enforcement laws by the Malaysian government after the Asian crisis and/or greater market pressures for increased disclosure.

TRANSP3 includes the disclosures required by IASs/US GAAP as at 2001 (including, but not restricted to, MASB disclosure requirements effective in 2002). In 2001, the MASB had not fully adopted all existing international accounting standards, such as those on segment reporting, goodwill, and financial instruments. With the exception of goodwill, the other two areas of accounting were adopted by the MASB at a later stage and became effective in 2002. We found that the majority of firm disclosures in our sample did not fully reflect these new accounting standards in their 2001 annual reports, as they were not required by the MASB as at 2001. In the absence of domestic standards on some of the accounting issues, we conjectured that some firms might have elected to surpass the domestic disclosure requirements by voluntarily adopting international standards in their 2001 annual reports. TRANSP3 captures that possibility.

In order to determine whether the transparency of Malaysian firms is influenced by international standards, TRANSP4 includes the disclosures required by IASs and/or US GAAP but not by MASBs in 2001 or 2002. To examine whether Malaysian firm disclosures are influenced by US GAAP rather than IASs, TRANSP5 includes the disclosures required by US GAAP but not by IASs or MASBs in 2001. Similarly, TRANSP6 includes the disclosures required by IASs but not by US GAAP or MASBs in 2001. Therefore TRANSPs 3–6 are measures of voluntary disclosure by Malaysian companies.

Regression models

We tested hypotheses H1 to H9 using the following cross-sectional multi-variate model.

$$TRANSP_{j,it} = \beta_0 + \beta_1 YEAR_{it} + \beta_2 AUDITOR_{it} + + \beta_3 INTAUD_{it} + \beta_4 AC_{it} + \beta_5 INDDIR_{it} + \beta_6 INDDSH_{it} + \beta_7 DUALLD_{it} + \beta_8 CNTRL + \beta_9 SMLSH_{it} + \beta_{10} SHNUM_{it} + \beta_{11} INSTSH_{it} + \beta_{12} LEVG_{it} + \beta_{13} LNTA_{it} + \beta_{14} SIZE_{it} + \beta_{15} PROFIT_{it} + \beta_{16} DIVF_{it} + \beta_{17} INDUSTRY_{it} + \in_{it}$$

The model was tested with each year separately, then both years pooled.

$TRANSP_{j,it}$ is the transparency index j of firm i at time t, where j represents each type of transparency measure (TRANSP1 to TRANSP6), and t equals fiscal year 1996 or 2001.

$YEAR_{it}$ equals 1 for 2001 and 0 for 1996. This variable only appears in the model which pools both years' data.

Several corporate governance variables were included, all based on prior research especially Haniffa and Cooke (2002), Ho and Wong (2001). $INTAUD_{it}$ equals 1 for the existence of an internal auditor, 0 otherwise; ACit is the number on the audit committee; $INDDIR_{it}$ is the number of independent directors and $INDDSH_{it}$ is the percentage of shares held by independent directors. Agency theory posits that the separation of chairperson and managing director roles provides checks and balances on management's performance and decisions (Argenti 1976). Forker (1992) provides evidence that a dominant personality, including dual leadership where a managing director is also the chairperson of the board, is associated with poor disclosure. Therefore we included dual leadership ($DUALLD_{it}$) in the model, assigning 1 for the existence of dual leadership, 0 otherwise.

$AUDITOR_{it}$ is a dummy variable that equals 1 for a Big Five auditor and 0 otherwise.

Shareholder dispersion is proxied by $SHNUM_{it}$, which is the number of shareholders of firm i at time t scaled by net assets; and also by $SMLSH_{it}$ equal to the total percentage of voting stock held by shareholders who each had 5% or less of the issued shares of firm i at time t; INSTSH$_{it}$ is the percentage of shares held by institutional shareholders.

LEVG$_{it}$ is the total debt/total assets of firm i at time t; and LNTA$_{it}$ is the natural logarithm of total assets of firm i at time t. DIVF$_{it}$ represents the degree of firm diversification (or complexity) and is the number of business segments the firm operates in.

CNTRL indicates the extent of control by one party or family group. Due to data limitations, CNTRL was measured differently in 2001 and 1996. In 1996, ultimate owners of companies could not be traced from annual reports because large holdings were often owned by nominee shareholders, and ultimate owners were not shown. Therefore, we measured CNTRL in 1996 (and in 2001 when both years were pooled) by TOPSH, the percentage holding of the largest shareholder. By 2001, companies were required to disclose the name/s behind nominee shareholdings, and directors' direct and indirect shareholdings were also disclosed. With those disclosures, we were able to use a scheme based on La Porta et al. (1999), to classify the ultimate ownership of each company. In 2001, CNTRL thus took three values: 0 = the company's shares are widely held, defined as no single shareholder owning 20% or more of the issued shares; 1 = 20% or more of the company's shares owned by a widely held corporation; 2 = 20% or more of the company's shares owned directly or indirectly by a family group or by the government. Like La Porta et al., we used a 20% threshold to determine concentrated ownership. Malaysian public companies disclose larger shareholders in their annual reports. If these were individuals or companies and none held 20% or more of the issued shares, the company was coded 0 and considered to be widely held. If at least one of these shareholders had 20% or more of the issued shares, and the shareholders were individuals or private companies, the public company was coded 2 and considered to be family controlled. If one or more of the large shareholders was itself a public company, we obtained that second public company's shareholding details from the KLSE website. If those major shareholders all held less than 20% of its issued shares, the original public company was coded 1 and classified as controlled by a widely held corporation. However, if an individual or private company held at least 20% of the second public company's issued shares, the first pub-

lic company was coded 2 and deemed to be family controlled. If a third public company held 20% or more of the second public company's issued shares,
the above process was repeated until the major shareholders were found to
be either individuals or a private company.

Table 2: Sample industry sectors.

Industrial Products	34
Trading Services	21
Properties	16
Consumer Products	11
Plantations	10
Construction	8
Finance*	3
Mining	1
Total Sample	**104**

* These are diversified firms, operating in finance, plantation, property and consumer
products industries.

Sample firms

Letters of request for 1996 and 2001 annual reports were faxed and/or mailed
to the 567 Malaysian companies listed on the KLSE at December 2001. Fif-
teen companies' annual reports were available online and 140 firms
responded to the faxed/mailed letters. The response rate was therefore 24.7%.
However, 34 firms could not be included because they had not provided a
1996 annual report. To increase the sample size, we included 13 firms that
provided a 1997 annual report but from which 1996 financial data could be
obtained from comparative figures. Eleven firms in the banking and insurance industries were excluded because their disclosures were regulated by the
Banking and Financial Institution Act 1989. A further five firms were ex-

cluded because their annual reports were incomplete and one firm did not have a 2001 annual report. The final sample consisted of 104 firms (i.e. 208 firm-years), which is 18.34% of the population of Malaysian publicly listed companies (table 2). As far as is known, there were no government-owned enterprises in the sample.

Results

Changes in transparency

Table 3 shows that each of the TRANSP indexes significantly increased between 1996 and 2001, thus supporting H1. Nevertheless, the actual level of each index is still very low, particularly for the voluntary disclosure indexes. The highest average TRANSP score is TRANSP2 at 0.3470 in 2001, and the highest maximum score is 0.5918 also for TRANSP2. TRANSP2 holds constant the MASB standards across both years, and its increase indicates that even compliance with older domestic standards improved after the crisis. Mean scores on the mandatory disclosure indexes TRANSP 1 and 2 exceed those for voluntary disclosure indexes TRANSPs 3–6: all the former are above 20%, all the latter are below 8%. Although TRANSP 3–6 all increase statistically significantly from 1996 to 2001, the actual improvement is very marginal.

Mandatory disclosure indexes TRANSPs 1 and 2

Table 4 presents ordinary least square regression results for the mandatory disclosure indexes TRANSPs 1 and 2 against all independent variables. The table shows regressions for each year separately first – TRANSP 1 for 2001, TRANSP 2 for 1996 – then both years combined with TRANSP 2, and finally change in TRANSP 2 (between 1996 and 2001) regressed on the independent variables for 2001.[5] When combining both years or looking at change in TRANSP between years, TRANSP 2 is used as the dependent variable be-

---

5 We also regressed change in TRANSP 2 on changes between 1996 and 2001 in all independent variables (excluding the industry dummies because they did not change). The regression equation was not statistically significant and so the results are not reported here.

cause it holds constant the MASBs in both years. For regressions covering 1996, the variable CNTRL was replaced by TOPSH. The regression which pooled both years has the YEAR dummy variable to capture the impact of the Asian financial crisis on TRANSP2; this regression was computed using the GLM univariate procedure in SPSS with YEAR as a fixed factor and other independent variables as covariates. All four regression equations are statistically significant. The first three have adjusted R^2s of 41.2%, 44.7% and 44.6% respectively, and the last (change in TRANSP 2) has 22.2%; all of which compares favourably with other disclosure index studies.[6]

YEAR is significant and positive in the pooled regression. Size is significant and positive in all four regressions, as are small shareholders and diversification in all regressions except that for change in TRANSP2. Equity raising and debt raising are significant and positive in two regressions each. Neither auditor nor any the corporate governance variables (internal auditor, audit committee, dual chair, independent directors' number and percentages of shareholding) were significant and positive. Indeed contrary to H2 and H4, audit committee and auditor were significantly negative for, respectively, two and three of the four regressions.

Voluntary disclosure indexes TRANSPs 3 and 4

Table 5 presents ordinary least square regression results for the voluntary disclosure indexes TRANSPs 3 and 4. As in table 4, table 5 shows regressions for each of 1996 and 2001, then both years combined, then change in TRANSP regressed on the 2001 independent variables. TRANSP 3 is used for the regression on 2001 variables; TRANSP 4 is used as the dependent variable for regressions covering 1996 only, both years, and the change in TRANSP on 2001. Unlike TRANSP 3, TRANSP 4 does not include IASs which became MASBs in 2002. For convenience, regressions for TRANSPs 5 and 6 are omitted from table 5 because they are not as strong as those for TRANSPs 3 and 4. All four regression models in table 5 are statistically sig-

---

6 For example, Haniffa and Cooke (2002, tables 6 and 7) have adjusted R2s of 46.3% and 47.9%; Gray et al. (1995) have adjusted R2s ranging from 14% to 46%.

nificant. They have adjusted R2s of 38.5%, 32.9% and 33.4% for the first three models and 14.2% for the change in TRANSP 4 model. Again, these compare favourably with other disclosure index studies.

Table 3: Changes in transparency.

Variables	Year	Min.	Max.	Mean	Standard deviation	Skewness	Paired t test probability	Wilcoxon test
TRANSP1	1996	0.0222	0.4111	0.2190	0.0855	-.077		
	2001	0.0889	0.5506	0.2968	0.1001	-.059	0.000**	0.000**
TRANSP2	1996	0.0192	0.5098	0.2786	0.1087	-.198		
	2001	0.0962	0.5918	0.3470	0.1181	-.120	0.000**	0.000**
TRANSP3	1996	0.0000	0.1690	0.0528	0.0352	.0843		
	2001	0.0000	0.2676	0.0795	0.0567	1.183	0.000**	0.000**
TRANSP4	1996	0.0000	0.1556	0.0582	0.0342	.812		
	2001	0.0000	0.2444	0.0750	0.0493	1.174	0.000**	0.000**
TRANSP5	1996	0.0000	0.1905	0.0376	0.0402	.913		
	2001	0.0000	0.1905	0.0509	0.0519	.960	0.002**	0.002**
TRANSP6	1996	0.0000	0.1481	0.0312	0.0376	.929		
	2001	0.0000	0.2222	0.0526	0.0576	1.256	0.000**	0.000**

*Significant at the 5% level (2–tailed).
** Significant at the 1% level (2–tailed).

Table 4: Regressions examining the association between MASB transparency indexes and the independent variables – unstandardized coefficients.

Variables	Pre-dicted Sign	TRANSP2 1996	TRANSP1 2001	TRANSP2 1996 and 2001	Change in TRANSP2 on 2001
Intercept	N/a	-0.352 (0.048)	-0.512 (0.002)	-0.413 (0.000)	-0.245 (0.218)
Auditor	+	-0.028 (0.074)	-0.001 (0.475)	-0.027 (0.037)	-0.051 (0.033)
Internal auditor	+	-0.005 (0.394)	-0.016 (0.277)	-0.147 (0.166)	-0.020 (0.246)
Audit committee	+	-0.017 (0.066)	-0.002 (0.426)	-0.012 (0.083)	-0.000 (0.493)
Independent direc-tors: no.	+	0.003 (0.296)	0.007 (0.208)	0.005 (0.137)	-0.006 (0.286)
Independent direc-tors: %Shareholding	+	0.091 (0.210)	0.231 (0.250)	0.061 (0.230)	0.168 (0.350)
Dual chairman	+	0.062 (0.026)	-0.037 (0.113)	0.006 (0.396)	0.026 (0.253)
Institutional share-holding	+	0.062 (0.279)	0.021 (0.347)	-0.010 (0.422)	-0.059 (0.194)
CNTRL / TOPSH	-	0.058 (0.208)	0.030 (0.012)	0.076 (0.077)	0.023 (0.083)
Small shareholders	+	0.080 (0.085)	0.078 (0.049)	0.101 (0.007)	-0.026 (0.332)
Number of share-holders	+	148.52 (0.024)	-116.95 (0.125)	54.708 (0.147)	-166.86 (0.099)
Equity-raising	+	0.090 (0.273)	0.319 (0.088)	0.168 (0.061)	0.201 (0.093)
Debt-raising	+	0.216 (0.011)	0.130 (0.186)	0.079 (0.097)	0.124 (0.254)
Leverage	+	0.012 (0.404)	-0.021 (0.124)	-0.012 (0.230)	-0.037 (0.058)

Variables	Pre-dicted Sign	TRANSP2 1996	TRANSP1 2001	TRANSP2 1996 and 2001	Change in TRANSP2 on 2001
Number of bankers	+	0.004 (0.122)	0.004 (0.104)	0.002 (0.191)	-0.000 (0.408)
Profit	+	0.000 (0.242)	-0.000 (0.308)	-0.000 (0.328)	0.000 (0.497)
Malay-chair	+	-0.810 (0.293)	0.017 (0.311)	0.002 (0.448)	0.033 (0.060)
Malay PCT	+	-0.000 (0.499)	0.026 (0.243)	0.002 (0.418)	0.026 (0.286)
Size	+	0.025 (0.004)	0.034 (0.000)	0.033 (0.000)	0.016 (0.047)
Diversification	n/a	0.023 (0.000)	0.012 (0.020)	0.019 (0.000)	0.004 (0.268)
Industries :					
Plantations	n/a	-0.050 (0.142)	-0.011 (0.372)	-0.033 (0.088)	-0.089 (0.034)
Consumer goods	n/a	0.022 (0.528)	0.013 (0.356)	-0.007 (0.391)	0.039 (0.378)
Industrial	n/a	-0.018 (0.437)	0.028 (0.153)	0.004 (0.419)	0.053 (0.133)
Trading	n/a	0.009 (0.733)	0.017 (0.262)	0.019 (0.160)	0.019 (0.581)
Year	+	n/a	n/a	0.057 (0.000)	n/a
F		4.043	4.413	7.951	2.228
Probability		0.000	0.000	0.000	0.005
Adj. R²		0.412	0.447	0.446	0.222

All probabilities in brackets are one-tailed except for n/a – signed variables.

Table 5: Regressions examining the association between IAS/USGAAP transparency indexes and the independent variables – unstandardized coefficients.

Variables	Predicted Sign	TRANSP4 1996	TRANSP3 2001	TRANSP4 1996 and 2001	Change in TRANSP4 on 2001
Intercept	N/a	-0.129 (0.027)	-0.256 (0.005)	-0.151 (0.001)	-0.154 (0.055)
Auditor	+	-0.010 (0.060)	0.000 (0.495)	-0.016 (0.004)	-0.019 (0.043)
Internal auditor	+	-0.004 (0.225)	-0.037 (0.006)	-0.011 (0.035)	-0.008 (0.241)
Audit committee	+	-0.006 (0.062)	-0.019 (0.004)	-0.010 (0.002)	-0.010 (0.049)
Independent directors : no.	+	0.016 (0.198)	0.003 (0.253)	0.003 (0.065)	-0.000 (0.421)
Independent directors: shareholding	+	-0.030 (0.209)	-0.146 (0.248)	-0.035 (0.202)	-0.105 (0.272)
Dual chairman	+	0.013 (0.102)	-0.011 (0.235)	0.005 (0.304)	0.018 (0.116)
Institutional shareholding	+	0.023 (0.253)	0.027 (0.214)	0.017 (0.203)	0.004 (0.444)
CNTRL/TOPSH	-	-0.015 (0.263)	0.001 (0.445)	0.003 (0.435	0.011 (0.056)
Small share-holders	+	0.022 (0.124)	0.019 (0.257)	0.012 (0.238)	-0.022 (0.180)
Number of share-holders	+	33.296 (0.085)	-21.229 (0.370)	-0.083 (0.449)	17.039 (0.371)
Equity raising	+	-0.050 (0.152)	0.007 (0.481)	0.004 (0.460)	-0.069 (0.284)
Debt raising	+	0.036 (0.115)	-0.047 (0.305)	0.016 (0.317)	-0.013 (0.429)

Variables	Predicted Sign	TRANSP4 1996	TRANSP3 2001	TRANSP4 1996 and 2001	Change in TRANSP4 on 2001
Leverage	+	0.015 (0.166)	0.000 (0.481)	0.008 (0.129)	0.009 (0.178)
Number of bankers	+	0.001 (0.108)	0.000 (0.319)	0.000 (0.476)	-0.002 (0.140)
Profit	+	-0.000 (0.114)	0.000 (0.035)	0.000 (0.156)	0.000 (0.040)
Malay chair	+	-0.002 (0.323)	0.004 (0.341)	-0.002 (0.336)	0.009 (0.163)
Malay pct	+	0.006 (0.336)	0.000 (0.487)	-0.007 (0.255)	0.004 (0.421)
Size	+	0.009 (0.003)	0.020 (0.000)	0.013 (0.000)	0.011 (0.003)
Diversification	n/a	0.005 (0.009)	0.002 (0.528)	0.002 (0.240)	-0.004 (0.204)
Industries :					
Plantations	n/a	0.005 (0.664)	-0.010 (0.612)	-0.003 (0.781)	-0.014 (0.402)
Consumer goods	n/a	0.007 (0.517)	-0.000 (0.981)	0.008 (0.447)	0.017 (0.334)
Industrial	n/a	-0.016 (0.043)	-0.008 (0.655)	-0.006 (0.370)	0.005 (0.739)
Trading	n/a	0.002 (0.852)	0.004 (0.796)	0.010 (0.198)	0.008 (0.586)
Year	+	n/a	n/a	0.016 (0.004)	n/a
F		3.804	3.114	5.322	1.715
Probability		0.000	0.000	0.000	0.042
Adj. R^2		0.385	0.329	0.334	0.142

All probabilities are one-tailed except for n/a – signed variables.

As with the mandatory TRANSP indexes in table 4, the variable YEAR is significant and positive when both years data are pooled, and size is significant and positive in all four regressions, thus supporting H1 and H6. For the other hypotheses support is patchy. Profit is significantly positively associated in 2001 with TRANSP 3 and change in TRANSP 4; while number of shareholders is significant only in 1996. Contrary to H2 and H4, auditor, and the corporate governance variables internal auditor, and audit committee are significantly negatively associated with the TRANSPs.

Robustness checks

As mentioned, in calculating the TRANSP indexes, all non-disclosed items were coded as 0 even if they appeared to be genuinely not applicable to particular companies. The resultant TRANSP scores are biased downwards. An attempt was made to recalculate the TRANSPs, adjusting the denominator TOTM for items thought to be not applicable. The adjusted TRANSP indexes are greater than those reported here, but when regressed against the independent variables, gave adjusted R^2s substantially lower than those reported in tables 4 and 5.

Discussion and conclusions

In this chapter, we examined the level of financial reporting transparency by Malaysian companies in 1996 and 2001; that is, before and after the Asian financial crisis, using two sets of indexes, one based on MASBs, the other based on IAS and/or US GAAP items not in MASBs. The former set measures mandatory disclosure, the latter voluntary disclosure. We investigated whether these transparency measures were significantly associated before and after the crisis with a set of explanatory variables drawn from the literature, and whether there has been any improvement in transparency following the crisis. The results show that there has been a statistically significant improvement in transparency, as measured by all our indexes, since the crisis. However, despite the increase, the average transparency scores of Malaysian companies in 2001 were still relatively low, both for mandatory disclosure (mean of TRANSP 2: 0.3470) and voluntary disclosure (mean of TRANSP 3: 0.0795). The low scores are driven only partly by the conservative coding strategy used. Overall, the results suggest that the transparency of Malaysian firms is still well below that required even by domestic accounting standards.

In both 1996 and 2001, all mandatory and voluntary TRANSP indexes were significantly positively associated with firm size, as predicted. The significance of the other independent variables depends on which TRANSP index and which year are being considered. Small shareholders are significantly positively linked with TRANSP 1 and TRANSP 2 in three of the four regressions in table 4, as are also equity raising and debt raising for two regressions each. The results suggest that in table 5, profit is significantly positively associated with TRANSP 4 and change therein; suggesting that companies doing well may try to signal that to the market by voluntarily disclosing more information.

The control variable diversification is significantly positive in three of the four regressions in table 4 (mandatory disclosure) but is significant in one regression only in table 5.

Neither the audit variable nor the corporate governance variables support hypotheses H2 or H4. Indeed, auditor, audit committee and internal audit have outcomes significantly opposed to these hypotheses, especially for voluntary disclosure TRANSPs 3 and 4, but also, to a lesser extent, for mandatory disclosure TRANSPs 1 and 2.

Our results are similar to those of Haniffa and Cooke (2002) in respect of size and profitability related to voluntary disclosure. However, unlike them, we found no support for an association between the ethnicity of boards of directors and board chairmen. Importantly, we have extended their study by examining disclosure in Malaysia before and after the Asian financial crisis and by investigating both mandatory and voluntary disclosure behaviour.

The significantly negative coefficients for auditor in tables 4 and 5 contrast with previous studies which found auditor type to have no significant role in determining the extent of voluntary disclosure by Malaysian firms (Hossain et al. 1994, Haniffa & Cooke 2002), or in some other Asian countries (Chau & Gray 2002). The univariate results show a significant increase in engagement of Big Five auditors from 1996 to 2001. However, the negative effect of auditor type on transparency in tables 4 and 5 may be due to external factors surrounding the Malaysian audit market. As part of foreign investment policy in Malaysia, Big Five auditors have to form an alliance with local Malaysian auditors in order to establish their business in Malaysia. Therefore the audit quality of the Malaysian Big Five auditors may not be as high as the quality of Big Five auditors in developed countries, where alliances with local auditors are not required. Certainly there appears to be no improvement in audit quality following the crisis. This observation of poor audit quality in East Asian countries in general, and in Malaysia in particular, is also made by Rahman (1998) and Capulong et al. (2000).

Unlike other East Asian countries, Malaysian audit fees are regulated.[7] Fan and Wong (2001) reported that Malaysia has the lowest audit fees in the East Asian region. It is possible that Malaysian economic policy, in restricting foreign ownership, together with the fact that many listed companies are family owned, results in less demand for audit service by firms with an international reputation (Simon et al. 1992). Evidence presented in previous auditing studies suggests a positive relationship between audit fee and audit quality. Accordingly, one implication of a regulated audit fee market is that it may negatively affect an auditor's incentives and hence audit quality and the level of transparency in financial reports.

The negative association between transparency and some corporate governance variables suggests that these corporate governance variables may be substitutes for disclosure rather than complements. On the other hand, given the widely held view that transparency and corporate governance were both inadequate before the crisis, and given that both significantly increased after the crisis, it is puzzling why the two should not be positively associated in tables 4 and 5. The negative association between transparency and corporate governance variables requires further investigation, because both are usually thought important for any company.

---

7 Simon et al. (1992) report that there is no Tier 1 (the Big Six/Five international accounting firms) audit fee premium found in the Malaysian audit market and that Tier 1 representation is less pronounced in Malaysia than in Singapore and Hong Kong. Simon et al. report that the size-adjusted market share of the then Big Eight in 1987 was only 48% in Malaysia, compared with at least 90% in both Hong Kong and Singapore.

Contrary to hypothesis H3a, CNTRL/TOPSH, used to measure family control of companies in 1996 and 2001 respectively, were significantly positively associated with TRANSP 1 and 2, mandatory disclosures, in three regressions in table 4, though transparency levels were relatively low. A possible explanation is that the measures of CNTRL/TOPSH do not adequately capture family control in our sample.

Our results have significant policy implications. Adopting international accounting standards as MASBs is clearly not sufficient in itself to achieve greater transparency. Malaysian regulators should employ more stringent mechanisms to enforce accounting standards and the listing requirements of the KLSE, and to enhance audit quality.

As in any research study, the current one has limitations. The transparency indexes are biased downwards because 'not applicable' items were coded as being not disclosed; but that coding does give a better model fit than our attempts to determine if items were 'not applicable' and to adjust the indexes upwards. The indexes are based on seven accounting areas – consolidation accounting, accounting for associates and joint ventures, foreign currency transactions, financial instruments, segment reporting and related party transactions – and so do not cover all aspects of disclosure. Nevertheless, the seven areas do cover issues arguably most likely to be the sources of unexpected bad news or important non-disclosures given the Asian financial crisis and the way in which Malaysian companies are financed and controlled. Also we cannot rule out that the increase in transparency observed between 1996 and 2001 was spurred not by the Asian financial crisis but by a long-term improvement in transparency as companies became more aware of the benefits of improved disclosure.

Future research may conduct similarly detailed single-country studies on other emerging markets so that international comparisons can be made. Such studies could also use a larger sample of both large and small firms covering more accounting areas to provide a more *complete* assessment of disclosure practices. It would also be informative to have knowledge about the effectiveness of emerging markets' firm-level corporate governance and how it relates to firm transparency and value.

References

Ang JS & Ciccone SJ (2001). International differences in financial transparency. Working paper, Florida State University.

Argenti J (1976). *Corporation collapse, the causes and symptoms.* New York: John Wiley & Sons.

Backman M (2001). *Asian eclipse: exposing the dark side of business in Asia,* rev edn. Singapore: John Wiley & Sons.

Ball R, Robin A & Wu JS (2003). Incentives versus standards: properties of accounting income in four East Asian countries. *Journal of Accounting and Economics,* 36: 235–70.

Barry CB & Brown J (1985). Differential information and security market equilibrium. *Journal of Financial and Quantitative Analysis,* 20: 407–22.

Botosan C (1997). Disclosure level and the cost of equity capital. *The Accounting Review,* 72: 323–49.

Botosan C & Plumlee MA (2002). A re-examination of disclosure level and the expected cost of equity capital. *Journal of Accounting Research,* 40(1): 2–22.

Capulong MV, Edwards D, Webb D & Zhuang J (2000). Corporate governance and finance in East Asia – a study of Indonesia, Republic of Korea, Malaysia, Philippines and Thailand. Volume 1 (A consolidated report). *Asian Development Bank.* www.adb.org

Chau GK & Gray SJ (2002). Ownership structure and corporate voluntary disclosure in Hong Kong and Singapore. *The International Journal of Accounting,* 37: 247–265.

Choi J & Wong TJ (2002). Auditor choice and legal environments: an international investigation. Working paper, Hong Kong University of Science and Technology.

Claessens S, Djankov S & Lang LHP (1999). Expropriation of minority shareholders in East Asia. Working paper, World Bank.

Claessens S, Djankov S & Lang LHP (2000). The separation of ownership and control in East Asian corporations. *Journal of Financial Economics,* 58: 81–112.

Coles JL & Loewenstein U (1988). Equilibrium pricing and portfolio composition in the presence of uncertain parameters. *Journal of Financial Economics*, 22(2): 279–303.

Coles JL, Loewenstein U & Suay J (1995). On equilibrium pricing under parameter uncertainty. *Journal of Financial and Quantitative Analysis*, 30(3): 347–64.

Craig R & Diga J (1998). Corporate accounting disclosure in ASEAN. *Journal of International Financial Management and Accounting*, 9(3): 246–74.

Fan JPH & Wong TJ (2001). Do external auditors perform a corporate governance role in emerging markets? Evidence from East Asia. Working paper, Hong Kong University of Science and Technology.

Fan JPH & Wong TJ (2002). Corporate ownership structure and the informativeness of accounting earnings in East Asia. *Journal of Accounting and Economics*, 33: 401–23.

Forker JJ (1992). Corporate governance and disclosure quality. *Accounting and Business Research*, 22(86): 111–24.

Francis JR, Khurana IK & Pereira R (2003). The role of accounting and auditing in corporate governance, and the development of financial markets around the world. *Asia-Pacific Journal of Accounting and Economics*, 10(1): 1–30.

Gelb DS & Zarowin P (2002). Corporate disclosure policy and the informativeness of stock prices. *Review of Accounting Studies*, 7(1): 33–52.

Gray SJ (1988). Towards a theory of cultural influence on the development of accounting systems internationally. *Abacus*, 24(1): 1–15.

Gray SJ, Meek GK & Roberts CB (1995). International capital market pressures and voluntary annual report disclosures by US and UK multinationals. *Journal of International Financial Management and Accounting*, 6(1): 43–68.

Handa P & Linn SC (1993). Arbitrage pricing with estimation risk. *Journal of Financial and Quantitative Analysis*, 28(1): 81–100.

Haniffa RM & Cooke TE (2002). Culture, corporate governance and disclosure in Malaysian corporations. *Abacus*, 38(3): 317–49.

Healy P, Hutton MA & Palepu KG (1999). Stock performance and intermediation changes surrounding sustained increases in disclosure. *Contemporary Accounting Research*, 16: 485–520.

Healy P & Palepu KG (2001). Information asymmetry, corporate disclosure and the capital markets: a review of the empirical disclosure literature. *Journal of Accounting and Economics*, 31(1–3): 405–40.

Ho SSM & Wong KS (2001). A study of the relationship between corporate governance structures and the extent of voluntary disclosure. *Journal of International Accounting, Auditing and Taxation*, 10: 139–56.

Hofstede G (1980). *Culture's consequences. International differences in work-related values.* Thousand Oaks, CA: Sage.

Hossain M, Tan LM & Adams M (1994). Voluntary disclosure in an emerging capital market: some empirical evidence from companies listed on the Kuala Lumpur stock exchange. *The International Journal of Accounting*, 29: 334–51.

Hung M (2000). Accounting standards and value relevance of financial statements: an international analysis. *Journal of Accounting and Economics*, 30: 401–20.

Johnson S, Boone P, Breach A & Friedman E (2000). Corporate governance in the Asian financial crisis. *Journal of Financial Economics*, 58: 141–86.

Klapper LF & Love I (2002). Corporate governance, investor protection and performance in emerging markets. Working paper, World Bank.

Kuala Lumpur Stock Exchange (KLSE) Listing Requirements 2001. klse.com.my.

Lang MH & Lundholm RJ (1996). Corporate disclosure policy and analyst behaviour. *The Accounting Review*, 71(4): 467–92.

La Porta R, Lopez-de-Silanes F, Shleifer A & Vishny R (1997). Legal determinants of external finance. *Journal of Finance*, 52: 1131–50.

La Porta R, Lopez-de-Silanes F, Shleifer A & Vishny R (1998). Law and finance. *Journal of Political Economy*, 106: 1113–55.

La Porta R, Lopez-de-Silanes F & Shleifer A (1999). Corporate ownership around the world. *Journal of Finance*, 54: 471–517.

La Porta R, Lopez-de-Silanes F, Shleifer A & Vishny R (2000). Investor protection and corporate governance. *Journal of Financial Economics*, 58: 3–27.

La Porta R, Lopez-de-Silanes F, Shleifer A & Vishny R (2002). Investor protection and corporate valuation. *Journal of Finance*, 57: 1147–70

Lemmon ML & Lins KV (2003). Ownership structure, corporate governance, and firm value: evidence from the East Asian financial crisis. *Journal of Finance*, 58: 1445–68.

Lim MH (1981). *Ownership and control of the one hundred largest corporations in Malaysia*. Oxford: Oxford University Press.

Lins K (2003). Equity ownership and firm value in emerging markets. *The Journal of Financial and Quantitative Analysis*, 38(1): 159–84.

Lins K & Servaes H (2002). Is corporate diversification beneficial in emerging markets? *Financial Management*, 31: 5–31.

Mahbob S (2000). The Asian crisis: what lessons have we learnt? *Forum Professional Muda Malaysia (Promuda)*, October 2000.

Mitton T (2002). A cross-firm analysis of the impact of corporate governance on the East Asian financial crisis. *Journal of Financial Economic*, 64(2): 215–24.

Morris RD (1987). Signaling, agency theory and accounting policy choice. *Accounting and Business Research*, 18(69): 47–56.

Morris RD, Ho BUS & Gray SJ (2004). Transparency of financial reporting before and after the Asian financial crisis: an empirical study of Indonesian company practices. *Asia-Pacific Journal of Accounting and Economics*, 11(2): 193–221.

Patel SA, Balic A & Bwakira L (2002). Measuring transparency and disclosure at firm-level in emerging markets. Working paper, Standard & Poor's, New York.

Poon S (1999). Malaysia and the Asian financial crisis – a view from the finance perspective. *African Finance Journal*, special issue.

Radelet S & Sachs J (1998). The onset of the East Asian financial crisis. Working paper, Harvard Institute for International Development.

Rahman MZ (1998). The role of accounting disclosure in the East Asian financial crisis: lesson learned? *UNCTAD Study: Accounting and Asian Financial Crisis.*

Rajan R & Zingales L (2002). Which capitalism? Lessons from the East Asian crisis. *Journal of Applied Corporate Finance,* 11(3): 40–48.

Reynolds JK & Francis J (2000). Does size matter? The influence of large clients on office-level auditor reporting decisions. *Journal of Accounting and Economics,* 30: 357–400.

Shleifer A & Vishny R (1997). A survey of corporate governance. *Journal of Finance,* 52: 737–83.

Simon DT, Teo S & Trompeter G (1992). A comparative study of the market for audit services in Hong Kong, Malaysia and Singapore. *The International Journal of Accounting,* 27: 234–40.

Vishwanath T & Kaufmann D (2001). Towards transparency: new approaches and their application to financial markets. *World Bank Research Observer,* 16: 41–57.

Welker M (1995). Disclosure policy, information asymmetry, and liquidity in equity markets. *Contemporary Accounting Research,* 11: 801–27.

Willard Report (1998). Report of the working group on transparency and accountability, G22 Working Group, October.

6

Formal rationality in the Spanish empire: government accounting in the Philippine tobacco monopoly, 1769–99

Maria Cadiz Dyball (Macquarie University)

*Abstract**

This historical study examines the role of government accounting systems as a formal mode of rationality in pursuit of a substantive end. In the early years of the Philippine tobacco monopoly, from 1766 to 1799, accounting played an enabling role in an elaborate system of control, surveillance and punishment deployed by the Spanish colonial state to increase its revenues. The Philippine tobacco monopoly reported cash surpluses which were remitted to the Royal treasury in Spain. Whilst the full potential of accounting appears not to have been fully attained, it was complicit in perpetuating a colonial project of domination and extraction of revenues from its colonized peoples.

'Power' does not necessarily mean just the capacity to apply force. More exactly, it can be applied to the underlying structures that made empire possible (Kamen 2002, pxxiii).

* This project was funded by a Macquarie University New Staff Research Grant. The author is grateful to Rod O'Donnell, Graeme Harrison and Salvador Carmona for their support for the project. The chapter also benefited from comments by Salvador Carmona and attendees of the 2006 Interdisciplinary Perspectives on Accounting Conference specially Chris Poullaos, Anne Pezet, David Cooper and Rodney Coyte.

This idea is supported by a rich body of accounting research that shows that underlying structures such as accounting practices were enmeshed within British and American colonial systems of government. Accounting practices worked in different ways to perpetuate British colonial policies of domination, subordination and exploitation of colonized peoples (Davie 2005, 2000; Neu 2000a, 2000b). The potency of accounting practices varied as colonized peoples actively resisted (Bush & Maltby 2004). In fledgling research on the American empire a passive form of resistance was alternatively used by colonized peoples by 'not-doing' accounting (Dyball et al. 2006, 2007). Thus research on the role of accounting in colonial relations shows that a healthy scepticism about accounting's potency as an agent in the enactment of imperialism, and in the construction and maintenance of empires, is to be encouraged (Annisette & Neu 2004).

A neglected context in accounting research is that of the Spanish empire. This chapter seeks to redress this gap by examining the role of accounting in the first 30 years of the Philippine tobacco monopoly (1769–99). This period is characterized by a compounding of motives for the Spanish colonial state to retain the Philippines as part of its empire. From beneficiaries of the Spanish colonial state's propagation of Christianisation, Filipino subjects were subsequently coopted as both agents and customers of a tobacco monopoly project. In particular, this chapter investigates the role of accounting practices in articulating an expansion of the substantive rationality of the Spanish empire's colonization of the Philippines. In Weberian (1978) terms, there was, in addition to a substantive rationality of propagation of the Catholic faith, a 'logic of action' for the Philippine-Spanish colonial state to financially support the Spanish empire.

My examination is largely based on primary materials on the Philippine tobacco monopoly that are stored in the Archivo General de Indias in Seville, Spain. Interpretations of these primary materials were supported by readings of secondary materials on the Spanish tobacco monopoly and the Philippine political, social and economic contexts during the 18th century.

The remainder of the chapter has five parts. The second section briefly surveys accounting research that exposes the role of accounting in colonial state administration and relations. It also reviews the role of accounting in the Spanish Royal Tobacco Factory 1760–90, an almost parallel period with that covered in this study, as analyzed by Carmona, Ezzamel and Gutierrez (1997, 1998). Section three explains Weber's (1978) description of substantive and formal rationalities and the role of bureaucracy and accounting in the pursuit of substantive modes of rationality. It also provides a background to the Spanish colonial state in the 18th century and articulates the requirements of a formal mode of rationality and bureaucracy, following the war against the British. It also provides a basis for my analysis in the fourth section where I describe the accounting practices in place for the tobacco monopoly. Section five provides an evaluation of the organization and administration of the monopoly. In the conclusion, I reflect on whether bureaucracy and government accounting practices facilitated the Spanish colonial state's pursuit of a substantive rationality of sustainable growth of the Spanish empire.

Literature review

Accounting and colonial relations

Accounting research on the mutually constitutive roles of a colonial state and accounting practices primarily focuses on the British experience (Annisette & Neu 2004), with fledgling research on the American empire. In pioneering work, Johnson and Caygill (1971) and Johnson (1982) explored how imperial Britain relied on an accounting infrastructure to manage the breadth of its empire. The expansion and consolidation of the British imperial state were shown to be associated with the imperial involvement of emergent accounting professional associations. A disturbing view was shown by Neu (2000a, 2000b) in the case of Canada, where accounting techniques were implicated in translating a British colonial policy which involved the subjectification of Canada's indigenous peoples. Specifically, accounting enabled the colonizer to exercise power over its colonial subjects through knowledge of them (Said 1979, cited in Neu 2000b, p165). A parallel theme is found in Davie's analyses of Fiji in which she saw accounting as involved in "the production of a calculative knowledge of imperialism" (2000, p330) and the "hierarchization and marginalization of the Fijian population" (2005, p77).[1] Both Neu and Davie dealt with cases where accounting enabled the colonizer to perpetuate a policy of domination of the colonies. In addition, Davie (2000) showed the potent role played by collaborative indigenous classes. These collaborators either shared the same ideology with the colonialists (Bakre 2004) or directly benefitted as agents in the implementation of the coloniser's policies (see also Petras 1981). However, there are also documented cases of failure of colonial policies and accounting to subdue indigenous subjects. Bush and Maltby (2004), for example, exposed how the West Africans resisted British colonial taxation resulting in a failed bid by the British to instil a 'self-disciplinary culture' into African subjects. Dyball et al. (2006; 2007) also suggested that accounting was not an active agent used by the American colonizer to appropriate spoils arising from its colonization of the Philippines. On the contrary, the rejection and subversion of accounting were critical elements in the successful appropriation by the Filipino political elites of the spoils arising from US colonial policy.

This brief review suggests that at different junctures in history: i) British accounting professional bodies were coopted in the administration of colonies by the British imperial state; ii) accounting techniques were used in the subjectification of colonial subjects; iii) indigenous collaborators were integral agents in the implementation of accounting controls but iv) there were also contrary tendencies on the part of colonial subjects to resist and subvert colonial policies and accounting practices. A unifying theme of the British colonial policies was a logic of action distinctive of capitalism. As Zeitlin (1972, p95) explains:

> Capitalism is a process in which capitalist imperialism establishes industries for the extraction of natural resources and organizes market for its commodities, both of which lead to a substantial transformation of the colonial socio-political, economic and cultural systems.

---

1 For Davie, 'knowledge of imperialism' is also in part a knowledge of subject races in that it involves structures of surveillance and accountability (2000, p334).

In contrast, colonial Spain's focal logic of action, that is, substantive rationality, in acquiring the Philippines as a colony in the 16th century was Christianisation (Scott 1982).[2] This changed in the late 18th century when a substantive rationality of a sustainable and financially viable Spanish empire was added. Under these circumstances we might ask whether accounting would operate effectively as part of the Philippine tobacco monopoly?

The observations made by Davie (2005, 2000), Neu (2000a, 2000b) and Annisette (1999) are also based on assumptions of a colonial state that is modernist and hence, strong.[3] A modernist and strong colonial state is assumed to have enhanced infrastructural capabilities to penetrate and extract from the colonized population (Weiss & Hobson 1995). As Davie (2000) explains, the British colonial state transformed Fijian chiefly structures into instruments of surveillance, control and accountability of the indigenous peoples thus becoming part of a British system of penetration and domination. These arrangements secured for the British imperial state an infrastructure for territorial expansion and for British capital investment to become profitable in Fiji. Implied in Davie's explanation was a requirement that the British colonial state had to have a bureaucracy for its domination of colonized peoples to succeed and for imperial business ventures to thrive. What was the situation in the Philippines?

Accounting in the Spanish Royal Tobacco Factory, 1760–90

Accounting practices in the Royal Tobacco Factory (RTF) in Seville, Spain, were examined by Carmona, Ezzamel and Gutierrez (1997, 1998). Informed by institutional theory and a view of accounting practices as a disciplinary

---

2 There are other views on why Spain was interested in the Philippines as a colony, namely: 1) the extractive or exploitative potential of the islands; 2) their strategic or military value to the Spanish empire; and 3) bullionist, mercantilist and commercial considerations (Bjork 1998). Headley (1995) partly agrees with Scott (1982), in giving primacy to religious explanations but adds that imperial factors were equally vital for the continued presence of Spain in the Philippines.

3 Weiss and Hobson (1995) generally describe modernist states as strong and traditional states as weak. The terms modern/modernist/strong and traditional/traditionalist/weak are used in this paper interchangeably.

regime, they analyzed the financial accounting systems and cost accounting techniques in the factory for the period from 1760 to 1790. They also describe the high and increasing dependence of the Spanish Crown on tobacco income (Artola 1982 as cited by Carmona et al. 1998) whilst facing a decline in the overall consumption of tobacco which became particularly pronounced after the 1770s. The purpose of the tobacco monopoly in Spain and in its colonies was to fill state coffers with tobacco revenue (Goodman 1994).[4] Although crucial, the RTF was only part of the value chain of the tobacco monopoly in Spain which included upstream and downstream players (e.g. suppliers of raw materials and distribution channels, respectively). The entire value chain was linked via the financial accounting system of the governing state apparatus, the tobacco agency. Within the RTF were cost accounting practices that demonstrated to the tobacco agency the superior quality of its products and their favourable cost attributes. The cost accounting system monitored quantity (e.g. physical checks, matching of actual results against targets) and quality (meeting pre-specified targets) which then created a framework within which performance could be assessed and reported (Carmona et al. 1997, p438). Whilst the potent roles of accounting practices were acknowledged, the authors nonetheless observe that the presence of these technologies did not result in full compliance of those subjected to their surveillance and disciplinary intentions. There was active resistance, and resilient means of beating the system were evident.

For the purposes of this chapter, these studies of accounting regimes in the RTF in Spain, show that there was a history of accounting practices firmly in place, which continued to be refined, to ensure that revenues were maximized for the Spanish Crown. It was highly likely that accounting regimes would be adopted in the administration of the tobacco monopolies in the Spanish colonies. As Meyer and Rowan (1977, pp343–44) put it, accounting practices are "highly institutionalized, rationalized and impersonal prescriptions" that specify, in a rule-like manner, ways of pursuing social

---

4 The royal tobacco monopoly had been introduced in the Spanish colonies of Cuba (1717), Peru (1752), Chile and La Plata (1753) before the reign of Carlos III.

purposes. This philosophical position by Meyer and Rowan harks back to Weber's thesis of substantive and formal rationality, which I will now explain.

Theoretical framework

Rationality, according to Weber, is the underlying force or reasoning behind the creation of some form of economic activity (Taylor 1994, Roth & Wittich 1978). Substantive rationality, in particular, is to think in a human way (Collins 1985, p95), where the thinking is oriented towards achievement or furtherance of some 'ultimate' value (past, present, or potential) (Weber 1978, p85). It is a criterion of ultimate ends and could be ethical, political, utilitarian, hedonistic, feudal, or egalitarian. Weber anchored substantive rationality in the 'self' as the underlying basis of the 'oughts'. Formal rationality, on the other hand, refers to the 'means' in the rationalization process. It is unambiguous and the purposeful calculation of the most efficient means to an end (Cockerham et al. 1993). Formal rationality is "the extent of quantitative calculation or accounting which is technically possible and is actually applied" (Weber 1964, pp184–85). Maximum calculability (that is, formal rationality) is "a generalized means that indiscriminately facilitates the purposeful pursuit of substantive ends" (Brubaker 1984, p37). Formal rationality is a matter of fact whilst substantive rationality is a matter of value. Given this means-ends dichotomy, it is notable that there could be a chasm between the two where the means (formal rationality) fails to achieve the ends (substantive rationality).

Formal rationality is, however, not 'value-free'. Weber himself alerts us to its morally and politically problematic institutional foundations. For example, maximum formal rationality requires centralized ownership and control of the means of production (1978, pp138, 161), the ability of owners to hire and fire workers at will to control the work process (1978, pp128–29, 137–38, 163), thoroughgoing market freedom (1978, pp161–62), and more generally, the 'struggle of man against man' in the marketplace (1978, pp93, 108). Likewise, the "formal rationality of money accounting does not reveal anything about the actual distribution of goods" (1978, p108), which determines whether or not actual production satisfies the needs or wants of a population. Thus there are limits to what formal rationality can reach and "in such cases substantive rationality would fill in the gaps" (Radcliffe 1997, p347). As Weber (1964, p185) notes "substantive rationality cannot be measured in terms of formal calculation alone, but involves a relation to the absolute values or to the content of the particular ends to which it is oriented". In other words, "the analysis of formal rationality alone tells us nothing about its direction or outcome" (Colignon & Covaleski 1991, p149).

Crucially also for this chapter, formal accounting practices are key elements of bureaucratic forms of domination and as Weber (1978, pp108, 987) explains, they are:

> associated with the social phenomena of shop discipline and appropriation of the means of production, and that means with the existence of a system of dominance ... Bureaucracy is the means of transforming social action into rationally organizing authority relations, bureaucracy was and is a power instrument of the first order for one who controls the bureaucratic apparatus. Where administration has been completely bureaucratized, the resulting system of domination is practically indestructible.

Weiss and Hobson (1995) elaborate on how the state, in particular, institutionalizes its relations with civil society. It is reliant on infrastructural power, of which bureaucracy is an integral element. Infrastructural power in turn has three dimensions, namely penetrative (the ability to reach into and directly interact with the populace); extractive (the ability to extract resources from the population), and negotiation power (the ability to coordinate political, industrial actors and social power groups) (1995, p7).

The substantive rationality of the Hispanic acquisition of the Philippines

> The most important thing His Majesty desires is the spread of our Holy Catholic faith and the salvation of souls of the infidels (Instruction from the Royal Audiencia of New Spain to Miguel Lopez de Legazpi, 1564 as cited by Doeppers 1976, p100).

This quote reflects the primary motive of Spain in colonizing the Philippines in the 16th century (see also Scott 1982). The Spanish crown was a 'patron' of the church in the Indies through the institution of 'royal patronage'. Thus, political (state) and spiritual (community) governance were conjoined in Spain's occupation of the Philippines (de Jesus 1982). The Spanish religious order of the Augustinians arrived in the Philippines in 1565, followed by the Franciscans in 1578, the Jesuits in 1581 and the Dominicans in 1587.[5] Active efforts by the clergy to resettle Filipinos in central church villages linked villagers to the network of Roman Catholicism Christendom (Doeppers 1976).[6] The authority of the clergy was strong. The friars constituted the largest, numerically, and most influential Spaniards in the Philippines (Leroy 1907, Kamen 2002). In 1722 there were said to be over 1500 friars in the Philippine islands, a figure that exceeded the total of the Spanish lay population (Schurz 1939).

The Spanish Crown bore the financial burden of sending and supporting missionaries to the Americas and the Philippines (Cushner 1971). It financially supported the *padres* (priests) by shouldering the costs of ocean voyage from Spain to the Philippines (via Mexico), and providing salaries, stipends, wine for mass, oil for cooking and funds to construct or rebuild churches or convents. A 1766 report on the financial affairs of the Philippines by a member of the royal *audiencia* (an administrative tribunal) of Manila stated that:

> the royal treasury spends in these islands much more than they can produce; and that the ecclesiastical estate – or, to speak more accurately, the religious orders – profit by and receive almost all the proceeds from the tributes (personal [head] taxes on Filipino subjects) (De Viana 1766, p87).

That tributes were the only source of government revenues as reported in the 1766 report is disputed elsewhere (see for example, Fradera 2004). It appears that the report was based on the assumption that the tributes were the revenues that should be covering the expenses relating to the 'salvation of souls of the infidels'. This observation is deduced from De Viana (1766, pp90–91) who lamented:

---

5 The religious orders were explicitly assigned to different areas in the Philippines by the Spanish Crown (Doeppers 1976).
6 Like its other colonies, the strength of the Hispanic colonial system in the Philippines, including both church and secular administration, rested on an urban or quasi-urban base (Mores 1972).

It is, then, apparently fully proved that what these Indians contribute to the king is not sufficient for the necessary expenses for their spiritual administration ... From this it follows: First, that all the profit of these Islands accrues to the ecclesiastical estate. Second, that in order to aid the Indians the royal revenue has been burdened, to the injury of other vassals, with the charge of the royal situado (subsidy) which comes annually from Nueva España (Mexico), in order to maintain the forts, troops, and courts and meet the other expenses of the royal treasury here.

The salaries and special funds, however, were apparently slow in arriving and insufficient (Cushner 1971, pp76, 78). Citing records kept at the Archivo General de Indias (Ultramar 613), Cushner reports that the tardiness and lack of financial support by the Spanish colonial state to the priests were in part compensated by Filipino men fishing for them and rowing their boats in trips to say Mass in nearby towns, Filipino women cleaning the village church and husking the rice for the priests' personal consumption, and Filipino boys cutting grass for the priests' horses for free. Nonetheless, the Spanish colonial state relied on the priests for local knowledge and control (McLennan 1973, Cruikshank 1982). For nearly three centuries, the only other Spanish political authorities visible at the *pueblos* (towns) were the notoriously corrupt Spanish *alcaldes* (provincial leaders – see Bourne nd, Cullinane 1982, Corpuz 1997).

Barangays were the smallest administrative political units and were pre-conquest kinship units. The *pueblos* were a consolidation of *barangays*, each one consisting of 30 to 100 families (Benitez 1932, Chandler et al. 1985). Colonial Spain accepted traditional socio-political arrangements and made the Filipino head of pre-conquest kinship units, the *cabeza de barangay* (head of the *barangay*). Moreover, another Filipino from the old pre-conquest ruling class was made the *gobernadorcillo* or head of the *pueblo*. Filipinos were generally confined to the political posts of the *gobernadorcillo* and *cabeza de barangay*. The political structure under the Spaniards did not allow for Filipinos to go beyond the post of *gobernadorcillo* and their political power remained within the *pueblo* (Owen 1971, Roces 1990). The *cabezas* and *gobernadorcillos, inter alia*, collected the tributes within their *barangays*, and delivered them to the *alcalde*. They were held accountable for full delivery of the tribute quotas. The quotas were pre-determined on the basis of registers of the tribute-payers in the *pueblos*. In return, the *gobernadorcillos*, *cabezas* and their deputies were exempted from paying tributes. They were also expected to remunerate themselves for their efforts (Chandler et al. 1987, p27).

In brief, the local government structure in 18th-century Philippines was highly reliant on the priests and the local leaders to reach and extract tributes from its Filipino subjects, who were to be converted to Catholicism. There was a notable lack of a rigorous approach to a quantitative calculation or accounting whose application might maximize the collection of tributes. On the contrary, the tributes were not sufficient to cover for the ecclesiastical expenses borne by the Spanish colonial state.

At this point a discussion of the Spanish colonial state's power is warranted to identify some of the issues that the Spanish colonial state had to confront when it imposed the tobacco monopoly in the Philippines. In regard to penetrative power, the Spanish colonial state was highly reliant on the *padres* and the local ruling clans to reach the Filipino population. Arguably the few Spaniards willing to reside in the Philippines made these arrangements essential (Pilapil 1973). Reliance on the *padres* and local leaders could be highly problematic because, with geographical distance, the state would be unable to monitor the *padres* and ruling clans (Weiss & Hobson 1995). The authority of the state is weakened significantly when subjects (in this case, the local officials and the priests) gradually acquire greater knowledge of the local population and their activities. In the Philippines there is evidence of the priests wielding strong authority over and commanding respect from the Filipinos (Pizarro 1827, Leroy 1907, McLennan 1973, Cruikshank 1982, Kamen 2002). Ezzamel (1997) also comments as evidence of a weakened state a much reduced level of state revenue, as the local leaders had enough power to minimize their tax payments to the state.

In the Philippines, the *cabezas* and *gobernadorcillos* remunerated themselves for their efforts to collect tributes from the Filipinos (as noted above). It was highly doubtful that they were reporting all the tribute-payers in their villages (de Viana 1765, 1766), thus denying the Spanish colonial state its full entitlement of tributes. The *padres* also put additional burden on the Filipinos as they also exacted tributes (de Viana 1766, Corpuz 1997). The church tributes were parish contributions which, unlike the annual government tributes, were rendered all year round. Arguably, these contributions to the church competed with the Spanish colonial state's ability to extract more taxes from the Filipinos such that the administration of the Philippines was subsidized by another Spanish colony, Mexico (de Jesus 1973).

Negotiation power was weak also, with economic development not a priority for the Spaniards in the two centuries prior to the introduction of the tobacco monopoly (Scott 1982). Until the mid-18th century, the galleon trade was the only foreign trade entered into in the Philippines (Schurz 1939). Manila was an entrepot for Chinese and other Asian goods, headed for Acapulco, Mexico (Fast & Richardson 1970). It was the exclusive privilege of Spaniards resident in the Philippines, which partly explains why most of the Manila-based Spaniards were disinterested in 'developing' the local economy beyond subsistence production (de Viana 1766). Two galleons sailed from Manila each year to Acapulco carrying merchandise from Persia, the Levant, India, Java, Sumatra, Banda, Maluco, Malacca, Borneo, Siam, Cambodia, Cochin-China, Japan and Formosa. Corpuz (1997, p40) alleged that successful voyages allowed these merchants "to live in ease as gentlemen for ten months of the year, attending to the business of their shipments for only two months" (see also Schurz 1939, p41). When the British captured Manila in 1762 they were profoundly disappointed by its poverty (Kamen 2002, p215). "The Philippines resemble the estates of those great lords whose lands remained uncultivated though they would make the fortune of a great number of families" (quoted in Schurz 1939, p42). The custom duties collected from the trade went to the Manila treasury and assisted in the administration of the Philippines. However, this was not enough and Mexico continued to subsidize the Philippine colony.

The Philippines' dependence on Mexico became quite untenable as a result of the seven-year war between Spain and Great Britain, which ended in 1762 (de Jesus 1973, Corpuz 1997). In addition to the cessation of subsidies from Mexico, the galleon trade between Manila and Acapulco also stopped during this period. The absence of import and export duties generated from the trade contributed to the bankruptcy of the Philippine treasury. The war also put an enormous drain on the finances of imperial Spain, making it vulnerable to more foreign aggression (Fradera 2004).

Pressed by the need to generate additional revenue, the Bourbon bureaucrats, led by Charles III, established a royal tobacco monopoly in its colony of Mexico in 1764. The Spanish Crown also had financial success in running a tobacco monopoly in Seville and Cadiz since the 16th century (Goodman 1994, Carmona et al. 1997, 1998). The Mexican tobacco venture quickly became profitable with its profits remitted back to Spain (Brading 1979, Corpuz 1997). Sicotte (1997) asserts that the establishment of the royal tobacco monopoly in Spanish America was a crucial element in revitalising the Spanish empire's fortunes. The monopoly had the same objective throughout the continent: to increase fiscal revenues and remit them directly to the metropolis. Thus in 1769, the Spanish crown ordered the extension of the tobacco monopoly to the Philippines and its other colonies (de Jesus 1973). Specifically in the case of the Philippines, the Spaniards also decided that tobacco would be the best product to sell to the Filipinos because they "noticed that they learned to smoke even before they learned to think" (de Jesus 1980, p99). Mexico was an exemplar for all the colonies and the Mexican tobacco monopoly was administered by government officials. The Philippines had to adopt Mexico's administrative arrangements, including its accounting system (Carvajal to Basco, 6 February 1782). As explained in the following section, the introduction of the tobacco monopoly in the Philippines further exposed the Spanish colonial government's initial dependence on the localized masters in the *padres*, *cabezas* and *gobernadorcillos*. Most importantly, it represented a major shift in the substantive rationality of the Spanish Crown in retaining the Philippine colony.

The Philippine tobacco monopoly

Introducing the Philippine tobacco monopoly

In 1769, an edict was made to establish a tobacco monopoly in the Philippines (de Arriaga to de Anda, 12 December 1769). However, due to lack of funds, it took another 12 years before it was implemented. On 13 December

1781, the Spanish Governor-General of the Philippines, Jose Basco y Vargas, announced that the government was assuming exclusive control over tobacco manufacture and trade in Manila and the adjoining eight provinces of Tondo, Cavite, Batangas, Tayabas, Laguna de Bay, Pampanga, Bataan and Bulacan. The Filipinos, who had been growing and smoking tobacco since the 16th century (Dampier, 1698), were then given five months to sell to the government, at government-set prices, private stocks of tobacco leaves and six months to dispose of manufactured tobacco (Basco to de Galvez, 15 May 1782a). This paved the way for the government tobacco shops to open in 1782 (Basco to de Galvez, 8 May 1782) to sell back to the Filipinos the tobacco products they had surrendered.

The tobacco monopoly was at that time the Spanish regime's largest economic venture in the Philippines, its prior commercial experience limited to the galleon trade. With the monopoly, it now had to manage the full breadth of the tobacco industry – from the growing of tobacco by Filipino farmers, to the purchase of tobacco leaves from the contracted farmers, the manufacture of tobacco products and finally the marketing and sale of tobacco products (Corpuz 1997). The monopoly required the Spanish colonial government to build an infrastructure with vastly enhanced powers of penetration, extraction and negotiation previously not 'needed' when Christianisation was the major goal.

The 'terms of rule' associated with the monopoly had to radiate from the centre (the state). Sovereignty had to be centralized as opposed to parcelized. The Spanish Crown also had learnt from prior experience that collecting revenue from tobacco was very difficult unless it was well supervised (Goodman 1994, p217). Clearly there was a need for bureaucracy to augment the state's extractive power. Ideally and typically, bureaucracy is the handmaiden of infrastructural power, through which the state is able to independently interact with society (Weiss & Hobson 1995, p35). Through bureaucratic staff, the state is able to dominate through accumulation of knowledge. Prior to the Philippine tobacco monopoly, the *padres* and the local leaders knew every Filipino in the *barangays* and *pueblos*. As already noted, the local leaders used their knowledge of the tribute payers to profit themselves and deny the Spanish colonial state its full share of the tributes.

Paradoxically, the institution of the tobacco monopoly now required that same knowledge to be captured by the centralising state. This was to be achieved through an accounting system which viewed the Filipinos as producers and consumers (rather than as souls to be saved) and required the local leaders to function as bureaucrats. They would have to choose whether to cooperate or resist.

Organizing the Philippine tobacco monopoly

Given the Spanish colonial state's reliance on the *padres* as its localized expression of authority, unsurprisingly, the tobacco monopoly was announced to the Filipinos as a "duty of a faithful subject". Filipinos were warned that disregard for the tobacco monopoly was a 'sin' requiring a confession to the *padre,* who would "demand restitution as a requirement for absolution" (Sancho de Santa Justa 1781, pp58–9, as cited by de Jesus 1973).

The Philippine tobacco monopoly was closely patterned after that of Mexico (de Jesus 1973; see also Basco to de Galvez, 15 May 1782a). A driving force behind the Philippine tobacco monopoly was Jose de Galvez, who was visitor-general to Mexico from 1765 to 1772. He held more power than the viceroy during most of his tenure. He exercised almost unlimited powers to examine and reform administration, create tribunals of justice and collect revenues. The primary aims of his tenure were financial: to increase the revenues of the Spanish crown (Hardwick 2005). De Galvez became the Minister of the Indies from 1776 to 1787 having had extensive experience in the establishment of the tobacco monopoly in Mexico (Deans-Smith 1992). The Mexican tobacco monopoly was the most vibrant and largest in Spanish America during the Bourbon period. Under de Galvez's direction, the tobacco monopoly in the colonies underwent major changes in its structure and administration reflecting a strategy of vertical integration (Perez Vidal 1959). Thus the Philippine monopoly had three main functions: the growing of tobacco leaves by contracted Filipino workers to be sold to the Spanish colonial state (*coleccion*), the manufacture of tobacco cigars, cigarettes and snuff (*fabrica*), and the sale of manufactured products (*administracion*) (Arenas 1850). In the Philippines, de Galvez's instructions were well received by the governor-general Jose Basco y Vargas, who was very supportive of the

tobacco monopoly. His tenure from 1778 to 1787 was progressive. He introduced the *Sociedad Economica de Amigos del Pais* (Economic Association of
Friends of the Country) and encouraged agriculture and the development of
other industries (Governors of the Philippines during the Spanish colonial
period, 2005). He encouraged the cultivation of indigo, cotton, tobacco,
cinnamon, pepper, sugar, silk, hemp, tea, coffee, and the opium poppy (Beck
2006).

Coleccion

Coleccion, which covered the growing, harvest and transport of tobacco to
the factory in the capital city of Manila, was outsourced by the Spanish colonial government to Filipinos (Director of the *Renta del Tabaco* to Basco, 23
January 1783). As incentive, farmers in the *coleccion* were exempted from the
mandatory corvee labour. This strategy can be explained in two ways: 1) the
approach taken by de Galvez, the Minister of the Indies had always been
supportive of cooptation of local interests (Deans-Smith 1992), and, 2) this
reflected a continuation of traditional political arrangements in the Philippines, whereby locals were integrated in the state's infrastructure.

For a period of three years from 1782, a Filipino contractor, Juan Tinio,
was responsible for ensuring that Filipinos in designated provinces complied
with the royal edict that they cultivated tobacco.[7] The *padre* was also coopted
as he was required to verify and revise, if required, a list of all inhabitants in
his parish, identifying also those who were old enough to help in the cultivation of tobacco (Jagor et al. 2005). According to Jagor et al. the list was used
to help the government verify the estimated tobacco production by the Filipino contractor. The contractor, Tinio, was provided 10,000 pesos to lend, as
he saw fit, to farmers to enable them to setup their land for tobacco cultivation. He was also provided with a detachment of 21 soldiers to safeguard the
money and tobacco. Exempt from the *alcalde*'s jurisdiction, he was directly

---

7 Juan Tinio won the contract against another bidder. Juan Tinio's proposed terms were
'more beneficial' to the Spanish colonial state primarily because Mr Tinio agreed to be
subjected to the government's grading of tobacco leaves (Basco to Tinio, 23 January 1782).

accountable to the officials of the monopoly. However, reflecting his privileged status, the contractor could demand labourers and means of transportation from the *alcalde*, as the need arose. Crucially, the contractor also had to sell all the harvested tobacco leaves to the government at pre-set prices. One could see that the sovereign Spanish colonial state initially co-opted the *padres* and a Filipino partner, bearers of power through their knowledge of the Filipino population, as agents in tobacco production. The Spanish colonial state was quite aware that it would have been 'not possible' to manage the *coleccion* itself due to the 'excessive amount' of the farmers, who individually "only sowed a tiny parcel of land" (Basco to Tinio, 23 January 1782), a practice now rendered untenable. In a meeting with Governor-General Basco, tobacco farmers, accompanied by their parish priests, demanded that the contract with Tinio, the contractor, be allowed to lapse on account of the low prices received for their tobacco (Basco to de Galvez, 18 June 1784). The presence and role of the *padres* as spokespersons for the Filipino farmers in meetings with government officials is notable. This is consistent with Pizarro's (1827) observation that the *padre* pleads for and protects his flock from oppression.

From that time on, the Spanish colonial state took over the *coleccion*, completing the vertical integration of the Philippine tobacco monopoly. This is a critical juncture in the ascent of formal rationality in the tobacco monopoly. Specifically, accounting procedures were put in place for the growing and harvest of tobacco leaves (Carvajal to Basco, 15 May 1782; also see de Jesus 1973, p64). An overseer, who was Filipino, was chosen from among the farmers on the basis of native intelligence, integrity, diligence and knowledge of Spanish. He and a Spanish guard were exempt from corvée labour and from paying tributes (de Jesus 1973, p78). Every year they each received two books with numbered pages, authenticated by the office of the auditor general. In the first, they entered an estimate of each farmer's probable harvest and, in the second, what the farmers actually produced. The two officials had to verify, by onsite inspection, claims of crop damage so that they could revise their estimate of the claimants' expected yield. Unaccounted discrepancies between entries in the two books were evidences of possible fraud.

At harvest time, one of the officials stayed to watch the warehouse, while the other patrolled the fields. When all the farmers had delivered their crops, the tobacco leaves were graded by the *aforadores*. A Spanish official appointed one *aforador* and another was elected by the farmers. To settle disputes between the two, the Spanish official added a third member whose decision was final. Upon agreeing on the grade and the equivalent price, the farmers were paid. After the farmers had signed the books attesting that payment had been received, the overseer and the guard certified the books with their own signatures and surrendered them for delivery to the office of the auditor general. Once the Spanish colonial state took over the *coleccion*, it was subjected to accounting controls. Variances, for example, between budgeted and actual harvests were used to detect possible cases of smuggling of tobacco leaves.

Fabrica and administracion

The organization of *fabrica* and *administracion* is shown in table 1. The organization of the functions of *fabrica* and *administracion* of the Philippine tobacco monopoly incorporated an accountability and accounting system that radiated from the centre (at the national level) to the workers in the *pueblos*. This centralizing tendency was reflective also of an organizing principle of the imperial Spanish state under the Bourbons (Carmona et al. 1997). The practice of accounting, however, mainly served the purpose of stewardship with the institution of the state as the owner, and the bureaucrats as the stewards.

In *fabrica*, there were also procedures to monitor, record and safeguard tobacco products and their production. The manufacture of tobacco leaves into cigars, cigarettes and snuff was initially in a factory in the capital city of Manila owned by the Spanish government.[8] Under the supervision of a foreman, factory hands worked from 6am to noon and from 2pm to 6pm.

---

8 The Dominicans loaned, without charge, their rest-house, which was adjacent to the parish church in Binondo in Manila to house the factory (Basco to Galvez, 15 May 1782b).

Table 1: Organization of the Philippine tobacco monopoly – *Administracion* and *Fabrica*. After CG Carvajal to JV Basco, 6 February 1782, no. 502, Filipinas 886, Archivos de Indias, Seville, Spain.

Position	Responsibility	Accounting reports/ records	Frequency
Director	In-charge of *administracion* (sale of tobacco products), *fabrica* (manufacture of tobacco products), and *coleccion* (purchase of tobacco leaves).		
Auditor general	Certified all movements of funds and tobacco		
	Audited all accounts		Monthly
	Prepared reports on the tobacco monopoly's performance		Monthly
	Kept all records		
	Reconciled orders of payment with Treasurer's accounts		Monthly
	Kept a key to the Treasury and General Stores		
Treasurer	Maintained records	Debit and credit ledgers	
	Deposited and withdrew monies		
	Prepared statements of accounts		Yearly
	Performed cash counts		Yearly and as required
General stores			
Weight comptroller	Stored tobacco to avoid deterioration or rot		
	Weighed and classified tobacco bales received	Invoices	
	Weighed boxes of tobacco products dispatched	Invoices	
Bookkeeper	Maintained records of deliveries and dispatches	Debit (deliveries) and credit (dispatches) ledger	

Position	Responsibility	Accounting reports/ records	Frequency
	Calculated yields – ratios of tobacco bales delivered to the factory to deliveries received by the general stores Reconciled records with the Weight comptroller's invoices		Monthly
Administracion			
General manager – national level	Performed inventory count of tobacco products and weighing equipment		Yearly
	Maintained a separate account of tobacco of inferior quality Ensured that tobacco products were sold according to prescribed prices Ensured that sales monies were deposited in coffers Secured approval of accountant for any payments and subsequent withdrawal of monies Prepared supporting documentation for payments Prepared statements showing tobacco sales, salaries and other expenses Maintained files of correspondence with administrators, inspectors and other employees in the provinces and reported areas of concern to senior management Suggested measures to improve tobacco sales	Balance sheet	Monthly
Provincial administrators	Maintained records of receipts and dispatches of tobacco products to wholesalers and retail tobacconists	Debit and credit ledger	Daily
	Maintained records of sales	Sales ledger	Not specified
Provincial accountants	In charge of tax/revenue collection; responsible for the tax/revenue agents Primarily responsible for checking that weighing scales were correctly calibrated and that tobacco products were accurately weighed before dispatch to wholesalers and retail tobacconists		

Position	Responsibility	Accounting reports/ records	Frequency
	Visited/inspected tax/revenue agents as often as possible Ensured that tax/revenue agents promptly remitted revenue collections		
Wholesalers	Sold tobacco products heavier than two ounces Remitted sales Performed inventory count Maintained list of buyers	Ledgers Buyers' list	Weekly Weekly & yearly Daily
Retail tobacconists	Maintained records of receipts of tobacco products and remittances of sales. Performed inventory count Remitted revenue collections	Ledgers	Daily & weekly
Tax /revenue agents	Distributed tobacco products to wholesalers and retail tobacconists based on anticipated weekly sales Maintained records of tobacco received and dispatched and revenue/cash remittances Reconciled records Maintained records of sales Provided accurate list of prices to wholesalers and retail tobacconists Appointed wholesalers and retail tobacconists Inspected wholesalers and retail tobacconists Monitored cultivation and sale of contraband tobacco products	Debit and credit ledgers Sales ledger	Weekly Twice weekly Monthly Daily At least monthly
Auditors/ guards/ corporals	Checked performance and background of all employees Did inspections/audits of tax collectors, wholesalers and retail tobacconists' records and inventory Reported and started proceedings against fraudulent employees		

Position	Responsibility	Accounting reports/ records	Frequency
Fabrica			
Supervisor	Ensured that tobacco leaves and tobacco products were stored in a secure place Maintained records of receipts of tobacco leaves and dispatches of tobacco products to the general stores Prepared statements of tobacco movement, on hand and shrinkage Maintained a database of factory workers Monitored factory workers and their performance	Debit and credit ledger Inventory report	Monthly
Accountant	Maintained records of dispatches of tobacco products to the general stores, specifying the types and classes of products, and, whether they came from *coleccion* or from confiscated contraband tobacco leaves; also maintained records of dispatches with details on recipients and types and classes of products Prepared and reconciled statements of tobacco movement with Supervisor Maintained records of finances Prepared orders of payment for salaries of factory workers and other expenses.	Debit and credit ledger Inventory report Debit and credit ledger	Yearly

The doors of the factory were shut at the strike of the clock at six in the morning and two in the afternoon when the workers were all in, and opened only when the shifts ended. The workers were not allowed to leave their posts unless absolute necessary. Pay was based on the volume of production. Most of the workers were Filipino women. It was thought that women worked with greater care and with less risk of fraud.

In *administracion*, there was accounting for the movement of tobacco through the meticulous recording of receipts and dispatches in each rung of the hierarchy. There was also a system to classify and record tobacco in different grades, including a separate category and account for rotten tobacco, and for regular inventory counts. Procedures to record sales on a daily basis and to remit cash collected at least twice weekly also supported the stewardship role of the employees in *administracion*. There were also control procedures in place to check on whether government employees were performing their stewardship roles, with the auditor general, for example, responsible for auditing all accounts. There were also provincial accountants who had to check that weighing scales were properly calibrated and auditors who had to inspect the records of, and tobacco inventory held by, the revenue/tax collectors, wholesalers and retail tobacconists. If judiciously applied, these accounting and accountability procedures would have provided some assurance to the Spanish colonial state that tobacco products reached their intended customers and that revenue was remitted back to the Treasury.

A feature of the government accounting system introduced for the functions of *fabrica* and *administracion* was that it created a bureaucracy and encouraged a vocation of office-holding. Indeed there was a potential for the bureaucracy to progress toward one which ideally and typically would be impersonal, expert, procedural and hierarchical (du Gay 2000, see also Weber 1978, p958ff). To illustrate the push for impersonal relations between employees, the Spanish colonial state painstakingly articulated in the rules governing the accounting system that the provincial accountants were not to invite the auditors in their houses for meals. The accountants were also instructed not to accommodate the auditors' horses nor lend the auditors money. Any attempt by the auditors to solicit these would have resulted in disciplinary action.

A comment on the government accounting system as a formal mode of rationality
The tobacco monopoly was the Spanish regime's first economic venture in the Philippines for which a distinct bureaucracy was organized (Corpuz 1997, p120). In previous discussions, we saw that bureaucratic positions were created in a clearly defined hierarchy of offices. The officials in the tobacco monopoly were expected to manage the sale and production of tobacco products. Management, in this case, meant "mobilising and co-ordinating

resources to carry out accepted policy" (Parker 1993, p170).[9] The bureau that the Spanish colonial government created was not simply, as Rohr (1979, p40) put it, a "neutral instrument of management" but rather had the potential to be "a mighty institution of government". It had the potential to be an "instrument of state power" (Hennessy 1995, p.121). The Spanish colonial state was to become the most dynamic element in Philippine economic and social development until the mid-19th century (Fradera 2004, p311). The tobacco monopoly was to be a catalyst in the transformation of the Spanish colonial state.

Description and analysis of the tobacco bureau revealed that an accounting system was integral but not the only requirement for the successful operation of the tobacco monopoly. Accounting procedures and accountability relationships were minutely articulated, indicating that the Spanish colonial government intended to rely on them for information to ensure, to some extent, that officials were held accountable for their conduct. The focus was on 'legality and fraud prevention', an approach likewise practised in the Royal Tobacco Factory in Seville during this time (Carmona et al. 1998, 1997). The hierarchy of offices and of accounting information meant there was a trail of accounting data connecting the Filipino farmer to the head office of the treasurer and auditor general. One could also track the movement of tobacco products from the debit and credit ledgers in the office of the manager of the general stores in the capital city of Manila to the ledgers of the retail tobacconists in the *pueblos*. Arguably, the accounting system gave the Spanish colonial state apparatus the potential to radiate from the centre (capital) to the *pueblos*, and also for revenues extracted from the consumers to flow back to the national treasury. In other words, the accounting system had the potential to assist the Spanish government to enhance its infrastructural power to reach and extract from the Filipinos. However, it is equally important to acknowledge that the acceptance and implementation of the tobacco monopoly, including the tobacco bureau and government account-

---

9 Management, in the accounting literature, has a different meaning, viz, "a focus on efficiency and profitability" (Macias 2002, pp44, 50).

ing system, were also initially dependent on the cooperation of the *padres* and the Filipino overseers and farmers. In other words, accounting as a technology for the Spanish colonial state was not sufficient for the tobacco monopoly to work. In the following section, an attempt is made to assess the success of the government accounting system and the tobacco bureau in general.

Implementing the Philippine tobacco monopoly – accounting, resistance, fraud and inefficiencies

The Philippine tobacco monopoly was a financially successful venture. It returned more revenues and became the longest-running state economic project ending in 1882 (de Jesus 1973, Corpuz 1997). The financial success was almost immediate. In the first nine months of its operations the monopoly yielded revenues of 96,850 pesos and net profits of 44,697 pesos. The reporting of healthy profits continued and for the next year in 1783, the monopoly earned 239,047 pesos, of which 150,000 pesos was remitted to the Spanish treasury and the Philippine colony subsequently became self-funded. Given the evidence of healthy profits, one could suggest that the Spanish colonial state was able to successfully enhance its penetrative and extractive powers. Not only was the Philippine colony self-funded, the colony was also remitting funds to the Spanish Crown's treasury. By 1795 it had contributed a total of 1,971,695 pesos (Estado de valores de la Renta del Tabaco, 1802).

Accounting appears to have played an enabling role from the very start. The accounting reports provided some feedback on whether the internal control procedures for the tobacco bureau were effective. These procedures involved a hierarchy of record-keeping. The accounting reports contained vital information on the cash position and existing tobacco inventory of the tobacco bureau. It was a barometer of the growing strength of the Spanish colonial state's penetrative and extractive powers.

An accounting report for the bureau's operations was first prepared for the period from 10 March 1782 to 31 December 1782, the initial nine months of operations (Basco to de Galvez, 31 May 1783). This first report comprised two distinct parts: a physical flow and costing of tobacco inventory and cash flow. The physical flow of tobacco units was segregated into different types of inventory, namely *fardos* (bales of tobacco leaves), *puros* (cigars), *cigarillos* (cigarettes), and *polvo* (snuff – tobacco in powder) and corresponding costs were provided. The section on cash flow provided descriptions and sums of sources of inflow as well as outflows. The major source of cash inflow was from sales of tobacco products. This being the first nine months of operations, the major cash outflow was the purchase of private stocks of tobacco products from the Filipinos with salaries and manufacturing costs ranking second and third, respectively. Reports continued to be generated by the accounting system in subsequent years.

Comparing this report to that for the year 1798, for example, it was found that the same information was being generated (Estado general de la Real Renta del Tavaco en las Islas Filipina, 1799). The first section still provided information on the tobacco inventory including beginning balances for the different types (quantity and costs), receipts and disbursements of tobacco products in and from the warehouses, sales and ending balances. The second section was still on the cash flow, with beginning and ending balances and cash inflows and outflows clearly specified. The main sources of cash were still tobacco sales and the major outflows were spent on salaries and wages and purchases of tobacco leaves from the farmers. The locations of the ending cash balance were also identified, such as the Treasury, the tobacco bureau, and in a number of government offices in the provinces. There was also a third section comparing previous year's sales and current assets with the current year's. The report for 1798 was positive showing increases in sales, cash balances and current assets. However, this did not necessarily indicate an acceptable level of performance as I found explanations for lower than expected harvests in some of the files for the Philippine tobacco monopoly. For example, in correspondence dated 7 May 1791, typhoons were blamed for the destruction of tobacco plants and a resultant epidemic killing some of the farmers (found in the file Ultramar 638). Looking back, though, there is confirmation that the tobacco monopoly was profitable in the period examined in this study (Estado de Valores de la Renta del Tabaco, 1802). However, as the next section will show, it was also apparent that more revenues could have been generated if there had not been resistance to the above arrangements, in part because they were constrained, as well as facilitated, by the traditionally embedded governing roles of the *padres* and local leaders in the Philippine *pueblos*.

Resisting through smuggling

When the Philippine tobacco monopoly was introduced, a comment was made that the "provinces where the monopoly was to begin were the most populous and the most notorious for 'vicious' men, and every little town, every little house, had its plot of tobacco" (Gonzalez to de Galvez, 19 December 1785). Filipinos, who had previously grown tobacco for their personal consumption, initially resisted the Spanish colonial state's monopoly of tobacco production. As a result for the first decade or so, tobacco grown with the *coleccion* was not being fully sold back to the state. Smugglers were striking at the monopoly's own supply lines (de Jesus 1973, p74).

The problem of tobacco smuggling is endemic to tobacco monopolies. Goodman (1994, pp216–17) observes that states which embarked on these projects, had "to contain powerful countervailing forces for contraband". He cited innumerable evidences that suggest that "smuggling was a perennial problem and was so highly organised" in tobacco monopolies everywhere. The reason, he says, is quite simple:

> no monopoly could monitor and police agricultural production, and there was therefore no way, of telling whether, and to what extent, a tobacco farmer was withholding some of his output for sale in the black market.

In the Philippines, the Spanish colonial government responded in two ways: 1) by co-opting the *padre* and the ruling clans of the *pueblos*, and 2) using its military strength, or as Mann (1988, p4; 1993, p55) put it, the state's "monopoly of the means of violence". The *padre*, who was the most visible Spanish authority in the locales, was involved in verifying the list of all inhabitants in his parish, identifying also those who were old enough to help in the cultivation of tobacco (Jagor et al. 2005). Jagor et al. report that those old enough included little children and this practice might have resulted in growing discontent amongst Filipinos. The *padre*, however, was also vocal in opposing aspects of the tobacco monopoly. The appointment of a Filipino overseer in the management of *coleccion* has also been previously discussed. The Filipino overseer, chosen from among the farmers on the basis of native intelligence, integrity, diligence and knowledge of Spanish, was placed at the head of a group of 50 farmers. Recall that the overseer had to maintain records to monitor production and that unaccounted discrepancies between entries in the books of estimated and actual harvests were evidences of fraud. Severe penalties applied to those caught smuggling, including confiscation of the contraband tobacco, a fine worth twice the value of the confiscated tobacco and cost of prosecution and, failing to pay the fine, a term in prison (Sancho de Santa Justa 1781, as cited by de Jesus 1973). To illustrate, acting on evidences of fraud, and applying the penalties for smuggling, on 8 February 1787, a regiment of soldiers was dispatched to destroy illegally-grown tobacco (del Castillo to de Galvez, 1787). However, the Filipino 'rebels' ambushed them, killing many soldiers. Within two days of the ambush, the Spanish colonial government responded by flexing its judicial and military might. Two of the alleged leaders of the ambush were arrested (Basco to de Galvez, 17 June 1787).[10]

The first few years of implementation of the tobacco monopoly was tumultuous and even the application of forceful sanctions by the Spanish colonial state was not a full deterrent to smuggling. The cooptation of the local leaders acting as overseers in *coleccion* was also at times inefficacious. The overseers and the Spanish officials in *coleccion* who were suppose to record each farmer's crop cooperated in concealing the fraud in return for a share in the profits. This meant that the accounting control of reporting variances between estimated and actual productions was undermined and that variances were not fully reported. This was because "smugglers could easily offer the overseers and officials eighteen to twenty pesos for a *fardo*

---

10 De Jesus (1973) provided innumerable accounts of how the Spanish colonial state used its monopoly of force to counter tobacco smuggling in the Philippines based on primary sources read from Archivos General De Indias in Seville, Spain. Sturtevant (1976) and Fradera (2004) also provided descriptions of significant Filipino uprisings and the emergence of banditry in some areas in the Philippines.

(bale of tobacco leaves) of tobacco – about four times what the monopoly would pay – and still net a profit of ten to twenty pesos" (de Jesus 1973, p149). However, over time resistance to the monopoly appear to have waned:

> As neither the life of the vagrant nor the outlaw could last for a long time, those who knew nothing but the cultivation and commerce of tobacco had to abandon it in the end: for time makes them forget the injury and the bitterness it had cost them to lose their trade which their livelihood depended and made them see that a way of making a living is never lacking to the diligent and the hard-working (Aguilar to Gardoqui, 22 July 1794).[11]

Opposition from the padres

Apart from acting as spokespeople for Filipino farmers, the *padres* held a strong view against the tobacco monopoly. In correspondence to the Governor-General between 1791 and 1799, the 'religious', notably the bishop of *Nueva Caceres*, continually expressed their opposition to the tobacco monopoly. The strong message conveyed was that it was an injustice to impose a second form of 'tribute' (personal tax) to the Filipinos by compelling them to buy tobacco products from the Spanish colonial state (e.g. correspondence dated 10 June 1783, 17 June 1793). Officials of the Spanish colonial state, however, thought that the tobacco monopoly also hurt the interests of the *padres*. Filipino parishioners, before the imposition of the tobacco monopoly, grew tobacco in their backyards. They gratuitously lavished their parish priests with tobacco. With the monopoly, this practice stopped. It was alleged that as a result of the financial cost of the tobacco monopoly to the Filipinos: 1) the *padres* had to buy their own tobacco, and 2) the *padres* received less church alms and dues (Gonzalez to de Galvez, 10 June 1787). Thus, the consent of the *padres* in supporting the state's tobacco monopoly project was, during this period, withheld at various times. The implication for the Spanish colonial state was that the *padre* resisted being coopted as this meant the

---

11 Rafael Maria de Aguilar and Diego De Gardoqui were, at this time, Philippine Governor-General and the Minister of the Indies, respectively.

Spanish colonial state was now directly and more aggressively competing for resources with the *padre*.

Fraud in the bureau

Fraud within the bureau was rampant (De Zuniga 1793, pp285–86), some of it observed by De Zuniga, a priest who arrived in the Philippines in 1786. De Zuniga described how Spanish *aforadores* downgraded the quality of tobacco leaves so that Filipino farmers were paid less. In the factory the best cigars were set aside as gifts for the Governor-General, the members of the royal court, the king's attorney, and others to whom it was the custom to give specific quotas during Christmas. The supervisors also had the pick of the choice leaf from which they made good cigars for sale at five pesos more than the rules allowed. This practice cascaded down the ranks as the cigars moved from the factory to the provinces' tobacco shops. The lower-ranked officials received a quantity of the remaining best, either for their own consumption or for sale at higher price. The Filipinos were apparently left with the poorest quality cigars.

There were other equally important challenges and obstacles to the tobacco monopoly that crucially encouraged fraudulent behaviour. Two are highlighted: the lack of cash in circulation in the Philippine colony and the low salaries for officials in the tobacco bureau. According to Bishop Juan de Santa Rosa (yet another priest), the Spanish colonial state was delayed in paying Filipinos the tobacco leaves they surrendered when the monopoly was initially imposed, forcing it to 'sell' the tobacco back to the Filipinos (de Santa Rosa to Basco, 4 April 1787). Within two years of the imposition of the tobacco monopoly, Santa Rosa alleged there was a shortage of cash, prompting people to barter with goods and services. This apparently resulted in fraudulent behaviour from tobacco retailers as they, for example, demanded fabric, which would have taken eight days to make, in exchange for seven to eight cigars, or about two days' tobacco supply. The low salary rates resulted in shortage of personnel and undoubtedly encouraged fraudulent behaviour. The salary rates were provisional when the monopoly started and were meant to have been doubled as soon as the monopoly stabilized (de Galarraga to Soler, 9 July 1800). Despite remitting cash back to the royal treasury in Spain after only nine months of operations and continually doing so, it was only in 1810 that salary adjustments were made (Ysla de Leon, as cited by de Jesus 1973, p145).

Concluding remarks

This chapter sought to further examine the role of accounting in colonial relations. Previous research has highlighted that accounting's potency as an agent in the enactment of British and American imperialism has risen and waned over time and at different places. Looking at a different place at a different time, we examined the Spanish-sponsored Philippine tobacco monopoly from 1769 to 1799. The chapter investigated the role of accounting practices in articulating an expansion of the substantive rationality of the Spanish empire's colonization of the Philippines. In addition to a substantive rationality of propagation of the Catholic faith, there was a compelling 'logic of action' for the Spanish colonial state in the late 18th century to help sustain the Spanish empire. This case was particularly interesting because there has been little research in the accounting literature on accounting practices in the colonies of the Spanish empire. My examination of the first 30 years of the Philippine tobacco monopoly exposed an expansion of the state's bureaucracy that relied on accounting practices as formal modes of rationality. Accounting came into play when there was an extension of substantive rationality from soul-saving to revenue-enhancement – an awkward pairing of 'ends' that put the *padres* in the position of both enablers of and resisters to the latter. The bureaucracy crucially required the cooptation of the *padres* (especially at the beginning) and local leaders (throughout the period examined), and the application of military force. Accounting reports supported a story of an increase in the penetrative, extractive and negotiation powers of the Spanish sovereign colonial state. The ultimate success barometer was remittance of cash surpluses to the royal treasury in Spain. Was the full potential of the government accounting system as a formal mode of rationality achieved? Apparently not, as resistance by the Filipinos, the *padres* and the government officials themselves, meant that the integrity of variances between estimated and actual production was compromised. If there was collusion and fraud between *aforadores* and overseers, the estimates and actual production numbers would have been inaccurate. The potency of accounting was undermined with the subversion of accounting controls. Likewise, accounting did not reveal anything about the actual distribution of tobacco which determines whether or not actual production satisfied the needs or wants of the population. The accounting reports could not tell that the best cigars were taken by government officials for their personal use and that the Filipinos were buying and consuming low-grade products. Thus there were clearly limits as to what accounting could report. Letters from the *padres* (whose support for the tobacco monopoly project wavered at times) to Spanish government officials exposed and explained the fraud and resistance. In supporting an imposed monopoly project, accounting was nonetheless complicit in perpetuating Spanish imperialism in the Philippines. On this point, I join the growing chorus of voices in the accounting literature that expose accounting as part of colonial structures that helped make empire possible.

References

Primary Sources

Archivo General de Indias, Seville, Spain:
Aguilar RM to Gardoqui D (1794). July 22, no. 71, Ultramar 636.
Basco JV to de Galvez J (1782). May 8, no. 493, Filipinas 886.
Basco JV to de Galvez J (1782a). May 15, no. 501, Filipinas 886.
Basco JV to de Galvez J (1782b). May 15, no. 504, Filipinas 883.
Basco JV to de Galvez J (1783). May 31, no. 589, Filipinas 883.
Basco JV to de Galvez J (1784). June 18, no. 745, Ultramar 636.
Basco JV to de Galvez J (1787). June 17, no. 1019, Ultramar 636.
Basco JV to Tinio J (1782). January 23, Filipinas 883.
Carvajal CG to Basco JV (1782). February 6, no. 502, Filipinas 886
Correspondences to the Governor General (1791–99). Filipinas 887.
De Arriaga J to de Anda (1769). December 12, Filipinas 883.
De Galárraga P to Soler MC (1800). July 9, Ultramar 631.
De Santa Rosa J to Basco JV (1787). April 14, Ultramar 636.

Del Castillo M to de Galvez J (1787). July 2, Ultramar 636.

Director of the Renta del Tabaco to Basco JV (1783). 23 January, Filipinas 883.

Estado de Valores de la Renta del Tabaco desde el ano de 1782, que fue su creacion hasta el de 1801 en Islas Filipinas (1802). July 6, Ultramar 631.

Estado general de la Real Renta del Tavaco en las Islas Filipinas (1799). May 8, Filipinas 887.

Gonzalez C to de Galvez J (1787). June 10, no. 201, Ultramar 636.

Report dated May 7 1791, Estanco de en Camarines y Albay, Ultramar 638.

Dampier W (1698). *A new voyage round the world*. London: James Knapton.

De Viana FL (1765). Memorial of 1765. In EH Blair & JA Robertson (Eds), *The Philippine Islands, 1493–1898*, XLVIII, (pp197–338). Cleveland: The Arthur H Clark Company.

De Viana FL (1766). Financial Affairs of the Islands, 10 July 1766. In EH Blair & JA Robertson (Eds), *The Philippine Islands, 1493–1898*, L, (pp77–116). Cleveland: The Arthur H Clark Company.

De Zuniga JM (1793). *Estadismo de las Islas Filipinas: mis viajes por este pais*. Madrid: Retana. (Trans by V Del Carmen (1973) as *Status of the Philippines in 1800*, Filipiniana Book Guild).

Jagor F, de Comyn T, Wilks C & Virchow R (2005). The former Philippines thru foreign eyes. [Online] Available at www.authorama.com/former-philippines-1.html. Accessed 29 September 2005.

Pizarro MB (1827). Reforms needed in Filipinas. In EH Blair & JA Robertson (Eds), *The Philippine Islands, 1493–1898*, LI, (pp182–274). Cleveland: The Arthur H Clark Company.

Secondary Sources

Annisette M (1999). Importing accounting: the case of Trinidad and Tobago. *Accounting, Business and Financial History*, 9(1): 103–33.

Annisette M & Neu D (2004). Accounting and empire: an introduction. *Critical Perspectives on Accounting*, 15(1):1–4.

Bakre, OM (2004). Accounting and the problematique of imperialism: alternative methodological approaches to empirical research in accounting in developing countries. *Advances in Public Interest ing*, 10: 1–30.

Beck S (2006). Pacific Islands to 1875. [Online] Available at www.san.beck.org/2-13-PacificIslands.html#4. Accessed 30 April 2006.

Benitez C (1932). *Philippine civics: how we govern ourselves*. Boston, MA: Ginn.

Bjork K (1998). The link that kept the Philippines Spanish: Mexican merchant interests and the Manila trade, 1571–1815. *Journal of World History*, 9(1): 25–50.

Bourne EG (1827). Historical Introduction. In EH Blair & JA Robertson (Eds), *The Philippine Islands, 1493–1898*, I, (pp19–88). Cleveland: The Arthur H Clark Company.

Brading DA (1971). *Miners and merchants in Bourbon Mexico, 1763–1810*. England: Cambridge University Press.

Brubaker R (1984). *The Limits of Rationality*. London: Allen & Unwin.

Bush B & Maltby J (2004). Taxation in West Africa: transforming the colonial subject into the 'governable person'. *Critical Perspectives on Accounting*, 15(1): 5–34.

Carmona S, Ezzamel M & Gutierrez F (1997). Control and cost accounting practices in the Spanish royal tobacco factory. *Accounting, Organizations and Society*, 22(5): 411–46.

Carmona S, Ezzamel M & Gutierrez F (1998). Towards an institutional analysis of accounting change in the Royal Tobacco Factory in Seville. *Accounting Historians Journal*, 25(1): 115–47.

Chandler DP, Roff WR, Smail JRW, Steinberg DJ, Taylor RH, Woodside A & Wyatt DK (1987). *In search of Southeast Asia: a modern history*, rev edn. St Leonards: Allen & Unwin.

Cockerham WC, Abel T & Luschen G (1993). Max Weber, formal rationality, and health lifestyles. *The Sociological Quarterly*, 34(3): 413–28.

Colignon R & Covaleski M (1991). A Weberian framework in the study of accounting. *Accounting, Organizations and Society*, 16: 141–57.

Collins R (1985). *Three sociological traditions*. New York; Oxford: Oxford University Press.

Corpuz OD (1997). *An economic history of the Philippines*. Quezon City: University of the Philippines Press.

Cruikshank B (1982). Continuity and change in the economic and administrative history of 19th century Samar. In AW McCoy & EC de Jesus (Eds), *Philippine social history: global trade and local transformations*, (pp219–50). Quezon City: Ateneo de Manila University Press.

Cushner NP Jnr (1971). *Spain in the Philippines: from conquest to revolution*. Quezon City: Ateneo de Manila University Press; Tokyo, Japan: Charles E. Tuttle Co.

Davie SSK (2005). Accounting's uses in exploitative human engineering: theorizing citizenship, indirect rule and Britain's imperial expansion. *Accounting Historians Journal*, 32(2): 55–80.

Davie SSK (2000). Accounting for imperialism: a case of British-imposed indigenous collaboration. *Accounting, Auditing and Accountability Journal*, 13(3): 330–59.

De Jesus EC (1973). *The tobacco monopoly in the Philippines*. PhD dissertation, Yale University.

De Jesus EC (1980). *The tobacco monopoly in the Philippines*. Quezon City: Ateneo de Manila Press.

De Jesus EC (1982). Control and compromise in the Cagayan Valley. In AW McCoy & EC de Jesus (Eds), *Philippine social history: global trade and local transformations*, (pp21–38). Quezon City: Ateneo de Manila University Press.

Deans-Smith S (1992). *Bureaucrats, planters and workers: the making of the tobacco monopoly in Bourbon Mexico*. Austin: University of Texas Press.

Doeppers D (1976). The evolution of the geography of religious adherence in the Philippines before 1898. *Journal of Historical Geography*, 2(2): 95–110.

Du Gay P (2000). *In praise of bureaucracy*. Thousand Oaks, CA: Sage.

Dyball MC, Chua WF & Poullaos C (2006). Mediating between colonizer and colonized in the American empire: accounting for government monies in the Philippines. *Accounting, Auditing and Accountability Journal*, 19(1): 47–81.

Dyball MC, Poullaos C & Chua WF (2007). Accounting and empire: professionalisation as resistance, the case of the Philippines. *Critical Perspectives on Accounting*, 18(4): 415–49.

Ezzamel M (1997). Accounting, control and accountability: preliminary evidence from Ancient Egypt. *Critical Perspectives on Accounting*, 8: 563–601.

Fast J & Richardson J (1970). *Roots of dependency, political and economic revolution in 19th-century Philippines*. Quezon City: Foundation for Nationalist Studies.

Fradera JM (2004). The historical origins of the Philippine economy: a survey of recent research on the Spanish colonial era. *Australian Economic History Review*, 44(3): 307–20.

Goodman J (1994). *Tobacco in history: the cultures of dependence*. New York: Routledge.

Governors of the Philippines during the Spanish colonial period (nd). [Online] Available at www.zamboanga.com/html/Spanish_governors_of_the_philippines.ht m. Accessed 4 July 2005.

Hardwick MR. Jose de Galvez: Visitor General of New Spain, 1765–1772 (nd). [Online] Available at www.militarymuseum.org/Galvez.html. Accessed July 4, 2005.

Headley JM (1995). Spain's Asian presence, 1565–1590: structures and aspirations. *Hispanic American Historical Review*, 75(4): 623–46.

Hennessy P (1995). *The hidden writing*. London: Victor Gollancz.

Hooper K & Pratt M (1993). The growth of agricultural capitalism and the power of accounting: a New Zealand study. *Critical Perspectives on Accounting*, 4: 247–74.

Johnson TJ (1982). The state and professions: peculiarities of the British. In A Giddens & G Mackenzie, *Social class and division of labour: essays in honour of Ilya Neustadt*, (pp168–208). Cambridge: Cambridge University Press.

Johnson TJ & Caygill M (1971). The development of accounting links in the Commonwealth. *Accounting and Business Research*, 1(2): 155–73.

Kalberg S (1980). Max Weber's types of rationality. *American Journal of Sociology*, 85(5): 1145–79.

Kamen H (2002). *Spain's road to empire: the making of a world power.* London: Penguin.

Leroy JA (1907). The Philippines, 1860–1898: some comment and bibliographical notes. In EH Blair & JA Robertson (Eds), *The Philippine Islands, 1493–1898*, LII, (pp112–207). Cleveland: The Arthur H Clark Company.

Meyer JW & Rowan B (1977). Institutionalized organizations: formal structures as myth and ceremony. *American Journal of Sociology*, 83(2): 340–63.

McLennan MS (1973). Peasant Hacendero in Nueva Ecija: the socio-economic origins of a Philippine commercial rice-growing region. PhD dissertation, University of California.

Morse RM (1972). A prolegomenon to Latin American urban history. *Hispanic American Historical Review*, 52: 359–94.

Neu D (2000a). Accounting and accountability relations: colonization, genocide and Canada's first nations. *Accounting, Auditing and Accountability Journal*, 13(2): 268–88.

Neu D (2000b). 'Presents' for the 'Indians': land, colonialism and accounting in Canada. *Accounting, Organizations and Society*, 25(2): 163–84.

Owen NG (1971). Introduction: Philippine society and American colonialism. In NG Owen (Ed), *Compadre colonialism, studies on the Philippines under American rule*. Michigan Papers on South and Southeast Asia, 3: 1–12. The University of Michigan Center for South and Southeast Asian Studies.

Parker R (1993). *The administrative vocation.* Sydney: Hale & Iremonger.

Parkin F (1982). *Max Weber.* London: Tavistock Publications.

Perez Vidal J (1959). *España en la historia del tabaco.* Madrid: Centro de Estudios de Etnología Peninsular. Biblioteca de dialectología y tradiciones populares.

Petras JF (1981). *Class, state and power in the third world, with case studies on class conflict in Latin America.* London: Zed Books.

Pilapil V (1973). Review: 'Spain in the Philippines: from conquest to revolution' by Nicholas P. Cushner. *Hispanic American Historical Review*, 53(2): 315–16.

Radcliffe V (1997). Competing rationalities in 'special' government audits: the case of NovAtel. *Critical Perspectives on Accounting*, 8: 343–66.

Roces MN (1990). *Kinship politics in postwar Philippines: the Lopez family, 1945-1989*. PhD dissertation, University of Michigan.

Roher J (1979). *Ethics for bureaucrats*. New York: Marcel Dekker.

Roth G & Wittich C (Eds) (1978). *Max Weber, economy and society*. Berkeley, Los Angeles: University of California Press.

Schurz WL (1939). *The Manila galleon*. New York: EP Dutton & Co.

Scott WH (1982). The Spanish occupation of the Cordillera in the 19th century. In AW McCoy & EC de Jesus (Eds), *Philippine social history: global trade and local transformations*, (pp39–56). Quezon City: Ateneo de Manila University Press.

Sicotte R (1997). Abstract – the Spanish royal tobacco monopoly in the viceroyalty of Peru, 1752–1813. [Online] Available at www.eh.net/pipermail/abstracts/1997-September/000601.html. Accessed 30 April 2006.

Sturtevant D (1976). *Popular uprisings in the Philippines, 1840-1940*. Ithaca: Cornell University Press.

Taylor PL (1994). The rhetorical construction of efficiency: restructuring and industrial democracy in Mondragon, Spain. *Sociological Forum*, 9(3): 459–89.

Weber M (1964). *The theory of social and economic organization*. New York: Free Press.

Weber M, Roth G, et al. (1978). *Economy and society : an outline of interpretive sociology*. Berkeley: University of California Press.

Weiss L & Hobson JM (1995). *States and economic development: a comparative historical analysis*. Cambridge: Polity Press.

Zeitlin M (1972). *Capitalism and imperialism: an introduction to neo-Marxian concepts*. Chicago: Markham Publishing Company.

7

Developing integrative performance management systems

Robert H Chenhall (Monash University)

Abstract

This chapter is concerned with the development of integrated performance management systems. Increasingly it is being argued that the effectiveness of performance management will depend on the extent to which performance measures form an integrated performance management system. The idea of integrative performance management can be found in the development of performance measurement in business disciplines other than management accounting. In this chapter, developments in the areas of manufacturing, marketing and human resource management are considered. In management accounting the balanced scorecard has evolved as the exemplar integrated performance management systems. Notwithstanding its popularity there have been criticisms of the BSC as an integrative performance management tool. The chapter examines these criticisms and provides suggestions as to how BSC may be elaborated to address the issues of concern.

This company has some sophisticated measurement systems in manufacturing and marketing but they operate independently. The current work they are doing on Balanced Scorecards seems to flow nicely from these innovations. It will be interesting to see how well the scorecard can enable the company to develop a fully integrated system, or whether this is too ambitious at this stage.[1]

The passage cited above dates from 2002 when many Australian firms were excited about improving their performance evaluation systems by moving from performance measurement to performance management. An outcome of the research being undertaken at this time between Bill Birkett and the author was that despite difficulties in adopting and implementing systems such as Balanced Scorecards (BSC), there was (and still is) great interest in the evolving sophistication of BSC-type systems and their potential to provide for a more integrated approach to management. This chapter is inspired by this quotation and explores how performance measurement innovations in manufacturing, marketing and human resource management helped management accountants grasp the importance of integrated performance measurement (IPM), culminating in the development of the BSC. The chapter also discusses some criticisms of the BSC as an integrating management system and suggests avenues to address these potential problems.

Assessing performance is an important element of management accounting. This has evolved from a traditional concern with performance measurement to one of performance management (Lebas 1995, Euske & Zander 2005, Folan & Browne 2005). Performance measurement has typically related to ways of articulating, in a quantitative way, the meaning of desired outcomes and to assess the effectiveness of the organization or the individual in achieving those outcomes. On the basis of this process, desired outcomes can be reviewed and, ideally, performance related to activities can be examined and developed to achieve the outcomes, usually taking into account changes in strategic and operating circumstances. Traditionally in management accounting, this was done by way of budgets, and financially-based performance reports with some attention being given to aggregate efficiency standards. In addition, performance measurement has been con-

---

1 Comment from Bill Birkett during research with the author into the role of Balanced Scorecards in a selection of Australian companies.

cerned with assessing aspects of production processes including suppliers and customers. This has been done by defining these outcomes in ways that can be measured readily. In recent years, measurement has extended to include difficult-to-measure dimensions such as social responsibility, intellectual capital and employee welfare. A distinctive aspect of traditional approaches has been their reductionalist approaches, where components of the organization, such as a production process or a division, are the subject for evaluation.

Concern with finding 'measures' for outcomes and the processes driving these outcomes is usually considered important to evaluating performance. However, the way in which these measures might tell us something about the intricacies of how the organization is going to achieve its objectives moves 'performance measurement' to 'performance management'. Performance management asks questions related to what causes performance and it attempts to capture how this occurs in terms of performance measures. In recent years this has moved performance evaluation away from reductionist approaches to a focus on how the various components of the organization interact to affect the whole. As such performance management encompasses performance measurement and performance measurement enables performance management.

Performance management requires us to understand the processes by which the organization achieves its objectives and this provides the basis to think about measuring these processes, establishing feedback on progress to achieve them, rethinking the objectives in changing operating situations, and using the measures in ways that encourage participants to focus on how they and the organization can achieve desired outcomes. This inevitably broadens the scope of performance evaluation to develop some form of model of how the various operations of the organization interact to effect desired outcomes and to include a broad range of information that relates to these models. This has moved performance management to focus on integrative aspects of performance measurement, or to the development of IPM. The integrative aspect of performance management is part of the development of more strategic resources management systems. These systems provide a way to ensure that operations can be related to strategies (a vertical connection) and that linkages across the value chain are made in ways consistent with delivering on strategy (Chenhall 2005). Birkett (1995) noted that when management accounting becomes a strategic resource management system, it will be able to participate in resource-related direction setting, in the design and implementation of organizational change, and in the development of control systems and performance measurements.

In this chapter two aspect of the IPM are considered. First, it is shown that the essence of IPM can be found in the development of performance measurement in business disciplines other than management accounting. Developments in the areas of manufacturing, marketing and human resource management (HRM) are considered. Second, it is concluded that to some, the BSC articulates an exemplar IPM. Notwithstanding its popularity there have been criticisms of the BSC as an integrative performance management tool. The chapter examines these criticisms and provides suggestions as to how BSC may be elaborated to address the issues.

The move to integrated performance management

Throughout the 1980s, consideration of performance measurement was an important part of a variety of disciplines such as manufacturing, marketing and HRM, as well as management accounting (Waggoner, Neely & Kennerley 1999, Chenhall & Langfield-Smith 2007). Consideration of these developments is part of the evolution of performance measurement where non-financial measures became important on their own and as supplements to financial measures. Within these disciplines innovations were developed that are part of the evolution towards IPM where non-financial and financial measures are connected into causal models. The following section provides an overview and illustrations from these disciplines of the application of a variety of performance measures and how these were employed to provide IPM, and how they helped develop performance management in management accounting.[2]

---

2 This section draws upon and elaborates on work done by Chenhall and Langfield-Smith (2008) published in the *European Management Journal*.

Manufacturing

Around the early 1980s, management accountants recognized that others working in operations or manufacturing had a focus on performance measurement. Drawing on ideas from manufacturing, Johnson and Kaplan (1987) claimed that the role of short-term financial measures had been undermined by rapid changes in technology, shortened product life cycles and innovations in production operations (Johnson & Kaplan 1987, pp254–55). The decreased reliance on direct labour, increased capital intensity and a stronger contribution made by intellectual capital and other intangible resources made it invalid to rely on traditional methods of matching revenue to costs and consequent short-term measures of profit as a measure of performance. They proposed that non-financial indicators should be employed, based on the organization's strategy, and include measures of manufacturing, marketing, and research and development. The new manufacturing environment with practices such as just-in-time (JIT) and total quality management (TQM) was also said to encourage a need for a more encompassing means for evaluating strategic investment decisions (Berliner & Brimson 1988).

For some time, manufacturing has stressed direct measures of operations that are in real time and in fine detail. As this discipline has matured, more complex approaches have recognized the interdependencies between the production, marketing, HRM and finance functions and have attempted to build performance measurement systems that capture these interdependencies (Harrison et al. 1990, Hall 1990, Vollmann 1990, Cooper & Turney 1990, Nanni et al. 1992). Examples include, Lynch and Cross' (1995) performance measurement hierarchy that articulates an integrated performance measurement system, from senior management level to the operational level, which addresses both market and cost considerations to support aspects of strategic importance. Another example is the performance prism (Neely & Adams 2001, Neely et al. 2002), consisting of five facets. The top and bottom facets are stakeholder satisfaction and stakeholder contribution, respectively, while the three side facets are strategies, processes and capabilities.

Many of the ideas for employing multiple measures to suit advanced manufacturing and to relate these to the business, found their way into main stream management accounting by writers such as Howell and Soucy (1987) and Bromwich and Bhimani (1989, pp56–57). Others provided details of using measures such as on-time deliveries, reduction in inventory, cooperation with suppliers, process cost reduction, quality, cycle time and product complexity (Mosconi & McNair 1987, Johnson 1988, Green et al. 1991). The thrust of these innovations in management accounting were captured by professional association with volumes such as *Performance excellence in manufacturing and service organizations* (AAA 1990). Other volumes followed, notably, *Measures of manufacturing excellence* (Kaplan 1990) and *Performance measurement, evaluation and incentives* (Bruns 1992). Since then manufacturing measures have been recognized as one of the key perspectives of IPM, such as the 'internal business process' perspective in the BSC, the internal 'processes' within the performance prism (Neely & Adams 2001), the 'business operating systems' in the performance pyramid of Lynch and Cross (1991), and 'process performance measures' of the quantum performance measurement matrix of Hronec (1993), (see also Folan & Brown 2005, for a discussion of IPM drawn from manufacturing).

Marketing

The marketing discipline has developed IPM that integrates customers and markets with other facets of the organization's activities and to financial outcomes. Prominent examples include *customer satisfaction measurement*, the *service profit chain* and *customer lifetime value* that have been developed as IPM.[3] Defining and measuring *customer satisfaction* and understanding how customer satisfaction, service quality and organizational performance are integrated has been studied for some decades in the marketing literature. For many years it was generally believed that market share was the main driver of profitability (Buzzell & Gale 1987). However, a range of studies found that customer loyalty was a more influential driver than market share (Reichheld & Sasser 1990, Reichheld 1996). This work led to a large body of

---

3 A useful review of the linkages between marketing and management control systems is provided in Foster and Gupta (1994).

research that explored the determinants of customer loyalty, including customer satisfaction (Heskett et al. 1994). This stream of marketing literature has been instrumental in flagging the need to build IPM to examine whether higher customer satisfaction improves financial performance, through increasing customer loyalty, reducing price elasticities, positive word-of-mouth advertising, reducing transaction costs and enhancing the firms' reputation (see, for example, Anderson et al. 1994, Fornell et al. 1996, Anderson et al. 1997).

The Service Profit Chain (SPC) is another example of a marketing-based IPM. It is the outcome of research that maintains that there are strong direct links between profit, growth, customer loyalty, customer satisfaction, the value of goods and services delivered to customers and employee capability, satisfaction, loyalty and productivity (Heskett et al. 1994). In particular, the strongest linkages have been found to be between profit and customer loyalty, employee loyalty and customer loyalty, and employee satisfaction and customer satisfaction. Given these connections, the development of the service profit chain has been likened to a form of BSC with its focus on drivers and means-end relationships (Heskett et al. 1994).

There has been relatively limited empirical research in the marketing literature examining the linkages between service quality and profitability (see Zeithaml 2000 for a review) or linking marketing effort to profitability (see the review in Bowman & Narayandas 2004). However recent research in the accounting literature has investigated the linkage between customer satisfaction and financial returns (Anderson et al. 1997, Ittner & Larcker 1998, Banker et al. 2000). A more integrative approach is found in work by Smith and Wright (2004) who extended the work of Ittner and Larcker (1998) and Banker et al. (2000) by applying the SPC framework to companies within the personal computer industry. Their approach sought to explain the causal relations between product value attributes (brand image, firm viability, product quality and post-sale service quality), product market attributes (average price and customer loyalty) and financial performance (sales growth and return on assets). They found that product value attributes directly and differentially impacts on the level of customer loyalty and selling prices.

Customer loyalty measures also explained levels of revenue growth and profitability.

Another tool of customer analysis advocated in the marketing literature that demonstrates integration between customers and financial outcomes is the *customer lifetime value* (CLV). CLV is the level of net profit to a firm from the lifetime of transactions of the customer with the firm (Jain & Singh 2002). It is assumed that customers who remain with an organization for a long period of time generate more profits than those who stay for a short time, due to price premiums paid by loyal customers, increased sales and new customers gained through referrals from those loyal customers, cost effectiveness of dealing with established customers, and revenue growth through increased sales from those customers (Reichheld 1996). As well as integrating customers with financial returns, this approach also acknowledges that a multi-period analysis is required to assess the impact of customer-based strategies. That is, returns from marketing initiatives are received over the long term. In its simplest form CLV may be measured as the present value of the future net cash flows that are expected to be received over the lifetime of a customer, consisting of revenue obtained from the customer, less the cost of attracting, selling and servicing the customer (Keane & Wang 1995, Berger & Nasr 1998). A more sophisticated approach that also involves consideration of time horizons involves customer-base analysis. These models take into account the past behaviours of customers to model the probability of purchases of individual customers in the next time period, to determine the customers who are active in future periods (Schmittlein et al. 1987, Reinartz & Kumar 2000). Outcomes of this modelling may be used to calculate CLV.

Human resource management and performance measures

A primary focus of HRM has been on performance measures as part of reward systems at the shop-floor level. Variable performance payments have been included in employee remuneration through piece-rates, gain-sharing and profit sharing, and appropriate non-financial and financial measures of performance have been important in determining the extent of rewards. The concerns of HRM with many aspects of management have helped inform the debate in accounting on how performance management should be developed to accommodate the 'human' element of the organization, which is often considered as an aspect of the learning and growth perspective of a BSC (Kaplan & Norton 1996).

Over the past few decades HRM has adopted an integrated approach that aspires to develop the entire management team with the aim of managing all organizational resources, of which employees are one. So while HRM is concerned with traditional practices of recruitment, training, development, communications and rewards, its purpose is to employ, explicitly, these practices to develop organizational values consistent with achieving desired strategic priorities. The primary outcome is to enhance the organization's financial performance, which moves the purpose away from placing the highest priority on the welfare of employees, to one that considers the organization's overall needs for human resources. This has involved efforts to develop IPM which relate HRM practices to other functions and to broader organizational goals. By way of illustration consideration is given to the development of *360 degree performance ratings, human capital index, multiple-attribute utility analysis* and *intangible assets*.

The innovation of *360 degree performance* ratings provides a way of gaining insight into an individual's performance from a variety of sources such as supervisors, peers, subordinates, customers and suppliers (Hazucha et al. 1993). The provision of information from a wide set of individuals who have close working relationships with the employee provides multiple perspectives of the individual's performance. There are considerable challenges in ensuring that performance measures used from multiple sources are consistent and valid. These include different raters using different dimensions of performance, or defining measures of these dimensions differently. Also, raters may use similar measures but weight them differently in making judgements on performance. Or different raters may use the same measures, weight them similarly but have different opportunities to observe individuals being rated and thus see different behaviours (Borman 1997, p302). Notwithstanding these difficulties, a 360-degree approach can act as an IPM system as it acquires information on how individuals are integrating their efforts across the organization.

There have been a variety of applications that have sought, explicitly, to relate HRM initiatives to other aspects of organizations' activities and outcomes. The consulting firm, Watson-Wyatt, has developed a methodology for calculating the correlation between HRM practices and shareholder value (Watson Wyatt 2005). The system provides a set of measures that quantify which HR practices and policies have the greatest association with shareholder value. Using these measures they assign a single *human capital index* (HCI) score to a company (0–100), with high scores indicating superior HR practices and being associated with higher share value. Another approach to quantitatively integrate HRM performance measures is *multiple-attribute utility analysis* (MAUA). This is an approach that attempts to build IPM by assessing how the multiple facets of job performance combine to affect desired outcomes (Boudreau 1991, Roth & Bobko 1997). MAUA involves four steps. First, the process involves determining multiple attributes related to the consequences or outcomes of a decision. Next, performance measures are determined for each attribute. Once measures are determined they are combined in a utility function to assist in making decisions. A key concern is to develop a series of utility functions that relate the multiple measures to a common metric, such as effectiveness. An ordering of the relative importance of different attributes is performed. The most appropriate way of combining different attributes and weighting their importance is a complex issue and of great relevance to management accountants who wish to employ IPM (Roth & Bobko 1997, pp354–59). Finally, a decision is made by determining the utility of possible decision options and then determining the robustness of the decision to changes in measures, weights and utility functions, employing simulation and sensitivity analysis.

More recently, innovations in measuring the workforce as *intangible assets*, or intellectual capital, have evolved as organizations recognize the key HRM principle that it is people who are the source of competitive advantage (Stewart 2001). HRM researchers have developed IPM frameworks that link various aspects of intellectual capital and, in some instances, link these to other perspectives including financial performance (Brooking 1996, Stewart 1997, Sveiby 1997, Edvinsson 2002, Andriessen 2004). These systems have contributed by helping to define the meaning and measurement of intangible assets and more generally have provided links between HRM practices and the economic value of the organization. This orientation was identified as a key component of the BSC in Kaplan and Norton's *Strategy maps* (2004, chapter 7).

The prior examples illustrate that the idea of employing IPM as a management system to integrate the activities of an organization to achieve desired outcomes is not unique to management accounting and has been employed across a range of disciplines for some time. However, in the 1990s management accounting provided an articulation of the potential benefits of IPM and offered, in a user-friendly way, a technique or way of thinking that uses a strategic orientation to integrate operations with financial outcomes. This was the advent of the BSC (Kaplan & Norton 1996, 2001, 2004, 2006, 2008) which since its inception has become as well known as other breakthrough innovations in management accounting, like activity-based cost management. While the BSC has gained a high profile and has great recognition, the practice has not been without its critics. The following section considers some concerns with the BSC as an IPM system and provides suggestions on how these potential problems can be addressed within a BSC approach to performance management.

Balanced Scorecards, criticisms and elaborations

Increasingly in management accounting it is being argued that the effectiveness of performance management will depend on the extent to which performance measures form an IPM system, that enables strategy and operations to be integrated and harmonized (Olve, Roy & Wetter 1999; Epstein & Birchard 2000; Epstein & Westbrook 2001; Banker et al. 2001; Inner & Larcker 2003). Empirical evidence on the effectiveness of IPM is limited. There is some evidence that integration within performance management systems is beneficial. Banker et al. (2001) and Sandt et al. (2001) found that the provision of systematic linkages between measures enhances satisfaction with the systems. Ittner et al. (2003) found that firms in the financial services sector that had more coherent performance measurement systems were associated with enhanced satisfaction with the PMS. Bryant et al. (2004) found that in well-designed BSC each outcome measure was associated with outcomes measures in all higher-level BSC perspectives. For example, higher levels of employee skills (part of the learning and growth perspective) was associated with higher levels of product introductions (internal business process perspective) and customer satisfaction (customer perspective). Chenhall (2005) found that performance management systems that provide integrative information were associated with effectiveness in achieving targeted strategies. While this evidence suggests benefits of IPM, it is not clear whether these systems are widespread. For example, Ittner and Larcker (2003) found that managers made little attempt to link non-financial performance measures to advance their chosen strategies. Moreover, only 23% of these managers were able to show that they built causal models and most did not validate the causal links.

The extent to which causal models do in fact help enhance performance has not been examined widely and evidence is mixed. A study by Rucci, Kirn and Quinn (1998) found that a business model predicted how employee attitudes affected customer attitudes which together enhanced financial performance, at the US firm Sears. However, in a study of the distribution operation of a large US firm, Malina, Nørreklit and Selto (2007) were unable to show that a business model that included aspects such as profitability, sales, customer satisfaction, inventory, and safety significantly predicted cause-effect relationships between these variables. However, despite this, within this firm, managers were highly satisfied with the business model and used it extensively.

Kaplan and Norton (1996, 2001, 2004, 2006, 2008) presented the BSC which has become recognized globally as a tool to explicitly integrate performance measurement systems with strategy. The BSC model emphasizes the need for balance between short-term and long-term measures across various strategic dimensions of the business (financial, customers, internal processes, learning and growth). The central role of linkages, or cause-effect relationships for connecting operations to strategy, was noted in the first book on the scorecard, *The Balanced Scorecard: translating strategy into action* (Kaplan & Norton 1996), and is elaborated as 'strategy maps' that are central to IPM in the book *The strategy focused organization* (Kaplan & Norton 2001) and in *Strategy maps* (Kaplan & Norton 2004). The following book titled *Alignment* (Kaplan & Norton 2006) employs cause-effect relationships and strategy maps to help align the efforts of business and shared service units to generate 'enterprise-derived value'. Also in *The executive premium* (Kaplan & Norton 2008) the aim of cause-effect relationships is to describe how organizations can establish strong links from strategy to operations so that employees' everyday operational activities will support strategic objectives. The book elaborates on the links between long-term strategy and daily operations.

What is cause-effect?

While developing cause-effect relationships between strategic outcomes and operations, structural units and employees is a key aspect of the BSC, the precise meaning of how this might be achieved has been debated. The meaning of cause-effect by way of strategy maps and BSCs is established and elaborated in the first three books by Kaplan and Norton (1996, 2001, 2004). Perhaps the clearest articulation of the centrality of cause-effect relationships within a BSC is in their first book, *The Balanced Scorecard* (1996). They note

> A properly constructed scorecard should tell the story of the business unit's strategy through a sequence of cause-and-effect relationships. The measurement system should make the relationships (hypotheses) among objectives (and measures) in the various perspectives explicit so that they can be managed and validated (p146).

Outcome measures in the form of lagging measures are seen as effects while performance drivers take the form of leading indicators and are the causes (p159). In this work it is stressed that to ensure tangible payoffs from change programs then "causal paths from all the measures on a scorecard should be linked to financial objectives" (p151). The critical importance of cause-effect modelling within the scorecard is clear with an output of the scorecard being a graphical model of how the measures are linked within the perspectives, and to measures or objectives in other perspectives (p307). This theme is elaborated further in their second and third books.

Cause-effect takes place in two interrelated ways. First, a strategy map is established to link, in generic terms, a strategy (expressed in financial terms) to what has to be done to achieve that strategy in the perspectives of customers, internal processes and learning and growth. Second, the different aspects of the generic linkages are elaborated by way of a BSC that refines the cause-effect linkages in more operational detail and provides measures with targets that invites reflection on opportunities for initiatives. Here cause-effect is central to understanding connections between strategy and operations with two principles being proposed: first, to translate the strategy to operational terms; and second, align the organization to the strategy (Kaplan & Norton 2001, pp9–12).

While the idea that organizations can be made more effective by understanding what operational decisions cause the achievement of desired outcomes has great appeal, the application of cause-effect within the BSC framework has not been accepted without critique. The most important of these include the following. First, it is not always clear that so called cause-effect relationships do in fact involve cause and effects. Second, the cause-effect relationships and strategy maps are too simplistic; they do not account for more complex relationships between variables; they are linear and sequential. Each of these will be critically examined in terms of the evolution of BSC and in terms of broader issues of organizational modelling.[4]

Do BSC examine cause-effect relationships?

The first criticism is that cause-effect relationships depicted in the BSC, particularly those that have a financial component, do not represent relationships where one variable causes an effect on a separate variable (Malina et al.

---

4 In this chapter consideration is given to the modelling aspect of BSC. There are other concerns that have been raised including: how BSCs relate to other aspects of the organization's management control system; how balance is achieved between BSC measures; issues of the suitability, or fit, of BSC to different contextual settings; and concerns related to the effective implementation of BSC.

2007, Nørreklit 2000, Oriet & Misiaszek 2004, Otley 1999). This criticism may be explained by way of an example drawn from a proposed cause-effect relationship in the BSC that involves the customer perspective (Kaplan & Norton 1996, p67). A relationship between improved customer profitability and enhanced segment financial performance does not involve cause and effect, rather it is a logical connection, which involves a tautological relationship. This follows as customer profitability is part of financial performance. To say that customer profitability causes improved financial performance is meaningless in terms of a cause-effect connection. Both variables have a financial component; specifically customer profitability is determined by considering number of customers and their financial impact, which is in fact an aspect of financial performance.

While it may be argued that logical relationships within BSC are not meaningful in terms of cause and effect, it is unclear whether their inclusion as part of a strategy map will necessarily result in misspecification and dysfunctional decisions based on the maps. Certainly in the example given, the stated relationship could be seen as redundant – seeing customer profit as part of the revenue and growth mix dimension of the financial perspective (Kaplan & Norton 1999, p52) *and* as part of the customer perspective (Kaplan & Norton 1996, p71). That is, it is not that customer profitability will improve profitability it is that customer profitability is improved profitability. One could argue that in BSC terms this moves customer profitability from the customer perspective to the financial perspective, as part of the construct of growth in net income.

From a formal modelling perspective, slippage between logical and cause-effect relationships can be addressed by standard procedures for defining constructs, such as the four perspectives of the BSC, and the various dimensions that elaborate these perspectives including identification of variables and measures that operationalize the dimensions as performance indicators. This involves, first, determining an agreed meaning of the dimensions, or their face validity. This may be driven by theoretical considerations, or more typically in the case of a BSC, meaning will be defined by practice. What is being sought is agreement on an underlying construct, such as customer satisfaction, and a selection of variables will then be employed related to that construct to reflect its meaning. For example, designers of BSC may agree that customer satisfaction is an underlying latent construct and its meaning will be reflected in operational excellence, customer intimacy and product leadership. Within the construct of operational excellence, elements will include product service attributes, customer relationship and brand image. Within these variables a performance measure will be devised to reflect its meaning. For product service attributes these might be product quality, timeliness and functionality (see Kaplan & Norton 2001, p96).

While such descriptions are unlikely to remain static, concern with careful definitions to arrive at an agreed definition, is a first step to developing valid BSC for an organization. If sufficient data are available on the application of the BSC, statistical tests, such as factor analysis, can be employed to see if the relationships between measures and their respective constructs in the BSC strategy maps are in fact valid (for examples see Stemsrudhagen 2004, Rejc & Slapničar 2004). It is also possible to test for discriminant validity which examines if particular measures belong only to their related construct and are not part of other constructs that are found within and between the different perspectives.[5] Once it is confirmed that measures belong to particular constructs it is possible to have some confidence that measurement errors will not contaminate the application of quantitative techniques to BSC cause-effect models.[6]

Is BSC too simplistic?

A further concern with identifying cause-effect relationships within BSC is that the approach is too simplistic. It is claimed that the illustrations provided by the proponents of BSCs do not include alternate or more complex explanations of the cause-effect relationships, and the strategy maps are too simplistic (Nørreklit 2000, Oriet & Misiaszek 2004, Reilly & Reilly 2000,

---

5 Structural equation modelling can be employed to conduct these tests (e.g. Hoyle 1995, Chin 1998).

6 For an elaboration of the importance of construct definition as an aspect of formal modelling in management accounting, see Bisbe et al. (2007).

Schonberger 2008). Also they are restricted to examining linear relationships, that the direction of causality may be reversed, and that they involve uni-directional causality, such that metric A causes B, when in fact A may cause B but B then causes A. Associated with these criticisms is the claim that the BSC does not recognize that variables have differing time horizons before effects are realized, with some occurring in the short-term while others take a longer period of time.

While it is always possible to provide alternate explanations for explaining and prescribing strategy, including additional and alternative paths, or reversed arguments for cause-effect, this is not a compelling criticism of BSC, per se. Proponents of BSC claim that it is important to recognize that the tool is related to strategy and as such it should examine those decisions that have a critical effect (Kaplan & Norton 1996, p162–65). As such the approach involves a broad-brush strategic orientation. Other techniques, such as 'KPI scorecards', can be used to examine what has to be done at a more detailed level to achieve the higher level issues identified in strategy maps and BSC (Kaplan & Norton 2001, p103).

Using models to learn about the business situation and to examining alternate explanations applies to all formal modelling techniques. Abernethy et al. (2004) in a study of casual mapping in a hospital found that developing causal performance maps enabled management to learn about the activities and processes necessary to achieve a well-functioning clinical program. The role of BSC to learn and test alternate assumptions to develop double loop learning is stressed in the BSC. In fact, in each volume of Kaplan and Norton's BSC there is increasing emphasis on using BSC as a mechanism to debate and test different assumptions and logics that may apply to strategy (1996, p269; 2001, chapter 12; 2004, ch. 10; 2006, p95; 2008, ch. 9). This process provides the mechanisms in practice where alternate models can be developed and the direction of causality tested.

When developing models, the assumptions of linearity, uni-directional causality and single-period analysis all aim to decrease the complexity of modelling. Increasingly in management accounting, it is being recognized that practice and research needs to recognize complexity. In as much as BSC employs these simplifying assumptions it is open to the criticism of being too simple. Oriet and Misiaszek (2004, p277) address the difficulty in determining what is the appropriate level of complexity to model organizational reality. They note that there are arguments for both simplifying and for addressing complexity in representations of reality. In an illustration of building causal maps, Abernethy et al. (2005, p152) stress that highly complex maps of performance drivers are unlikely to be feasible or desirable to implement performance measurement systems as sufficient data usually are not readily available, and the use of excessive complexity can lead to information overload or selective focus on the most easily achievable measures.

The level of complexity in BSC models depends on the purpose of the model. If the intent is to consider issues related to strategy, an approach that considers broad constructs and critical relationships would seem sensible. If there are issues that are of concern in understanding more micro attributes that lie beneath some constructs or relationships then a more fine-grained approach is warranted, particularly if they invalidate the understanding provided by the more simplified model. In essence we choose a simple model over a more complex approach when the additional details in the complex approach do not invalidate the predictions under consideration. Perhaps designers of BSC should be conscious of the principle of 'Ockham's razor' (entities should not be multiplied unnecessarily) which suggests that when faced with a choice between BSCs, with either a high level of complexity or a more simplified representation of reality, we should first study the simplest of models, unless it is clearly wrong when considering more details. That is not to say simpler models will be correct, it just establishes priorities.

Are the assumptions of BSC unrealistic?

In the main, the relationships depicted in BSC involve linear connections between causes and effects. In business cause-effect relationships, linearity is usually unlikely, particularly when considering the affects of either very small or large changes of one variable on another. As non-linear change is not based on a simple proportional relationship between cause and effect, the change can be abrupt, unexpected and difficult to predict. This can be difficult to model. However, typically, in many business situations the non linearity can be predicted. For example, the magnitude of changes will be small at the start of an intervention, it will grow in the size of the effects and then diminish – a typical S-shaped relationship. A change in quality of a product may start with small increases in sales and then as information on the product improvement spreads, sales increase at a greater rate and then as a consequence of saturation or competition, sales decline.

In some situations divergence from linear relationships may not be great and not much damage is done by assuming linearity. In other situations, while non-linearity may apply to the whole range of changes involving cause and effect, the specific level of changes may be approximated by a linear relationship. For example, the effect of product improvements on sales during the period where product improvements have been recognized in the market and demand is high, may approximate a linear relationship. In this relevant range, linearity may be adequate, as long as conclusions are not extrapolated beyond the relevant range. If it is believed or can be shown that assumptions of linearity will lead to erroneous conclusions it is relatively easy to model nonlinearity and to test models using nonlinear statistics.

Usually, modelling can involve 'what if' analysis by examining the model with varying assumptions as to the degree of effects at different levels of the cause. Mathematical approaches can be used to model non-linear relationships, such as quadratic functions. Also, modelling techniques such as systems dynamics provide a way of including nonlinearities into modelling (Roberts 1978). In some instances it may be desirable to transform nonlinear relationships into linear ones. However, this is done to enable the analysis to use more powerful linear-based statistical routines. If nonlinearities are involved in the BSC models then this is important information and should be accommodated directly.

Another criticism related to simplifying assumptions is that BSC assume unidirectional cause-effect relationships, when in fact reverse or recursive causality may be evident. Clearly, the direction of cause-effect is best considered at the time of developing strategy maps. For example, in the first instance it may be considered that an investment in a new technical innovation will provide new product characteristics and this will have an effect on improving customer loyalty. However, on reflection it may be that suggestions for improved products come from a loyal customer base and this is the cause for efforts to acquire new technology to generate innovative product characteristics. This type of adjustment is not exclusive to BSC and applies to all modelling. Recursive causality is more complex and involves considering multi-period effects. While BSC recognizes that different interventions may have either short- or long-term effects, on the whole, they do not present situations where decision A effects outcome B, and as a consequence B has an effect on A. For example, an improvement in technology may provide product features that enhance customer satisfaction which increases financial returns. It may then be that the improved financial return provides the ability to invest further in the technology which then further enhances customer satisfaction and financial returns.

More generally, concerning time lags, it has been claimed that BSC does not take account of the different timing effects of interventions (Nørreklit 2000, p71–72; Haas & Kleingeld 1999, p244; Otley 1990, p376). Effects of changes in existing internal processes, such as continuous improvement programs may have effects within the short term, while investments in research and development may take a longer period of time and be more uncertain requiring continual monitoring. In using BSC for planning, different time horizons can readily be built into strategy maps. Kaplan and Norton distinguish between lagging and leading indicators which recognized that some measures relate to the past and some to future possible outcomes (1996, p150). While important to the BSC, this relates only to the measurements and considers only desired outcomes, and not the dynamics implicated in strategy maps. However, there is ample evidence in the five Kaplan and Norton books of a dynamic approach to the use of BSC and of including different planning horizons within strategy maps and BSC (e.g. 1996, p100; 2001, p85; 2004, p47–48, 2006, p24; 2008, p62–66). Clearly, as the planning situation extends into the future it is likely to become more uncertain, which decreases the level of confidence in cause-effect relationships.

As indicated earlier, within the BSC literature it is recommended that the BSC be used like many other long-range planning tools to monitor the effectiveness of outcomes, and to use feedback from these outcomes for double-loop learning, to correct for faulty assumptions and for rethinking action plans and even strategies (e.g. 1996, p17; 2001, pp274–76; 2004, pp300–06 as knowledge management systems; 2006, pp285–86 as strategy review meetings; 2008, p251–79 as testing and adapting the strategy). There are many opportunities to include time lags into formal performance models including time series data, such as pooled sample data or panel data. The use of statistical testing to include time lags is noted by Kaplan and Norton, particularly in the latest volume (2008, pp260–73). Examples of models in accounting that include examining management decisions through time include Banker, Chang and Majumdar (1993); Banker, Chang and Majumdar (1996); Banker, Datar and Kaplan (1989); and Banker, Field, Schroeder and Sinha (1996).

Using BSC for dynamic learning

Many of the criticisms that have been levelled at the BSC as an IPM system are applied to the formal modelling stage of planning and control. For some commentators these problems are so significant that they believe that cause-effect modelling is not appropriate and 'softer' approaches that identify means-end relationships are more satisfactory. Here the aim is to establish coherence between all groups to ensure they contribute to the desired outcomes of the organization (see Nørreklit 2000, pp83–85; Hass & Kleingeld 1999, pp240–41). A means-end approach considers that the cause-effect interrelationships taking place as the business seeks coherence is something of a black box that cannot be understood with precision (Lane 1986). The black box has the complications of nonlinearity, recursive causality, and requirements for short-term imbalances that may pre-empt the achievement of long-term objectives. Certainly, if the business situation is very complex and uncertain this may be the most realistic approach. However, before that, much can be learned by considering the procedures for 'best-practice' modelling to clarify the reasonableness of the assumptions and nature of the cause-effect relationships.

Using strategy maps and BSC in an 'interactive way' (Simons 1995) provides a useful way for obtaining knowledge from across the organization on strategies, both deliberate and emerging, and on the connections between financial performance, customers, internal processes and learning and growth, to sustain optimal linkages in both the short and long terms. Once established, the strategy maps and BSC can be used to learn about the effectiveness of strategies, assumption and operations. Attention to defining the meaning of the perspectives within a BSC and its dimensions and associated measures can address issues of the validity of constructs within the BSC model. Assumptions of linearity, uni-directional causality and a concern with the short-term can be justified as a first step to get a feel for models. This will certainly be useful in situations where some predictions are possible, perhaps based on probabilities that may be revised with experience as in Bayesian methods (Jaynes 2003). It is not a difficult task to examine if these assumptions invalidate models and make adjustments through time.

If statistical and econometric methods are to be used there are many techniques that can accommodate relaxation of these simplifying assumptions. While it is beyond the scope of this chapter to detail these, standard methods to model nonlinearities are available from the popular statistical packages. For more advanced applications, techniques such as systems dynamics provide a way to frame, understand, and discuss complex issues and problems. This approach deals with nonlinearities, recursive causality and time delays, usually as an exploratory way to understand the business situation under consideration (Roberts 1978). Exciting leading edge methods can be applied where there is great uncertainty and little understanding of cause-effect, such as artificial intelligence (Trigueiros & Taffler 1996), neural networks (Lisboa et al. 2000), fuzzy set methods (Ragin 2000, Abdel-Kader 1999) and chaos theory (Etheridge 1993, Tse 1994).

Conclusion

At the outset of this chapter a quotation from Bill Birkett was used to pose the question whether it is too ambitious for organizations to design performance management systems to achieve fully integrated systems. This question has been addressed in the chapter by considering how developments in disciplines other than management accounting have been helpful in integrating performance measures, related to the particular discipline, into broader management concerns. Management accounting is well placed to draw on these ideas as it is the primary location for organization-wide performance management. The BSC is an innovation that has been promoted as the pre-eminent vehicle to develop IPM. While the BSC is well known to many organizations concerned with performance management, it is not without its critiques. In this chapter, issues concerned with the design of BSC have been examined. The most important revolve around the role of cause-effect modelling that lies at the heart of BSC. For some there is lack of clarity as to when associations between dimensions of BSC models reflect true cause and effect and when they are statements of logical connection. These issues can alert designers of BSC to be concerned as to whether they are defining different components of a single construct or cause-effect associations between different constructs. Another issue common to a string of criticisms is the oversimplification of BSC models. Decisions around these issues may involve the level of detail that should be modelled. It was noted that this will likely depend on the purpose of the BSC with more strategic concerns requiring broader modelling. It was also noted that using BSC modelling for double-loop learning can help target key concerns that need to be included as plans unfold. There are also a series of more technical issues that involve unrealistic assumptions in BSC models concerning linearity, causality and time horizons. These are simplifying assumptions that can be justified when first attempting to understand the situation to be modelled. The chapter noted that there are readily available modelling techniques to relax these assumptions.

The developments in recent years of popular IPM, like BSC, do mention many of the potential problems with the scope of modelling and the unrealistic nature of implied assumptions. But these tend to be made in passing and there have been few developments in accounting to show how the problems can be addressed. As implied in the Bill Birkett quotation, it is probably a mistake for organizations to be too ambitious in the expectations for realistic, comprehensive IPM models. Rather, the main benefits would seem to be to motivate strategic thinking about how different areas have an influence on strategy and how they may impact horizontally across the value chain. IPM can help identify and define variables that drive strategy and alert managers to how they interact through time to have effects. Moreover, using IPM in a dynamic way to assist in learning would seem to be a strong justification to persist with developing IPM.

References

AAA (1990). *Proceedings of the Third Annual Management Accounting Symposium.* San Diego, CA: American Accounting Association.

Abdel-Kader M (1999). Evaluating investment decisions in advanced manufacturing systems – a fuzzy set theory approach. *European Accounting Review*, 8(3): 575–87.

Abernethy MA, Horne M, Lillis AM, Malina MA & Selto FH (2005). A multi-method approach to building causal performance maps from expert knowledge. *Management Accounting Research*, 16: 135–55.

Anderson EW, Fornell C & Lehmann DR (1994). Customer satisfaction, market share, and profitability findings from Sweden. *Journal of Marketing Research*, 58(3): 53–66.

Anderson EW, Fornell C & Rust RT (1997). Customer satisfaction, productivity, and profitability: differences between goods and services. *Marketing Science*, 2: 129–45.

Andriessen D (2004). *Making sense of intellectual capital: designing a method for the valuation of intangibles.* Boston, MA: Butterworth Heinemann.

Banker RD, Chang H & Majumdar SK (1993). Analyzing the underlying dimensions of firm profitability. *Managerial and Decision Economics*, 14(1): 25–36.

Banker RD, Chang H & Majumdar SK (1996). A framework for analyzing changes in strategic performance. *Strategic Management Journal*, 17(9): 693–712.

Banker RD, Datar SM & Kaplan RS (1989). productivity measurement and management accounting. *Journal of Accounting, Auditing and Finance*, 4(4): 528–54.

Banker RD, Field JM, Schroeder RG & Sinha KK (1996). Impact of work teams on manufacturing performance: a longitudinal field study. *Academy of Management Journal*, 39(4): 867–90.

Banker R, Janakiraman SN, Konstans C & Pizzini MJ (2001). Determinants of chief financial officer's satisfaction with systems for performance measurement. Working paper, University of Dallas.

Banker R, Potter G & Srinivasan D (2000). An empirical investigation of an incentive plan based on nonfinancial performance measures. *The Accounting Review*, 75(1): 65–92.

Berger PD & Nasr N (1998). Customer lifetime value: marketing models and applications. *Journal of Interactive Marketing*, 12(1): 17–30.

Berliner A & Brimson JA (1988). *Cost management for today's advanced manufacturing – the CAM-I conceptual design*. Boston, MA: Harvard Business School Press.

Birkett WP (1995). Management accounting and knowledge management. *Management Accounting*, 77(5): 44–48

Bisbe J, Batista-Foguet JM & Chenhall RH (2007). Defining and measuring attributes of management control systems: a methodological note on the risks of theoretical misspecification. *Accounting, Organizations and Society*, 32(7–8): 789–820.

Borman WC (1997). 360 degree ratings: an analysis of assumptions and a research agenda for evaluating their validity. *Human Resource Management Review*, 6(3): 299–315.

Boudreau JW (1991). Utility analysis and decisions in human resource management. In MD Dunnette & LM Houbh (Eds), *Handbook of Industrial and Organizational Psychology*, 2, (pp621–745). Palo Alto, CA: Consulting Psychologists Press.

Bowman D & Narayandas D (2004). Linking customer management effort to customer profitability in business markets. *Journal of Marketing Research*, 41(4): 433–47.

Bromwich M & Bhimani A (1989). *Management accounting: evolution not revolution*. London: The Chartered Institute of Management Accountants.

Brooking A (1996). *Intellectual capital: core assets for the third millennium enterprise.* London: Thompson Business Press.

Bruns WJ (1992). *Performance measurement evaluation and incentives.* Boston, MA: Harvard Business School Press.

Bryant L, Jones DA & Widener SK (2004). Managing value creation within the firm: an examination of multiple performance measures. *Management Accounting Research,* 16: 107–31.

Buzzell RD & Gale BT (1987). *The PIMS principles: linking strategy to performance.* New York: Free Press.

Chenhall RH (2005). Integrative strategic performance measurement systems, strategic alignment of manufacturing, learning and strategic outcomes: an exploratory study. *Accounting, Organizations and Society,* 30(5): 395–422.

Chenhall RH & Langfield-Smith K (2007). Multiple perspectives in performance measurement. *European Journal Management,* 25(4): 266–82

Chin WW (1998). Commentary: issues and opinion on structural equation modelling. *MIS Quarterly,* 22(1): vii-xvi.

Cooper R & Turney PBB (1990). Internally focused activity-based cost systems. In RS Kaplan (Ed), *Measures for manufacturing excellence,* (pp 291–305). Boston, MA: Harvard Business School Press.

Edvinsson L (2002). *Corporate longitude: what you need to know to navigate the knowledge economy.* London: Brookhouse.

Epstein M & Birchard B (2000). *Counting what counts: turning corporate accountability to competitive advantage.* Cambridge, MA: Perseus Books

Epstein M & Manzoni J-F (2004). Performance measurement and management control: superior organizational performance. *Studies in managerial and financial accounting,* 14:265–301.

Epstein M & Westbrook R (2001). Linking actions to profits in strategic decisions management. *Sloan Management Review,* 42(3): 39–49.

Etheridge HSR (1993). Chaos theory and non-linear dynamics: an emerging theory with implications for accounting research. *Journal of Accounting Literature,* 12: 67–100.

Euske KJ & Zander LA (2005). History of business performance measurement. *Encyclopedia of social measurement*, 2:227–32.

Folan P & Browne J (2005). A review of performance measurement: towards performance management. *Computers in Industry*, 56: 663–80.

Fornell C, Johnson MD, Anderson FW, Chia J & Bryant BE (1996). The American customer satisfaction index: nature, purpose and findings. *Journal of Marketing*, 60: 7–18.

Green FB, Amenkhienan F & Johnson G (1991). Performance measures and JIT. *Management Accounting*, 72(8): 50–53.

Hall RW (1990). World-class manufacturing: performance measurement. *Proceedings of the Third Annual Management Accounting Symposium*, (pp103-10). San Diego, CA.

Harrison JM, Holloway CA & Patell JM (1990). Measuring delivery performance: a case study from the semiconductor industry. In RS Kaplan (Ed), *Measures for manufacturing excellence*, (pp309–51). Boston, MA: Harvard Business School Press.

de Hass M & Kleingeld A (1999). Multilevel design of performance measurement systems: enhancing strategic dialogues throughout the organization. *Management Accounting Research*, 10: 233–62.

Hazucha JF, Hezlett SA & Schneider RJ (1993). the impact of 360^0 feedback on managerial skill development. *Human Resource Management*, 32: 325–51.

Heskett JL, Jones TO, Loveman GW, Sasser WE Jnr & Schlesinger LA (1994). Putting the service-profit chain to work. *Harvard Business Review*, March–April: 164–74.

Howell RA & Soucy GR (1987). Cost accounting in the new manufacturing environment. *Management Accounting*, 68: 42–9.

Hoyle RH (Ed) (1995). Structural equation modeling: concepts, issues, and applications. Thousand Oaks, CA: Sage.

Hronec S (1993). *Vital signs, using quality, time and cost performance measurements to chart your company's future.* New York: Arthur Andersen and Co.

Ittner CD & Larcker DE (1998). Are non-financial measures leading indicators of financial performance? An analysis of customer satisfaction. *Journal of Accounting Research*, 36 (supplement): 1–35.

Ittner CD & Larcker DF (2003). Coming up short on nonfinancial performance measurement. *Harvard Business Review*, November: 88–95.

Jain D & Singh SS (2002). Customer lifetime value research in marketing: a review and future directions. *Journal of Interactive Research*, 16(4): 34–46.

Jaynes ET (2003). *Probability theory: the logic of science.* Cambridge: Cambridge University Press.

Johnson HT (1988). Activity-based information: a blueprint for world-class management accounting. *Management Accounting*, June: 23–30.

Johnson HT & Kaplan RS (1987). *Relevance lost: the rise and fall of management accounting.* Boston, MA: Harvard Business School Press.

Kaplan RS (1990). *Measures of manufacturing excellence.* Boston, MA: Harvard Business School Press.

Kaplan RS & Norton DP (1996). *The Balanced Scorecard – translating strategy into action.* Boston, MA: Harvard Business School Press.

Kaplan RS & Norton DP (2001). *The strategy focused organization: how Balanced Scorecard companies thrive in the new business environment.* Boston, MA: Harvard Business School Press

Kaplan RS & Norton DP (2004). *Strategy maps – converting intangible assets into tangible outcomes.* Boston, MA: Harvard Business School Press.

Kaplan RS & Norton DP (2006). *Alignment–using the Balanced Scorecard to create corporate synergies.* Boston, MA: Harvard Business School Press.

Kaplan RS & Norton DP (2008). *The executive premium-linking strategy to operations for competitive advantage.* Boston, MA: Harvard Business School Press.

Keane TJ & Wang P (1995). Applications for the lifetime value model in modern newspaper publishing. *Journal of Direct Marketing*, 9(7): 59–66.

Lane J-K (1986). The logic of means-end analysis. *Quality and Quantity*, 20(4): 339–56.

Lebas MJ (1995). Performance measurement and performance management. *International Journal of Production Economics*, 41(1–3): 23–35.

Lisboa PJG, Vellido A & Edisbury B (2000). *Business applications of neural networks the state-of-the-art of real-world applications*. New Jersey: World Scientific Publishing Company.

Lynch RL & Cross KF (1995). *Measure up! Yardsticks for continuous improvement*. Cambridge, MA: Basil Blackwell.

Malina M, Nørreklit HSO & Selto F (2007). Relations among measures, climate of control, and performance measurement models. *Contemporary Accounting Research*, 24(3): 935–82.

Mosconi W & McNair CJ (1987). Measuring performance in an advanced manufacturing environment. *Management Accounting*, 69(1): 28–31.

Nanni AJ, Dixon JR & Vollmann TE (1992). Integrated performance measurement: management accounting to support the new manufacturing realities. *Management Accounting Research*, 4: 1–19.

Neely A & Adams C (2001). Perspectives on performance: the performance prism. *Journal of Cost Management*, 15(1): 7–15.

Neely A, Adams C & Kennerley K (2002). *The performance prism: the scorecard for measuring and managing business success*. London: Financial Times Prentice Hall.

Nørreklit H (2000). The balance on the Balanced Scorecard – a critical analysis of some of its assumptions. *Management Accounting Research*, 11: 65–88.

Olve N-G, Roy J & Wetter M (1999). *Performance drivers: a practical guide to using the Balanced Scorecard*. Chichester: John Wiley & Sons.

Oriot F & Misiaszek E (2004). Technical and organizational barriers hindering the implementation of a Balanced Scorecard: the case of a European space company. In M Epstein & J-F Manzoni (Eds), *Performance measurement and management control: superior organizational performance. Studies in managerial and financial accounting*, 14. Amsterdam: JAI.

Otley D (1999). Performance management: a framework for management controls systems research. *Management Accounting Research*, 10: 363–82.

Ragin CC (2000). *Fuzzy-set social science*. Chicago: The University of Chicago Press.

Reichheld FF (1996). *The loyalty effect: the hidden force behind growth, profits and lasting value*. Boston, MA: Harvard Business School Press.

Reichheld FF & Sasser WE Jnr (1990). Zero defections: quality comes to services. *Harvard Business Review*, September–October: 105–11.

Reinartz W & Kumar V (2000). On the profitability of long lifetime customers: an empirical investigation and implications for marketing, *Journal of Marketing*, 64(4): 17–35.

Reilly GP & Reilly RR (2000). Using a measure network to understand and deliver value. *Journal of Cost Management*, November–December: 5–14.

Rejc A & Slapničar S (2004). Determinants of performance measurement system design and corporate financial performance. In M Epstein & J-F Manzoni (Eds), *Performance measurement and management control: superior organizational performance. Studies in managerial and financial accounting*, 14, (pp47–73). Amsterdam: JAI.

Roberts EB (1978). *Managerial applications of system dynamics*. Cambridge: MIT Press.

Roth PL & Bobko P (1997). A research agenda for multi-attribute utility analysis. human resources management. *Human Resource Management Review*, 7(3): 341–68.

Rucci AJ, Kirn SP & Quinn RT (1998). The employee-customer-profit chain at Sears. *Harvard Business Review*, 76(1): 82–97.

Sandt J, Schaeffer U & Weber J (2001). Balanced performance measurement systems and manager satisfaction-empirical evidence from a German study. Working paper, WHU-Otto Beisheim Graduate School of Management.

Schmittlein DC, Morrison DG & Colombo R (1987). Counting your customers: who are they and what will they do next? *Management Science*, 33: 1–24.

Schonberger RJ (2008). Lean performance management (metrics don't add up). *Journal of Cost Management*, January–February: 5–10.

Simons R (1995). *Levers of control*. Boston, MA: Harvard Business School Press.

Smith RE & Wright W (2004). Determinants of customer loyalty and financial performance. *Management Accounting Research*, 16: 183–206.

Stemsrudhagen JI (2004). The structure of Balanced Scorecards: empirical evidence from Norwegian manufacturing industry. In M Epstein & J-F Manzoni (Eds), *Performance measurement and management control: superior organizational performance. Studies in managerial and financial accounting*, 14, (pp303–21). Amsterdam: JAI.

Stewart TA (1997). *Intellectual capital: the new wealth of organizations.* New York: Doubleday.

Stewart TA (2001). *The wealth of knowledge – intellectual capital and the twenty-first century organization.* London: Nicholas Brealey Publishing.

Sveiby KE (1997). *The new organizational wealth: managing and measuring knowledge-based assets.* San Francisco: Barrett-Kohler.

Trigueiros D & Taffler R (1996). Neural networks and empirical research in accounting. *Accounting and Business Research*, 26(4): 347–55.

Tse NSF (1994). Dynamical systems theory applied to management accounting: chaos in cost behaviour in a standard costing system setting. *Journal of Intelligent Material Systems and Structures*, 16(5): 269–79.

Vollmann T (1990). Changing manufacturing performance measurements. *Proceedings of the Third Annual Management Accounting Symposium*, (pp53–62), San Diego, CA.

Waggoner DB, Neely AD & Kennerley MP (1999). The forces that shape organizational performance measurement systems: an interdisciplinary review. *International Journal of Production Economics*, 60–61(20): 53–60.

Watson Wyatt (2005). *Maximizing the return on your human capital investment.* Human Capital Index Report, New York.

Zeithaml VA (2000). Service quality, profitability, and the economic worth of customers: what we know and what we don't know. *Journal of the Academy of Marketing Science*, 29(1): 67–85.

8

Intellectual capital statements and the development of organizational knowledge management strategies

Jan Mouritsen (Copenhagen Business School) and Christina Boedker (UNSW)

Abstract

The intellectual capital statement reports on a firm's knowledge management activities and strategies. It is an accounting system that brings distance to the firm's knowledge by presenting it as a constellation of knowledge resources that are summarized in various types of containers such as e.g. human, structural and relational capital. The act of bringing distance has two opposing effects. First, it stops the flow of action within which knowledge is developed and mobilized in a stream of inseparable activities. The statement distances knowledge from its specific organizational embeddedness and yet, curiously, through narrative it reconstructs a panorama of achievement within which and over time, organizational knowledge management activities gain and lose properties. By creating distance it develops visibility so that it is possible to see more aspects of knowledge resources and intervene to increase or decrease them. Visualizing knowledge resources implies intervening on knowledge resources.

Intellectual capital is related to knowledge, but precisely what this relation is, is ambiguous. A preliminary and provisional definition of intellectual capital is that it consists of human, structural and relational capital (Abeysekera 2006, Andriessen 2004, Edvinsson & Malone 1997, Petty & Guthrie 2000, Sveiby 1997). It suggests that knowledge can be found in certain places such as in people, in structural arrangements or with suppliers and customers. To intellectual capital, knowledge is placed somewhere, but it is not a proposition about what this knowledge is. To mobilize knowledge, intellectual capital may, as some research says or hopes, propose that the relations between these three types of capital will predict the value of an entity such as a firm or a nation state etc. (e.g. Bontis 2004, Bontis & Fitz-enz 2002, Wang & Chang 2005). Three types of intellectual capital are often presented as a causal model which is understood to predict the development of value: investments in human capital affect increases in structural capital and relational capital, which then in turn increase financial value. Following from this, the ambition of intellectual capital research is to demonstrate stable and durable relations between intellectual capital and value (Marr et al. 2003).

Such a view, however, has the unfortunate limitation that it marginalizes how intellectual capital is to be managed. There is little room for management because durable (statistical) relations already specify that increased investment is always reasonable: increased value results from increasing investments in human, structural and relational capital. The solution is given and therefore there is no choice but to follow an agenda of continual expansion. There are no trade-offs. Thus, there is no management (e.g. Mouritsen 2006).

This ambition to make management an integral part of intellectual capital requires that intellectual capital is understood as something different from a predictive model which takes over the tasks of managing from managers. Instead, intellectual capital may be seen as an accounting system that is an input to management, supplying information that proposes the size of intellectual capital, investments in intellectual capital and effects of intellectual capital. As an accounting system, intellectual capital presents numbers – and text and pictures – which describe the composition of, investments in and effects of knowledge resources (see Boedker et al. 2005, Mouritsen et al. 2002, Mouritsen & Larsen 2005). This is parallel to a conventional financial accounting system which describes assets, cash-flows, investments and profitability of an entity such as a firm. While the conventional accounting system describes the financial resources of the firm, the intellectual capital statement uses a parallel format to describe the knowledge resources of the firm. Just as the accounting system is not the same as the firm's economy, the intellectual capital statement is not the same as the firm's knowledge. The difference between accounting information and the firm's economy produces a space for managerial action; a similar difference between intellectual capital and the firm's knowledge also produces a space for managerial intervention.

Treating intellectual capital as an accounting system has the characteristic that it proposes only to describe knowledge resources rather than knowledge. As an accounting system, intellectual capital does not presume that there are stable links between its elements on the one side and value creation on the other. It proposes to organize a structured description of a firm's knowledge resources but it does not claim to have presented a finite business model of its relations. Relations between elements of intellectual capital are the domain of those who take intellectual capital information into consideration. They are the domains of management. This makes an intellectual capital statement similar to an accounting system which provides a description of the development of categories in the accounting system rather than the economy of the firm; likewise the intellectual capital statement provides a description of the development of knowledge resources rather than of knowledge.

This rendering of intellectual capital focuses its presentation of the development of knowledge resources. Drawing on a set of intellectual capital statements developed by Lands, an Australian public sector organization, it is possible to show how an intellectual capital statement gains form and traction over time. This development interlaces accounts of numbers and narratives that together constitute the intellectual capital statement.

Understanding intellectual capital as an accounting system

Understanding intellectual capital as an accounting system asks the question how we should understand what an accounting system is and does. Drawing on Latour (1986), it may be described as visualization – a mechanism to inscribe disparate traits and present them in tabular, graphical or diagrammatic form. Typically, an intellectual capital statement is rich in visualization and contains tables of numbers, graphs of development in, or composition of, employees and customers, and diagrams of the firm's organization. These inscriptions are everywhere and they combine internal and external entities; they inscribe the past and the future.

The intellectual capital statement is a report – it is a visualization organized in a two-dimensional inscription of the three-dimensional world. As such, the intellectual capital statement has certain properties. First, it is a report which is *mobile*. It can be moved and transported into and out of offices, onto the internet, through to external audiences. It is not as heavy as the firm itself but light and transportable. Intellectual capital statements move the firm effortlessly into offices or onto the internet.

Second, even if it can travel, it is also *immutable* and remains stable. The intellectual capital statement's numbers, diagrams and pictures remain stable even if they are transported. Thus the firm, as it is presented in the intellectual capital statement, has durability.

Third, the intellectual capital statement has a *flat surface* which hinders hidden or convoluted statements. Everything is in open light as the intellectual capital statement's flat surface presents things to the eye directly. It is not necessary to look on the back of the page because all is on its front.

Fourth, the *scale* of the elements brought into the intellectual capital statement *is modifiable* so that anything can be rearranged and be put next to anything. A building can be reduced in size to fit a page, and a microchip can be increased in size to fit the page – and suddenly it is possible to see the firm and the chip it produces at the same time. Modifiable scales enable anything to be presented in the same intellectual capital statement.

Fifth, an intellectual capital statement is *reproducible and spreadable*. It can be produced in any number and sent to any constituency in any location. The more copies of the intellectual capital statement, the more it moves around.

Sixth, the intellectual capital statement is *recombinable* with other texts e.g. annual financial reports or other inscriptions that are presented via tables, diagrams and pictures. That is, the intellectual capital statement can be inserted into new contexts it was not designed to relate to. When being recombined the intellectual capital statement may gain new, or lose some, properties.

Seventh, intellectual capital statements can *superimpose* images and diagrams on each other and invent new things. When diagrams of individuals' competency profiles are superimposed on each other they create a notion of an organization's investment in competency.

Eighth, the intellectual capital statement makes tables and diagrams *part of a text*. Numbers, diagrams and tables are narrated within the universe of a knowledge strategy.

Finally, the eight movements described above are the elements in rendering a three-dimensional world understandable in a two-dimensional space. The world has been made a text including numbers, diagrams and words. The intellectual capital statement is a construction whose durability depends on how it is able to move the elements which it engages in its mobilization. When mobilized, it not only constructs its own visualization, it also acts on the setting from which it extracts its cues. As Latour states:

> If you wish to go out of *your* way and come back heavily equipped so as to force others to go out of *their* ways, the main problem to solve is that of *mobilization*. You have to go and to come back *with* the 'things' if your moves are not to be wasted. But the 'things' have to be able to withstand the return trip without withering away. Further requirements: the 'things' you gathered and displaced have to be presentable all at once to those you want to convince and who did not go there. In sum, you have to invent objects which have properties of being *mobile* but also *immutable, presentable, readable* and *combinable* with one another (Latour 1986, 6).

The visualization found in the intellectual capital statement is thus related to intervention. An intellectual capital statement has parallel characteristics to financial statements and it is therefore, in principle, 'equally' good for the purposes of management or intervention – either through the management of the firm or the decisions made in the capital market. An intellectual capital statement creates knowledge about how knowledge is created, developed and applied in the firm (Boedker et al. 2005). It summarizes the firm's efforts to develop and use knowledge resources. The intellectual capital statement creates distance from the ongoing affairs of the firm, and in this way it facilitates evaluation. Presenting the composition, upgrade and use of knowledge resources over time (Mouritsen et al. 2002), the intellectual capital statement puts forward evaluative questions: Do we like it? Where should it be changed? Can we agree on new measures? Such questions are managerial ones because they help managers to change knowledge resources and direct them towards new strategies. As a managerial technology, intellectual capital statements can do the following:

1. Capture the on-going affairs of the business and transport them to a locality where they can be debated and assessed independently of the day-to-day concerns of operations.

2. Establish a distanced perspective on the myriad of actions that go on all the time to use and qualify knowledge.

3. Induce evaluative and normative reflection by assessing knowledge management activities.

4. Allow decision making because there is time to contemplate on the future of knowledge resources, with the realization of activities and the results turning up in a subsequent intellectual capital statement.

In principle, the intellectual capital statement facilitates intervention, either from the perspective of internal readers or from external ones. Knowledge about the development and application of the firm's knowledge resources is integral to the mobilization of a systematic kind of knowledge management. Here, the interest in intervention is stronger than in representation. Or, alternatively, the interest in intervention drives interest in measurement in the sense that 'good' measurement allows intervention to occur. This type of argument persuades Latour (1991, p160) to say that

> the problem of correspondence becomes crucial only for those who want to act at a distance. If you are not at a distance, or do not wish to act upon other settings, the notion of correspondence vanishes, and so does the problem of the referent.

To act at a distance means acting to influence others; inscription is connected to power. This is not happenstance because one of the key features of the knowledge society is to make phenomena discussable and transformable. It is characteristic that

> the reflexivity of modern social life [is] that social practices are constantly examined and reformed in the light of incoming information about those very practices, thus constitutively altering their character (Giddens 1990, 38).

Consequently, in modern life, information about it is used to alter it. It transforms practices. Therefore, when we consider intellectual capital measurement it is useful to look not only at its descriptive qualities, but also at its performative qualities (Mouritsen 2006).

As a report – as an inscription – an intellectual capital statement presents the firm and its environment in one place. It

> makes changes in the set of elements and concepts habitually used to describe the social and the natural worlds. By stating what belongs to the past, and of what the future consists, by defining what comes before and what comes after, by building up balanced sheets, by drawing up chronologies, it imposes its own space and time. It defines space and its organisation, sizes and their measures, values and standards, the stakes and rules of the game (Callon & Latour 1981, p286).

This may be translated into the specifics of the intellectual capital statement in the following way:

> [it] literally defines elements (knowledge narrative challenges, efforts, and indicators), literally lays out what comes before and after (the flow of the narrative and the sequences of numbers in reports), literally builds balanced sheets (the numbering of knowledge resources), literally defines measures (indicators for portfolio, development and effects of knowledge resources), literally defines values (use values and exchange values), and literally defines the stakes (the possibility of a knowledge based organisation in knowledge society), (it) presents a technology for stabilising and managing knowledge society/economy (Mouritsen & Flagstad 2005, p222).

This rendering of the intellectual capital statement has important corollaries in the literature on the role and effects of accounting systems where its mobilization is highlighted (Andon et al. 2006, Briers & Chua 2001, Cuganesan et al. 2007, Mouritsen et al. 2001, Mouritsen 2006, Quattrone & Hopper 2006, Robson 1991). These authors explain that accounting systems have two opposite properties. On the one hand they present performance that a manager cannot escape. Performance, as defined by the accounting system – the inscription, the visualization – demands response. However, it is also fragile because it is it not mobilized and if nobody listens to its propositions, it is virtually dead. Accounting systems, such as intellectual capital statements, are not primarily to be understood as 'ready-made' but as constructions 'in the making'. As a consequence, accounting systems such as intellectual capital statements are not primarily adopted in a firm; they are adapted because they influence the situation at hand and have to develop along the path taken by its mobilization.

Studying and understanding intellectual capital statements

Intellectual capital has been said to be best conceptualized as a process of organizational discovery and development (Roos et al. 1997). "Value does not (only) imply calculating a value, but to understand the creation and development of value" (Mouritsen 2004, p261). Indeed, "what is important about intellectual capital is the implicit importance, not of the investment in the stock of intellectual capital, but of the flow – the utilization of that stock in pursuing the purposes of management" (Collier 2001, p441).

Studying intellectual capital as a process of value creation has been done in different ways e.g. through semi-structured interviews, internal management reports, or through external reports, such as annual reports or intellectual capital statements. The focus of such inquiry is how knowledge-management activities are mobilized in the relation between an aspiration about effects of knowledge and indicators about the size and constellation of knowledge resources; the approach concerns the flow of knowledge in the constitution of the firm's activities (Boedker et al., 2005). It reports mechanisms that make knowledge manageable and propose how the resources of the organization are composed and bundled together in order to create value (Mouritsen, Larsen & Bukh 2001). With Fincham and Roslender's (2003, p12) words, business reporting is no longer solely about the financial representation and the valuation of assets but its emphasis is

> on telling the story of how different assets and values within the organisation evolve jointly and coalesce. The new business reporting is a theory of what creates value, one that is set in narrative form, albeit a reliable and valid form (Fincham & Roslender 2003, p12).

In the following, the case study of an organization's reporting of intellectual capital via its intellectual capital statements over a three-year period is analyzed and discussed.

Intellectual capital and organizational knowledge management at the NSW Department of Lands: an analysis of Land's intellectual capital statements over three years

The NSW Department of Lands is an Australian public sector organization. It manages the land titling register and all crown land in the state of NSW.[1] The department started its journey to produce an intellectual capital statement in 2003 when the director general declared that the department would produce an intellectual capital statement next year, and in an interview he justified this by a grand proposition of the value of firms in modern societies:

> The greatest value of organisations in today's business environment is in intangible assets. However, in most organisations, senior executives pay little attention to the greatest asset in their organisations; that is the knowledge or intellectual capital. Decision-making is skewed towards short-term materialistic gains, which undervalues the real value and influences whether an organisation is sustainable or not. At the moment, organisations are undervaluing their true wealth. We need to develop a greater sense and appreciation and awareness of the true value of what the intangibles are, and in doing so, be able to better allocate financial and other related resources. We need to be able to, in a structured sense, have an objective discussion about where we should be cutting or increasing our resource allocation. Our objective is to get a better understanding of what constitutes the organisation, the value of the organisation, and how we can use that knowledge generally, augmented with other tools, to bring about better decision making.

This was followed by the first intellectual capital statement in the next accounting year, 2004–05. The intellectual capital statement introduced some reasons for its own role:

> Traditionally, like many organizations, our reporting processes have focused on the financial aspects of our business. We acknowledge that changes in re-

---

1 The department was created in April, 2003, integrating three separate operating divisions: Land and Property Information (LPI), the provider of land and property information for NSW; Crown Lands, the administrator of all crown lands comprising over half of all land in NSW (which includes around 29mn hectares of land valued at over $8.3bn); and Soil Services, a specialist conservation earthmoving and soil consultancy business.

porting are occurring in the private sector, particularly in relation to intangible assets, and recognise that this style of reporting brings added value to the way in which we manage and plan for the future (Intellectual Capital Statement 2004–05, p7)

Figure 1: Knowledge containers at NSW Department of Lands.

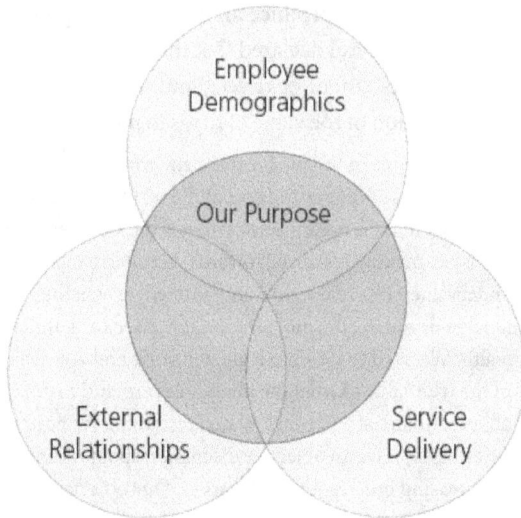

Employee
Demographics

Our Purpose

External
Relationships

Service
Delivery

Source: Intellectual Capital Statement (NSW Dept of Lands *Annual Report*, 2004–05, p10).

The first intellectual capital statement produced contours of an organizational knowledge management strategy. This addressed three management challenges (see figure 1), including: 1) employee demographics, specifically an ageing workforce and how to retain existing staff; and 2) service delivery, specifically IT automation and new technology required to service customers more timely and efficiently. Both were connected to 3) broader concerns of creating public value and meeting community and external stakeholder needs. The first intellectual capital statement noted:

> In this first Lands Intellectual Capital Statement we seek to report on the three areas of managerial effort – employee demographics, service delivery and the management of external relationships. As indicated earlier, it is our

intention that, over time, these indicators will change to reflect our improved understanding of these areas of management focus (Intellectual Capital Statement 2004–05, p10).

As knowledge is inaccessible, the intellectual capital statement produced a series of knowledge containers that were hoped and expected to correlate with knowledge. These containers were people, technology and community. These three containers were connected; for example people were presented as a requisite for good customer services and community relations; similar powers were ascribed to technology. Yet, the containers were also fragile because they reported not on knowledge but on knowledge resources. So, the age structure of the workforce was not the same as knowledge. But the age of the workforce entered a narrative of recruitment, and additional strategies were presented to address and find solutions to the problem of recruitment, such as efforts around internal seminars, mentoring and training. These were reported on in the 2004–05 statement:

> However, the tacit knowledge of our workforce – the know-who, know-how, know-why, know-where – the informal networks, recollections and experiences that enable our staff to respond to more complicated issues is more difficult to transfer. One solution involved a retiring staff member conducting a series of internal seminars or lectures to present an overview of his work and experiences and for questions and answers about particular issues. Other options are also being explored include support networks, mentoring arrangements and training program (Intellectual Capital Statement 2004–05, p11).

Issues concerning service delivery were presented largely as IT projects. Again IT projects were not similar to knowledge but they were related to the intensity of transformation towards an IT-based organization where customers engage in self-service. IT suddenly swapped competencies with customers – organizational capital with relational capital; and it probably also reduced the severity of the ageing workforce allowing a substitution of employees for technology:

> The demand for continuous, integrated, quality service delivery requires us to think 'smarter' about our internal processes and to use available technology and communication solutions to deliver cost effective and equitable services to our clientele wherever they are located (Intellectual Capital Statement 2004–05, p12).

Table 1: Emerging indicators. After *Intellectual Capital Statement* (2004–05, pp11–12).

Employee demographics	02/03	03/04	04/05	Desirable trend
Number of full time equivalent employees at 30 June	1458	1441	1427	→
Average age of employees	-	-	45	↘
Learning and development – external courses – no. of staff attending	-	246		↗
Learning and development – internal courses – no. of staff attending	-	462		↗
% of staff who identify as being of NESB*	15.3	15.7	15.3	↗
Women as a % of total staff as at 30 June* *further information about trends in EEO groups can be found in the Annual Report appendices	34.8	35	36.4	↗
Service delivery	02/03	03/04	04/05	Desirable trend
Average number (monthly) internet feedback requests (based on 9 months of records)	-	-	285	↗
Average number (monthly) hits on Lands web site	-	-	1,848046	↗
External relationships	02/03	03/04	04/05	Desirable trend
Number of significant committees and statutory bodies involving Lands representatives	40	32	35	→
Research partnerships	2	2	6	↗

The first statement did present numbers, although not many (see table 1). These were directed at visualising progress in each of the three knowledge containers. There was also an arrow showing management's 'desired trend' and whether they hoped the numbers would go up or down.

Over time the intellectual capital statement changed – new narratives showing new strategies and projects were added and more numbers were added. Black and white images and figures such as the one shown previously in figure 1 above were replaced with colourful images and pictures.

New narratives with more detailed solutions and strategies to address management challenges such as the ageing workforce came into play. The 2005–06 report notes the following:

> For example, the Land and Property Information Division (LPI) has a slightly higher age profile than some other areas of Lands and a very experienced and specialised workforce. During the reporting year LPI took significant steps to integrate strategies relating to staff profile and skills development, internal process and improved partnerships into its corporate and operational plans … Several projects have already commenced including reviewing and documenting processes, engaging graduates from secondary and tertiary schools and working with staff to identify issues and potential remedial actions (Intellectual Capital Statement 2005–06, p10).

Here the report was part of a dialogue where new things were added over time. In later years, the intellectual capital statement even gave rise to the production of entirely new documents and reports inside different business units. For example, the concern with an ageing work force gave rise to the creation of a 60-page document called Vision 2013 in the Land and Property Information business unit. The aim of this was to develop a vision till year 2013 for human resources and business-planning action plans at the local workplace level. This document used a combination of performance measures and narrative to define the problems and go into greater detail by, for example, explaining and measuring the age profile of staff in different areas of operation (see table 2 and figure 2). The Vision 2013 document was communicated and discussed by a team of senior management in 23 sessions with all 773 members of LPI's staff thus enrolling many more actors in the discourse and knowledge management activities related to the intellectual capital statement.

Similarly, new solutions emerged with regard to improving customer-service delivery through IT projects:

> Lands continues to examine and develop processes which provide support to and improve our service delivery options. We are currently undertaking projects in relation to manual and old system titles involving the conversion of information to our digital titling system. The Data Conversion and Cleansing Program also includes the capture of our film-based aerial photography in digital form to enable wider access to the important historical material and reducing the risk of handling fragile film medium. Overall these projects will collectively enable greater equity of access to our land and spatial information products (Intellectual Capital Statement 2005–06, p10).

Table 2: Staffing in key operation areas at LPI – examples of numbers and images used in the Vision 2013 document.[2]

Function	2006 Staff	Turned 60 years 2006– 2013	Staff under 60, February 2013
Conversions & Data Cleansing	64	22	42
TRS	217	70	147
PIS	70	22	48
Valuation Services	107	46	61
Map Sales	13	7	6
Spatial Information Services	101	35	66
Survey	61	20	41
Graphic Services	42	4	38
Legal Services	23	4	19
ICT	75	12	63
Total	773	242	531

---

2 Source: NSW Department of Lands, Lands and Property Information Consultation Draft, 'Vision 2013: a seven- year business and workforce plan for LPI', Barry Douse, July 2006, Version 4.0 (pp7, 18 and 21).

Figure 2: LPI Age Profile.

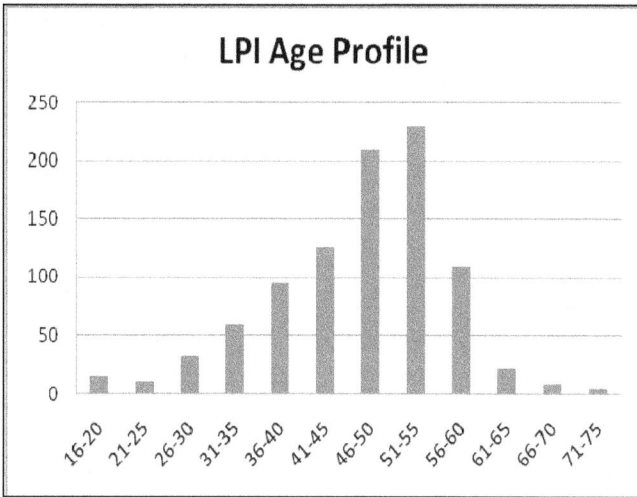

These examples show that the intellectual capital statement was not decoupled from the affairs of the firm, but instead a centre for creating new dialogues and a catalyst for coming up with new solutions and management strategies to direct more efforts, energy and resources towards managing knowledge. The ambition to manage knowledge resources strengthened over time and the statement was both a product of the network of which it was a part, and also as an actor that designed new context.

The statement also designed new context through more calculations about the issue at hand. More numbers were added. For example, indicators about external/customer relations entered into the statement. Customer-related measures increased from two in the first report to 22 in the 2005–06 report (see table 3). Also new ratios were introduced and 'percentage change' was now calculated, another addition to previous statements. The intellectual capital statement gained strength over time as more was added to it and it resulted in new calculations. Through calculations and visualizations the intellectual capital statement took on new forms, gained traction and enabled the knowledge management strategies to broaden in scope and reach.

Table 3: Adding numbers. After *Intellectual Capital Statement* (2005–06, p14).

Key performance indicators	Division	2004/05	2005/06	% change	Expected Trend
Customer/community					→
Land title transactions registered	LPI	806,965	810,037	0.4%	→
Plans registered	LPI	13,181	11,912	-10%	→
Copies of land title related documents supplied to customers	LPI	4.25m	4.27m	0.5%	→
Boundary determinations	LPI	17	16	-6%	→
New land valuations issued to Office of State Revenue	LPI	2.4m	2.4m	-	→
New land valuations issued for rating purposes	LPI	683,000	817,000	20%	→
Supplementary valuations issued	LPI	46,806	41,987	-10.3%	→
Land valuation objections received	LPI	16,515	11,000	-33%	→
Land valuation objections processed	LPI	10,179	14,400	41%	→
Percentage of land valuations changed as a result of objection	LPI	29%	36%	24%	→
Survey enquiries (including SCIMS searches)	LPI	88,081	78,970	-10%	→
Number of formal customer complaints	SCS	4	3	-25%	→
Number of new clients					
- Consult	SCS	22	25	14%	↑
- Works	SCS	269	226	-16%	↑
- Operations	SCS	5	6	20%	↑

Key performance indicators	Division	2004/05	2005/06	% change	Expected Trend
Percentage of perpetual leases converted	CL	-	36.48%	-	→
Percentage of enclosure permits granted	CL	-	22.57%	-	→
Number of Community Trust Boards	CL	658	661	0.5%	→
New State Parks established	CL	-	1	-	↑
New Regional Reserves established	CL	-	3	-	↑
no. of internet feedback requests (monthly av.)	Dept/ICS	285	232	-19%	↓
no. of hits on website (monthly av.)	Dept/ICS	1.8m	2.3m	28%	↑

Also during this time, the name of the report changed from 'intellectual capital statement' to 'extended performance report' which acknowledged that in Australia at the time, this more general concept was increasingly preferred by firms to the more specific concept of intellectual capital statement. However, this change was in name primarily and any change in layout or in content was not discernible.

Numbers about the organization's financial performance were also added in the 2005–06 report. And these grew and expanded in the 2006–07 report, to now reach 13 indicators (table 4).

Table 4: Adding financial indicators. After *Extended Performance Report* (2006–07, p17).

Financial					
Total operating revenue	Lands	$164.6m	$172.4m	$188.3m	9% ▲
Value of PPE and In-tangible assets	Lands	$116.8m	$140.7m	$164.2m	17% ▲
Maintenance costs as a % of asset value	Lands	3%	2%	1%	1% ▲
Revenue from adminis-tered activities (Crown Entity)	CL	$115.4m	$64.1	$98.5m	54% ▼
Revenue collected from developed or vacant land and land sold to NSW government agencies	CL	$54.2m	$21.06m	$19.54	-7.2% ►
Revenue collected from leases, permissive occu-pancies, royalties, water licences etc on behalf of the Crown Leasehold Entity	CL	$45.57m	$40.65m	$41.04m	1% ▲
Operating profit before income tax	LPI	$17m	$94.5m	$75.1m	-21% ▼
Return on assets	LPI	12%	63%	38%	-40% ▼
Total debt to total assets	LPI	112%	54%	38%	-30% ▼
Profit margin	LPI	11%	61%	46%	-25% ▼
Revenue (SCS) Consult Works Operations	SCS	$6.6m $7.4m $2.9m	$7.6m $7.4m $3.1m	$11.5m $7.9m $4.5m	51% ▲ 7% ▲ 45% ►

Adding numbers, whether financial or non-financial, created new dimensions to the intellectual capital statement. The statement differed to previous versions which favoured narratives. Whilst the intellectual capital statement expanded activities around knowledge, the numbers also provided a point of stabilization as they figured out the constellation of itemized knowledge resources at a point in time. In contrast, the narratives more closely resembled a flow, a totality connecting things. There were two forms of expression about knowledge – one itemized knowledge resources and rendered them visible separately; the narrative in contrast linked knowledge resources and paid attention to their interrelationships. Numbering produced distance and amplified certain traits; narrative produced entangled presentations that combined the past and the future without a concern to separate knowledge resources.

New images also started to appear. The 2006–07 report showed the organization's reception area. It was a pleasant environment – a nice place for customers to be serviced, and for employees to work (see figure 3).

New numbers were added again in the 2006–07 report when the department undertook customer satisfaction surveys for the first time:

Demonstrating public value

93% of respondents to SCS's customer satisfaction survey rated overall performance as good to exceptional.

90% of respondents to LPI's online survey rated their satisfaction with online services between seven and 10 (10 being the highest).

Improving customer services

Launch of Online Survey Services Portal (SSP) to deliver online survey related products and services to NSW Registered Surveyors.

Introduction of new electronic service delivery (ESD) products and services including the Cadastral Records Enquiry (CRE) and online objections to land valuations.

Introduction of a consumer feedback system within the Crown Lands division (Extended Performance Report 2006–07, p12).

Figure 3: Adding colourful image. Photo of reception at NSW Department of Lands, LPI, Extended Performance Report (2006–07, p10).

Narratives also changed and started to take on a more future-oriented focus. For example, both the 2006–07 and 2007–08 reports had added descriptions for each knowledge container labelled 'future focus'. The 2007–08 report, for example, talked about the future focus for employees:

> Develop and begin the implementation of a Management and Leadership Program that references and integrates the NSW Public Sector Capability Framework.
>
> Develop a Manager's and Supervisor's Toolkit which can be readily accessed by all staff.
>
> Pilot the department's new online Induction Program.
>
> Encourage the participation and development of women at all levels of the organisation through workplace initiatives and programs (Extended Performance Report 2007–08, p17).

The language and narratives also changed during this time, from being full sentences to being shorter points or bullet-point statements that all started with a verb as shown above.

Table 5: Trends in number of employees.

Indicators/ activity		2004/ 05	2005/ 06	2006/ 07	Target for 07/08	Actual for 07/08	% change against 06/07	Expected trend
Learning and growth								
% of staff turnover	Lands	7.5%	5.1%	6%	n/a	7.2%	1.2%	▲
Number of employees as at 30 June	Lands	1,427	1,453	1,551	n/a	1,591	0.03%	▲
Average age of employees	Lands	45	46.49	46.48	n/a	46	0%	-

Yet, numbers which were intended to go down, due to new strategies and projects, did not always go down. Indeed, some went up. For example, the many attempts to manage an ageing workforce by retaining staff and reduce average age did not produce the effects they set out to achieve. In fact, in 2008, staff turnover had increased by 1.2% and from 2005 to 2007 average age had gone up (table 5).

Understanding the operation of the intellectual capital statement

Characteristics of the intellectual capital statement

Intellectual capital is not the same as knowledge. The inscriptions produced in intellectual capital statements are presentations of organizational knowledge management strategies. Just like a balance sheet and profit and loss statement are not the same as the firm's value and prospect yet related to them, the intellectual capital is not the same as the firm's knowledge but related to it. Four observations can be made.

First, intellectual capital inscribes knowledge resources rather than represents knowledge. The statement expanded the array of solutions sought and projects implemented. The intellectual capital statement not only represented knowledge, it also translated knowledge into many new strategies and projects (such as 'figuring out what the customer can tell us about us', new recruitment processes, new IT systems, online services, training programs, seminars etc). The statement included new things and strategies over time. These new things were partly an effect of the insight and visibility produced by the intellectual capital statement when it was mobilized. The statement was involved in the network of which it became a part – as an actor it influenced and constructed its context. It was both a network element and an actor.

Second, both numbers and narratives played roles in managing knowledge and developing solutions. Narratives had to be strengthened and this required new numbers to be constructed and calculated. Intellectual capital developed dynamically and gradually, gaining more formation as numbers were added. Intellectual capital did not have its representations *a priori* but developed its properties over time as new calculations and numbers strengthened the technology. Thus the statement was in search of items to represent. Indeed, there was no logical end to things that could have been presented and therefore the gradual inclusion and exclusion of items over time reflects how intellectual capital was equipped with capabilities and how knowledge management strategies changed and adapted over time.

Third, the intellectual capital statement consisted of two related but different propositions about knowledge resources. Indicators about the size and effects of knowledge resources *separated* items of knowledge. Another part is the narratives where people, technology and customers were related and acted as a *totality* to develop something for an audience.

Yet, and fourth, a new accounting technology such as intellectual capital statements can neither 'capture the world' nor necessarily produce the effects set out to achieve. Indeed, at this organization some numbers about human capital – the ageing workforce – went *up* when they were supposed to go down.

The knowledge of an intellectual capital statement

The practices of Lands illustrate that intellectual capital statements reflect on a firm's process of developing, sharing and maintaining its knowledge base. It assigns purposes to this process and surveys its accomplishments through a series of numbers. The intellectual capital statement shows the firm's efforts to monitor, to qualify and to orchestrate its knowledge resources. It is aimed at persuading an internal or external audience that it develops its knowledge resources so as to develop the relationships between knowledge resources and the firm's aspirations to be innovative, flexible and customer-oriented.

For some, such a story line is not easily acceptable and therefore there is a demand for more measurement and accountability (Marr et al. 2003). However, as the discussion presented above suggests, it is not measurement as such that is in demand; it is the provision of explanation. This explanation has to be about how relations between knowledge containers occur and are made productive. Relations in knowledge have to be drawn up before they are intelligible and this is where the intellectual capital statement may have a role. One possible conclusion is that the intellectual capital statement is the only place where intellectual capital is actually visible. The inscriptions in the intellectual capital provide all the means to construct intellectual capital. We only know it via the statement. It cannot be seen by the naked eye because the naked eye has to live with a three-dimensional world with huge frictions of time and space; the intellectual capital statement reduces this friction by all the characteristics of a visualization defined by Latour: in effect the intellectual capital statement is an inscription of things that can be evaluated via their visualization.

What is then outside intellectual capital? It is possible to enrol a huge variety of transactions into an explanation that we call intellectual capital. Just as profits in the financial statement are only there on paper, intellectual capital may just be there on the paper. Profits, after all, are the result of all kinds of valuation processes and it cannot be directly seen if the financial statement were not in place. So, perhaps intellectual capital only exists on the paper and the relation to practices has to be pointed out.

How are such practices pointed out? Either they are not pointed out because by and large, we already know them. This is the case of the financial accounting statement. We know, for example, which industry a particular firm belongs to and thus also its primary technology, markets and competition. We have prior knowledge. Or the practices have to be outlined on the paper. This is what intellectual capital statements do. They show how, for some firms, intellectual capital is a story line that explains – or proposes – how various sorts of activities can be attached to the movement of intellectual capital and thus all the disparate singular events that can be seen in practices are integrated with each other and put into a large storyline about the functioning of intellectual capital and about how management looks toward it to upgrade it and monitor its effects.

Then it is suddenly clear that narratives and numbers are related. They are inseparable because they help to constitute each other. Narratives of achievement, e.g. in the production of quality of life for some people, or flexible education and training etc. can suddenly be integrated with 'small' efforts to develop training, IT and customer relations. By putting narrative, efforts, indicators, pictures and ambition together suddenly it becomes clear what kind of knowledge resource is interesting to firms (Mouritsen et al. 2002). Then the world is inscribed on paper. It is pulled in and capable of evaluation. And by combining and recombining the elements of the intellectual capital statement itself, it may change and transform people's ideas about what happens in the firm. Sometimes the intellectual capital statement changes the firm in the eyes even of management (see also Gröyer & Catasus 2006). It is interesting to note Latour's (1993) point about such paper work:

> All these inscriptions can be superimposed, reshuffled, recombined, and summarized, and totally new phenomena emerge, hidden from the other people from whom these inscriptions have been extracted.

Paperwork (inscriptions) is highly flexible. It is possible to add, subtract, multiply or divide numbers and new phenomena will emerge. It is possible to integrate indicators with efforts and narratives and suddenly get a new version of what intellectual capital is, and is doing, in the firm. It is noteworthy that such accomplishments will not emanate from practices as such. They will have to be motivated somewhere. They require reflexivity and therefore they require some notion that the present could be different from the future. For this to happen, the flexibility of learning from inscriptions – all the things that are already available on the paper that constitute the intellectual capital statement – it is possible to redefine the world. It is a potentiality. It may not always happen, but the prospect is central to how we see such things as intellectual capital that, in principle, is said to develop firms.

Conclusion

The intellectual capital statement reports on a firm's knowledge management activities and strategies. It is an accounting system that brings distance to the firm's knowledge by presenting them as a constellation of knowledge resources that are summarized in various types of containers such as e.g. human, structural and relational capital. The act of bringing distance has two opposing effects. First, it stops the flow of action within which knowledge is developed and mobilized in a stream of inseparable activities. The statement distances knowledge from its organizational embeddedness and thus in a sense creates a mirage of knowledge. It destroys the processes where knowledge is integral for the purpose of visualization.

The visualization destroys the precise representation of knowledge; it is clear that knowledge is a flow. However, by creating distance it also develops visibility, so that it is possible to see more about the resources that embody knowledge, and by separation between knowledge containers it is suddenly possible to perform new operations on knowledge. It is possible to count knowledge containers – their size, investments in them and effects pertaining to them. In addition, as a visualization, the intellectual capital statement also offers a variety of mechanisms such as tables, diagrams and pictures which together creates a firm by moving all sorts of entities close to each other. It is possible to 'see' the buildings, employees, the products and technologies, profitability, investments in HR development and customer relations in one presentation in two-dimensional format. It is possible to construct a whole that is larger than any eye can see. Yet, by seeing the intellectual capital statement, a whole has been created that presents the firm easily without the friction of time and space offered by nature. Even if this is no representation of the firm in the sense of a copy of the firm, it is a visualization that itself creates knowledge about the firm by the things that are put together.

The intellectual capital statement is an accounting system in the same sense as a financial accounting system. The financial accounting system is related to the firm's economy but is not its economy. The intellectual capital statement is related to the firm's knowledge but is not the same as its knowledge. It is a technology of managing which requires to be mobilized. It does not copy the world and is thus no bottom line found at the end of the day. It is an input defined at the beginning of the day so that managers and others have something to do during the day, spending their time translating the knowledge developed in intellectual capital statements into activities that impact the flow of knowledge embedded in integrated organizational processes.

References

Abeysekera I (2006). The project of intellectual capital disclosure: re-searching the research. *Journal of Intellectual Capital*, 7(1): 61–77.

Andon P, Baxter J & Chua WF (2003). Management accounting inscriptions and the post-industrial experience of organizational control. In A Bhimani (Ed), *Management accounting in the digital economy*. Oxford: Oxford University Press.

Andriessen D (2004). IC valuation and measurement: classifying the state of art. *Journal of Intellectual Capital*, 5(2): 230–42.

Bontis N (2004). National intellectual capital index: a United Nations initiative for the Arab region. *Journal of Intellectual Capital*, 5(1): 13–39.

Bontis N & Fitz-enz J (2002). Intellectual capital ROI: a causal map of human capital antecedents and consequents. *Journal of Intellectual Capital*, 3(3): 223–47.

Boedker C, Guthrie J & Cuganesan S (2005). An integrated framework for visualising intellectual capital. *Journal of Intellectual Capital*, special edition: 'Management Consulting Practices on Intellectual Capital', 6(4): 510–27.

Caddy I (2000). Intellectual capital: recognizing both assets and liabilities. *Journal of Intellectual Capital*, 1(2): 129–46.

Catasús B & Gröjer J-E (2006) Indicators: on visualizing, classifying and dramatizing. *Journal of Intellectual Capital*, 7(2): 187–203.

Cuganesan S (2005). Intellectual capital-in-action and value creation: A case study of knowledge transformations in an innovation project. *Journal of Intellectual Capital*, 6(3): 357–73.

Edvinsson L & Malone MS (1997). *Intellectual capital*. London: Piatkus.

Giddens AG (1990). *The consequences of modernity*. Cambridge: Polity.

Latour B (1986). Visualisation and cognition: thinking with eyes and hands. In H Kuklick (Ed), *Knowledge and society studies in the sociology of culture past and present*, 6, (pp1–40). Stanford: JAI Press. (The version used is downloaded from www.bruno.latour which is formatted to 32 pages).

Latour B (1991). The politics of explanation: an alternative. In S Woolgar (Ed), *Knowledge and reflexivity - new frontiers in the sociology of knowledge*. London: Sage.

Marr B, Gray D & Neely A (2003). Why do firms measure their intellectual capital? *Journal of Intellectual Capital*, 4(4): 441–64.

Mouritsen J, Bukh PD, Larsen HT & Johansen MR (2002). Developing and managing knowledge through intellectual capital statements. *Journal of Intellectual Capital*, 3(1): 10–29.

Mouritsen J (2004). Measuring and intervening: How do we theorize intellectual capital management? *Journal of Intellectual Capital*, 5(2): 257–67.

Mouritsen J & Flagstad K (2005). The making of knowledge society: intellectual capital and paradoxes of managing knowledge. In B Czarniawska & T Hernes (Eds), *Actor-network theory and organizing*, (pp208–29). Malmø: Liber & Copenhagen Business School Press.

Mouritsen J & Larsen HT (2005). The 2nd wave of knowledge management: re-centring knowledge management through intellectual capital information. *Management Accounting Research,* 16(3): 371–94.

New South Wales Dept of Lands (2004–2005). *Annual report* (including Intellectual capital statement).

Petty R & Guthrie J (2000). Intellectual capital literature review: measurement, reporting and management. *Journal of Intellectual Capital,* 1(2): 155–76.

Quattrone P & Hopper T (2006). What is IT? SAP, accounting, and visibility in a multinational organization. *Information and Organizations,* 16: 212–50.

Robson K (1991). On the arenas of accounting change: the process of translation. *Accounting, Organizations and Society,* 16(5–6): 547–70.

Roos J, Roos G, Edvinsson L & Dragonetti NC (1997). *Intellectual capital: navigating in the new business landscape.* Houndsmills, Basingstoke: Macmillan.

Roslender R & Fincham R (2003). Intellectual capital as management fashion: a review and critique. *European Accounting Review,* 12(4): 781–95.

Sveiby KE (1997). *The new organizational wealth: managing and measuring knowledge-based assets.* San Francisco: Berrett-Koehler.

Wang W-Y & Chang C (2005). Intellectual capital and performance in causal models. Evidence from the information technology industry in Taiwan. *Journal of Intellectual Capital,* 6(2): 222–36.

9

Supply chain management: enhancing performance through performance measurement systems

Kim Langfield-Smith and David Smith (Monash University)

Abstract

The aim of this chapter is to explain how performance measurement systems can enhance supply chain performance and to outline various approaches that may be taken in designing and implementing such systems and the challenges. Through the use of a case study, the chapter demonstrates how performance measurement and targeted performance improvement activities located in one segment of a supply chain can lead to improved performance for other supply chain partners. Additionally, the chapter discusses various models from the literature that can be used to design and implement performance measurement systems in supply chains. The chapter concludes by considering future challenges for management accounting in the field of SCM.

One of the most significant paradigm shifts of modern business management is that individual organizations can no longer compete as solely autonomous entities, but rather as supply chains (Lambert 2008, p1).

The term 'supply chain management' (SCM) has a variety of meanings in research and in practice. A quick internet search reveals that many websites concerned with SCM focus on software packages and present SCM solutions which are mainly technical approaches, often based on software for streamlining the internal operations of a business and sometimes linking systems to immediate customers or suppliers. While some researchers have restricted their view of SCM to interlinked activities within a single organization, more broader perspectives describe SCM as "the management of a network of interconnected businesses involved in the ultimate provision of product and service packages required by end customers" (Harland 1996, pS64). In the academic literature there has been limited conceptual development of SCM and much of the published research is based on observation and anecdotal evidence, tending to focus on case studies of successful (or unsuccessful) implementations of supply chain approaches (Harland et al. 2004).

SCM can provide organizations with effective ways of working with suppliers and customers to achieve improved performance across the supply chain, in the face of increasing global technological and competitive pressures (Gunasekaran et al. 2001, Elmuti 2002). SCM may involve partners working on joint solutions to problems and on ways to improve the efficiency of the supply chain, enabling performance improvements for individual partners and the overall supply chain (Langfield-Smith & Smith 2005). Such solutions and improvements take advantage of operational and performance interdependencies between partners and the quality of the relationships between supply chain partners, which can lead to innovations that could not be achieved by partners working alone.

The potential benefits of SCM include cost savings through inventory reductions and process efficiencies, reduction in waste, reduction in transaction costs across the supply chain, faster responses to changes in market demands, lower product development costs and increased competitiveness and profitability (LaLonde 1997, Brewer & Speh 2000). Internationally, many consultants have built up large practices in the area of SCM implementation, and over the past decade, a range of practitioner articles and conferences have been dedicated to the topic. Despite the high levels of activity and interest, and the widespread adoption of SCM approaches by businesses, there remains a lack of clarity in the academic literature as to what constitutes SCM, how the benefits of SCM can be achieved and how performance measurement systems can be designed and implemented to contribute to SCM success (Gunasekaran & Kobu 2007).

The aim of this chapter is to explain how performance measurement systems can enhance supply chain performance and to outline various approaches that may be taken in designing and implementing such systems. The remainder of this chapter is structured as follows. The next section considers the definition and scope of SCM, while the third section considers the relevance of SCM to accounting. In section four, a case study demonstrates how performance measurement and targeted performance improvement activities located in one segment of a supply chain can lead to improved performance of other supply chain partners. Section five outlines some models that may be used to conceptualize and design supply chain performance measurement systems. The final section presents challenges and issues that need to be addressed to advance knowledge in this area.

What is supply chain management?

Even though the term SCM has been used since at least the early 1980s, many researchers and managers differ in their definitions of the concept. Oliver and Webber (1982) viewed the supply chain as the integration of business functions of purchasing, sales and distribution within the one organization. This internal focus is still held by some researchers and managers today. So SCM becomes just another name for logistics or materials management. Another view is that SCM is the linking of the organizations to either suppliers or to customers. Researchers in the operations management and supplier management fields (see, for example, Christopher 1992, Ellram 1991) have sometimes drawn on industrial economic theories of Coase (1937) and Williamson (1991) to view supplier relationships as alternatives to vertical integration and to focus on the nature of contracts between organizations. Other researchers have focused on relationships between organizations and suppliers, involving just-in-time management, supplier base reduction and the development of collaborative partnerships (Harland 1996). Researchers in the marketing field have focused their perspectives of SCM on the relationships between the organization and its customers. From a performance measurement perspective, the focus of some of this research is on matching the expectations of customers with the perceptions of managers

(Morgan 2004). For example, the well-known SERVQUAL model (Zeithaml 1990) focuses on measuring key service dimensions that include reliability, responsiveness, courtesy, credibility, and security, and identifying gaps between customer expectations and manager perceptions.

Other researchers take a broader approach, regarding SCM as encompassing the wider network of interlinked partners. For example, Lambert (2008) views SCM as the management of *relationships across the supply chain*. Thus, the supply chain is not really a chain; it is a network of businesses and relationships. Figure 1 (Lambert 2008, p3) provides an illustration of a simplified supply chain network structure and the SCM processes required to integrate functions across the supply chain. This supply chain has two tiers of suppliers and customers, and eight SC management processes that are implemented within each organization in the supply chain. Corporate and functional silos are viewed as barriers to the integration of the eight processes across the supply chain. For example, as Lambert (2008) notes, incentive systems and performance metrics are often used to emphasize and reward the performance of each function. Lambert claims that a key to successful SCM is moving away from managing individual functions (a vertical approach) to integrating activities into supply chain processes (a horizontal approach).

Lambert views customer relationship management and supplier relationship management as the two critical linkages across the supply chain. While relationship building will benefit individual supply chain partners, a difficult issue is reaching agreement on how gains from joint improvement efforts will be shared. Another issue is deciding what data or information will be shared between supply chain partners. Accurate profit reports and performance metrics provide important data to assist in supply chain improvement.

However, supply chains are more complex than this. Figure 2 (Lambert, Garcia-Dastugue & Knemeyer 2008, p207) shows a more complex supply chain. This supply chain is presented from the perspective of the 'focal' company. The supply chain will look different, depending on where you are located within a network. While this network may look unmanageable, to achieve cross-organizational integration not all links need to be closely

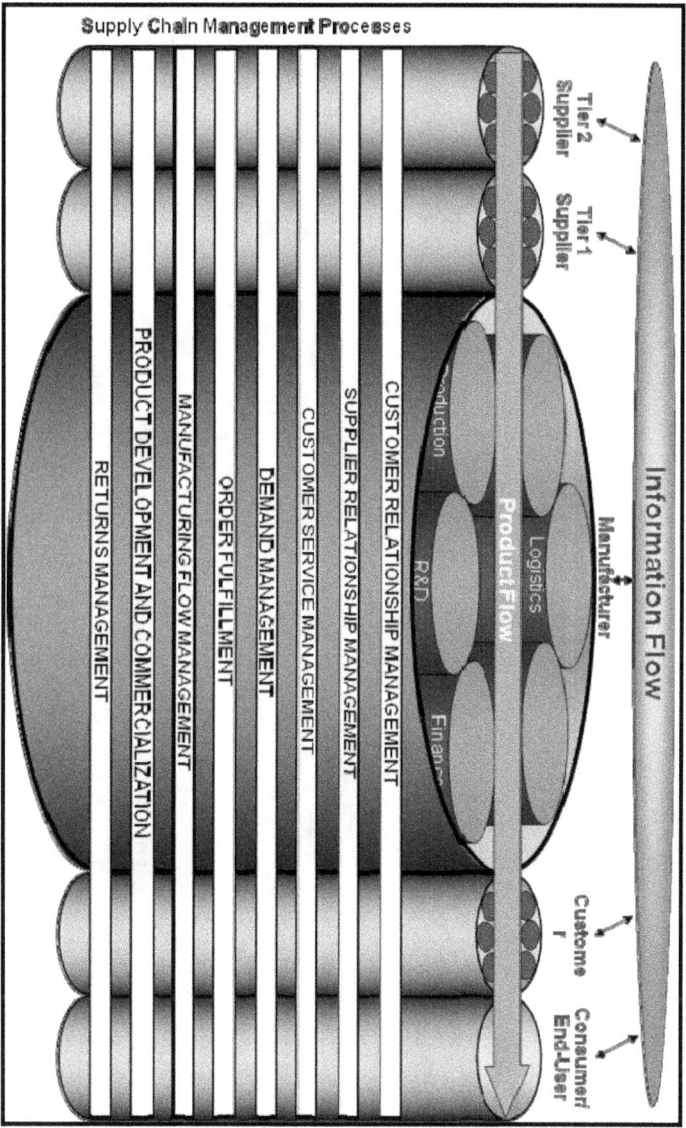

Figure 1: Integrating business processes across the supply chain. After Lambert (2008, p3).

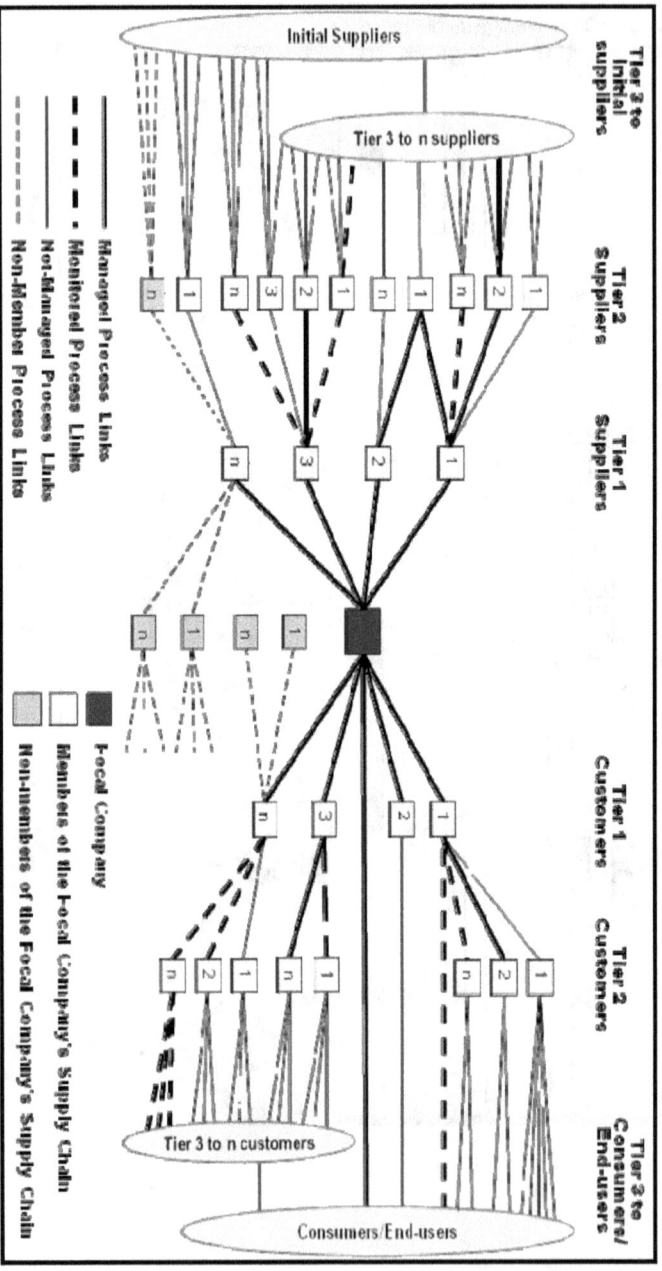

Figure 2: Supply chain network with different forms of links. After Lambert et al. (2008, p207).

managed by the focal company. Also, some entities that are included in this diagram are not members of this particular supply chain, as they do not have a direct or indirect relationship with the focal company. Supply chains do not exist in isolation; an organization may be a member of a number of different supply chains.

Different parts of the supply chain may be given different degrees of management attention, but some relationships are more critical than others. This is indicated in figure 2 by four different levels of process links:

- *Managed process links* are those links that the focal company regards as critical, and thus need to be integrated and managed. The organization will integrate and manage process links with their immediate customers and suppliers, as well as with other organizations in the supply chain.

- *Monitored process links* are regarded by the focal company as less important, however, the focal company is still motivated to ensure that the process links are integrated and managed by other members of the supply chain. These links are therefore monitored by the focal company rather than actively managed.

- *Non-managed process links* are not actively managed or monitored by the focal company. The focal company relies on other members of the supply chain to manage these links.

- *Non-member process links* highlight that managers in the focal company need to be aware that their supply chains are influenced by other connected supply chains. For example, an organization that is a supplier to the focal company may also supply product to a major competitor of the focal company. This may cause the focal company to carefully consider how much attention is provided to developing and improving the operating systems of that supplier and how much data to share with the supplier. It might also mean that the supplier may wish to contribute only limited resources to the focal company's product development processes. While non-member organizations and links are not part of the focal company's supply chain, they may affect the performance of the focal company and its supply chain partners. For example, if a tier 2 supplier has a shortage of product and cannot supply all its customers, it may favour customers with which it has the closest relationships and which are the major customers. If a tier 1 supplier is not one of those favoured customers then it may not receive supply, and this material shortage may have significant implications for the focal company.

The relevance of accounting to SCM

As accountants, why should we be interested in SCM? SCM is of interest to accountants as an effective supply chain can make an impact on corporate financial performance through improved inventory management, more efficient operational processes and enhanced customer service and supplier relationships. Also, accounting has direct relevance for SCM as it can provide the information and the tools to help achieve effective SCM.

An important contributor to supply chain performance is the development of appropriate supply chain performance measurement systems, but as various authors have noted, this is a neglected aspect of SCM practice and research (Brewer & Speh 2000, Lohman et al. 2004, Lambert 2008). Other authors have noted that appropriate development of PMS has also been a problem in the introduction of a range of operational innovations including TQM, JIT, Manufacturing Resource Planning (MRPII) and business process re-engineering (Oakland 1995, Harrison 1992, Luscombe 1993, Hammer & Stanton 1995, Schonberger 2001).

While it can be difficult to design performance measures that integrate operations across the supply chain within an organization, the development of performance measures that span the broader supply chain is particularly challenging and there is limited research and possibly limited applications in practice to draw on. Prior research has argued that effective performance measurement systems are essential for the attainment of SCM objectives (Chan & Qi 2003, Morgan 2004) so it is curious that there should be limited research and applications. The benefits that effective performance measurement can bring to a supply chain include the alignment of operational processes across multiple organizations, the targeting of the most profitable market segments, and the identification of cost drivers that allow the causes of costs to be determined, which will reduce costs across the supply chain (Lambert & Pohlen 2001, 2008; Langfield-Smith & Smith 2005).

Organizational performance measurement systems have been researched widely across several fields including management accounting, operations management and marketing. Management accounting research has contributed significantly to this field of inquiry, due to its emphasis on design and implementation issues relating to performance measurement systems (see, for example, Ittner & Larcker 1998, Otley 1999, Ittner et al. 2003, Chenhall & Langfield-Smith 2003, Banker et al. 2004). Several well-known performance measurement frameworks have been developed, including the Balanced Scorecard (Kaplan & Norton 1996) and the performance measurement pyramid (Lynch & Cross 1992) to guide the design of performance measurement systems. However, these frameworks and most of the empirical research in this area have focused on performance measurement systems *within an organization*, not on performance measurement systems that extend *beyond the boundaries of the organization*. Some normative frameworks have been proposed to guide the design of supply chain performance measurement systems. These are mostly focused on supply chains within an organization, and occasionally address performance measurement systems that cross-organizational boundaries (see, for example, Brewer & Speh 2000; Lambert & Pohlen 2001, 2008; Gunasekaran et al. 2004, 2005). Later in this paper, these frameworks will be discussed.

A case study of performance measurement and supply chain performance

The way that performance measurement can deliver performance outcomes for a supply chain and for individual partners will be illustrated by focusing on a case study from the auto-textile industry.

In 2001 in Melbourne, a supply chain project was undertaken to improve efficiencies and reduce waste along the supply chain for manufacturing seat

Figure 3: The auto-textile supply chain.

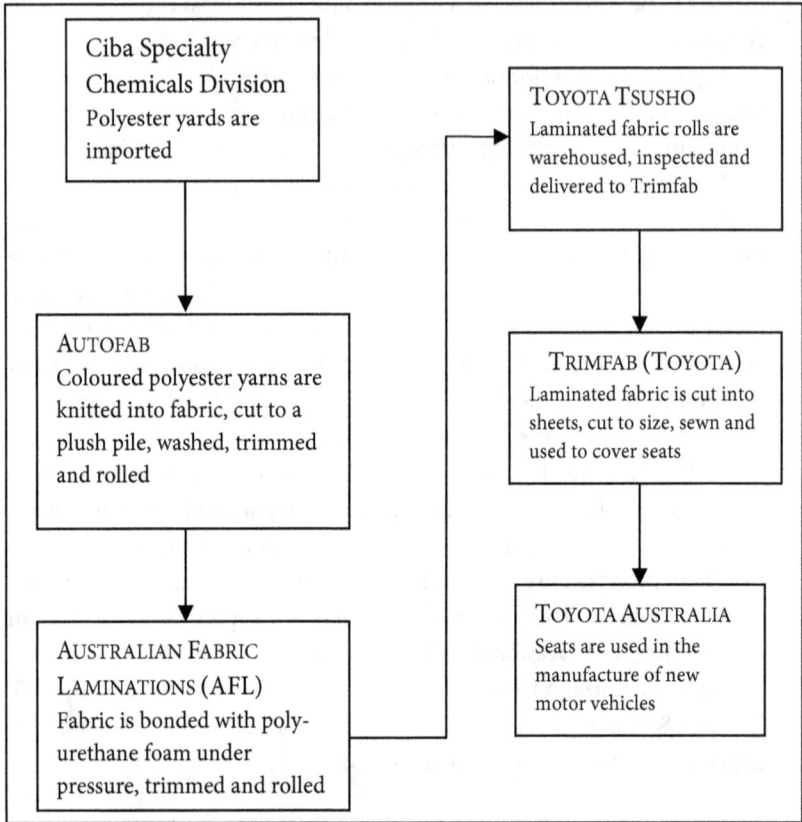

```
┌─────────────────────────────────────────────────────────────────────┐
│  ┌──────────────────────┐                                            │
│  │ Ciba Specialty       │          ┌─────────────────────────┐       │
│  │ Chemicals Division   │          │ TOYOTA TSUSHO           │       │
│  │ Polyester yards are  │───────┐  │ Laminated fabric rolls are │   │
│  │ imported             │       └─▶│ warehoused, inspected and │    │
│  └──────────────────────┘          │ delivered to Trimfab      │    │
│          │                          └─────────────────────────┘       │
│          ▼                                     │                      │
│  ┌──────────────────────┐                      ▼                      │
│  │ AUTOFAB              │          ┌─────────────────────────┐        │
│  │ Coloured polyester   │          │ TRIMFAB (TOYOTA)         │       │
│  │ yarns are knitted    │          │ Laminated fabric is cut into │  │
│  │ into fabric, cut to a│          │ sheets, cut to size, sewn and│  │
│  │ plush pile, washed,  │          │ used to cover seats      │       │
│  │ trimmed and rolled   │          └─────────────────────────┘        │
│  └──────────────────────┘                      │                      │
│          │                                      ▼                      │
│          ▼                          ┌─────────────────────────┐       │
│  ┌──────────────────────┐           │ TOYOTA AUSTRALIA        │       │
│  │ AUSTRALIAN FABRIC    │           │ Seats are used in the   │       │
│  │ LAMINATIONS (AFL)    │           │ manufacture of new      │       │
│  │ Fabric is bonded with│───────────│ motor vehicles          │       │
│  │ poly-urethane foam   │           └─────────────────────────┘       │
│  │ under pressure,      │                                             │
│  │ trimmed and rolled   │                                             │
│  └──────────────────────┘                                             │
└─────────────────────────────────────────────────────────────────────┘
```

Source: Adapted from Langfield-Smith and Smith (2005).

covers in the auto textile industry (Infotech Research 2002).[1] Auto textiles are used by motor vehicles manufacturers in the seating and trim. The textiles

---

1 Dr John Cummings from Infotech Research undertook this supply chain project on behalf of Environment and Heritage. The case material is based on discussions with Dr Cummings and his documentation of the project and was also reported in Langfield-Smith and Smith (2005).

consist of a knitted polyester fabric with foam backing. The companies that were involved included Ciba Australia, an importer of dyes and finishing chemicals; Autofab, a fabric manufacturer; Australian Fabric Laminators (AFL), a fabric and foam laminator; Toyota Tsusho, a warehousing and distribution company; and Trimfab which manufactured seats for use by Toyota in their motor vehicles. The supply relationships between these companies are illustrated in figure 3.

The objective of the supply chain project was to develop a partnership between the supply chain participants to focus on environmental improvement though waste reduction. Specifically, the aims were to:

1. establish a system of communication on environmental issues that couples the partners in the supply chain
2. provide an environmental management system (EMS) that evaluates environmental impacts and waste and which develops solutions across the supply chain
3. establish the system as an integral function of the participants' EMS efforts
4. develop improvement opportunities and implementation plans (Infotech Research, 2002).

The factor that led to the initiation of the project was the high level of waste that was generated at various stages of the supply chain. The loss of raw materials across the supply chain was considerable: more than 22% at fabric manufacture, about 8% at lamination, 0.3% at distribution and 27% in seat manufacture. Across the supply chain, the yield for polyester yarn was only 53% and for polyurethane foam was 72%. Thus, for every kilogram of polyester yard that Autofab ordered from Ciba, only about 53% ended up in the seats that were manufactured by Trimfab. Overall, approximately 1419kg of raw material was wasted across the supply chain each day. There were limited opportunities for reprocessing laminated fabric waste, which occurred through reject rolls, trim waste, and off-cuts. Most waste was disposed of in landfill. In addition, approximately 180kg of packaging waste was generated per day, consisting of cardboard boxes, plastic wrap, plastic spindles, cardboard cores and plastic roll ends. While some of the cardboard cores were returned to suppliers for reuse, each supply chain partner recycled most of the cardboard and plastic waste through external recyclers.

A supply chain approach enabled the recognition of the full extent of the wastage across the supply chain and allowed the causes of the wastage to be detected. In particular, it highlighted how activities and practices followed by companies early in the supply chain could lead to waste in companies further down the supply chain.

Waste auditing, waste streamlining, causal analysis and the testing of waste reduction opportunities were applied across the supply chain. Material waste was reduced through changing lengths of rolls of fabric to reduce off-cut waste, using more optimal cutting pattern layouts, and investigating ways to recycle off-cuts to avoid landfill. Initiatives to reduce packaging waste – including boxes, plastic wrap, cardboard cores and spindles – involved the reuse of packaging, reduced packaging, and increased pulping and recycling by external recyclers. The supply chain approach enabled performance improvements in one partner to have positive impacts on the performance of other partners down the supply chain. For example, when AFL increased the standard length of the fabric roll from 22 metres to 25 metres, this led to a saving of 43kg of waste materials per day for Trimfab. The return of all cardboard cores to partners along the supply chain and the recycling of packaging waste resulted in cost savings for all partners. These improvements diverted 36,000kg of waste from landfill per year.

The development of performance measures and the setting of targets and timelines were important for encouraging change and for monitoring improvements. Some examples of these measures, targets and responsibilities are listed in table 1. While the measures focused primarily on waste reduction, which was the focus of the project, the outcome of this waste reduction activity was also considerable cost savings. For example, the savings from reduced laminated fabric waste was estimated at $800,000 per year across the supply chain.

Table 1: Performance measurement in the auto-textile supply chain.

Target	Measure	Responsibility	When	Document
Roll off cut waste reduction by 20%	Waste audit at Trimfab	Toyota Trim-fab	May 2002	Waste audit report
Trim reduction by 30%	Trim requirement in specification	AFL	June 2002	Minutes of SC meeting
Packaging waste recycling	Waste audit at all sites	Autofab, AFL, Toyota Trim-fab, Toyota Tsusho	November 2002	Waste audit report
Core recycling 100%	Waste audit	Autofab, AFL, Toyota Trim-fab, Toyota Tsusho	November 2002	Waste audit report
Autofab waste water treatment to COD<500 mg/L	Waste water monitoring	Autofab	July 2002	Minutes of SC meeting
Air emission compliance at Autofab and AFL	Stack emission monitoring	Autofab and AFL	Dec 2001 and June 2002	Site EMS documents

Source: Adapted from Infotech (2002, p2).

In implementing this project and developing performance data, several difficulties were encountered. The supply chain was a mix of small companies (Autofab and AFL) and very large companies (Ciba and Toyota). Thus, information systems, performance measurement systems and data availability were at different levels of sophistication. Unlike the larger companies, the smaller companies did not have on hand the required data to measure performance. However, in the larger companies the data were not always in the form required for the supply-chain analysis. Thus, in the smaller companies the consultant who managed the project developed simple systems to measure the physical data. In the larger companies, data needed to be aggregated from various sources within the businesses.

Other difficulties included sustaining enthusiasm and motivation among participants, maintaining a supply chain perspective, and creating effective means of communication between supply chain partners. Employees who were directly involved in the supply chain project were also involved in other operating aspects of their business that may have been considered more critical to their individual organization. Therefore, for some employees, the time available to devote to the project was limited and enthusiasm and motivation may have been difficult to sustain in the light of other competing company priorities. In some companies, employee incentives emphasized individual company goals, and these did not always encourage a high level of motivation for the project or commitment to a supply chain perspective. The auto-textile supply chain, outlined in figure 3, was not a major activity for either Ciba or Toyota. However, for Autofab and AFL, the auto-textile supply chain represented a significant part of their production activity.

In light of these difficulties, effective and ongoing communication between the supply chain participants was difficult to achieve. Communication initially took the form of an internet site where participants could share and pool performance data and monitor performance and solutions. This was not very effective due to busy schedules and other competing commitments of participants. This was followed by the encouragement of email communications, and then finally the consultant met directly with supply chain participants to progress the analysis and the project.

There was little resistance to the sharing of information between supply chain partners. This may have been a function of the data that were collected, which consisted of basic cost data, waste and other physical measures, rather than more sensitive profit or sales revenue data. Another advantage was that as the focus was on minimizing environmental waste, performance improvements were immediate and highly visible. However, the limited focus may also have been a barrier to gaining higher levels of commitment and visibility of the project in the partner organizations.

Performance improvements that were obtained by companies in the auto-textile supply chain would not have been possible without collaboration between the partners and their willingness to make the necessary changes. The collaborative efforts revealed the opportunities for performance improvements and led to effective solutions. The focus for the performance measurement and improvements was confined to a single dimension – waste reduction – and that made the project manageable, achievable and non-threatening to partners. However, gaining cooperation and maintaining enthusiasm and motivation for supply chain projects may be more difficult when the project is broader and the focus is more central to the operations of the partners. Performance measurement and monitoring was important to set expectations, encourage progress and to assess improvements.

An important issue in supply chain performance improvement projects, which has the potential to derail projects, is the potential for a mismatch between the partners that bear the costs and undertake the efforts to introduce improvements and the partners that reap the benefits. This was an issue in the auto-textile supply chain project; the benefits from the changes that were made by Autofab accrued primarily to Trimfab.

An advantage of supply chain improvement projects is that they can provide smaller companies, which do not have the financial resources or the expertise to devote to performance improvement, the opportunity to engage with larger, more sophisticated supply chain partners, to benefit from their expertise and from the broader supply chain collaboration. However, those same supply chain partners may have limited incentives to engage with small suppliers or with particular supply chains that are considered a low priority. The auto-textile supply chain represented a large part of the operating activity of Autofab and AFL, but was only one of many supply chains for Ciba and Toyota.

Supply chain performance measurement systems

Developing frameworks that provide guidance for the design and implementation of supply chain performance measurement systems is a complex and difficult task. *Design* includes defining the criteria that best captures different aspects of supply chain performance (such as on-time delivery, reduced material waste, cycle time, customer satisfaction), deciding how those criteria should be measured, and constructing the measures. *Implementation* includes creating new IT systems to capture the appropriate data and produce performance reports, and 'selling' the new systems and administrative processes to managers and employees who may be resistant to change. In a multi-organizational supply chain, many of these aspects need to be negotiated with managers working in supply chain partners, so the 'success' of these activities will be influenced by various factors as outlined below.

The design and implementation of performance measurement systems across supply chains may vary due to *contextual factors*, which include industry type, organizational size and the strategy of each of the supply chain partners. The success of designing and implementing performance measurement systems that cross many organizational boundaries may also be influenced by *technical factors,* which may focus on the compatibility of IT systems, data formats and data definitions across the organizations in the supply chain. *Relational factors* can also create barriers or enhance implementation. These include the degree of willingness of partners to share information, the quality of the relationships between partners (including trust), the degree of dependence of a supply chain partner on other supply chain partners, and the level of acceptance or resistance to change of managers across the supply chain.

As depicted in figure 4, the scope of supply chain performance measurement systems can be viewed across three levels: within the organization (level 0); between the organization and its tier 1 suppliers and customers (level 1); and between the organization, tier 1 suppliers and customers, tier 2 suppliers and customers, and other partners in the supply chain (level 2).

Figure 4: The scope of supply chain performance measurement systems.

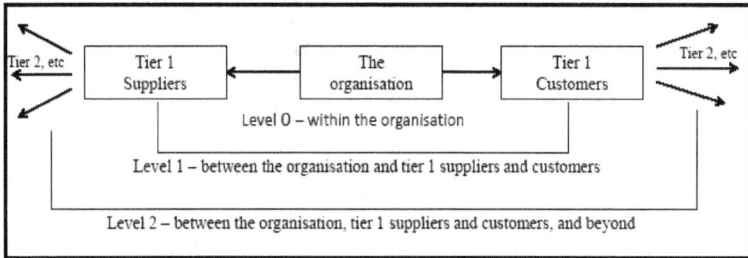

```
 Tier 2, etc        Tier 1              The              Tier 1           Tier 2, etc
                    Suppliers        organisation       Customers

                          Level 0 – within the organisation

              Level 1 – between the organisation and tier 1 suppliers and customers

            Level 2 – between the organisation, tier 1 suppliers and customers, and beyond
```

Within the organization (level 0), performance measurement systems can be used to monitor and manage an organization's performance across its functional areas. This includes implementing financial and non-financial measures that capture performance at various points along the internal supply chain (Flapper et al. 1996, Fransoo & Wouters 2000). However, a broader supply chain management perspective entails taking a process orientation which crosses supply chain partners. Some research has focused on developing performance measurement systems that include tier 1 suppliers and customers (level 1) (see, for example, Gunasekaran et al. 2001, Langfield-Smith & Smith 2005). However, there appears to be limited published research that explores the design and implementation of performance measurement systems that go beyond tier 1 suppliers or customers to cross the broader supply chain (level 2 measures). What follows are a variety of frameworks that have been developed to accommodate SCM performance measurement systems.

Brewer and Speh's (2000) Balanced Scorecard approach

Brewer and Speh (2000) designed a Balanced Scorecard for supply chain performance measures that involved intra-organizational and inter-organizational functional integration, sharing and cooperation. This scorecard was structured around what they saw as the four main goals of SCM, namely waste reduction, time compression, flexible response, and unit cost reduction.

Figure 5: Balanced Scorecard for SCM.

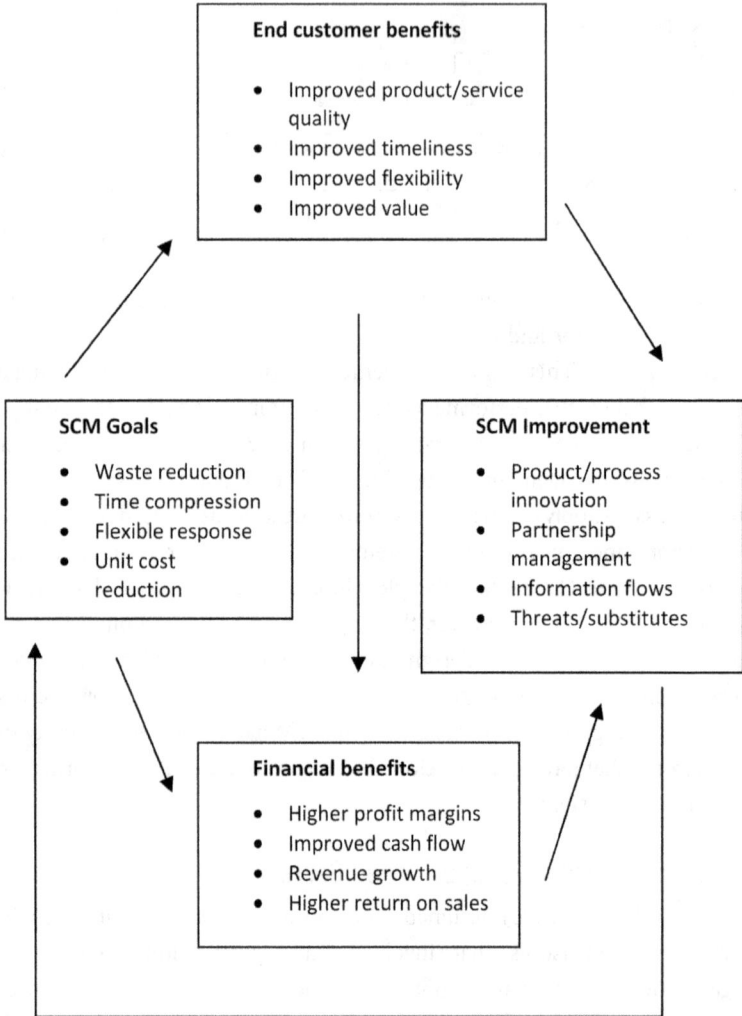

End customer benefits

- Improved product/service quality
- Improved timeliness
- Improved flexibility
- Improved value

SCM Goals

- Waste reduction
- Time compression
- Flexible response
- Unit cost reduction

SCM Improvement

- Product/process innovation
- Partnership management
- Information flows
- Threats/substitutes

Financial benefits

- Higher profit margins
- Improved cash flow
- Revenue growth
- Higher return on sales

Source: Brewer and Speh (2000), p78.

- *Waste reduction across the supply chain* can be achieved through reducing duplication of activities, harmonizing operations and systems, and improving the quality of products, operations and assets. This can lead to cost reduction and improved customer satisfaction.
- *Compression of the cycle time from customer order to delivery* can be activities. This can lead to reduced inventory levels, provide a visible realized through process improvement and waste-reduction diagnosis of cumulative problems enabling a quick response, enhanced cash flow and improved customer responsiveness.
- A *flexible response to customer requirements* across the supply chain can be achieved through the way an order is handled and the customising of products to meet customer needs in a cost-effective way. This will enhance customer satisfaction, and possibly reduce cost.
- In *reducing unit costs*, there needs to be a balance between cost reduction and the level of service offered to customers.

As shown in figure 5, these four goals lead to end-customer benefits, SCM improvements and financial benefits. However, the four goals also correspond with the four perspectives of Kaplan and Norton's (1996) Balanced Scorecard. Specifically, Brewer and Speh (2000, p85) argue that their SCM Goals perspective is linked with the Internal Business Process perspective, Customer Benefits links to the Customer Perspective, Financial Benefits links to the Financial Perspective, and SCM Improvement links to the Innovation and Learning Perspective. Four measures were identified for each dimension, as outlined in table 2.

Brewer and Speh (2000) also introduced a dynamic element to their framework, by recognizing that organizations must continually innovate to improve SCM and to ensure future profitability for all supply chain partners. Thus, members of a supply chain can achieve SCM improvements through:

- redesigning product and processes across the supply chain
- improving collaboration across the supply chain and leveraging the knowledge of partners in the supply chain
- improving information management across the supply chain to improve decision making

- engaging in improved monitoring of the external market to detect new competitor activities.

Table 2: Measures for a SCM Balanced Scorecard.

Perspective	Goals	Measures
Financial	1. Profit margin 2. Cash flow 3. Revenue growth 4. Return on assets	1. Profit margin by supply chain partner 2. Cash-to-cash cycle 3. Customer growth and profitability 4. Return on supply chain assets.
Customer	1. Customer view of product/service 2. Customer view of timeliness 3. Customer view of flexibility 4. Customer value	1. Number of customer contact points 2. Relative customer order response time 3. Customer perception of flexible response 4. Customer value ratio
Internal business process	1. Waste reduction 2. Time compression 3. Flexible response 4. Unit cost reduction	1. Supply chain cost of ownership 2. Supply chain cycle efficiency 3. Number of choices/average response time 4. % of supply chain target costs achieved
Innovation and learning	1. Product/process innovation 2. Partnership management 3. Information flows 4. Threats and substitutes	1. Product finalization point 2. Product category commitment ratio 3. Number of shared data sets/total data sets 4. Performance trajectories of competing technologies

Source: Adapted from Brewer and Speh (2000, p86).

The SCM Balanced Scorecard includes measures that integrate across the supply chain to encourage partners to focus on the interdependencies that exist between supply chain partners (for example, supply chain cost of ownership and supply chain cycle time), while other measures are not integrated, to help partners focus on problems within their own organization (Langfield-Smith & Smith 2005).

Subsequent papers that have emphasized a BSC approach to SCM performance measurement systems include Bhagwat and Sharma (2007) and Kleijnen and Smits (2003). Using a case study methodology, Bhagwat and Sharma observed that limited consultation between organizations was a barrier to the successful implementation of a SCM Balanced Scorecard. Kleijnen and Smits (2003) present a range of simulation methodologies to demonstrate how the values of specific performance measures within a supply chain BSC change, once the cause and effect relationships between measures are modelled. They state that simulation modelling may help managers understand causality and can be used as a forecasting tool to assess the outcomes of alternative design strategies. However, this approach provides a technical solution, and relational issues are not emphasized.

The strengths of Brewer and Speh's Balanced Scorecard approach lie in its ability to balance both financial and non-financial measures, to link measures with the strategy of the supply chain, and to measure performance across the entire supply chain (Langfield-Smith & Smith 2005). Yet Brewer and Speh indicate that there is little evidence that organizations have implemented their Balanced Scorecard in supply chains. Further, subsequent work has failed to provide much insight into how contextual, technical and relational issues affect Balanced Scorecard design, implementation and use in the case of SCM.

Gunasekaran et al. (2004) framework

Based on an empirical analysis and an earlier theoretical paper (Gunasekaran et al. 2001), Gunasekaran et al. (2004) developed a framework that maps four major supply chain (SC) activities – plan, source, make and deliver – against the strategic, tactical and operational management decision levels. This classification provides a means for grouping SC measures. Table 3 provides an example of this classification. Thus, supplier delivery performance relates to sourcing activities and tactical planning, while percentage of defects is an operational measure relating to the 'make' activity.

While Gunasekaran et al. (2004) state that their framework is a first step for organizations to better understand SC metrics, it clearly is focused on the single organization, not the wider supply chain. Gunasekaran et al. recognize this and state that a 'good' SCM program will lead to improved cross-functional and intra-organizational planning and control and more complete SC integration, and suggest a wider supply chain performance measurement system is needed. However, apart from highlighting the importance of this development and that "care must be exercised in developing such a system in order that it promotes mutually advantageous exchange among participants, so that relationships endure the test of time" (p346), there is no guidance on what such a performance measurement framework would look like or how it could be developed. Further, Gunasekaran et al.'s framework is essentially a 'laundry list' of measures sourced from the prior SC literature. While the authors acknowledge this, and that performance metrics need to be developed to reflect the unique needs of each supply chain partner, the framework provides no guidance as to how relevant contextual factors may influence the development of appropriate SC measures. For example, Gunasekaran et al. (2004, p345) note in relation to their framework that "the importance of individual metrics presented herein might not apply to all supply chains in all industries". Similarly, the framework does not seek to account for how technical and relational factors may influence the development and implementation of SC measures.

Table 3: Three levels of supply chain performance measures. Adapted from
Gunasekaran et al. (2004, p345).

Supply chain Activity/process	Level of managerial planning		
	Strategic	Tactical	Operational
Plan	Level of customer value of product, Variances against budget, Order lead time, Net profit vs. productivity ratio, Total cycle time, Total cash flow time, Product development cycle time	Customer query time, Product development cycle time, Accuracy of forecasting techniques, Planning process cycle time, Order entry methods, Human resource productivity	Order entry methods, Human resource productivity
Source		Supplier delivery performance, Supplier lead time against industry norm, Supplier pricing against market, Efficiency of purchase order cycle time,	Efficiency of purchase order cycle time, Supplier pricing against market
Make/assemble	Range of products and services	Percentage of defects, Cost per operation hour, Capacity utilization, Utilization of economic order quantity	Percentage of defects, Cost per operation hour, Human resource productivity
Deliver	Flexibility of service system to meet customer needs, Effectiveness of enterprise distribution planning schedule	Flexibility of service system to meet customer needs, Effectiveness of enterprise distribution planning schedule, Effectiveness of delivery invoice methods, Percentage of finished goods in transit, Delivery reliability performance	Quality of delivered goods, On time delivery of goods, Effectiveness of delivery invoice methods, Percentage of urgent deliveries, Delivery reliability performance

Linking measures to a supply chain strategy

Another approach to the development of supply chain performance measures is presented by Lambert and Pohlen (2001, 2008), who devised a framework that explicitly considers the relationship between measures and supply chain strategy. This framework focuses on a series of steps:

1. Map the supply chain from point-of-origin to point-of-consumption to identify the key linkages.
2. Use customer/supplier relationship management processes to analyze each link (customer-supplier pair) and reveal opportunities for improvements and additional value creation.
3. Measure customer and supplier profit, to assess how the relationship impacts on the profitability and shareholder value of the two organizations.
4. Realign supply chain processes and activities to achieve performance objectives.
5. Establish non-financial performance measures that encourage individuals to achieve supply chain objectives and financial goals.
6. Compare shareholder value and market capitalization across the two organizations with the supply chain objectives, and revise process and performance measures as required.
7. Replicate the above steps for each link of the supply chain.

This framework has the advantage of simplifying a potentially very complex process, by first focusing on the linkages in the focal company and then moving outward across the supply chain, one linkage at a time. It also provides alignment between process improvements, performance measures, organization and supply chain objectives and individual behaviour. This may enhance the possibility of achieving some of the synergistic performance outcomes associated with SCM. Like Brewer and Speh (2000), Lambert and Pohlen's (2001, 2008) work indicates that further research needs to be undertaken to test their proposed framework in an actual business setting. Further, like Gunasekaran et al.'s (2004) framework, Lambert and Pohlen's framework is largely silent on the potential role of contextual and relational factors in the development, implementation and use of supply chain performance measures.

Measuring up in practice

However, it appears in practice broad supply chain performance measurement systems are largely underdeveloped and this may limit the extent of supply chain performance improvements. This is supported by a recent survey of Bain and Company, who studied 162 managers and found that although more than 85% of the managers indicated that improving supply chain performance was one of their top priorities, less than 10% were adequately measuring supply chain performance, and less than 7% were collecting the information necessary to enable them to track their progress (Cook & Greenspan 2003). They also found that an increasing gap between the supply chain 'stars' and the laggards. Four reasons were provided for the inability of many organizations to achieve supply chain performance improvements:

- There is a lack of visibility of supply chain performance data across the company and supply chain.
- Too many companies have a narrow definition of supply chains, and failed to recognize that their supply chain extends beyond their first tier suppliers and customers.
- Managerial incentives do not reward supply chain improvements.
- There is a tendency to rely on sophisticated software to address supply chain problems, rather than looking at more fundamental solutions.

The Bain and Company study concluded that if the performance of the whole supply chain is not tracked then companies are in the dark as to the cost of their supply chain inefficiencies. They emphasized that good supply chain practices needed to run on data, not on instinct!

Conclusion

The aim of this chapter was to explain how performance measurement systems can enhance supply chain performance and to outline various approaches that may be taken in designing and implementing such systems. The relevance of SCM to accounting lies in the potential for accounting to play a role in the design and implementation of effective supply chain performance measurement systems. As revealed in the auto textile case study, when accompanied by process improvement activities, performance measurement, targets and reporting can lead to significant performance improvements that have the potential to benefit companies across the supply chains. The case also demonstrates that performance measurement activities need not be 'all-encompassing' or 'permanent' systems, but may be implemented as a one-off project that selectively targets particular problem areas.

The challenge in designing and implementing supply chain performance measurement systems lies with gaining cooperation, commitment and motivation from supply chain partners. While only a few frameworks have been developed for designing supply chain performance measurement systems, these are largely technical models that do not take into account the human or the relational factors that may determine the success of an implementation. Gattorna (2006) argues that in the future, successful management of the human factors in a supply chain will be the primary source of performance improvement.

The primary challenge for management accountants working in this area are to consider the relevant factors that may influence the success of initiatives to develop supply chain performance measurement systems that span the entire supply chain. This requires more than just an understanding of technical issues; an understanding of the relevant contextual and relational factors that influence the design and implementation of supply chain performance measures is required. Research can assist in developing our understanding of how these factors are implicated in the appropriate design and implementation of supply chain performance measures.

References

Banker RD, Chang H & Pizzini MJ (2004). The Balanced Scorecard: judgemental effects of performance measures linked to strategy. *The Accounting Review*, 79: 1–24.

Bhagwat R & Sharma MK (2007). Performance measurement of supply chain management: a Balanced Scorecard approach. *Computers and Industrial Engineering*, 53: 43–62.

Brewer PC & Speh TW (2000). Using the Balanced Scorecard to measure supply chain performance. *Journal of Business Logistics,* 21(1): 75–93.

Chan FTS & Qi HJ (2003). Feasibility of performance measurement system for supply chain: a process-based approach and measures. *Integrated Manufacturing Systems,* 14(3): 179–90.

Chenhall R & Langfield-Smith K (2003). Performance measurement and reward systems, trust and strategic change. *Management Accounting Research,* 15: 117–44.

Christopher MG (1992). *Logistics and supply chain management.* London: Pitman Publishing.

Coase R (1937). The nature of the firm. *Economica,* 4(16): 386–405.

Cook M & Greenspan N (2003). Why companies fail the supply-chain basics. *European Business Journal,* 15(2):74–78.

Ellram LM (1991). Supply chain management: the industrial organisation perspective. *International Journal of Physical Distribution and Logistics Management,* 21(1): 13–22.

Elmuti D (2002). The perceived impact of supply chain management on organizational effectiveness. *The Journal of Supply Chain Management,* 38(3): 49–57.

Flapper SD, Fortuin L & Stoop PPM (1996). Towards consistent performance measurement systems. *Journal of Operations and Production Management,* 16(7): 27–37.

Fransoo JC & Wouters MJF (2000). Measuring the bullwhip effect in a supply chain. *Supply Chain Management,* 5(2): 78–89.

Gattorna J (2006). *Living supply chains.* Harlow, UK: Pearson Education.

Gunasekaran A & Kobu B (2007). Performance measures and metrics in logistics and supply chain management: a review of recent literature (1995–2004) for research and applications. *International Journal of Production Research,* 45(12): 2819–40.

Gunasekaran A, Patel C & Tirtiroglu E (2001). Performance measures and metrics in a supply chain environment. *International Journal of Operations and Production Management,* 21(1–2): 71–87.

Gunasekaran A, Patel C & McGaughey RE (2004). A framework for supply chain performance measurement. *International Journal of Operations and Production Management*, 87: 333–47.

Gunasekaran A, Patel C & McGaughey RE (2005). Performance measurement and costing systems in new enterprises. *Technovation*, 25: 523–33.

Hammer M & Stanton SA (1995). *The reengineering revolution handbook*. London: Harper Collins.

Harland C (1996). Supply chain management: relationships, chains and networks. *British Journal of Management*, 7, special issue: S63–S80.

Harland C, Zheng J, Johnsen T & Lamming R (2004). A conceptual model for researching the creation and operation of supply networks. *British Journal of Management*, 15: 10–21.

Harrison A (1992). *Just in time in perspective*. London: Prentice Hall.

Infotech Research (2002). Auto textiles supply chain partnership for environmental management. Infotech Research, May, Melbourne.

Ittner CD & Larcker D (1998). Are non-financial measures leading indicators of financial performance? An analysis of customer satisfaction. *Journal of Accounting Research*, 36: 1–35.

Ittner CD, Larcker D & Randall T (2003). Performance implications of strategic performance measurement in financial services firms. *Accounting, Organizations and Society*, 28(7–8): 715–41.

Kaplan RS & Norton DP (1996). Using the Balanced Scorecard as a strategic management system. *Harvard Business Review*, January-February: 75–85.

Kleijnen JPC & Smits MT (2003). Performance metrics in supply chain management. *Journal of the Operational Research Society*, 54: 507–14.

LaLonde B (1997). Where's the beef in supply chain management? *Supply Chain Management Review*, 33(3): 9–10.

Lambert DM (2008). Supply chain management. In DM Lambert (Ed), *Supply chain management: processes, partnerships, performance*, (pp1–24). Sarasota, FL: Supply Chain Management Institute.

Lambert DM, Garcia-Dastugue SJ & Knemeyer AM (2008). Mapping for supply chain management. In DM Lambert (Ed), *Supply chain man-*

agement: processes, partnerships, performance, (pp197–216). Sarasota, FL: Supply Chain Management Institute.

Lambert DM & Pohlen TL (2001). Supply chain metrics. *International Journal of Logistics Management*, 12: 1–19.

Lambert DM & Pohlen TL (2008). Supply chain management performance measurement. In DM Lambert (Ed), *Supply chain management: processes, partnerships, performance*, (pp283–302). Sarasota, FL: Supply Chain Management Institute.

Langfield-Smith K & Smith D (2005). Performance measurement in supply chains. *Australian Accounting Review*, 15(1): 39–51.

Lohman C, Fortuin L & Wouters M (2004). Designing a performance measurement system: a case study. *European Journal of Operational Research*, 156: 267–86.

Luscombe M (1993). *Integrating the business: MRP II, a practical guide for managers*. London: Butterworth Heinemann.

Lynch RL & Cross KF (1992). *Measure up! Yardsticks for continuous improvement*. Cambridge, MA: Blackwell.

Morgan C (2004). Structure, speed and salience: performance measurement in the supply chain. *Business Process Management Journal*, 10(5): 522–36.

Oakland JS (1995). *Total quality management*. London: Butterworth Heinemann.

Oliver RK & Webber MD (1982). Supply chain management: logistics catches up with strategy. In M Christopher (1992). *Logistics: the strategic issues*, (pp63–75). London: Chapman and Hall.

Otley D (1999). Performance management: a framework for management control systems research. *Management Accounting Research*, 10(4): 363–82.

Schonberger R (2001). *Let's fix it! Overcoming the crisis in manufacturing: how the world's leading manufacturers were seduced by prosperity and lost their way*. New York: Free Press.

Williamson O (1991). Comparative economic organization: the analysis of discrete structural alternatives. *Administrative Science Quarterly*, 36: 269–96.

Zeithaml VA, Parasuraman A & Berry LL (1990). *Delivering quality service: balancing customer perceptions and expectations*. New York: Free Press.

10

Performance measurement and managerial behaviour

Anne Lillis (University of Melbourne)

Abstract

This chapter reflects on three studies relating to the broad issue of the way accounting performance measurement impacts on managerial behaviour. The first study relates to evidence of a shift in employment patterns which is not explained by economic fundamentals but appears to be driven by managerial decisions to avoid the persistence of accounting losses. The second study draws on evidence from manufacturing firms relating to the difficulty of pursuing strategies focused on customer responsiveness when conventional management accounting performance measures focus on efficiency and productivity. The final study examines the role of the Balanced Scorecard in mitigating the dysfunctional consequences of accounting performance measurement on managerial decision making. This latter study highlights the importance of aligning evaluation and incentives with performance measurement innovation. Overall this chapter draws on contemporary research to revisit a question with deep historical roots in the accounting literature.[1]

In this chapter, I reflect on contemporary research issues related to performance measurement and managerial behaviour. While the chapter focuses on relatively recent research, both the research themes and findings resonate

---

1 A version of this chapter was presented as an inaugural professorial lecture, which is reproduced in *Insights*, 4, Nov 2008 (University of Melbourne, Faculty of Economics and Commerce).

with quite early seminal writings on the topic of performance measurement and managerial behaviour. In 1975, Steven Kerr wrote the seminal paper 'On the folly of rewarding A while hoping for B' and in 1965 Solomons outlined the potential for underinvestment in capital projects in circumstances where managers who have significant investment influence are evaluated on annual performance measures such as return on assets. In effect, potentially good decision rules (such as net present value) would be overruled by evaluation protocols that draw attention to the impact of decisions on annual accounting performance measures, such as return on assets. These studies are now dated. However, their themes remain surprisingly current in contemporary research.

The general problem of performance measurement and managerial behaviour can be reflected in a simple decision dilemma where a manager may be guided by two different information sets. Managers faced with strategic, investment and operating decisions are generally faced with two sets of financial and non-financial information that may convey quite different messages:

1. Decision-facilitating information – information provided to decision makers prior to decision making, in order to help resolve uncertainties in decision problems (Demski & Feltham 1976). This role is also commonly referred to as the belief revision role to acknowledge that the information contained within the reported measures is informative for decision making (Narayanan & Davila 1998). For example, for a potential acquisition such information might include:
   - analysis of strengths and capabilities of the target company
   - discounted cash flow analysis of potential financial consequences of the acquisition over a five-year horizon
   - discounted cash flow analysis of the implications of choosing not to go ahead with the acquisition.

The dominant characteristic of decision-facilitating information is relevance to the decision at hand. Such information will generally, at a minimum, cover estimated financial impacts for the duration of the decision (e.g. a capital project).

2. Decision-influencing information – information collected by higher level management to evaluate the performance (decision outcomes) of sub-unit managers. By making the performance measurement parameters available to the subordinate manager, the need to ultimately report on performance against the measure *influences* subordinate managerial decisions (Demski & Feltham 1976, Narayanan & Davila 1998). For example, common performance measures used for periodic managerial performance measurement and bonuses include divisional profit and return on assets, measured quarterly or annually. These and other financial and non-financial measures form the basis for managerial performance measurement and bonuses.

The two decision signals may conflict. In the example given, a full project life analysis (discounted cash flow) will frequently give a different investment-decision signal to a single-period measure of accounting impact (such as annual return on assets). Stated in more general terms, routine performance measurement cuts arbitrary cross-sections through the lifetime performance of the manager and the division. These measures will never be completely reflective of the quality of managerial decisions. Many managerial decisions generate short-term costs and delayed benefits. It is the multi-period analysis that gives the more comprehensive picture of events. Yet we know accounting is generally locked into arbitrary reporting cycles.

Accounting does not exist in an organizational vacuum. Performance measurement is a critical control mechanism, but not the only mechanism in operation. Organizations rely on different leadership styles (more or less results driven), organization culture (cultivating a long-term commitment, long-serving managers) and informal control mechanisms that may 'balance' the influence of accounting performance measurement. Nonetheless, the importance of performance measurement in signalling desired behaviour and directing effort is widely acknowledged both theoretically and empirically.

In this chapter, I reflect on three research projects which examine aspects of the broad issue of performance measurement and managerial decision making from quite different perspectives. These are:

1. The way an important capital market metric (the accounting profit/loss threshold) induces decision making that cannot be explained by economic fundamentals.

2. The challenge manufacturing firms face in trying to implement strategies focused on flexibility and responsiveness when conventional manufacturing performance measurement practice creates the incentive to be efficient and productive (but not flexible and responsive).

3. The potential for recent performance measurement innovations such as the Balanced Scorecard to reduce the problem of accounting-focused decision making by broadening the basis of performance measurement away from a short-term financial focus.

Study 1: (Pinnuck & Lillis 2007)

Pinnuck and Lillis (2007) examine the impact of capital market based performance measurement on managerial decision making. The study focuses particularly on managerial decision making regarding the level of investment in employees. Drawing on the decision-facilitating/decision-influencing terminology used in the introduction to this chapter, decisions regarding the level of investment in employees should be facilitated by information about the economic fundamentals of the firm, especially activity levels. However Pinnuck and Lillis (2007) argue that decisions regarding the level of investment in employees are also significantly influenced by less rational responses to capital market pressures to avoid the reporting of accounting losses.

There are many forms of managerial behaviour that appear to be driven by capital market expectations. The most common is earnings management and there is a wealth of literature on this (Burgstahler & Dichev 1997, Hayn 1995, Dechow et al. 2003). While earnings management is largely focused on the use of discretionary accruals in order to manage the level of reported earnings (for example to avoid reporting losses or to smooth earnings), the focus of Pinnuck and Lillis (2007) is on real operating and investment decisions that are affected by capital market performance expectations. In particular, this study looks at patterns in decision making that arise from the reporting of accounting losses. The accounting profit/loss threshold represents a powerful decision heuristic for two reasons:

1. The reporting of a loss acts as a trigger for outside intervention (e.g. by boards, regulatory agencies, equity markets and lenders)
2. Firms reporting small losses appear to be asymmetrically devalued relative to those reporting small profits. In economic terms firms reporting small profits and small losses are in fact fundamentally similar, and are most likely all reflecting underlying *economic* losses.

Firms that cross the profit/loss threshold into an accounting loss position are under intense capital market pressure to get back to reporting a profit as quickly as possible. What can managers do when faced with this extreme performance tension? They have presumably exploited all available potential for accounting discretion that would have enabled them to report a small profit (but failed). They now need drastic action to improve the bottom line as quickly as possible. Action can include discarding less productive investments that may have been 'carried' during more profitable times. That is, there is a tendency for projects that have become unprofitable (in net present value terms) to accumulate when firms are consistently profitable and capital market pressures are minimal (a form of agency problem). Managers are reluctant to divest such projects because of reputation effects and the potential to incur high one-off restructuring or abandonment costs (Jensen 1986, Boot 1992). Thus managers may avoid divestment when they can get away with it, which may be the case when the firm is consistently profitable. Reporting a loss potentially leads to the resolution of some of these agency problems as managers divest non-performing projects to try to regain profitability as quickly as possible. Other options available to management also include cost cutting in discretionary areas like research and development. Investments in fixed assets are frequently lumpy and irreversible, rendering asset divestments less useful as a way of generating quick bottom-line impacts. Cutting employee numbers turns out to be a highly valuable 'response' lever in this situation. Changes in the level of investment in employees provides a continuum (non-lumpy) of divestment potential. It is also relevant that cost cutting in relation to employees is universally available whereas the potential to cut discretionary spending, such as research and development, is applicable to a limited range of settings where such expenses are incurred. Pinnuck and Lillis (2007) test two main hypotheses:

H1: *Ceteris paribus*, firms that report an accounting loss have a lower level of incremental investment in employees than economically equivalent firms that report an accounting profit.

H2: Firms that move from reporting an accounting profit to reporting an accounting loss have an abnormal negative change in investment in employees.

To test these hypotheses Pinnuck and Lillis draw on a sample of 77,711 firm-year observations from Compustat firms over the period 1983 to 2003. The study finds that:[2]

- The average percentage growth in number of employees is systematically lower for loss-making firms than for profit-making firms. There is a significant discontinuity at the threshold rather than a continuous distribution and the difference is not explained by differences in economic fundamentals between small loss and small profit firms. This is reflected in figure 1.

- Firms that cross the threshold from a profit to a loss disproportionately reduce their investment in employees in the year that they cross the threshold (reducing investment in employees seems to be reactive).

- The effect is more significant in the year following the threshold crossing – consistent with firms taking some time to decrease their investment in fixed labour.

- The employment decisions of firms that crossed the threshold are compared with a benchmark sample of firms with a similar earnings drop that did not cross the threshold. Across all quartiles of earnings decreases, the firms that switch from reporting a profit to reporting a small loss have statistically greater negative change in labour than any other firms with a similar earnings drop.

---

2 Refer to Pinnuck and Lillis (2007) for full model, regression results and robustness tests.

- Employment patterns are examined for the same cross section of firms based on cash flows. A similar kink in employment patterns is not observable (either visually or statistically) at the zero cash flow threshold. The observation of the discontinuity in employment patterns around the zero accounting profit threshold but not the zero cash flow threshold suggests that it is the accounting loss heuristic which is affecting the decisions of corporate managers.

Figure 1: Average annual percentage change in the number of employees by firms as a function of different levels of net income either side of the zero net income threshold (Pinnuck & Lillis 2007).

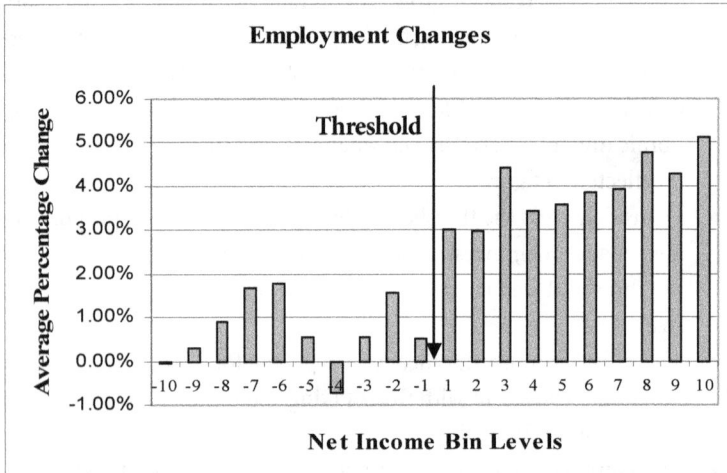

To summarize the findings of this study, the use of the accounting profit/loss threshold as a performance benchmark in a capital market setting causes this profit/loss threshold to act as an anxiety-inducing decision heuristic which has significant economic consequences. The reporting of a loss impacts on managerial behaviour as decisions are directed at quickly restoring profitability. Most notably, the observed shift in employment patterns at the threshold is above that which is explained by the decline in volume of activity. The availability, liquidity and divisibility of employees may render them particularly susceptible to 'management' to meet capital market performance expectations focused on accounting performance metrics. The determination to report an accounting profit appears to be a reaction to the decision influence of capital market pressures rather than such decisions reflecting the fundamental economics of the firm which should inform such decisions.

Study 2: Implementing manufacturing flexibility (Abernethy & Lillis 1995, Lillis 2002)

This section reflects on the results of two studies that address the influence of performance measurement on managerial behaviour from quite a different perspective. These studies examine how performance measurement within manufacturing sub-units affects managerial behaviour in the context of their 'buy-in' to strategies focused on responsiveness and flexibility. Conventional measures of manufacturing performance focus on efficiency and productivity (cost variances, scrap, downtime etc). These measures are well suited to manufacturing firms with high levels of product standardization, stable production processes and a focus on cost minimization (Brownell & Merchant 1990, Govindarajan 1988). However these attributes are no longer reflective of current strategic priorities in manufacturing. In figure 2, Lillis (2002) documents contemporary strategic priorities across a sample of 36 Melbourne-based manufacturing companies.

Figure 2 demonstrates the prevalence of multiple strategies focused on quality, service, customer responsiveness and dependability rather than low cost.

The market-driven shift in contemporary manufacturing priorities is captured in a quote from a local manufacturer producing heavy-duty men's work clothes. They "used to do long runs of '97 regulars' or efficient combinations of '82 regulars' and '112 stouts' put them in inventory and sell them" but are now facing demand for a varied mix of products at short lead times. While the product range in this example has remained relatively stable the firm has significantly increased its responsiveness to customers by shortening lead times and meeting greater within-order variety. These market-initiated changes have increased the rate of production changeovers, reduced batch sizes and increased disruption.

Figure 2: Classified summary of strategic orientations (Lillis, 2002).

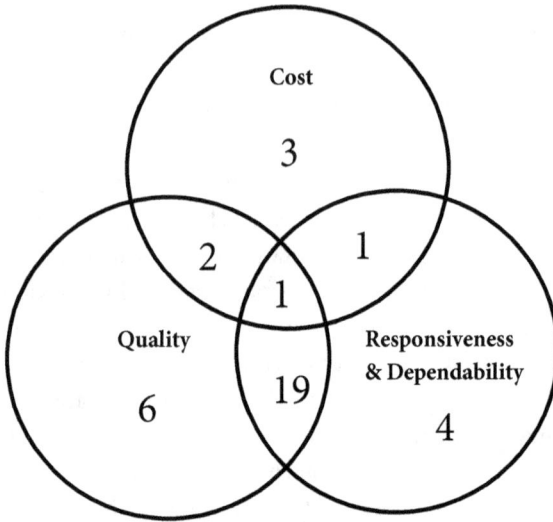

This imposes a management challenge of how to elicit responsiveness from manufacturing sub-units. Manufacturers facing these changed demands are superimposing customer-focused strategies on organizations where the management control infrastructure is not aligned with these strategies (Kaplan 1990). In order to be flexible enough to meet variable customer demands and associated short lead times, manufacturing and sales need to work much more collaboratively than has historically been the case (Parthasarthy & Sethi 1993, Bowen et al. 1989). Interdependencies are described as 'reciprocal' rather than sequential as manufacturing and sales managers negotiate 'joint' optimal solutions, rather than manufacturing determining optimal scheduling and efficient batch sizes (Van de Ven et al. 1976). To the extent that customer-focused strategies in manufacturing are superimposed on structural and performance measurement infrastructure that best supports manufacturing efficiency, it is difficult to get strategic 'buy-in' from manufacturing sub-units. How do you shift the mindset of efficient lot sizes and maximum throughput to allow for the costs of disruption associated with frequent changeovers, reduced batch sizes and greater product variety?

In settings with a strong commitment to customer responsiveness, the absence of standardization makes it increasingly difficult to specify unambiguous performance standards (Abernethy & Lillis 1995). Yet firms seem somewhat wedded to the use of efficiency measures in manufacturing. Lillis (2002) documents the performance measurement practices of the same firms profiled in figure 2. In figure 2, the strategic profile of these 36 firms was reflected in a strong emphasis on differentiation through a combination of quality, service and responsiveness strategies with little emphasis on low cost. Figure 3 shows the performance measurement practice in these same firms emphasizes cost, efficiency and productivity measurement in conjunction with a range of quality and customer service measures.

Figure 3: Classified summary of performance measures used to measure manufacturing performance (Lillis, 2002).

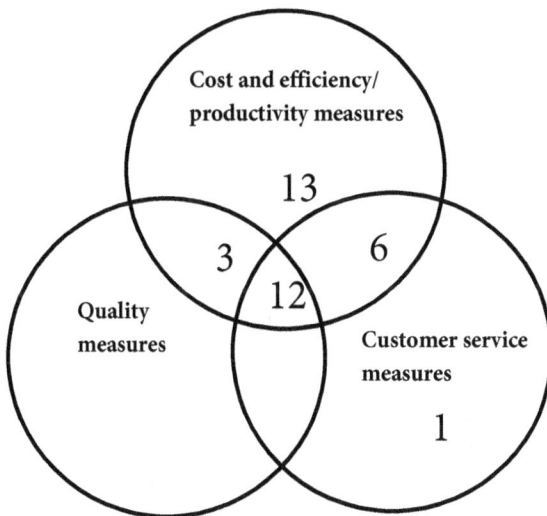

The emphasis on cost in performance measurement in figure 3 is somewhat incongruous given the strategic profile of the sample. While the performance measurement profile indicates the use of multiple measures which is consistent with advocated contemporary performance measurement practice, the extensive reliance on cost and efficiency/productivity measures is paradoxical. While it is clearly not the case that manufacturers focused on flexibility and responsiveness can ignore cost, flexibility and responsiveness are not low cost manufacturing options and on a day-to-day basis these strategic priorities involve trade-offs that require less than optimally efficient manufacturing. Lillis (2002) documents the challenge this poses. The continued emphasis on efficiency and productivity in manufacturing appears to occur because these are conventional management accounting and performance measurement practices that are difficult to dislodge. Yet profit centre managers speak of the difficulty of getting manufacturing managers 'on board' with strategies focused on responsiveness and flexibility (Lillis 2002):

> We're nowhere near as flexible as we would like. We always liken it to a battleship where it takes miles to turn it around.

> Production is so intent on meeting their weekly targets, if a special order comes in they tend to say "Oh no what a nuisance", rather than looking at the opportunity presented. And that's fair enough, that's where they're valued at ... That's their whole reward system. Yes [the special order does get done], but it takes a lot of management effort to tell people that they are going to do it.

> Setters [who set up machines for operators] and leading hands [who coordinate small groups of machine operators] are imbued with this view that the line must not stop and try as we may we cannot get that out of their thinking. The trouble is we have far too many long serving employees and they know that they have to get 25,000 products off that line this shift and they will do it ... They'll believe that they have done a good job and in fact there may be even some of the management mechanisms that tell them they're doing a good job. But it might not match the customer service angle and that's what's wrong.

The problem appears to be the internal inconsistencies among the multiple measures that are used to support complex strategies. Multiple measures of customer service and low cost may work well at the profit centre level where the impact of responsiveness can be gauged in terms of both cost and revenue functions. However, manufacturing sub-units are unable to evaluate these tradeoffs. In effect, the cost of disruption and short runs resides in the manufacturing sub-unit and the revenue benefits arising from customized, responsive sales flow to other parts of the firm.

Performance standards in manufacturing sub-units are generally constructed in the form of standard product costs that specify standard expectations in relation to material, labour and overhead input per unit of output. Such standards are set to reflect a specific efficiency or productivity level (assumed labour standard to assemble a certain number of units per hour). It is possible of course that the cost and efficiency measures used in these contemporary settings can be adapted to capture the costs of a quality and service focus. In an ideal world, it should be possible to reconfigure standard manufacturing performance measures to reflect the demands of responsiveness. It is, for example, possible to simply redevelop standard cost estimates (standard labour and material estimates) as quality expectations change. Efficiency standards can be altered and multiple measures can be used to encourage 'line stopping' to correct quality problems and reduce reject rates. Customer responsiveness is, however, a little different. The manufacturing cost implications of flexibility are inherently difficult to track. The manager of the industrial clothing manufacturer quoted above also said that he had "no idea of what responsiveness is costing and whether [the firm] should be refusing some level of responsiveness".

Responsiveness is by its nature unpredictable and disruptive. The costs are 'knowable' in the sense of additional setups and product customization costs but there is nothing standard about these costs. The number of setups and costs of customization vary depending on both the incidence and nature of specific customer requests. Firms struggle with this as they are unable to rewrite efficiency standards to incorporate the costs of disruption, but they want manufacturing sub-units to be prepared to 'wear' the disruption in the interests of customer responsiveness. In effect, these firms engage in the folly of rewarding efficiency while hoping for responsiveness. The way firms deal with this is to 'play down' the pressure around cost budgets and efficiency standards. In effect they rely less on accounting performance benchmarks as they would be 'counter-strategic'. Lillis (2002) documents that the most common mechanism for managing the inherent challenges in being responsive and efficient was to reduce the severity of reactions to variances.

Not only are conventional management accounting practices designed with cost-based manufacturing in mind, conventional structures within manufacturing firms also tend to support mass production at low cost. Efficiency was historically encouraged in manufacturing sub-units through task segregation or by 'buffering' manufacturing sub-units from the vagaries of markets and customers. Sales sub-units were charged with responsibility for dealing with customers (Bowen et al. 1989). Interdependencies between manufacturing and sales were always high but they were sequential in nature, with the sales and manufacturing interface managed through scheduling (Parthasarthy & Sethi 1993). While there is variation in the way scheduling is managed, the emphasis tends to be on manufacturing efficiency. In order to enhance flexibility many firms not only reduce the pressure to meet efficiency and productivity targets, they also make structural adjustments (Abernethy & Lillis 1995).

The structural response involves investing in integrative structural arrangements that facilitate cross-functional coordination and interaction (Bowen et al. 1989, Abernethy & Lillis 1995). Manufacturers enhance the levels of functional integration and collaboration required where strategies focus on responsiveness by adopting more organic, less mechanistic structures (Parthasarthy & Sethi 1993). These structural mechanisms include cross-functional teams, task forces and daily cross-functional meetings. The aim of these devices is to link the efficiency and productivity-focused mindset of manufacturing with the customer-focused mindset in sales, and to facilitate the joint development of optimal production solutions.

As indicated by the earlier quotations, flexibility implementation is frequently problematic but for those who juggle the performance measurement and structural requirements of flexibility, it works. "We have a fairly informal management structure. It's run a bit like a big milk bar."

From an accounting perspective, what is notable here is that performance measurement has not kept up with strategic change and the disaggregation of performance measurement into functional sub-units creates tensions. While decisions regarding optimal production scheduling and optimal levels of responsiveness should be informed by an organization-wide cost/benefit analysis, disaggregated performance measures that capture only part of the value chain influence managerial decision making and act as an impediment to strategy implementation.

Study 3: The Balanced Scorecard – a mechanism to reduce the dysfunctional consequences of managing by accounting outcomes (Grafton, Lillis & Widener 2008)

This section considers the question of whether performance measurement innovations, such as the Balanced Scorecard (BSC), solve the problem of performance measurement and dysfunctional managerial behaviour by broadening the base of performance measurement, identifying performance measures that are critical indicators of effective strategy implementation, and by capturing the dynamic nature of performance through a model of leading indicator and lagging outcome measures (Kaplan & Norton 1992, 1996). The prior sections suggest some of the dysfunctional consequences that arise from performance measurement that is locked into accounting metrics, short arbitrary timeframes, and 'silos' within firms. To some extent the BSC tries to address these issues by drawing on non-financial measures, by capturing multiperiod effects through leading and lagging measures and by focusing on the value chain of the firm rather than sub-unit optimization. Nonetheless the prior section raised a particular problem in performance measurement that the BSC may not resolve – the issue of disaggregation of a comprehensive profit centre scorecard to functional units which, by necessity, only partially reflect the firm's value chain. This section considers the broader potential of the BSC to reduce dysfunctional behaviour associated with over-reliance on accounting performance measures.

The Balanced Scorecard is a performance measurement innovation designed to specifically counter the adverse effects of managing directly by accounting numbers. This literature emphasizes that managing internal sub-units using metrics such as profits etc. focuses on outcomes but does not signal to managers what they have to do to improve outcomes (Kaplan &

Norton 1992). The BSC focuses on identifying and capturing useful information regarding performance on a set of 'leading' indicators – i.e. indicators that are causally linked with improvements in future financial performance. For example, a BSC might capture a measure such as customer retention on the basis that if you monitor customer retention it gives an early warning about how the firm might be tracking in relation to customers which will ultimately drive changes in revenue and profit. Regardless of the rationale underlying this key performance measurement innovation, the result is a broadening of performance measurement convention to embrace a wide-ranging set of financial and non-financial metrics that should have a causal link with future profits. The effect should be to encourage a medium to long-term focus, investment in intangible sources of growth and full development of business unit capabilities (Kaplan & Norton 1992, 1996). At a minimum, the effect should be to dilute the influence of accounting in evaluation, and thus reduce the extent to which managerial decision making is distorted by the need to 'perform' in short-term accounting terms.

However, there are challenges in reality associated with the implementation of a BSC. Some of these challenges relate to the potential for evaluation mechanisms to subvert the good intentions of the BSC. The BSC is fundamentally designed as a decision-facilitating tool. It provides a dashboard of measures that are basically designed to enhance the information available to managers in decision making. By targeting leading indicators, managers who seek to make decisions that improve on the BSC metrics should theoretically be implementing strategy effectively, and driving future financial performance improvements.

This rhetoric assumes that the BSC is a neutral management tool that will be used exactly as it was designed to be used to enhance managerial effectiveness. This literature has been either silent or equivocal on how this performance measurement innovation interacts with the mechanisms used to evaluate the performance of managers (Kaplan & Norton 1996). If decision-facilitating and decision-influencing measures remain disconnected, we may be back where we started. The BSC may be a good decision tool that just might not be used if the decisions it signals are not consistent with evaluation mechanisms. What if the manager is expected to use the BSC in decision making, but her bonus depends on sub-unit profit? Other researchers have documented that firms initially using a BSC try to reinforce the use of the scorecard by attaching incentives to performance on the full range of metrics. The problem is that perceptions of validity and reliability of metrics for evaluation and bonuses are somewhat different from the way the same criteria would be applied to information considered relevant for decision making. There are documented tendencies in practice to over-rely on conventional financial metrics when it comes to evaluation even when firms employ BSCs (Malina & Selto 2001; Lipe & Salterio 2000; Banker, Chang & Pizzini 2004). This appears to occur for a variety of reasons:

- They are well understood
- They are relatively 'reliable' and valid compared with softer measures such as employee and customer satisfaction, quality and responsiveness measures (Malina & Selto 2001)
- They are 'common' to all sub-units, whereas many other measures on the BSC may be situation-specific and thus not offer the opportunity for relative evaluation (Lipe & Salterio 2000)
- Compensation formulae become overly-complicated with too many metrics. Thus the complete BSC tends to be whittled down over time, and the accounting metrics tend to be the survivors (Malina & Selto 2001).

Thus there is scope to suggest that despite a very significant performance measurement innovation that is specifically designed to overcome the limitations of accounting, it is unlikely that the "folly of rewarding A while hoping for B" is fully resolved. Grafton, Lillis and Widener (2008) address this question directly. The researchers asked managers about two sets of performance measures – the measures they consider the most informative for running the business (typically a BSC-type set of measures) and the measures that are used by their superior management to evaluate their performance. Grafton, Lillis and Widener (2008) seek to establish how decision making patterns alter as the degree of commonality between the two sets of measures varies.

This study finds that:

- Among the managers interviewed there is a moderate degree of overlap between the measures they considered 'best' for running the business, and those used to evaluate performance (approximately 62% average commonality).
- The weighting on aggregate financial measures in evaluation is significantly greater than their usefulness in running the business (figure 4). Managers consider disaggregated financial information useful for running the business (measures such as sales by sub-unit/product line, costs, cash flows etc.). They consider aggregate financial measures such as profit and return on assets less useful. Yet there is a disproportionate reliance on aggregate financial measures in evaluation.
- Outcomes improve when firms do broaden evaluation protocols to embrace more of the measures that managers consider important. Grafton, Lillis and Widener (2008) find that the higher the level of commonality between the two sets of measures, the more the managers actually use the measures that are identified as important in running the business (and conversely the lower the level of commonality, the less they use these measures). The use of these measures improves the firm's ability to exploit its capabilities, both existing and future (as managers are using more effectively the range of 'high quality' measures available to them). In turn, the cases with higher commonality produce better financial performance outcomes. This result appears to be a function of greater use of the range of decision-facilitating measures and enhanced strategic responsiveness, not just a direct result of measuring accounting performance and driving improvement on that metric.

So does the BSC work? It is a performance-measurement innovation that has gained traction in practice. It has led to a significant shift in performance-measurement practice *within* organizations in that managers rely less on broad accounting performance measures than they did a decade ago. However there are still challenges. The BSC is designed primarily to facilitate decisions. Whether or not it manages to do so depends very much on how it links with performance evaluation (decision-influencing mechanisms) throughout the firm.

Figure 4

Summary results – decision-facilitating measures.

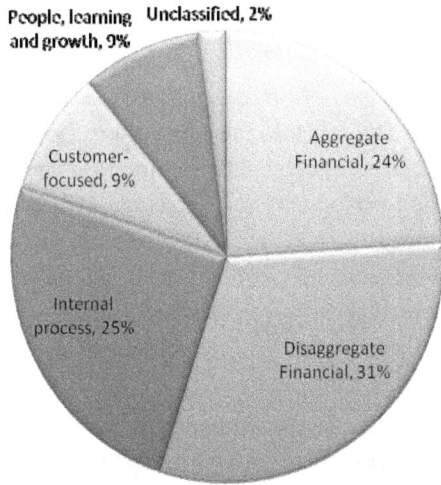

Summary results – decision-influencing measures.

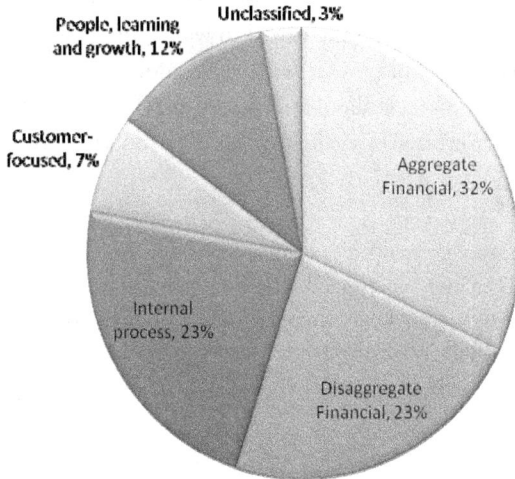

Firms could broaden performance evaluation protocols to fully exploit the content of a BSC. However there are impediments to doing this and firms seem reluctant to do it. Many measures that are effective for decision facilitation are too 'soft' and 'subjective' for use in performance evaluation (Banker et al. 2004, Malina & Selto 2001). In any case, evaluation still changes the agenda. The measures are no longer there just because they are important as a decision facilitator. The fact that they are used in evaluation shifts the agenda and introduces more potential for gaming and manipulation. To the extent that evaluation protocols remain accounting-focused and disconnected from the array of decision-facilitating measures that managers want to use, the potential remains for dysfunctional decision making, driven by performance measures that are 'incomplete' for any one of a range of reasons.

Concluding comments

In this chapter I have examined the link between performance measurement and managerial decision making from a range of perspectives. Dysfunctional decision making is attributed to capital market pressure to meet accounting benchmarks and to internal firm pressures to meet intra-organizational, silo-focused performance measures that only partially capture the firm's value chain. The chapter also examines the extent to which, in broad terms, the BSC is in fact a tool that induces long-term value adding decisions as it is promoted to do. What is notable about this discussion is its historical origins: the decision distortion created by evaluation has deep roots in the literature. To quote Kerr (1975):

> in the absence of formal reinforcement some soldiers will be patriotic, some presidents will be ecology minded, and some orphanage directors will care about children. The point, however, is that in such cases the rewarder is not causing the behaviors desired but is only a fortunate bystander. For an organization to act upon its members, the formal reward system should positively reinforce desired behaviors, not constitute an obstacle to be overcome.

It is evident in the contemporary research discussed in this chapter that firms still struggle with this tension, and it appears unlikely that performance measurement innovation such as the BSC has all the answers. However the genesis and broad-scale adoption of technologies such as the Balanced Scorecard and Economic Value Added (EVA) reflect the fact that there is broad awareness of accounting-induced decision myopia and the desire to correct it. Performance measurement innovation has become a critical concern among both academics and practitioners over the past two decades. While the issues addressed in this chapter are not, and indeed may never be, fully resolved, there is ample evidence of both research and consulting attention to the fundamental dilemma of how to induce value-adding, long-term decision making in organizations.

References

Abernethy MA & Lillis AM (1995). The impact of manufacturing flexibility on management control system design. *Accounting, Organizations and Society,* 20: 241–58.

Banker RD, Chang H & Pizzini MJ (2004). The Balanced Scorecard: judgmental effects of performance measures linked to strategy. *The Accounting Review,* 79(1): 1–23.

Boot A (1992). Why hang on to losers? Divestitures and takeovers. *The Journal of Finance,* 47: 1401–23.

Bowen DE, Siehl C & Schneider B (1989). A framework for analysing customer service orientations in manufacturing. *Academy of Management Review,* 14(1): 75–95.

Brownell P & Merchant KA (1990). The budgetary and performance influences of product standardization and manufacturing process automation. *Journal of Accounting Research,* 28(2): 388–97.

Burgstahler D & Dichev I (1997b). Earnings management to avoid earnings decreases and losses. *Journal of Accounting and Economics,* 24: 99–126.

Dechow P, Richardson S & Tuna I (2003). Why are earnings kinky? An examination of the earnings management explanation. *Review of Accounting Studies,* 8: 355–84.

Demski JS & Feltham GA (1976). *Cost determination: a conceptual approach.* Ames: Iowa State University Press.

Govindarajan V (1988). A contingency approach to strategy implementation at the business unit level: integrating administrative mechanisms with strategy. *Academy of Management Journal*, 31(4): 828–53.

Grafton J, Lillis AM & Widener S (2008). The influence of evaluation mechanisms on the use of decision facilitating performance measurement information. Working paper.

Hayn C (1995). The information content of losses. *Journal of Accounting and Economics*, 20: 125–53.

Jensen M (1986). Agency costs of free cash flow, corporate finance and takeovers. *The American Economic Review*, 76: 323–29.

Kaplan RN (Ed) (1990). *Measures for manufacturing excellence*. Boston, MA: Harvard Business School Press.

Kaplan RS & Norton DP (1992). The Balanced Scorecard – measures that drive performance. *Harvard Business Review*, 70(1): 71–79.

Kaplan RS & Norton DP (1996). *The Balanced Scorecard*. Boston, MA: Harvard Business School Press.

Kerr S (1975). On the folly of rewarding A, while hoping for B. *Academy of Management Journal*, 18(4): 769–84.

Lillis AM (2002). Managing multiple dimensions of manufacturing performance – an exploratory study. *Accounting, Organizations and Society*, 27: 497–529.

Lipe MG & Salterio S (2000). The Balanced Scorecard: judgmental effects of common and unique performance measures. *The Accounting Review*, 75(3): 283–96.

Malina MA & Selto FH (2001). Communicating and controlling strategy: an empirical study of the effectiveness of the Balanced Scorecard. *Management Accounting Research*, 13: 47–90.

Narayanan VG & Davila A (1998). Using delegation and control systems to mitigate the trade-off between the performance-evaluation and belief-revision uses of accounting signals. *Journal of Accounting and Economics*, 25(3): 255–82.

Parthasarthy R & Sethi SP (1992). The impact of flexible automation on business strategy and organizational structure. *Academy of Management Review*, 17(1): 86–111.

Pinnuck M & Lillis AM (2007). Profit versus losses: does reporting an accounting loss act as a heuristic trigger to exercise the abandonment option and divest employees? *The Accounting Review*, 82(4): 1031–53.

Solomons D (1965). *Divisional performance: measurement and control*. Illinois: Irwin.

Van de Ven AH, Delbecq AL & Koenig R Jnr (1976). Determinants of co-ordination modes within organizations. *American Sociological Review*, 41(2): 322–38.

11

Framing strategic resource management

Rodney Coyte (University of Sydney)

Abstract

This essay is presented in three parts. First, it situates the unfolding development of the concept of strategic resource management and indicates how it
was constituted by and helped reconstitute, the discourse and paradigm of
the community of practice of management accounting in the late 1980s to the
beginning of the 21st century. Second, it elaborates the evolved concept, explaining its integrating ideas and components, and identifies the
improvement methodologies and calculative technologies 'enrolled' in its
construction. Finally, it concludes by discussing the contribution made and
its contemporary relevance.

In 2008 I was kindly asked to contribute to a volume in honour of the work
of Professor Bill Birkett. I was both delighted to be involved and daunted by
the task of concisely encapsulating his extensive work reconstituting and
situating management accounting within a rapidly evolving strategic framework. Bill was a brilliant colleague and wonderful man who motivated and
inspired all those who worked with him across the wide breadth of subject
areas addressed in this volume, not the least of which was strategy and resource management. I got to know Bill in the early 1980s initially as a
Masters student in a Corporate Planning class he gave (and later as his PhD
student and colleague). As with everything he did, the class was interesting,
engaging, informed, enjoyable, rigorous, well structured and visionary. His
work in developing the concept and discipline of strategic resource management was no exception.

Bill was a master of the use of diagrams to represent complex ideas and interrelationships about the phenomena he explored. Diagrams were used extensively in the many practitioner and academic forums in which he framed strategic resource management and visualized a reconstituted management accounting practice of the future. Diagrams were a powerful form of visual representation for work which often tied together previously unrelated strands of such extant literatures as strategic management, management practice, business improvement, finance theory, and the sociological institutions and psychological attributes which govern knowing, thinking and meaning creation. Several of the diagrams from the initial framing and more recent 'evolved' framing of strategic resource management form an important resource for this essay.

Framing strategic resource management: developing management accounting

Before embarking on a detailed discussion of the evolved concept of 'strategic resource management' it is important to spend some time sketching the antecedents of this concept and how its development was intertwined (Modell & Weisel 2008) with the changing nature and importance of the accounting and finance function, particularly that part which constitutes management accounting work.

Introduction and background

By the late 1980s it was widely accepted that increasing the effectiveness of the development, management and deployment of resources was vital to the effective implementation and realization of enterprise strategy (Barney 1991, Grant 2002). From antecedents in evolutionary economics (Penrose 1959), the resource-based view of strategy (Nelson & Winter 1982), an alternative to the design or planning school (Andrews et al. 1965, Ansoff 1979), had been articulated.

Rather than 'fitting' the organization to the external environment the focus on achieving competitive advantage turned inwards. Internal capabilities, based on combinations of resources, developed from learning generated in situated organizational practices (Cook & Brown 1999), offered a competitive edge. Core competences (Hamel & Prahalad 1989, 1990) existed where these capabilities provided long-term advantages that could not be directly replicated by competitors. Capability development required that organizational resources be better understood, more actively managed and explicitly exploited in realizing strategy.

At the same time, the management accounting profession, as constituted in Anglo-Saxon countries[1] (Bhimani 1996, Birkett 1998), and 'management accounting work' as commonly performed by management accountants,[2] were seen as losing relevance (Johnson & Kaplan 1987). The focus on cost management, in the form of 'traditional'[3] product and process costing and variance analysis, could not provide the information for decision-facilitation information (Demski 2002; Demski & Feltham 1977; Christensen & Feltham 2003, 2005; Kupper 2009) required to maintain competitiveness in a business environment characterized by accelerating change and 'hyper-competition'.

Much of what constituted management accounting work at the time was cost accounting and this was both reflected in, and reinforced by, the accounting courses of the major teaching institutions. The role of management accounting was subordinate to financial accounting work in most organizations, generally not strategic in its orientation, nor reflective of the firm's position within an overall value creating system (Porter 1985). But advances were happening in practice (Simmonds 1981), in the situated learning that occurred within more innovative firms and with their professional advisors

1 Management accounting work is performed by professionals with varying educational and practice backgrounds in different countries, under different functional labels. The role of 'management accountant' is most clearly defined and more likely to be labelled as such in Anglo-Saxon countries. By contrast, in Germany and France, management accounting work is more likely to be performed by engineers and industrial economists, than by accounting trained professionals.

2 It is clear that many 'contemporary management accounting techniques' are adopted and claimed by other non-accounting professionals in other organizational functions. See, for example, Langfield-Smith 2008.

3 'Traditional' means full-absorption costing rather than an activity-based costing approach (Johnson & Kaplan 1987).

(Howell & Soucy 1987). Improvements were being made which enhanced the relevance of management accounting work and academics were beginning to respond by reframing management accounting work as strategic management accounting (Simmonds 1981, Bromwich & Bhimani 1989, Bromwich 1990) or strategic cost management (Shank & Govindarajan 1988, 1989; Shank 1989). However, due to institutionalized beliefs, and likely due to inadequacies in management accountant skill sets (Cooper 1996a, 1996b), the diffusion process, through mimetic and normative isomorphic processes (Di Maggio & Powell 1983), was slow and lacked coordination.

Against this backdrop, the Australian Centre for Management Accounting Development (ACMAD) was established at the beginning of the 1990s, with the co-sponsorship of major universities, the Federal Government, business members (in several states) and support from the professional accounting bodies. ACMAD's overall aim was to advance management accounting practice. It pursued this by helping to reorient and expand management accounting work, to enhance its relevance to business strategy (both its creation and realization), and to do this in a manner that raised its organizational profile. A key aspect of this aim was achieved by increasing academic involvement with the practitioner network to inform accounting practices, teaching and research. ACMAD aimed for a virtuous cycle of learning through the broadening and development of this 'community of practice' (Lave & Wenger 1991) where practitioners and professional bodies could share experiences both to inform, and derive greater benefits from, academic research and teaching.

Professor Birkett acted as the centre's director for over a decade, enrolling (Callon 1999, Law 1992) various actors (accounting and non-accounting professionals, academics and consultants) in this practice network, developing its scope and level of activity, establishing connections with other accounting bodies, and influencing the agenda around the (re)constitution of management accounting. An example of the latter is the contributions made by ACMAD to the issue agenda and concept publications of the International Federation of Accountants, Management Accounting Committee.[4]

From cost management to strategic resource management

As is clear from the breadth of work in this volume, not only was Professor Birkett the director and driver of ACMAD he also acted as a 'thought leader' in many aspects of management accounting work and the arenas it affected. Situating management accounting strategically was a key part of this work, as was positioning it within what was termed 'a world-class accounting/finance function'. The latter (detailed in figure 1 below) affects an opening of mindsets to include activities and change methodologies not traditionally viewed as part of the arena of operation of accountants and accounting work, and allows management accounting involvement in financial, stakeholder, systems and functional management. For example, this includes (stakeholder) management of customers, suppliers and employees; culture, capabilities and benchmarking within the accounting function; and systems management of process variables and information.

'Strategic resource management' was framed as a vision for practice, research and teaching, and to signal a clear break from the cost management and costing focus of the past. This vision encompassed strategic management, financial management and cost and process management, and provided a framework for the enactment of the 'world-class finance/accounting function'. It became a key overriding theme of many ACMAD endeavours from practitioner presentations, breakfast forums, seminars, cooperative research projects, publications, training programs, and education courses (such as the Management Accounting Qualification courses developed by ACMAD for practitioners). Strategic resource management operated as an umbrella term to enrol and tie the various actors to the agenda of advancing management accounting research and practice, and its theme was communicated in many forms. For example, the importance of the strategic management of resources is described in the IFAC professional concept statement:

---

4 For example, Coyte (1995) and Birkett (1998b).

Figure 1

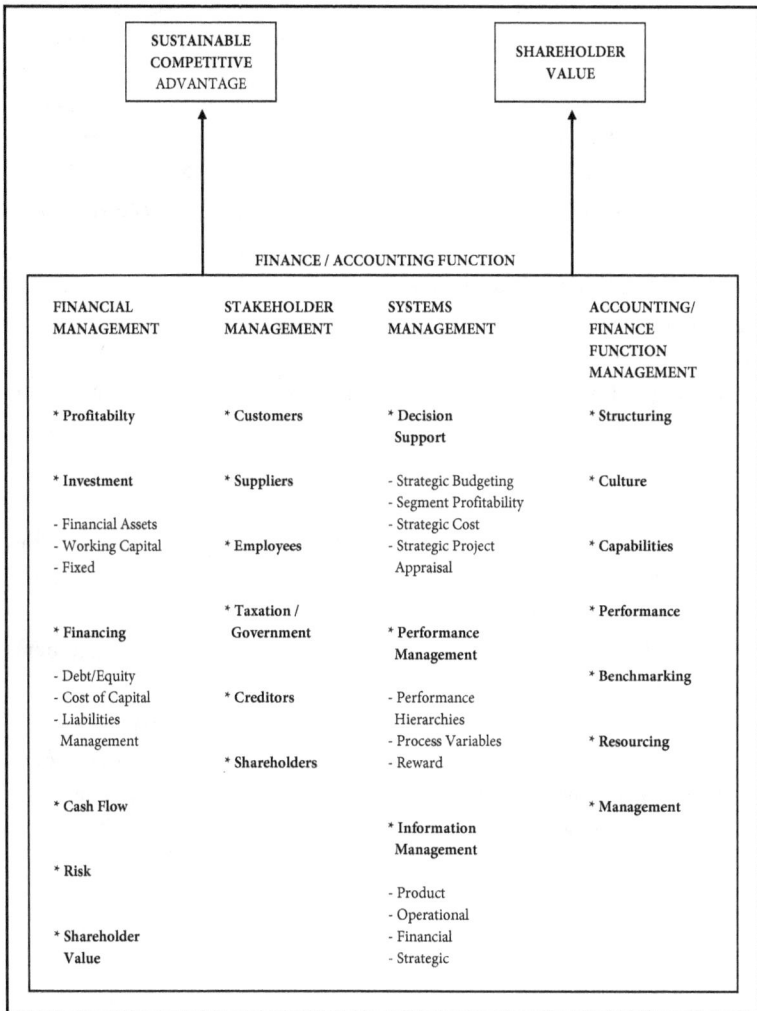

SUSTAINABLE COMPETITIVE ADVANTAGE			SHAREHOLDER VALUE

FINANCE / ACCOUNTING FUNCTION

FINANCIAL MANAGEMENT	STAKEHOLDER MANAGEMENT	SYSTEMS MANAGEMENT	ACCOUNTING/ FINANCE FUNCTION MANAGEMENT
* Profitabilty	* Customers	* Decision Support	* Structuring
* Investment	* Suppliers	- Strategic Budgeting	* Culture
- Financial Assets		- Segment Profitability	
- Working Capital		- Strategic Cost	
- Fixed	* Employees	- Strategic Project Appraisal	* Capabilities
	* Taxation /		* Performance
* Financing	Government	* Performance Management	
- Debt/Equity			* Benchmarking
- Cost of Capital	* Creditors	- Performance	
- Liabilities Management		Hierarchies	
	* Shareholders	- Process Variables	* Resourcing
		- Reward	
* Cash Flow			* Management
		* Information Management	
* Risk			
		- Product	
		- Operational	
* Shareholder Value		- Financial	
		- Strategic	

Source: Prof WP Birkett, School of Accounting, UNSW, c1994.

The management of resourcing and resource use is integral to both strategy realization and organizational change; effective resource deployments are necessary to support organizational objectives and strategies, and ongoing organizational change is likely to require ongoing redeployments of resources. Indeed the success of management in securing the vitality and endurance of the organization is likely to be dependent on the effectiveness with which it deploys and redeploys resources (Birkett 1998b, paragraph 24).

The concept of 'strategic resource management' was not fixed (Emsley 2008) but 'malleable' and evolved through the 1990s to encompass changes in the strategic environment and the opportunity these provided for expanding management accounting work and the skill set of management accountants. The concept was also a means of aligning and positioning 'management accounting technologies' for operational and process improvements within the enactment of strategy.

Initial framing of strategic resource management

Strategic resource management was initially centred on a concept of 'the duality of strategy' representing the supporting structures and processes for strategy realization, and the organizational tension in pursuing the simultaneous creation of value for the two key stakeholders: owners and customers. It is described as follows:

> Strategic resource management focuses on ways in which organizations utilize all available resources to generate value over time. Attention is given to the drivers of both shareholder and customer value as guides to organizational performance in capital and product/service markets. The transformation of financial resources in and out of financial forms is at issue, as is the elimination of waste in the process. The key question is: How does resource deployment effectively support strategy in the midst of organizational change? (Management Accounting Qualification, *Introduction to Strategic Resource Management*, 1996, p6).

In this concept the goals of owner and customer value creation are privileged over other stakeholders. Attention is drawn to strategies for financing (to minimize the cost of capital) and to the efficiency and effectiveness of the deployment of financial resources to long-term and operational asset acquisitions, and to resourcing organizational processes (i.e. to people acquiring and using assets and information resources to produce products or provide services which create value for customers). In this view customer value is generally defined as the excess of benefit received over the price paid, and owner value is measured by economic profit or the surplus remaining from profit after the costs of capital are recovered.[5] The concept of the duality of strategy is detailed in the value creation strategies illustrated in figure 2. Customer value is created through business strategies around product/service offerings. It is a necessary but insufficient criterion for shareholder value creation. The latter requires that investment in resourcing product/service strategies be managed and financed (through the lowest achievable cost of capital) in a manner which results in economic profit. Over investment and/or a high cost of capital, due to a sub-optimal financing structure, could result in shareholder value destruction even with success in the marketplace, a lesson learned from the 1980s economic boom.

Framing strategic resource management as integral to a 'world-class finance/accounting function' had its affect on management accounting by communicating and sanctioning change, and by repositioning management accounting work as strategic in nature and management accountants as having more powerful strategic roles.

---

5 In simple terms, economic profit is the surplus after all costs, including the cost of capital employed, are recovered. However, it could be measured in subtly different ways depending on which 'shareholder value' measurement approach is adopted. Some widely used techniques at the time included Stewart's EVA™ (Stewart 1995); Rappaport's shareholder value analysis (SVA) and the Boston Consulting Group's Total Shareholder Return (TSR). See Barbara and Coyte (1999) for a detailed comparison of these approaches.

Figure 2

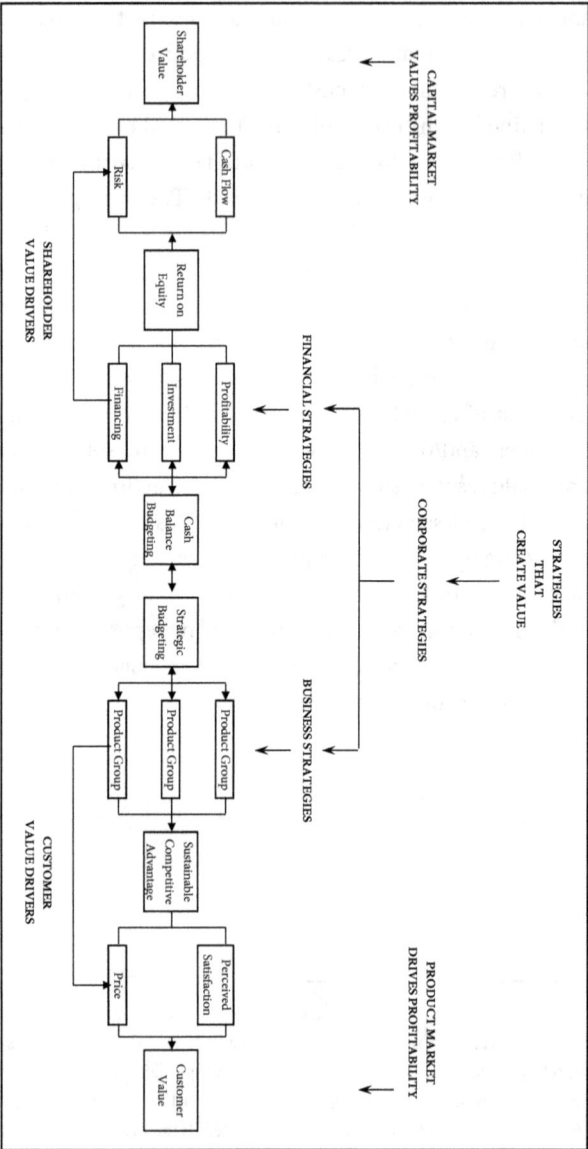

Figure 2

Source: Prof WP Birkett, School of Accounting, UNSW, c1994.

Opening spaces

The initial construct facilitated efforts to legitimate a particular reproduction of management accounting. Importantly, 'strategic resource management' was sufficiently flexible to allow a range of management and organizational improvement methodologies to be embraced as 'contemporary management accounting technologies'. This assisted ACMAD to enrol participants and colonize techniques not developed by 'management accountants' and those not previously considered within the purview of management accounting practice.[6] These techniques were developed in more general areas of practice improvement around business processes in manufacturing enterprises and included: benchmarking, just-in-time manufacturing, Kan Ban, Kaizen, business process re-engineering, process value analysis, cost driver analysis, and total quality control. They were perceived as appropriate ways of improving and managing resource use in product/service market strategies, financing strategies and in supporting processes. The early strategic resource management construct established process management as a key element, helping to legitimize accounting interest and involvement in the effectiveness of the deployment of resources to processes providing and supporting product/service offerings.

Being labelled 'management accounting techniques' signified that these methods were a normal part of the community of practice, and helped generate a broader understanding of the knowledge, technical skills, and change (and people) management abilities that were needed by 'management accountants' to manage resources strategically.

Managing meaning

The term 'strategic resource management' allowed scope for actors to attribute meaning in ways that related to their own situated context. *Strategic* can connote product/service market endeavours, enterprise-wide effects, integral

---

6 The opposite is generally taken for granted in extant literature. That is, the view portrayed is that these are management accounting techniques which are implemented by others (Langfield-Smith 2008, p222).

to success, sponsored by senior management, and be either planning or acting or both. *Resource* connotes anything that could be used to achieve ends or objectives and broadened mindsets to consider intangible as well as financial and physical resources. Although the construct did not initially focus directly on intangible resources it provided the scope for this to occur (as it did towards the end of the 1990s with ACMAD-sponsored forums on the subject presented by Karl Sveiby [1997, 2001], a thought leader and pioneer in the area and by the corporate psychotherapist, Margot Cairns [1998], of the softer skills needed by management accountants). *Management* connotes planning, coordination and control over any type of organizational process and activity, clearly signalling higher-level organizational activities than transaction processing, costing and variance analysis characterized in the traditional role.

Enhancing power

The legitimization conferred and meaning conveyed by strategic resource management supported the enhancement of the position, profile and power of the management accountant and management accounting work. Scope was provided for management accounting involvement (intervention) into resource deployment, consumption and conversion aspects of almost every type of organizational process, and to operate at the most senior levels of the organization. ACMAD facilitated this repositioning through involvement of senior management in the numerous and regular business issue forums, other networking activities, and the many other activities mentioned earlier.

Figure 3

	COST ACCOUNTING		MANAGEMENT ACCOUNTING		(STRATEGIC) COST MANAGEMENT		STRATEGIC RESOURCE MANAGEMENT
	PRIOR TO 1950	*Absorption *Constitution →	1965 1950 → 1965 1965 → 1985	*Consolidation *Reformation →	1985 1985 → 1999	*Absorption *Redefinition →	2000 1995 → 2010
	Antecedent Generation		**Classic Generation**		**Contemporary Generation**		**Coming Generation**

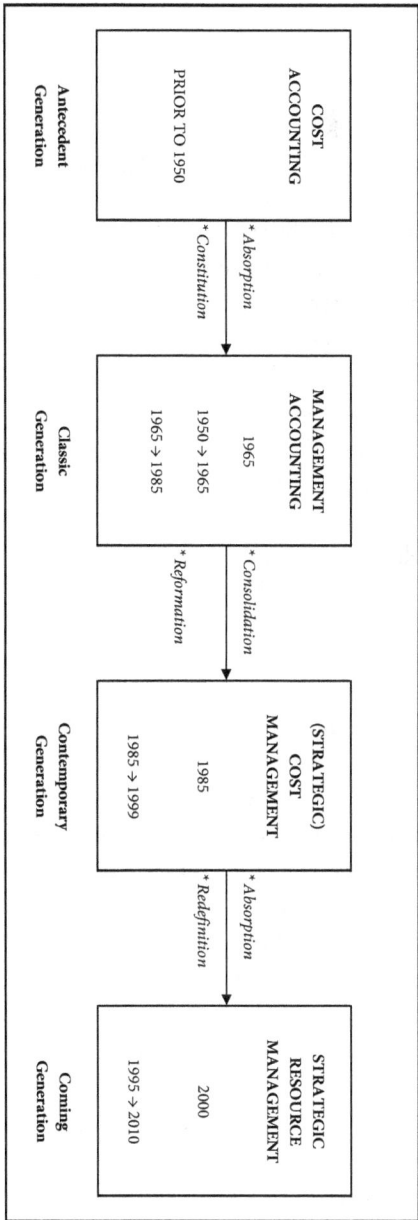

Source: Prof WP Birkett, School of Accounting, UNSW, Address to the National Institute of Accountants National Congress, October 1996.

Situated in time

Strategic resource management was also positioned as the future of management accounting. Figure 3 illustrates how the conception of management accounting had progressed from 'costing' to 'strategic cost management' and was becoming 'strategic resource management'. The change in terminology from 'cost' to 'resource' broadened the paradigm of management accounting work allowing it to be constructed according to the situation of the organization in terms of its key stakeholders, competitive situation and organizational objectives. It would 'absorb' strategic cost management technologies and be 'redefined' as more vital to organizational success and with few constraints to the application of its skill set to organization processes and decisions. In this way it envisioned the future for management accounting, past strategic cost management (regarded as the "third stage of the development of the management accounting discipline" (Shank 2007 cited in Langfield-Smith 2008, p207) and elevated thinking above the debate taking place in the field at the time.

A confluence of factors

A confluence of factors provided the opportunity for a more strategic resource-based orientation for management accounting and for the development of commensurate skills in management accounting professionals. This vision for management accounting was constituted within a complex intertwining of forces in the business environment, practice and research which affected the development of ACMAD and were affected by it. Management accounting was reproduced as 'strategic resource management' within this process.

The business environment of the time was changing rapidly. The economic boom of the late 1980s ended in a severe recession in the early 1990s. So significant were the many large corporate bankruptcies that some of the major Australian banks recorded their first ever loss. The regulatory environment was tightened in response to societal pressures to prevent what was generally referred to at the time as the 'corporate excesses of the 80s' from ever happening again. Corporate balance sheets were being rebuilt; financial resources were scarce and had to be managed more conservatively. Share-holder value (economic profit) metrics (Rappaport 1986) had increased their influence on business financing decisions and performance evaluation methods and decisions made by institutional investors (Barbera & Coyte 1999).

In response to the 1991–92 recession, increased efforts were made to reduce waste and inefficiency in organizational processes, and resource deployment was more carefully scrutinized for the 'value' created. These efforts built on earlier changes resulting from the previous recession and an overall decline in the 1970s and early 1980s of competitiveness compared to Japanese manufacturing firms, the latter which had increasingly prompted adoption of quality and process improvement practices in (non-Japanese) Western firms. In addition to total quality management, these practices included benchmarking, business process re-engineering, empowered teams, continuous improvement, manufacturing resource planning, target costing, process value analysis, and just-in-time throughput control and inventory management. Business conditions of the early 1990s were, once again, driving a change in perspectives about resources and their deployment in value creating processes. Business improvement efforts were encouraged by government funding of initiatives to research, model and diffuse best practice throughout the Australian business community. The National Industry Extension Service (NIES) was established to liaise with business organizations and centres such as ACMAD, and collaborative research projects were established (see, for example, Birkett et al. 1992). Programs such as the Best Practice Demonstration Program were funded to research, document and disseminate corporate examples as models for the Australian business community (Rimmer et al. 1996). 'Best practice' organizations were supported with funding and encouraged to disseminate their approach by presenting at forums, participating in benchmarking programs and facilitating visits by other organizations. At the same time productivity gains in information and communications technology (ICT) were rapidly expanding the capability to automatically capture, store and process information, and were providing new opportunities for efficiency, through enhanced coordination and reduced transaction costs, in areas as diverse as supply chain management and marketing. These gains accelerated through the 1990s as the World Wide

Web made such interorganizational connections feasible for organizations with insufficient transaction volumes or which were too small to economically operate the electronic data interchange systems of the 1980s and early 1990s.

As mentioned above, during the late 1980s and early 1990s, debate raged in academic and practitioner literature about the role and relevance of management accounting work. Situated in the world of cost control and cost management the status and value of traditional management accountant roles were under challenge (Johnson & Kaplan 1987). The emphasis on transaction processing, report preparation and variance analysis in these roles made them more vulnerable than financial controllership to the rapid advances in integrated business applications, such as manufacturing resource planning (MRP II) and, later, enterprise resource planning (ERP) systems, which were often implemented by other organizational functions. Automation of transaction processing reduced the value and status of the traditional cost accounting role. By contrast, the profile and status of the financial roles were growing with the increasing sophistication of financial instruments and changes in capital management techniques which provided opportunities to enhance shareholder value from existing operations. Framing management accounting work as strategic resource management provided scope to lift the relevance and status of management accounting work.

Management accounting syllabi at academic institutions significantly lagged behind developments in practice, as did the most widely used textbooks of the late 1980s and early 1990s. By the early 1990s practitioner-oriented journals were including work on strategic cost management and value chain analysis (Govindarajan & Shank 1992) as frameworks within which cost analysis and value analysis could be performed. However, neither provided the comprehensiveness of strategic resource management. Through the planning and influence of Professor Birkett the undergraduate and postgraduate streams in management accounting at University of New South Wales were redesigned in the mid-1990s to encompass the scope of strategic resource management. In the redesigned stream, the first course addressed process management and the second strategic value management. In addition, the Management Accounting Qualification was developed by ACMAD to provide a postgraduate qualification to enhance the skills of accounting professionals and business managers. It included subjects in strategic resource management, business strategy, and current developments in management accounting and managing.

The framing of the concept also constituted an elaboration of the skill set required to manage resources strategically. The view of what constituted management accounting work needed to be matched by the ability of management accountants. However, 'management accounting work' could, and was, being performed by 'others'. For example, process analysis by engineers and business analysts and industrial economists; benchmarking by a variety of 'others'; capital project appraisal by engineers; economic profit measurement by finance professionals; some aspects of performance management and reward setting by human resource professionals; and customer value and profitability analysis by marketing analysts. What then would differentiate management accountants from other professionals with the skills to implement some of these techniques? To conduct the new role envisioned, the management accountant would "need to develop not only sufficient technical skills but also social skills" (Langfield-Smith 2008, p220). They would need: the ability to deal with both quantitative and qualitative information; strong communication skills in dealing with all levels of the organization; political abilities; skill at building relationships and networks; a broad interest in and understanding of a range of business issues; a willingness to be involved and proactive; an ability to think strategically; and an ability to work in a team environment. They would need a strategic perspective, an understanding of the change needed, of the techniques available and of the ability to manage their implementation. Many ACMAD initiatives, within the framework of strategic resource management, as well as more progressive university and professional education and training courses, were structured to provide these skills.

Strategic resource management evolved

The first part of this essay briefly explained the initial concept of strategic resource management and recounted its framing, situatedness and unfolding conceptual development to show how it was constituted by, and helped re-constitute, the discourse and paradigm of the community of practice of management accounting in the 1990s.

In this section the evolved framing of 'strategic resource management' in the early 21st century will be examined in detail to explain its integrating ideas and components. The improvement methodologies and calculative technologies 'enrolled' will be identified.

Integrating notions

The duality of strategy: aligning resource mobilization with strategic management to enhance current and future value creating capability

The major theme underlying strategic resource management continued to be the 'duality of strategy' as illustrated in figure 4. In this view however, strategic duality represents the simultaneous management of:

- the mobilization of resources to generate and sustain capabilities to provide and support the *current* portfolio of products and services
- the capacity to develop new capabilities to sustain the value creating potential of the enterprise into the 'unknowable' distant and remote *future.*

The evolved duality of strategy is predicated on a particular view of how macro environmental issues faced by organizations (Johnson et al. 2005) are changing in the 21st century. Macro environmental influences both constrain strategic choice and create opportunities that can be exploited by strategy. They are categorized as more general factors such as: political, economic, social, technological, environmental and legal influences; and more specific competitive influences which constitute a second level of the macro envi-ronment and effect competition in the industry, sector or strategic group in which the firm operates.

Figure 4

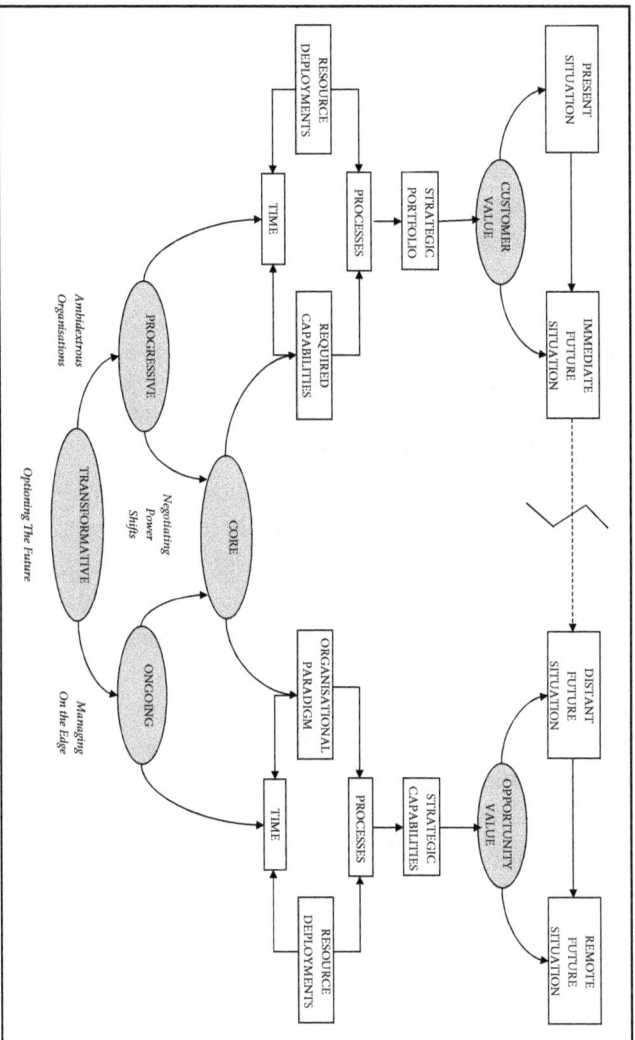

Source: Slide 15 in Managent Accounting: what is the future? Prof WP Birkett, IMM Finance Conference, 22/05/2000.

While these conceptions of the levels of macro environmental analysis have existed since the 1980s, it is the way environmental influences are changing, and what such change means for organizational strategy and resource management, which is the focus of the evolved framing of strategic resource management. This framing extends Toffler's (1980) theory of three waves of economic and technological change to a fourth wave recognising ecological and social issues that must be dealt with by strategic management. Hope and Hope (1997, p2) describe these waves as:

> the agricultural wave, which lasted from 8000 B.C. to the mid-eighteenth century; the industrial wave, which lasted until the late twentieth century; and finally, the information wave which began in the 1960s. The first wave was driven by physical labour, the second wave by machines and blue-collar workers, and the third by information technology and knowledge workers.

The third wave is characterized by the impact of technology (outsourcing, virtual organizations, integrated supply chains); the global market (investment of financial and knowledge resources without geographic restrictions); government-driven changes (deregulation and privatization, lowering of protection); the changing face of competition (blurring of industry boundaries, alliances); the changing pattern of employment (contracting and casualization); and the rise of knowledge as *the* key economic resource (Hope & Hope 1997, pp5–10).

The transition from the second to the third wave is portrayed in strategic resource management to be an evolution from: a repetitive environment (before 1950) that could be dealt with by extrapolation (capacity planning for expanded demand) after 1950; to discontinuous (fluctuations and shifts in demand) from the 1960s; accelerative (change) from the 1970s; and chaotic from the 1990s. In the fourth wave, from 2000 onwards, the macro environment is characterized as constrained. The latter periods reflect an increased rate of change, the impact of the World Wide Web and social and ecological sustainability imperatives. In the fourth wave organizations must deal with environments constrained by the need to create value for major stakeholders without destroying value for any stakeholder either in the present or the future. (This somewhat prophetic characterisation of the future also provides a framework for dealing with the increased regulatory environment arising from the global financial crisis of 2008–09).

In this evolved frame the meaning of the duality of strategy has changed with shareholder and customer value creation repositioned within an organizational sustainability model.[7] Over the long term, organizational sustainability requires the creation of value in the present and provision for value generation in the future. Customer and owner value are created through the existing strategic portfolio of products and services derived from current capabilities and competences and resourced through existing processes. Value generation in the 'remote' and 'distant' future, framed as 'opportunity value', is derived from the generation of new strategic capabilities. Such capabilities are developed through innovation in technologies, processes and modes of organising, through managing options, and through constant renegotiation of the organizational paradigms about products, services, markets, technologies, stakeholders and values. This environment will also be characterized by 're'-regulation, as society loses confidence in the ability of unfettered free markets to achieve sustainability objectives.

Traditionally, organizations have been influenced by, and have focused attention on, their most powerful stakeholders. However, in the contemporary business environment the ability to sustain value creation is also dependent on enterprise awareness and management of the potential sources of value destruction (or risks to value creation) for a broader range of stakeholders, inter-temporally. In this view organizations must manage their strategy, capabilities and competences, and pay attention to *all* stakeholders, to mitigate risks to value creation in the present and in the future. The notion of the 'duality of strategy' raises awareness and directs behaviour to manage value-creating enterprises in the contemporary environment and the 'fourth wave' environment of economic, social and ecological accountability.

---

7 See, for example, Elkington (1997) who proposes that organizations manage to a new, expanded 'triple bottom line' which incorporates economic, social and natural /environmental dimensions of enterprise performance.

Figure 5

	Before 1950	By 1965	By 1985	By 2000	Beyond 2000
Label	Cost Accounting	Management Accounting	(Strategic) Cost Management	Strategic Resource Management	Strategic Value Management
Evolutionary Landscape	Repetitive	Extrapolative	Discontinuous, Accelarative	Chaotic	Constrained
Outcome Focus	Cost	Profitability	Waste	Innovation	Stewardship
Organisational Problematic	Co-ordination	Congruence	Seamless	Virtual	Communitarian
Focus of Technologies	Budgeting, Costing	Planning, Control	Strategy, Change	Value Generation, Leveraging Capabilities	Value Exploration, Inclusive Creativity
Central Metric	Statistical	Financial	Non-financial	Opportunity Value	Tripple Bottom Line
Mode of Rationality	Calculative	Information Provision	Process Management	Time/space Management	Sustainability

Source: Slide 16 in Manageent Accounting: what is the future? Prof WP Birkett, IMM Finance Conference, 22/05/2000.

The transition from strategic resource management to the post-2000 fourth wave environment is represented in figure 5 as a shift to a yet broader concept of 'strategic value management', which incorporates strategic resource management. This vision of the future presents an inter-generational perspective which values diversity, is cognisant of externalities and enacts responsibility within a goal of stewardship over resources.

In the evolved framework the traditional focus on dominant stakeholders such as shareholders and customers, while essential for economic sustainability, is constrained by social forces and increasing regulation. In this view, value for shareholders and customers can no longer be achieved at the expense of 'other' stakeholders. Although, the 'other' may appear to be much less powerful and influential, value destruction (both current and inter-generational) can invoke external responses such as legal action, social and moral sanction, and destruction of reputational resources followed by financial resource destruction. For an enterprise which destroys value for some stakeholders in the pursuit of customer and shareholder value, diminution of intellectual and knowledge resources may also occur. For example, highly-skilled people (with employment choice) may not want to join such an enterprise and some of those already with the enterprise may choose to leave, seeking other opportunities, rather than be identified with or be seen as apologists for enterprises facing legal action or social sanction.

This vision of the fourth wave highlights a global domain, a more open organizational structure and increased virtuality, broader networks of inter-relationships, and the need for management to align their actions with social and environmental responsibilities, through responsible business practices. In the fourth wave competitive products and services, especially those that can be digitized, can emanate from outside geographic or national boundaries, as can resources. Relationships are increasingly important in drawing together the resources necessary to compete. Organizations rely on partnerships such as alliances and joint ventures, outsourced goods and services, contracted expertise, and complementary product and service providers to construct their own offering. Ownership and employment are less important than access and control over important resources. Networks, operating on trust and mutual value creation, become increasingly important. Virtual structures confer advantage by being more flexible and adaptable than more traditionally structured competitors. In this view organizations must deal with continual change and inherent contradictions in their competitive environments. For example, competitors in one market place may be collaborative partners in another spawning the awkward term 'co-opetition' in contemporary strategy literature (Brandenburger 1998).

Interlinked value generation

The evolved framing of strategic resource management stresses the increasingly interlinked mode of value generation. Financial, physical and human resources develop (other) intangible resources (such as reputation, intellectual property and technical and market knowledge). In turn, intangible resources generate financial resources (through, for example, revenue growth and enhanced profitability). Over time, failure to deliver value to, and sustain relationships with, resource contributors and customers will result in value destruction for owners.

In the fourth wave the focus is on value; not just its creation but also its maintenance. Value is exposed to loss and resources to waste. Risk to value is managed through performance appraisal systems and option management, and loss through waste is minimized through resource allocation and process management. Performance management systems are designed to move organizations towards value creation and away from value destruction. In this view, risk management becomes a key role of management accounting. Environmental, strategic, operational and reputational risk (Simons 2000) must be managed to prevent value destruction.

Resources and value creation are constituted by values

Broadly, organizations are formed to create value through the effective acquisition, generation and deployment (combination and mobilization) of resources and manage this process by setting strategy. Within the constraints of economic, social and environmental responsibilities and intergenerational outcomes, organizations should provide value for all resource contributors, with the organization's nature, structure, aims and raison d'être, determining the focus of value creation efforts. For example, a charity will direct effort to creating value for major benefactors and service recipients; a public enterprise will focus on the government, the public and the service recipients; and, in a business enterprise, focus is on creating value for shareholders and customers.

What constitutes both a 'resource' and 'value creation' will be determined by the value systems of stakeholders. A resource is "anything that is or could be entirely or partially of some use for something else – whatever 'things' are and however the use and ends are defined and interpreted" (Diefenbach 2006, p409). For things to become thought of and drawn upon as resources they must be valued. A 'thing' will not be regarded as a potential resource unless it is valued by someone or some group, that is, unless it is perceived to be of value or useful for developing value for a stakeholder in some context. What is considered to be of value will be based on value systems.

Rethinking resources

Strategic resource management entails an understanding of what 'things' (physical, conceptual, behavioural and affective) are constituted as resources of actual or potential value for an organization and its stakeholders, and how they can be used to achieve long-term strategic objectives and sustainable value creation. The evolved concept more explicitly details types of resources and provides the basis for expanding thinking and enhancing understanding of what constitutes organizational resources, essential if they are to be effectively managed.

Figure 6 provides an expansive view of resource types and provides a sense of process. Process is reflected in the transformation of financial resources into other types of resources, resulting in value creation or waste. In this evolved framing intangible resources are central and their combination with financial and physical resources in the value-creating process is emphasized. This reflects the growing recognition of the importance of intangibles through the 1990s and beyond, and can be contrasted with the initial concept, where resources were described more generally and attention tended to be on financial and physical resources along with cost, time and value attributes. Now 'core competences' confer 'strategic capabilities' and forms of

Figure 6

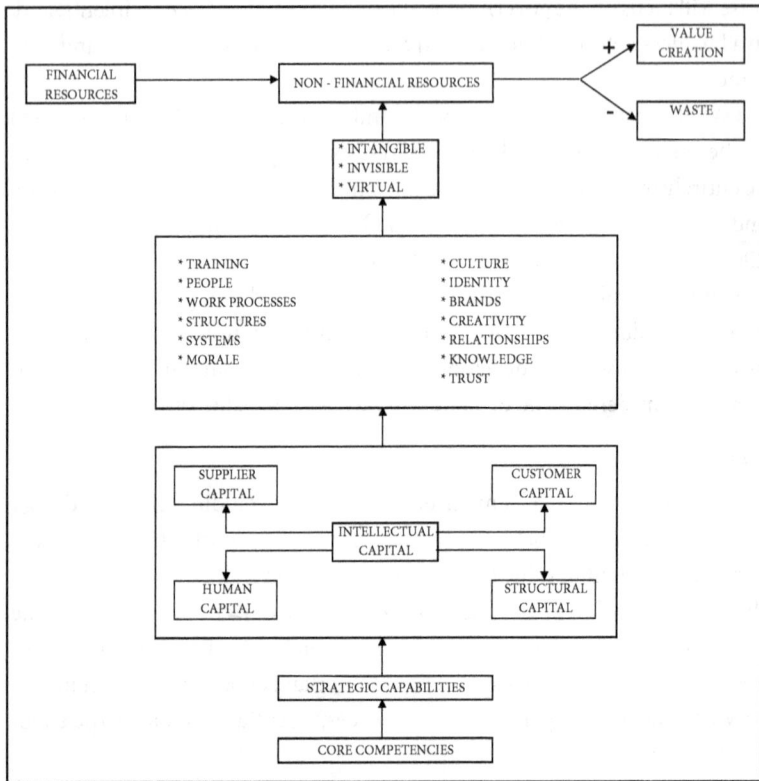

Source: Slide 13 in Manageent Accounting: what is the future? Prof WP Birkett, IMM Finance Conference, 22/05/2000.

intellectual capital are based on intangible, 'invisible' and 'virtual' things such as knowledge, trust, relationships and morale.

Resources available to organizations are of many types and have widely different attributes; they are seen to exist externally as well as internally. They can be owned, leased, employed, accessed when needed (supplier networks and distribution channels) or drawn upon in activities (such as trust, relationships and reputation).

The 'intangible', 'invisible' and 'virtual' labels convey the problematic character of resources, their transitory nature, the difficulty in measuring their value (which will depend on the way they are deployed in combination) and their potential to grow with use (for example, knowledge, trust and reputation). This characterization also highlights the potential fragility of many types of intangible resources. For example, reputation can take a long time to build but can be lost overnight if risk is poorly managed.

Tools and techniques to examine the effectiveness of strategic resource management

In summary, strategic resource management guides organizations in choosing modes of operation and cooperation and in improving and evaluating the effectiveness with which they mobilize resources to realize strategy and manage risks to value. Strategic resource management highlights the nexus between strategy, resourcing, organizing and change.

Given the more comprehensive framing of strategic resource management there is scope for inclusion of a wide variety of techniques in its application. As mentioned at the beginning of this essay, strategic resource management is not fixed but a malleable concept which may be used to colonize any type of performance analysis or evaluation technique; and any improvement method that can be applied in the pursuit of value-creation endeavours. In this section, the tools commonly regarded as part of the antecedent frameworks of strategic management accounting (SMA) and strategic cost management (SCM) will be identified before expanding this list to incorporate the tools and techniques used in the framing, application and teaching of the strategic resource management approach to management accounting work.

In comparison with strategic resource management, SMA and SCM are earlier and more traditional approaches to the development of a strategic orientation to management accounting practice (Anderson, 2007). Essentially, they remain within the realm of financial information analysis, based (mostly) on internally generated information.[9] SMA includes "target costing, life-cycle costing, strategic cost analysis, competitor cost analysis, activity-based costing, activity-based management, attribute costing, life-cycle costing and strategic performance measurement systems" (Langfield-Smith 2008, p206). SMA is regarded by some as 'broader than SCM' which is described as "the blending of the financial analysis elements of three themes from the strategic management literature – value analysis, strategic positioning analysis, and cost driver analysis" (Langfield-Smith 2008, p206).

Compared to SMA and SCM, strategic resource management is a much broader and more complete framework for directing, evaluating and improving resource management to realize strategy in a way that mitigates risk, optimizes financing and manages constraints. It encompasses techniques which not only deal with financial resources but also focus on the drivers of resource consumption and value generation – quality, time, waste, opportunity cost and option value. Figure 7, which elaborates on a vision for the future of management accounting, is annotated with the range of techniques that can be applied in the process of strategic resource management and the areas in which each applies. It illustrates the integral role of strategic resource management and its future evolution (as portrayed in 2000) into a role within a 'strategic value management' focus. This vision also helps open the practice to many techniques which analyze non-financial information to understand drivers of future value creation.

Contribution and conclusion

The framing of strategic resource management broadened and repositioned management accounting work for accounting and management practitioners, academics and management accounting students enrolled in this practice network with national and international reach. This is particularly so in the Australian context and in Anglo-Saxon countries in which management accounting practice has a traditional lineage.

---

9 The exceptions being competitor cost analysis and the use of non-financial performance measures in strategic performance management systems (SPMS).

Figure 7

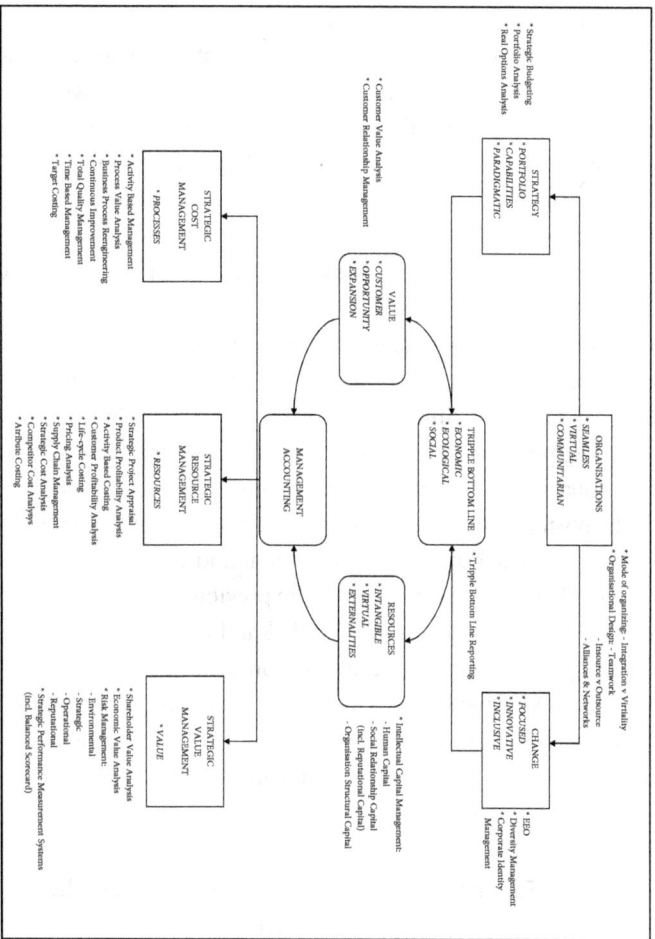

STRATEGY
* PORTFOLIO
* CAPABILITIES
* PARADIGMATIC

* Strategic Budgeting
* Portfolio Analysis
* Real Options Analysis

ORGANISATIONS
* SEAMLESS
* VIRTUAL
* COMMUNITARIAN

* Mode of organising: - Integration v Virtuality
* Organisational Design: - Teamwork
  - Insource v Outsource
  - Alliances & Networks

CHANGE
* FOCUSED
* INNOVATIVE
* INCLUSIVE

* EEO
* Diversity Management
* Corporate Identity Management

STRATEGIC COST MANAGEMENT
* PROCESSES

* Customer Value Analysis
* Customer Relationship Management

* Activity Based Management
* Process Value Analysis
* Business Process Reengineering
* Continuous Improvement
* Total Quality Management
* Time Based Management
* Target Costing

VALUE
* CUSTOMER
* OPPORTUNITY
* EXPANSION

MANAGEMENT ACCOUNTING

TRIPPLE BOTTOM LINE
* ECONOMIC
* ECOLOGICAL
* SOCIAL

* Tripple Bottom Line Reporting

STRATEGIC RESOURCE MANAGEMENT
* RESOURCES

RESOURCES
* INTANGIBLE
* VIRTUAL
* EXTERNALITIES

* Strategic Project Appraisal
* Product Profitability Analysis
* Activity Based Costing
* Customer Profitability Analysis
* Life-cycle Costing
* Pricing Analysis
* Supply Chain Management
* Strategic Cost Analysis
* Competitor Cost Analysys
* Attribute Costing

* Intellectual Capital Management:
  - Human Capital
  - Social Relationship Capital
  (incl. Reputational Capital)
  - Organisation Structural Capital

STRATEGIC VALUE MANAGEMENT
* VALUE

* Shareholder Value Analysis
* Economic Value Analysis
* Risk Management:
  - Environmental
  - Strategic
  - Operational
  - Reputational
* Strategic Performance Measurement Systems
(incl. Balanced Scorecard)

Adapted from Slide 19 in Manageent Accounting: what is the future? Prof WP Birkett, IMM Finance Conference, 22/05/2000.

Whilst research has not been conducted to assess the adoption of the holistic and visionary strategic resource management framework as a comprehensive plan for organizational strategic management, what is clear is that its promotion as a way of thinking has influenced a great many management accounting practitioners and their professional bodies. In addition, it has influenced the many management professionals who became involved in the frequent and various ACMAD activities, as well as academic research and teaching, and the curricula of management accounting and management courses.

The framing of strategic resource management has also helped increase the awareness, understanding and adoption of SMA/SCM concepts throughout organizational functions. Importantly, it has played a role in giving meaning to the alignment of individual action and decision making with group and functional implementation of improvement techniques; and consequently with business unit or corporate strategic management of product/service portfolios, capability development and risk management. What the framework does better than any of the previous frameworks such as SMA and SCM is to provide a more detailed and interlinked basis for understanding alignment than any technique on its own, including the widely used SPMS, the Balanced Scorecard. It has provided a way of thinking, tying together traditionally disparate areas within a sophisticated conceptual framework, in a manner not previously attempted.

References

Anderson S (2007). Managing cost and cost structures throughout the value chain: research on strategic cost management. In CS Chapman, AG Hopwood & MD Shields (Eds), *Handbook of management accounting research*, 1, (pp481–506). Oxford: Elsevier.

Andrews KE, Learned CR, Christensen R & Guth W (1965). *Business policy: text and cases*. Homewood, US: Richard Irwin.

Ansoff I (1979). *Strategic management*. New York: John Wiley & Sons.

Barbera M & Coyte R (1999). Shareholder value demystified: an explanation of methodologies and use. *The Australian Centre for Management Accounting Development*. Sydney: UNSW Press.

Barney J (1991). Firm resources and sustained competitive advantage. *Journal of Management*, 17: 99–120.

Bhimani A (1996). *Management accounting: European perspectives*. Oxford: Oxford University Press.

Birkett WP, Barbera MP, Chua WF, Fatseas VA, Luckett PF & Macmullen JS (1992). Cost management in small manufacturing enterprises. *The Australian Centre for Management Accounting Development*. Sydney: UNSW Press.

Birkett WP (1998a). Management accounting in Europe: a view from Down-Under. *Management Accounting Research*, 9: 485–94.

Birkett WP (1998b). *Management accounting concepts*. New York: International Federation of Accountants.

Brandenburger A (1998). *Co-opetition*. New York: Doubleday.

Bromwich M & Bhimani A (1989). *Management accounting: evolution not revolution*. London: Chartered Institute of Management Accountants.

Bromwich M (1990). The case for strategic management accounting: the role of accounting information for strategy in competitive markets. *Accounting, Organizations and Society*, 15(1–2): 27–46.

Callon M (1999). Actor-network theory – the market test. In J Law & J Hassard (Eds), *Actor-network theory and after*. Oxford: Blackwell.

Cairns M (1998). *Approaching the corporate heart: breaking through to new horizons of personal and professional success*. Sydney: Simon & Schuster.

Christensen PO & Feltham GA (2003). *Economics of accounting, volume 1: information in markets*. Boston, MA: Kluwer.

Christensen PO & Feltham GA (2005). *Economics of accounting, volume 2: performance evaluation*. Boston, MA: Kluwer.

Cook SD & Brown JS (1999). Bridging epistemologies: the generative dance between organizational knowledge and organizational knowing. *Organization Science*, 10(4): 381–400.

Cooper R (1996a). Look out, management accountants, part 1. *Management Accounting*, 77(11): 20–26.

Cooper R (1996b). Look out, management accountants, part 2. *Management Accounting*, 77(12): 35–41.

Coyte R (1995). The role of management accounting in the emerging empowered teams approach to work. *Management Accounting Committee Issue Statement no. 5*. New York: International Federation of Accountants.

Demski JS (2002). Management accounting. In H-U Kupper & A Wagenhofer (Eds), *Handworterbuch unternehmenschrechnung und controlling* (*Lexicon for accounting and controlling*), (pp1231–43). Stuttgart: Poeschel Verlag.

Demski JS & Feltham GA (1977). *Cost determination: a conceptual approach*. Iowa: Amis.

Diefenbach T (2006). Intangible resources: a categorical system of knowledge and other intangible assets. *Journal of Intellectual Capital*, 7(3): 406–20.

Di Maggio PJ & Powell WW (1983). The Iron Cage Revisited: Institutional Isomorphism and Collective Rationality in Organizational Fields. *American Sociological Review*, 48(2): 147–60.

Elkington J (1997). *Cannibals with forks*. Oxford: Capstone.

Emsley D (2008). Different interpretations of a 'fixed' concept: implementing Juran's cost of quality from an actor-network perspective. *Accounting, Auditing and Accountability Journal*, 21(3): 375-97.

Govindarajan V & Shank J (1992). Strategic cost management: tailoring controls to strategies. *Journal of Cost Management*, 6: 14–24.

Grant RM (2002). The concept of strategy. *Contemporary strategy analysis: concepts, techniques, applications*, 4th edn. Cambridge, MA: Blackwell.

Hamel G & Prahalad CK (1989). Strategic intent. *Harvard Business Review*, 67(3): 63–76.

Hamel G & Prahalad CK (1990). The core competence of the corporation. *Harvard Business Review*, 68(3): 79–91.

Hope J & Hope T (1997). *Competing in the third wave: the ten key management issues of the information age*. Boston, MA: Harvard Business School Press.

Howell RA & Soucy GR (1987). Cost accounting in the new manufacturing environment. *Management Accounting* (US), 69(2): 42–48.

Johnson G, Scholes K & Whittington R (2005). *Exploring corporate strategy: text and cases*, 7th edn. Harlow, UK: Financial Times Prentice Hall.

Johnson HT & Kaplan RS (1987). *Relevance lost: the rise and fall of management accounting*. Boston, MA: Harvard Business School Press.

Kupper H (2009). Investment-based cost accounting as a fundamental basis of decision oriented management accounting. *Abacus*, 45(2): 249–74.

Langfield-Smith K (2008). Strategic management accounting: how far have we come in 25 years? *Accounting, Auditing and Accountability Journal*, 21(2): 204–28.

Lave J & Wenger E (1991). *Situated learning: legitimate peripheral participation*. Cambridge: Cambridge University Press.

Law J (1992). Notes on the theory of the actor-network: ordering, strategy and heterogeneity. *Systems Practice*, 5: 379–93.

Modell S & Wiesel F (2008). Marketization and performance management in Swedish central government: a comparative institutionalist study. *Abacus*, 44(3):251–83.

Nelson RR & Winter SG (1982). *An evolutionary theory of economic change*. Cambridge, MA: Belknap Press.

Penrose ET (1959). *The theory of the growth of the firm*. Oxford: Oxford University Press.

Porter ME (1985). *Competitive advantage: creating and sustaining superior performance*. New York: The Free Press.

Rappaport A (1986). *Creating shareholder value: the new standard for business performance*. New York: The Free Press.

Rimmer M, Macneil J, Chenhall R, Langfield-Smith K & Watts L (1996). *Reinventing competitiveness: achieving best practice in Australia*. South Melbourne: Pitman.

Shank JK (1989). Strategic cost management: new wine or just new bottles? *Management Accounting Research*, 1: 47–65.

Shank JK (2007). Strategic cost management: upsizing, downsizing, and right (?) sizing. In A Bhimani (Ed), *Contemporary issues in management accounting*, (pp355–79). Oxford: Oxford University Press.

Shank JK & Govindarajan V (1988). Making strategy explicit in cost analysis a case study. *Sloan Management Review*, 29(3): 19–29.

Shank JK & Govindarajan V (1989). *Strategic cost analysis – the evolution from managerial to strategic accounting*. Homewood, IL: Irwin.

Shank JK & Govindarajan V (1992). Strategic cost management and the value chain. *Journal of Cost Management*, 6(3): 5–21.

Simons R (2000). *Performance measurement and control systems for implementing strategy: text and cases*. Upper Saddle River, NJ: Prentice Hall.

Simmonds K (1981). Strategic management accounting. *Management Accounting*, 59(4): 26–30.

Stewart GB (1991). *The quest for value: the EVA™ management guide*. New York: Harper Business.

Stewart TA (1995). Getting real about brainpower. *Fortune*, 132(11): 201–03.

Sveiby KE (1997). *The new organizational wealth: managing and measuring knowledge-based assets*. San Francisco: Berrett-Koehler.

Sveiby KE (2001). A knowledge-based theory of the firm to guide in strategy formulation. *Journal of Intellectual Capital*, 2(4): 344–57.

Toffler A (1980). *The third wave*. London: Pan.

12

Strategic resource management and technology innovation: an Australian story

Paul Andon, Jane Baxter and Linda Chang (UNSW)

Abstract

This chapter narrates the strategic resource management practices of the Bishop Technology Group, an innovative Australian organization. The case study focuses on this in the context of the creative and commercial aspects of technology innovation. The creative aspects of technology innovation were managed through the development of a creative culture, an open management style, participation in decision making, supportive structures, the use of performance measures, and patenting. The commercial aspects were addressed via the development of the firm's business model. The coupling of these creative and commercial elements of technology innovation may be understood in terms of key themes characteristic of the notion of strategic resource management championed by Birkett (see Coyte 2009 in this publication), namely balancing tensions between short- and long-term perspectives, continuity and change, focus and flexibility, and adequacy and expectations with respect to organizational resourcing.

Everybody loves the garage tinkerer who sells his brainchild to a big company and becomes a billionaire; and everybody sympathises with the plucky entrepreneur seeking venture capital for his little start-up company (*The Economist*, 12 February 1999, p12).

This chapter owes much to the work and insight of the late Professor Bill Birkett. First and foremost, this chapter is based on a series of interviews that were undertaken in conjunction with Bill from 1999 to 2001, investigating the strategic resource management practices (Birkett et al. 1992, Coyte 2009) of an innovative Australian organization. These interviews characterized the shifts in relation to strategic resource management that were occurring as organizational participants sought to maintain a creative and agile, yet relatively small, Australian organization capable of being competitive in a global marketplace. Second, this chapter was made possible because of the institution building that was Bill's signature competence and passion throughout his academic career. In particular, as Professor of Accounting at UNSW, Bill developed the Australian Centre for Management Accounting Development (ACMAD), which flourished under his leadership and promoted knowledge-sharing within a diverse and very active network of practitioners and academics. Our research was sponsored by ACMAD as part of this endeavour. In the chapter which follows, we pick up strands of the dialogue that ACMAD sought to sustain, seeking to encourage the diffusion of, and reflection on, a range of organizational practices. In particular, this chapter outlines the case of the Bishop Technology Group, an innovative Australian organization which fascinated Bill. The narrative focuses on the ways in which resources were furnished and mobilized to maintain and develop this organization's core creative capabilities, which underpinned its strategy of technology innovation.[1]

---

1 This case study was conducted between September 1999 and May 2001. Data were collected by interviewing and some document study. Interviews were conducted with a variety of organizational participants, including: the founder; the CEO; finance director; heads of each of the four business units; and a number of team leaders and innovators (of varying ages and levels of experience). Fourteen semi-structured interviews were conducted, with verbatim transcripts being produced from each audio-taped interview. In addition, four unstructured interviews were conducted, with notes taken. Interviews ranged from 45 minutes to two hours each. Proprietary documents cited in this study were made available by the CEO.

An innovative Australian organization

The Bishop Technology Group (BTG) was established by Australian inventor, the late Dr Arthur Bishop. Arthur Bishop left school at 17, embarking concurrently on an apprenticeship in fitting and turning and a diploma in mechanical engineering. The technological core of BTG stemmed from the wartime employment of Arthur Bishop. During World War II, he was involved in solving the problem of a 'violent shimmy or wobble' in aircraft landing gear supplied from the UK, which proved to be unsuitable for the condition of Australian runways.[2] Based on a mechanism used in film projectors, he was able to overcome this problem by developing a "variable ratio hydraulic damper". A resulting down-payment from the US Air Force, and a steady and substantial stream of royalties, enabled Arthur Bishop to continue his quest for technology innovation in Australia under the auspices of BTG.

BTG is a dynamic and fluid organization. At the time of our study, BTG was organized around four distinct business units.

1) *Bishop Steering* embodied the emotional and historical core of BTG. It leveraged and exploited the first inventions of Dr Arthur Bishop in the global automotive marketplace, with Bishop steering technology being used in over 20% of vehicles worldwide.

2) *Bishop Manufacturing* made high precision tooling and machinery.

3) *Bishop Innovation* constituted the 'sand pit' of BTG, investigating new technologies and patenting, as well as commercializing them.

4) *Bishop Austrans* emerged from Arthur Bishop's desire to create an automated people mover. It was a cash-hungry, risky and ambitious systems development.

This structure was augmented by a number of joint ventures and licence agreements.

---

2 See speech by A Bishop (1990) and www.bishopsteering.com/Company.htm.

The business of technology innovation

The core business of BTG was technology innovation. The commercialization of new technologies provided financial resources enabling BTG to
sustain a virtuous cycle of technology innovation and market development.
BTG relied on both *product* and *process* innovations for this (Drucker 1998,
Leifer et al. 2000, Kash 1989, Kok & Biemans 2009).

Figure 1: Bishop variable ratio technology – rack and pinion steering.

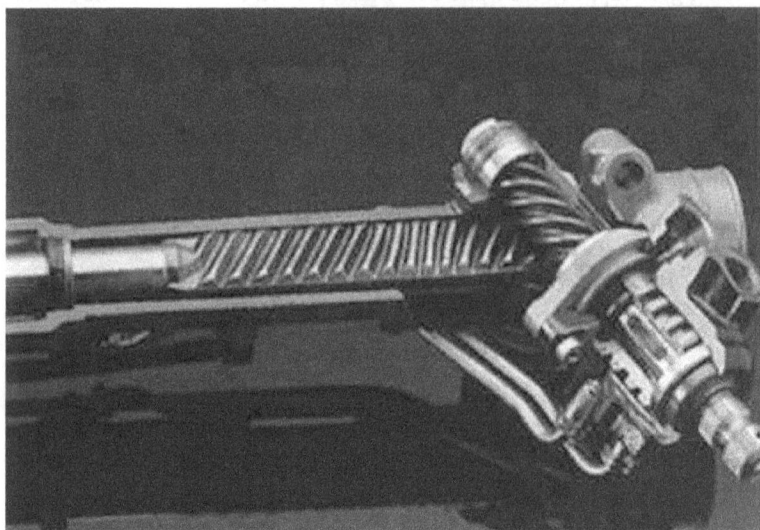

Source: www.bishopsteering.com/VR.htm

The seminal product innovation of BTG was variable ratio steering technology. Arthur Bishop developed variable ratio steering technology by
exploiting knowledge that he acquired from working on aeroplane steering
during the World War II. Variable ratio steering technology is based on a
rack and pinion gear (see figure 1).

The most distinctive feature of this technology is the uneven (or variably
spaced) teeth on the rack. The teeth on the pinion, in comparison, are evenly
spaced. Yet they mesh together smoothly when a car is steered. To mechanical engineers this is 'quite amazing'. Variable ratio steering technology

enables automotive engineers to achieve better vehicle suspension and safety. This technology has been the object of continuous innovation and improvement by BTG.

Whilst the invention of variable ratio steering technology helped solve a number of problems associated with steering in cars, it created a major problem for BTG. It was 'excruciatingly difficult' to make. Yet the commercialization of this technology required a corequisite capability to manufacture it at a level of cost, quality and rate of output acceptable to incumbents in the automotive industry. Consequently, there was a need to develop new methods of manufacture. Substantial process innovation was required as a result of the invention of variable ratio racks. A number of different process technologies were tried before converging on an innovative 'black art' known as warm forging.

In warm forging, the metal to be formed into the rack is washed, and then heated by an induction heater to about 760°C. The hot metal is rolled by two side punches into a toothed die. Automotive manufacturers may purchase the Bishop Y-Forging Die equipment (see figure 2) to produce racks using warm forging. The Y-Forging Die produces cost-effective, high quality steering racks in 12 seconds, while minimizing the amount of waste material and finishing required in relation to rival process technologies.[3]

Warm forging exemplifies a guiding principle of technology innovation within BTG:

> we have always done [this] with all of our processes. We've always offered automation so that you have absolute control. You don't have ... labour influencing the quality.

The capacity of BTG to engage in both product *and* process technology innovations conferred benefits on the group. First, it unlocked and enhanced the creative capacity of organizational participants, removing the constraints of incumbent technologies and methods of manufacture. Second, the coupling of product and process innovation also enabled BTG to commercialize

---

3 For technical specifications refer to the 'Bishop Y-Forging Die' fact sheet.

systems of interconnected technology innovations (Hughes 1999), a potentially lucrative approach to commercialization.

Figure 2: Bishop Y-Forging Die.

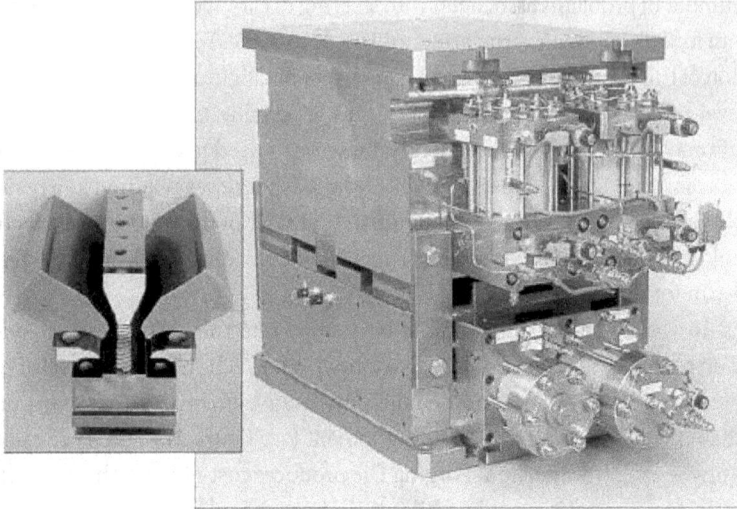

Source: www.bishopsteering.com/Ydie.htm

Managing the creative context of technology innovation

The foundation of BTG's innovative core revolved around an ability to foster and develop creativity. Arthur Bishop expressed this most eloquently:

> I like to think that a large part of innovation stems from mental activity within the subconscious – a spinoff of dreaming, which we all experience. Accessing these thoughts, which are often much freer of constraints than conscious thinking, may, for many potential inventors, lie dormant and unused.[4]

---

4 This quote is from an email by Arthur Bishop reflecting on issues raised in an interview.

Consequently, managers within BTG adopted a number of stratagems to facilitate creativity and the envisioning of future value.

Fostering creativity

First, managers at BTG encouraged the development of a creative culture (Amabile 1998, Herbold 2002, Chang & Birkett 2004). The formation of small teams, enabling ideas to be bounced back and forth, was one such practice. Injecting new blood and new perspectives into teams was another method adopted to maintain a creative culture. A research and development (R&D) manager explained:

> I've probably put on about 15 people in the last three years and the great thing about bringing the new people in is they challenge everything you've done. And so it's been good.

Nevertheless, there was little doubt that the creative core of BTG relied on the selection and retention of highly motivated staff. An R&D manager stated:

> It's a job of the heart. I mean, a lot of people, you know, have a passion and you have to be passionate to actually innovate. Our best innovators are all very passionate people.

Second, the CEO worked hard to ensure a relatively open management style (Amabile 1998). Openness was promoted to maintain the circulation of ideas throughout the Group. Consequently, managers positioned themselves as 'teachers' of innovation in their relations with subordinate staff:

> I've learned over the years that you can teach the innovation process to some extent but there are definitely people that are innovative and people who are less innovative ... I mean we teach the innovation process here at Bishop as a matter of routine ... We have a whole course structured.

Third, encouraging participation in decision processes was another important practice aimed at maintaining the creativity of BTG (Amabile 1998, Herbold 2002). There was a long history of striving to achieve engagement and consensus, with the organization being run by a management committee for a number of years. This approach did have its detractors with claims that some individuals' ideas were given priority over others'. Also, it was argued that ultimately BTG required the strong identifiable leadership that a vision-ary individual could offer. A senior manager stated:

> Oh, I think it's very important in innovating companies to have a kind of a fearless leader. I think Arthur [Bishop] has provided that kind of fearless leader over the years; a figurehead ... I mean a real technical fearless leader.

Fourth, adaptive organizational structures were also built to facilitate BTG's creative core over the lifecycle of its growth (Burns & Stalker 1959, Hansen et al. 2000, Hamel 1999, Strebel 1987). Significant growth entailed abandoning BTG's executive committee structure in favour of a more conventional 'pyramid organization', incorporating the four discrete business units out-lined above. This form of functional and hierarchical differentiation was welcomed by some, such as the finance director:

> I mean, in the last two years we've restructured into quite clear business units instead of basically having one, one big one, which encapsulated everything. This is paying off. We've been able to see a much better focus.

A young innovator was more ambivalent:

> If you want to start bouncing ideas off people you should always get a good spectrum of people to bounce ideas off, so get rid of physical walls and also in that respect get rid of the management structure for saying that, okay, you are a research engineer in the product division, therefore, you must research on a product. There is no reason to say that you can't develop a product or you can't research on processes for manufacturing.

Long-term employees also mourned the loss of a 'sense of family' as the innovation process became increasingly compartmentalized. But it was rec-ognized that "as you're growing, you know, you have to sort of departmentalise".

Fifth, performance-measurement practices were also adopted both to motivate the creative process and to place boundaries on its accomplishment (Simons 1995). Performance measures were used quite flexibly within the innovative divisions of BTG. However, the profit-oriented segments of the business were increasingly scrutinized in terms of both financial and non-financial performance measures. Nonetheless, there was a preparedness to experiment with and refine performance measures, which included a desire to introduce economic value-added calculations.

Sixth, a further important aspect of the creative milieu of BTG involved the management of intellectual property by using patents to erect a 'picket fence' around product and process technology innovations (Australian Academy of Technological Sciences and Engineering n.d., IP Australia 2000, Rivette & Klein 2000, Sullivan 1998). The patents were written and filed by relevant staff members, with this being seen as a core element of the creative processes of BTG:

> technical innovators are the best person to write the patent in my experience. I mean, you obviously want people who can rub two words together, who can actually write, but most of our people here can write and reason out good technical English and providing they can do that they can be taught the process of writing a patent. And the innovator is the most passionate person to write the patent. He is the person who actually, he or she is the person who actually has contributed to the idea. So, it is in their best interest to get a good patent.

Overall, being responsible for the development and lodgement of a patent was seen as a 'good pressure to be under' by research and development staff. These basic practices aimed at sustaining the creative context of BTG are summarized in figure 3.

Managing the commercial context of technology innovation

There was more to BTG than a capacity to dream, the sustenance of creative practices and a supportive organizational context (Chang & Birkett 2004, Christensen 1999, Herbold 2002, Van de Ven et al. 1999). Arthur Bishop stated:

> The complementary skill of successfully commercialising innovation depends rather on rational thinking – not being carried away by the new idea, requires a balance that is essential in the process.

Figure 3: Managing the creative context of BTG.

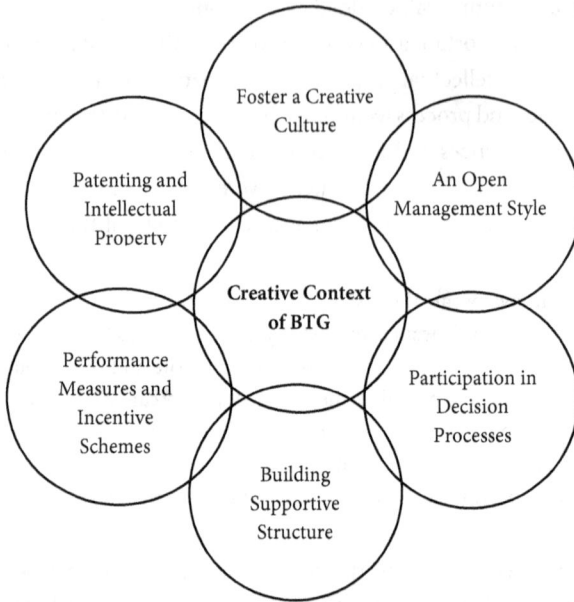

This 'balance' was provided by members of the managerial and administrative team who were responsible both for acquiring sufficient and suitable resources to sustain the innovative core of BTG, as well as configuring ways of extracting value from the process of commercialization.

Resourcing technology innovation

One of the greatest constraints on technology innovation in BTG was a shortage of funds. Over the years, the Bishop family strongly supported the financing of technology innovation, as the founder stated:

> We've never had a single dividend since the company was started, so the money went back into R&D. And it's very difficult to bridge that solely on royalties.

However, the growing requirements of BTG were re-shaping its resource profile. Government funding was acquired to support innovation activities, such as Austrans. Also new relationships were developed with financial institutions. Banks were approached to securitize royalty streams from established technology innovations, and finance was secured on favourable terms from overseas financial institutions. More significantly, outside equity was attracted to BTG. Daimler-Chrysler purchased 30% of the Group in August 2001. Strategically, the Daimler-Chrysler investment was seen to introduce 'smart money' to the Group, creating new opportunities for leveraging BTG innovations on an international scale.

At an operational level, the resourcing of innovations was managed through a series of very carefully constructed cash-flow projections. The finance director used a revolving 12-month forecast to anticipate the cash requirements of the Group. He indicated these forecasts were essential because of the 'lumpy' nature of the business:

> See our royalties don't come in every month. They're every quarter. And fairly predictable, so we've got a bit of a cycle. Also as well as getting an income from the manufacture of products using our technology, royalties, we also get the margin on sales of machines which are patented by us and that is very lumpy.

Nonetheless, an issue which continued to worry and frustrate the finance director was the *magnitude* of resources devoted to technology innovation: BTG has unquestioningly reinvested all of its profits into R&D. The finance director stated:

> We are spending too much money on R&D relative to our income generation, there isn't a linkage ... So I see that as a negative and I mean I'm not just sitting here telling you, I've told the others too that we've got to control that because it is, we're not building a cash bank which gives us opportunities to do other things.

Creating value from technology innovation

Given the resource constraints of BTG and a desire to grow, the commercial architecture of BTG underwent a number of transitions as managers aimed to reconcile the demands of the present and the resourcing of the future; balancing new research and development projects with the commercial exploitation of extant technology innovations (see Birkett et al. 1992, Coyte 2009).

The basic business model

BTG's basic business model is illustrated in figure 4.

Figure 4: BTG's basic business model.

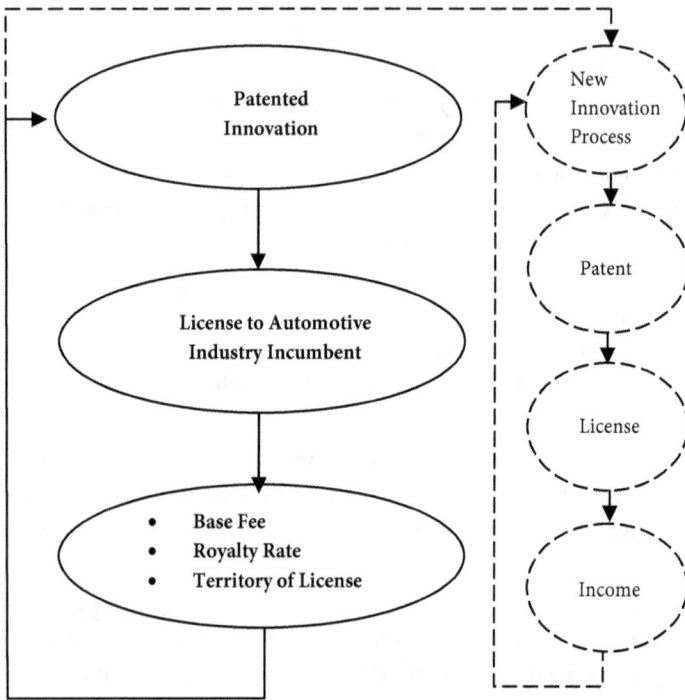

This model centred on the development of technology innovations which could be patented and commercialized through licensing. In working towards commercialization, BTG concentrated on 'blue sky' technologies – innovations which pre-empted or anticipated a market (Hamel & Prahalad 1994). The finance director explained:

> The main areas that we look for are virgin territory, very strong patent ability. We can pre-empt the market sometimes and the power steering was like that in the early days. Very much a luxury item, very few cars had it. So we came

in on this sort of crest of the wave. Pays for a lot of what you see around you and so on. But they're our main objectives that we tried to achieve … And because of our approach to IP and our core competency and patenting prior research, we are able to pick the areas to cover ourselves with a network of patents, we've got a monopoly and all we have to do is actually achieve.

Once a patent has been registered, BTG entered into a series of licence agreements. The licensing income stream consisted of up-front and ongoing payments. The emphasis on licensing stems from the resource and risk profile of BTG. As a relatively small business, BTG lacked resources to manufacture on a mass scale. Moreover, manufacturing entailed too much risk, given the cost pressures in the automotive industry. As a result, BTG required the income stream from its license agreements to sustain its research and development activities, as well as its operating infrastructure. There were few problems receiving royalties from licensees, and audit provisions were invoked rarely. In short, this basic business model served BTG well.

Modifying the business model

Time and taste combine to shape the trajectory of technology innovations. Whilst BTG excelled in developing mechanical solutions for the automotive industry, the knowledge-base of the industry as a whole had been shifting. It was acknowledged that a transition was occurring – from hydraulic to electric steering using fibre optic cables.

An innovation manager stated that BTG had reached a 'crossroads':

Undoubtedly, the biggest challenge the Bishop group faces today is the transition from hydraulic power steering to electric power steering and, you know, whether we invest our resources into developing the next generation electric steering or whether we move to something new and invest in something else other than automotive even.

BTG's basic business model was then *expanded* and *augmented* as a consequence (see figure 5).

Figure 5: Extending BTG's business model.

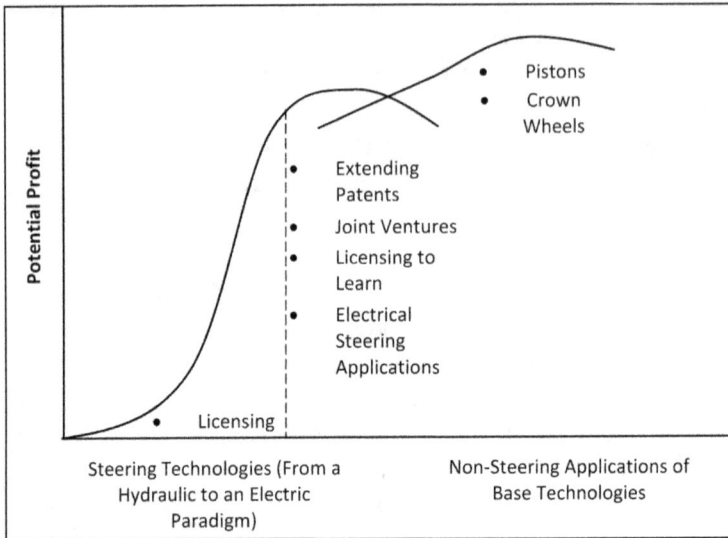

Expanding the business model

The expansion of BTG's business model involved 'stretching' the value extracted from mature technologies (Hamel & Prahalad 1993, Danneels 2002).
One approach involved extending the life of patents protecting core technology innovations, that is, variable ratio steering and warm forging production
techniques. The founder of BTG encouraged the re-visiting of patents in an
attempt to maintain an economic monopoly over these seminal inventions:
"So now we can point out the short-comings of the original concept and
argue for an inventive step, which we do quite frequently". On a more pragmatic front, the imminent expiry of strategically important patents motivated
BTG to form cooperative licensing agreements (Doz & Hamel 1998) with
major automotive manufacturers in a bid to promote the longevity of its
steering technology innovations:

> With our technology being old and in other words, you know, rack and pin-
> ion is pretty … all of that has been subject to patents many years ago. So the

tendency now is to run that down and more getting into cooperative arrangements.

BTG had been successful on this front developing a joint venture with Mercedes in Eastern Germany, enabling direct and efficient knowledge transfer to Mercedes. The venture was also beneficial to BTG because it embedded its products and processes in the basic design and production activities of an original equipment manufacturer (OEM), facilitating BTG's aspiration to capture value both earlier and more comprehensively within the automotive industry value chain.

In addition to being an economically advantageous relationship, the joint venture with Mercedes also changed the way BTG approached licensing. Involvement in the start-up of the East German manufacturing plant, and ensuring that racks were produced in 12 seconds as claimed, involved substantial organizational learning. A manager from Bishop Steering stated:

> We all probably have different ideas there and ideally a good licensee would be one you can say here is a license and, you know, they sign it and they make parts and send you royalties and they never have any problems and you never have to spend any more money on it. But I think, from my point of view, the ideal licensee is one where you have a relationship … and we not only bring the set of technology or, you know, grocery bag of technology and say here pick and choose what you want and use it and implement it, you work out the bugs. It's one where we're integrally involved in that process because the more we learn about their process the more capable we are to continue the innovation or to continue the improvements and a lot of times it's just making it better and sometimes it's just finding the completely new, better way because of what you learned from that relationship. So that's, my view is that the stronger the relationship the more information exchange there is between the parties the better the license or licensee relationship will be.

As a result, the ideal licence agreement has been reconfigured to accommodate both economic advantages *and* knowledge spill-overs.

BTG's business model was also expanded by promoting variable ratio racks for use with electric steering, although staff from Bishop Steering acknowledged that there were reputational hurdles to overcome in doing this:

Steering is going through a transition in itself, in technology not just the market, but we're moving hydraulic steering to electric steering. Well, Bishop is known to be an innovator in hydraulic steering and in our customers' minds they say, 'well you really don't have anything to offer in electric steering'.

Similarly, new automotive applications were sought for warm forging. Originally designed to produce precision steering racks, this forming technology was perceived to have applications in the manufacture of other automotive components, such as crown wheels and pinions.

Augmenting the business model

BTG also looked to other arenas of technology innovation. There was a perception that steering technology no longer provided sufficient innovative challenges or economic returns. An R&D manager stated:

There is a view, and I think this is across the company, that power steering has become systematised. Now, what that means is that you can basically build power steering to fit an electric steering [unit] almost by a Lego block approach. You don't need to be ... a technologist in electric steering anymore because you can buy all the individual bits and stick them together and then program the software to control it all. If it doesn't work you just re-change the program. A lot of our expertise in the original hydraulic power steering was developed in the day where you had to hard program on to metal parts what [the relevant] performance characteristic was. Nowadays you just dial that up with a bit of software. So, it isn't necessarily the smart end of town to be in anymore.

Consequently, there was a concerted effort to seek commercial opportunities in new fields, with photonics being regarded as a particularly fruitful pathway for future technology innovation.[5] Photonics was perceived as having huge market potential; in addition to leveraging the capabilities of the group (see figure 6). A manager from Bishop Innovation stated:

---

5 Photonics involves using photons of light, rather than electrons, to achieve greater bandwidth and speed of response.

we want to be in something where we can leverage our mechatronics skill. We probably have the best skill base in mechatronics in all of Australia, here at Bishop. We probably have the best mechatronics team of anybody in Australia. And the question you then ask is, 'how do you then best gear the intellectual property generated by mechatronics engineers?' and the answer is photonics – because photonics is dying for a mass production approach to that industry.

Figure 6: Disciplinary foundations of the BTG's business model.

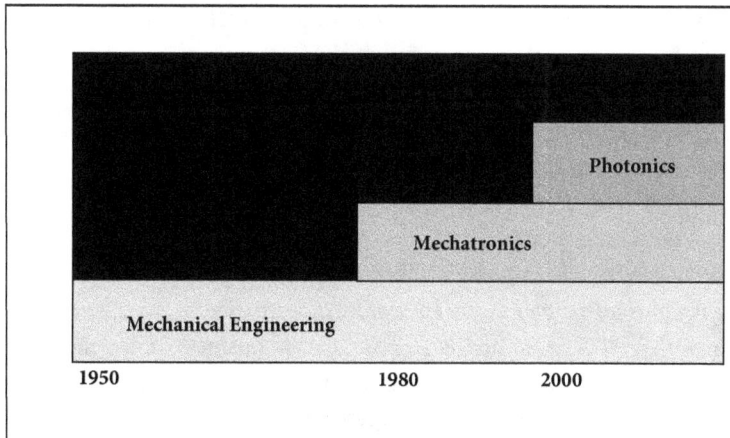

The search for commercial opportunities based on photonics was pursued in two ways. First, the established BTG approach of developing automated process technologies was mobilized as a template for value generation in this area. An R&D manager stated:

If you look at photonics companies, they are all just low-skilled workers working in clean rooms with masks and goggles and things on, working through microscopes, assembling stuff ... So what we want to do is automate [photonics applications]. The same way that power steering used to be handmade and then it became automated.

Second, the quest for commercial potential was pursued by further applying knowledge from photonics to other components in the automotive industry (such as torque and angle sensors), as well as to other industries (such as telecommunications and medicine), which were amenable to the application of this knowledge base.

Building a future

Overall, the practices of BTG were informed by a gradual realization that the environment had changed irrevocably (Castells 1996, Harvey 1989) – the future environment was more threatening and less munificent. In particular, a number of threats in the automotive industry environment had been identified by management and communicated to staff of BTG. These included:

- Increasing cost pressures from vehicle manufacturers
- Increasing consolidation of the automotive industry
- Increasing incorporation of electric steering systems in cars
- Excess capacity in hydraulic steering supply capability in North America, Europe and Japan
- Declining profitability of steering gear suppliers
- Noted decreasing profitability in relation to product technologies.

These insights into the industry environment were used by management to reinforce that BTG could no longer base its core business on the development and supply of hydraulic steering technologies, given a shift to electric steering and declining profitability in the steering gear segment of the automotive industry. Nonetheless, BTG aspired to significant levels of future growth. Consequently, there was a need to reframe the vision of BTG.

Reframing BTG's vision involved a complex dynamic. It involved both stabilizing the core competencies of the organization, whilst leveraging these capabilities in relevant adjacencies (Zook & Allen 2001). In a business plan it was stated:

> Bishop's core business was the creation, development and licensing of intellectual property related to products and processes for hydraulic power steering systems.

> The tension lies between redefining or protecting the core (while not creating a static state) on the one hand and expanding it into the right adjacencies (without abandoning the core) on the other.

As BTG wished to retain its role as a supplier to, and technology innovator, in the automotive industry, significant departures from past activities were envisaged also.

First, as the augmented business model of BTG indicated (refer to figure 6), there were plans to expand the range of components produced for the automotive industry. Warm forging process technology was to be used to generate other components, in addition to the variable ratio steering racks currently being produced. Also new product technologies, based on photonics, were planned to be supplied to system integrators in the automotive industry. Not only was BTG hoping to reposition itself within the automotive industry supply chain as a result of its increased product offerings, it was envisaged that a greater proportion of value would be extracted by increasing the volume of each component sourced from BTG.

Second, BTG's vision also entailed further change in terms of the scope of its strategy. BTG planned to enter new industries. Both extant and new technology innovations were to provide a platform for this transformation. Established manufacturing skills were to be leveraged in the provision of precision tooling and machinery for the biomedical and telecommunication industries, as well as to existing customers in the automotive industry. Similarly, a quest for 'blue sky' product technologies was to be extended to applications in the telecommunications industry.

BTG's vision, coupling existing and new capabilities, is captured in table 1. Embedding this vision in organizational functioning and reaping its anticipated financial rewards would not be easy, particularly as much of BTG's anticipated growth was to stem from *new* capabilities.

BTG *was* at a 'crossroads'. The automotive industry and informing technologies were changing rapidly. On one hand, there were opportunities to entertain significant changes in both organizational functioning and identity – albeit in the face of great uncertainty. On the other, there were opportunities to consolidate the core values of innovation and unassuming engineering excellence too.

Table 1: BTG's vision – leveraging existing and new capabilities (adapted from Danneels 2002)

	Technological Capability		
		Existing in BTG	New to BTG
Customer Capability — Existing in BTG	Existing in BTG	Exploiting variable ratio steering technology in emerging markets Exploiting warm forging technology in the automotive industry (steering rack, crown wheels and pinions)	Developing photonics applications for the automotive industry (torque and angle sensor, electric power assisted steering)
Customer Capability — New to BTG	New to BTG	Leveraging warm forging technology in the biomedical and telecommunications marketplace	Exploring photonic applications for the telecommunications marketplace

However, as a manager from Bishop Innovation stated: "It's not just engineering excellence – it's business". Central to the implementation of BTG's strategic initiatives was a capability to fuse the creative and commercial aspects of organizational functioning via the practices of staff. The process of strategic resource management had an important role to play in this respect, providing a capability to enable sufficient resourcing of and value extraction from technology innovation, whilst sustaining organizational processes facilitating the creative use of organizational resources and a market-orientation in innovation activities.

Strategic resource management and technology innovation

The BTG case highlights the dynamic tensions which underpin strategic resource management in organizations (Birkett et al. 1992, Coyte 2009). These dynamic tensions are accentuated by the nature of the core business of technology innovation in BTG. In short, the case indicates four such arenas of dynamic tension in relation to resource management practices concerning: first, short- and long-run orientations in resource management; second, continuity and change in resource management practices; third, focus and flexibility; and, fourth and finally, the coupling of adequacy and expectations in resource management (refer to figure 7).

Figure 7: Dynamic tensions in managing technology innovation

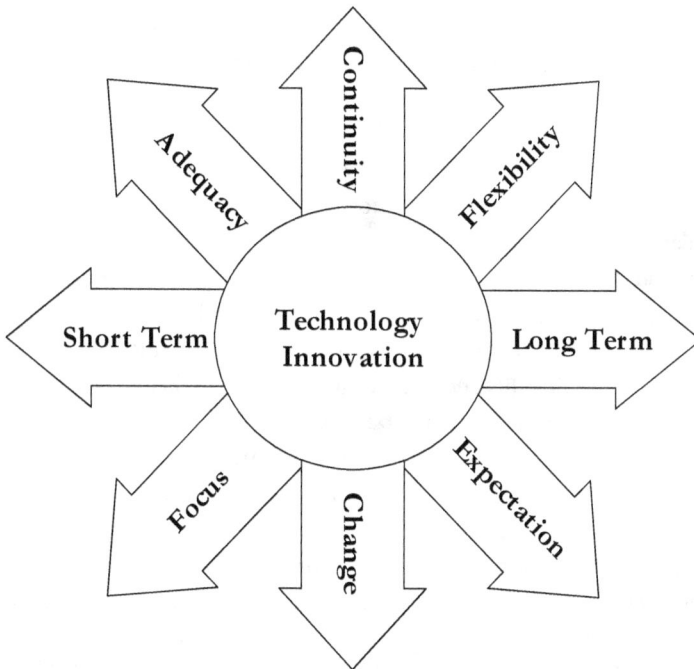

Continuity

Adequacy

Flexibility

Short Term

Technology Innovation

Long Term

Focus

Change

Expectation

The first of these dynamics – between short- and long-term orientations in resource management – illustrates tensions between the priorities of extant and envisioned forms of organizational functioning (see Birkett et al. 1992; Coyte 2009; Kaplan & Norton 1996, 2004, 2006). In the case of BTG, this involved balancing the resource needs of existing organizational structures and a portfolio of incumbent product and process innovations, whilst maintaining a virtuous cycle of technology innovation that enabled experimentation (Ciborra 2002) with new technology innovations and their possibilities. In the short term, BTG focused on resourcing the continuous improvement of its variable ratio steering product and the warm forging manufacturing process, as well as the patents that protected these technology innovations. With a view to the longer term, BTG resourced the development of new capabilities drawing on different knowledge bases (such as photonics). There was also a pull for resources to be mobilized in the development of novel forms of licensing and joint ventures that aimed to reposition BTG within the industry value-chain (Porter 1980, 1985) to increase its future revenues.

The second dynamic concerned tensions between continuity and change in strategic resource management. How was a balance to be negotiated between maintaining extant organizational practices and new directions in organizational functioning with potentially different resourcing requirements and risk profiles? Whilst the historical practices of BTG lay in designing and licensing steering technologies in the global automotive industry, there was a desire to grow and change. There were ambitions to increase sales revenue, profitability and staff numbers. Likewise, there was a desire to enter new industries, such as mass transportation, health and telecommunications. The prioritization and resourcing of this transition was to be guided by the notion of 'core' and 'adjacencies' (Zook & Allen 2001) that had been adopted by the CEO and his immediate senior management team. By connecting change to the historical core of the organization and BTG's espoused competencies in the areas of mechanical/mechatronic engineering excellence, intellectual property protection and licensing, a boundary system (Simons 1995) or way of framing the 'acceptable domain' (Simons 1995, p39) of change had been instituted. A form of risk management had become attached to resource allocation practices.

The third dynamic exemplified by the practices of BTG involved the coupling of focus and flexibility in strategic resource management. Whilst flexibility is considered a 'virtue' in a rapidly changing marketplace, such as the global automotive industry which BTG inhabited, in the face of increasing cost pressures and consolidation of the industry supply chain, flexibility is also a resource-consuming practice to maintain (Mouritsen 1999). Management needs to be alert to developing new possibilities; however, resources are scarce and focus needs to be achieved through the appropriate resourcing of reliable revenue streams. Developing uncertain options for future value creation diverts resources from the maintenance and development of core revenue streams. BTG struggled to achieve a resolution between focus and flexibility. It was acknowledged that BTG had failed to fully exploit the position that it enjoyed in terms of the 20-year monopoly period offered by the patents on its core products. The market for steering technology was shifting; however, BTG had not managed to achieve the extent of market penetration that may have been possible had there been a more focused application of resources to this strategic thrust. The emotional heart of BTG resided in its all-consuming and resource hungry innovation activities. Bishop Innovation, or the 'sand pit' was instituted to develop innovative options; these were its raison d'être. In more recent years, however, even this unit was 'feeling the pinch' from the resourcing requirements of the voracious Austrans project. It was a difficult balancing act.

The fourth dynamic highlighted concerns the adequacy of the resourcing of organizational functioning and expectations and aspirations for this. There was little doubt that BTG's aspirations for resourcing outstripped the reality of its resource profile (Grant 2002). As with any organization, visions for the future were constrained by the magnitude and mix of resources available to implement strategies. This was particularly acute in the case of BTG's financial resources. BTG had 'bootstrapped' its activities, transforming itself from a small postwar start-up to a recognized leader in technology innovation (Australian Academy of Technological Sciences and Engineering n.d.). The initial rapprochement between adequacy and expectations in resourcing was enabled by the values of the founder, Arthur Bishop. The Bishop family did not receive any dividends or lavish benefits. A belief in the business and its prospects resulted in all returns being reinvested in the business, with this reinvestment being directed substantially towards innovation activities. As the resource gap widened between the adequacy of available resources and the expectations embedded in the expanding and evermore ambitious visions for BTG, more innovative approaches to resourcing were adopted, consistent with the ideas of 'stretch' proposed by Hamel and Prahalad (1993). The CEO and finance manager explored new ways of resourcing BTG's activities. Licensing revenue was securitized to favourably change the timing of cash inflows. Government grants were sought and achieved. Off-shore funding was organized. More pertinently, the management of this ongoing dialectic between the adequacy of, and expectations for, resourcing highlights an area in which accounting and finance personnel are able to contribute in a very positive and distinctive way to the strategic resource management of an organization.

Conclusion

This chapter narrates the case of BTG, an Australian organization that has relied on the development, protection, and commercialization of a limited number of key product and process technology innovations to survive and grow. Innovation comprised the heart of this organization. The facilitation of a creative culture was an important part of BTG's success. Organizational practices promoting this centred on embedding creativity as a key value and practice in BTG's culture, as well as participation, an open management style, patenting, the building of supportive structures and a judicious use of appropriate performance measures. The resourcing of BTG's innovative core changed over time as the vision for the organization shifted and as expectations for growth became more ambitious. The basic business model of resourcing operations through the reinvestment of licensing income was augmented and expanded, resulting in the articulation of a vision that sought to shift BTG's activities into new industries, forms of relationships and products and processes. These shifts were to be informed by the expansion of the historical core of BTG into relevant 'adjacencies'. The case was argued to illustrate perennial issues in strategic resource management, portraying the dynamic tensions between practices informing first, the short- and long-term dimension of resource management; second, continuity and change in resourcing; third, focus and flexibility in resourcing, and finally, the adequacy of and expectations for the resourcing of organizational functioning.

References

Primary Sources

Bishop AE (1999). Acceptance speech of the James N. Kirby Memorial Award presented to Arthur E. Bishop by Institution of Production Engineers, May 24th.

Bishop AE (2001). Email to Jane Baxter, 2nd February.

Bishop Austrans Pty Ltd, (n.d.). Bishop Austrans (brochure).

Bishop Steering Technology Limited (2001). Bishop variable ratio technology (fact sheet).

Bishop Steering Technology Limited, (n.d.). Bishop y-forging die (fact sheet).

Bishop Technology Group, (n.d.). Austrans: the smart people mover – for today, www.austrans.com. Accessed 9th April, 2009.

Bishop Technology Group, (n.d.). Bishop steering technology. www.bishopsteering.com. Accessed 9th April, 2009.

Bishop Technology Group, (n.d.), Bishop Technology Group. www.aebishop.com. Accessed 9th April, 2009.

Bishop Technology Group (1999). Innovation as a core competency, (internal report).

Bishop Technology Group (2002). Business plan introduction: support documentation (internal document).

Grey B, (n.d.). Sustaining and commercialising innovation. Lecture at University of Technology Sydney, Sydney.

IP Skills Team, Bishop Technology Group, (n.d.). IP skills: a core competency of the Bishop Group (internal report).

Secondary Sources

Anon (1999). Leaps of faith. *The Economist*, February 20: 5–24.

Amabile TM (1998). How to kill creativity. *Harvard Business Review*, 76: 77–87.

Australian Academy of Technological Sciences and Engineering, (n.d.). Bishop Technology Group – the power of patenting.

www.powerhousemuseum.com/australia_innovates. Accessed May 4, 2009.

Birkett WP, Barbera MR, Chua WF, Fatseas VA, Luckett PF & Macmullen JS (1992). *Cost management in small manufacturing enterprises*. Sydney: Australian Centre for Management Accounting Development.

Burns T & Stalker GM (1959). *The management of innovation*. London: Tavistock Press.

Castells M (1996). *The rise of the network society*. Oxford: Blackwell.

Chang L & Birkett WP (2004). Managing intellectual capital in a professional service firm: exploring the creativity-productivity paradox. *Management Accounting Research*, 15: 7–31.

Christensen CM (1999). *Innovation and the general manager*. Boston, MA: Irwin McGraw-Hill.

Ciborra C (2002). *The labyrinths of information: challenging the wisdom of systems*. Oxford: Oxford University Press.

Coyte R (2009). Framing strategic resource management. In J Baxter & C Poullaos (Eds). *Practices, profession and pedagogy in accounting*, ch. 11. Sydney: Sydney University Press.

Danneels E (2002). The dynamics of product innovation and firm competences. *Strategic Management Journal*, 23: 1095–21.

Doz YL & Hamel G (1998). *Alliance advantage: the art of creating value through partnering*. Boston, MA: Harvard Business School Press.

Drucker PF (1998). The discipline of innovation. *Harvard Business Review*, 76(6): 149–157.

Grant R (2002). *Contemporary strategy analysis: concepts, techniques, applications*, 4th edn. Malden, MA: Blackwell.

Hamel G (1999). Bringing Silicon Valley inside. *Harvard Business Review*, 77(5): 71–84.

Hamel G & Prahalad CK (1993). Strategy as stretch and leverage. *Harvard Business Review*, 71(2): 75–84.

Hamel G & Prahalad CK (1994). *Competing for the future*. Boston, MA: Harvard Business School Press.

Hansen MT, Chesbrough HW, Nohria N & Sull DN (2000). Networked incubators: hothouses of the new economy. *Harvard Business Review*, 78(5): 74–84.

Harvey D (1989). *The condition of postmodernity*. Cambridge: Basil Blackwell.

Herbold RJ (2002). Inside Microsoft: balancing creativity and discipline. *Harvard Business Review*, 80(1): 72–79.

Hughes TP (1999). Edison and electric light. In D MacKenzie & J Wajcman (Eds), *The social shaping of technology*, 2nd edn (ch. 3). Buckingham: Buckingham Open University Press.

IP Australia (2000). *The patents guide: the basics of patenting explained*. Canberra: Canberra Printing.

Kaplan R & Norton D (1996). *The Balanced Scorecard*. Boston, MA: Harvard Business School Press.

Kaplan R & Norton D (2004). *Strategy maps: converting intangible assets into tangible outcomes*. Boston, MA: Harvard Business School Press.

Kaplan R & Norton D (2006). *Alignment: using the Balanced Scorecard to create corporate synergies*. Boston, MA: Harvard University Press.

Kash DE (1989). *Perpetual innovation: the new world of competition*. New York: Basic Books.

Kok R & Biemans W (2009). Creating a market-oriented product innovation process: a contingency approach. *Technovation*, 29(8): 517–26.

Leifer R, McDermott C, O'Connor G, Peters L, Rice M & Veryzer R (2000). *Radical innovation: how mature companies can outsmart upstarts*. Boston, MA: Harvard Business School Press.

Mouritsen J (1999). The flexible firm: strategies for a subcontractor's management control. *Accounting, Organizations and Society*, 24: 31–55.

Porter M (1980). *Competitive strategy: techniques for analyzing industries and competitors*. New York: The Free Press.

Porter M (1985). *Competitive advantage: creating and sustaining superior performance*. New York: The Free Press.

Rivette K & Kline D (2000). *Rembrandts in the attic: unlocking the hidden value of patents*, Boston, MA: Harvard Business School Press.

Simons R (1995). *Levers of control*. Boston, MA: Harvard Business School Press.

Strebel P (1987). Organizing for innovation over an industry cycle. *Strategic Management Journal*, 8: 117–24.

Sullivan PH (1998). Extracting value from intellectual property. In PH Sullivan (Ed), *Profiting from intellectual capital: extracting value from innovation*. New York: John Wiley & Sons.

Van de Ven AH, Polley D, Garud R & Venkataraman S (1999). *The innovation journey*. New York: Oxford University Press.

Zook C with Allen J (2001). *Profit from the core: growth strategy in an era of turbulence*. Boston, MA: Harvard Business School Press.

13

Competency profiles for management accounting practice and practitioners

Bill Connell, FCMA

Abstract

Bill Birkett and I both believed it was important for theory and practice to be articulated in response to change in the management accountant's world. This point is illustrated in Bill's work with IFAC to develop competency profiles (IFAC Study 12) for managements accountants as the focus of management accounting shifted from the creation of value to the management of 'value at risk'. The focus of Study 12 is the articulation and development of competences which will enable the management accountant to play a role in strategic value management. This chapter shows how Study 12 linked competence and resource mobilization through the notion of competence and the articulation of key roles and competence profiles for various levels of management accounting practitioners (novice, assistant, competent, proficient and expert). It also shows how the competency standards were applied by the BOC Group.

I worked for The BOC Group for 40 years in a variety of roles and was responsible for a number of change management projects affecting the role of the management accountant. My special interest was strategy and risk. In all these projects, my first action was to try to identify best practice and then adapt it to the project in hand. I also represented the Chartered Institute of Management Accountants (CIMA) on the committee of the International Federation of Accountants (IFAC) which focused on Professional Accountants in Business (PAIB). This committee was formally called the Financial and Management Accounting Committee (FMAC) and I had the pleasure of chairing it for six years.

I met Bill Birkett at my first PAIB meeting and was immediately impressed by his academic approach to management accounting. He stated that when practice is ahead of theory then there is a need to review and research practice. He had the ability to review and understand the history of the accounting profession, but importantly the ability to envisage its future direction and emerging trends. His rigour was impressive and he was never happier than when he was producing a diagram to explain his thoughts! It was a pleasure for the practitioner to work with this academic on emerging topics. I also had the pleasure of awarding Bill with an outstanding achievement award from IFAC for his contribution to management accounting.

A subject close to both of us was competencies and Bill chaired the sub-group which produced Study 12, *Competency profiles for management accounting practice and practitioners* (IFAC 2002). Needless to say, when Bill completed this it was 294 pages! Study 12 has been used by CIMA to update its qualification requirements for students and it was stated as being helpful in this process.

My copy of Study 12 still has Bill's autograph and the inscription, 'Thanks for the inspiration and support'. As part of the project I arranged for Bill Birkett to visit the UK and interview a number of practitioners both in BOC and other well-recognized UK-based global companies. Competencies were critical in the finance development program in BOC. The finance graduate scheme relied heavily on competency profiles and won five awards in the UK. The BOC Group career development program and succession planning also relied on competencies.

Study 12 prompted a number of other publications that I will explain later in this chapter. It was therefore important for theory and practice to be articulated for competency profiles, particularly as the world of business and management accountants is constantly changing.

The world of business and the management accountant is constantly changing

The types of changes which informed thinking about the relevant competencies for management accounting were highlighted at a finance conference of IFAC focusing on the need to reduce the cost and improve the effectiveness of the finance function. The following extracts from an IFAC presentation in India are relevant.

Extract From IFAC presentation in India

Critical Imperatives for Finance

1. Must improve and cost reduce its core business processes to allocate additional resource to more strategic activities

2. Must undertake value-added business analysis

3. Must oversee management of financial and non-financial risk and balance them with non-traditional growth opportunities

4. Must develop performance measurement systems (financial and non-financial measures) that help managers achieve strategic and shareholder value goals

Implications for People

5. Accountants must be as familiar with Shareholder Value Analysis as General Ledger

6. Knowledge of business essential to add value

7. Need for assessment of competencies (move from processing to strategic)

8. Departments will be a smaller number of highly skilled professionals

9. Accountants will be experienced in working in cross-functional teams

Conclusions

10. The role of finance and the CFO is changing dramatically

11. There is a distinct move into strategy/risk and value creation

12. The core requirement for ethics/integrity is stronger than ever

13. Boards require robust information for corporate governance and strategic success

14. Many accountants with the correct experience, competencies and leadership qualities are moving into general management.

Two studies preceding the work on competencies (Study 12) made it abundantly clear management accountants' competencies were changing. These
changes were important because they created a platform for Study 12.

The first study (IFAC 1998) traced the evolution of the management accounting function from the early 1960s and clearly identified the emerging
changes. The following figures show these dramatic changes. As such, the
activities encompassed by modern management accounting have evolved
through four recognizable stages, with each representing an adaptation to
new conditions and challenges (refer to figure 1).

With reference to figure 1, in stage 1 (that is, prior to 1950) the focus was
on cost determination and financial control. In stage 2 by 1965, the focus had
shifted to the provision of information through the use of such technologies
as decision analysis and responsibility accounting. In stage 3 by 1985, attention was focused on waste reduction in business practices using process
analysis and cost management technologies. By stage 4, 1995, attention had
shifted to the creation of value through the effective use of resources and
through the use of technologies that examined the drivers of customer value,
shareholder value, and organizational innovation. It was my belief and also
that of Bill Birkett that stage 5 would focus on the management of 'value at
risk' and we had scoped out our thoughts on this, then sadly Bill died.

The second study which was instrumental in starting the competency
work was *A profession transforming from accounting to management* (IFAC
2001). Twelve member bodies were asked to write about their experiences
and their output produced this unique study. The findings were remarkably
common across all twelve bodies from both large and small countries and
can be summarized in two parallel movements. The first is the importance of
performing corporate governance, a topic that continues to dominate our
business life, and the second is the movement of accounting and accountants
into the management processes. The study concluded: "This has risks and
opportunities for all accountants, but importantly the competencies of successful accountants are changing".

Figure 1: Evolution of management accounting.

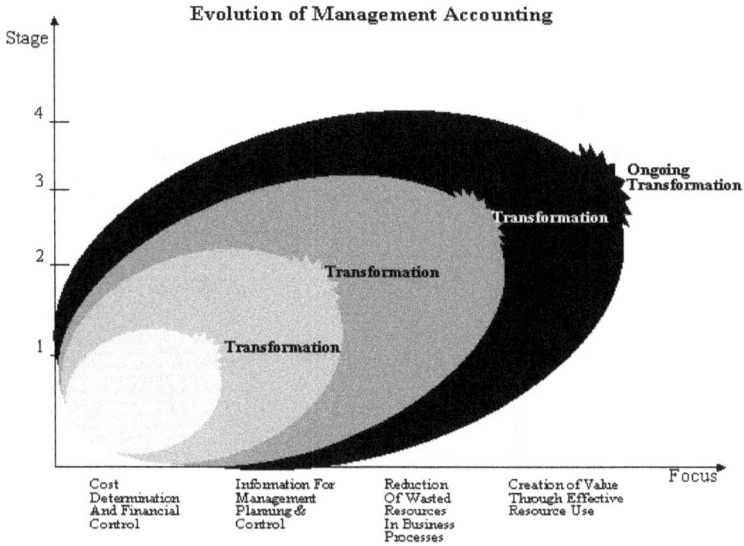

Evolution of Management Accounting

Given these envisaged changes in the finance function beyond 2000, it had become clear that a comprehensive study on competency profiles for management accounting practice and practitioners was essential. This was published as Study 12 in January 2002 by IFAC. I have extracted salient extracts from Study 12 in the next section.

These changes in the work context and competences of management accounting are demonstrated by comparing the finance function of the 1980s with that of the finance function beyond 2000. These two figures were included in the competency study (refer to figures 2 and 3).

Figure 2: The finance function of the 1980s.

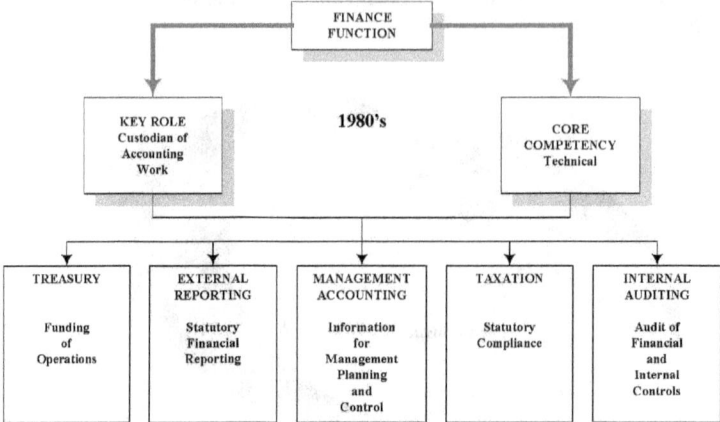

```
                          ┌──────────────┐
                          │   FINANCE    │
                          │   FUNCTION   │
                          └──────────────┘
          ┌──────────────────────┼──────────────────────┐
          ▼                      │                       ▼
  ┌───────────────┐            1980's          ┌───────────────┐
  │   KEY ROLE    │                            │     CORE      │
  │  Custodian of │                            │  COMPETENCY   │
  │   Accounting  │                            │   Technical   │
  │     Work      │                            └───────────────┘
  └───────────────┘
```

TREASURY	EXTERNAL REPORTING	MANAGEMENT ACCOUNTING	TAXATION	INTERNAL AUDITING
Funding of Operations	Statutory Financial Reporting	Information for Management Planning and Control	Statutory Compliance	Audit of Financial and Internal Controls

Figure 3: The finance function beyond 2000.

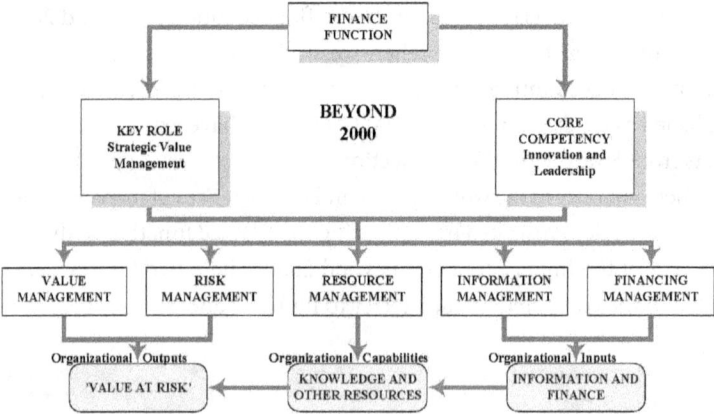

```
                          ┌──────────────┐
                          │   FINANCE    │
                          │   FUNCTION   │
                          └──────────────┘
          ┌──────────────────────┼──────────────────────┐
          ▼                      │                       ▼
  ┌───────────────┐         BEYOND             ┌───────────────┐
  │   KEY ROLE    │          2000              │     CORE      │
  │ Strategic Value│                           │  COMPETENCY   │
  │  Management   │                            │ Innovation and│
  └───────────────┘                            │  Leadership   │
                                               └───────────────┘
```

VALUE MANAGEMENT	RISK MANAGEMENT	RESOURCE MANAGEMENT	INFORMATION MANAGEMENT	FINANCING MANAGEMENT

Organizational Outputs | Organizational Capabilities | Organizational Inputs

| 'VALUE AT RISK' | ◄── | KNOWLEDGE AND OTHER RESOURCES | ◄── | INFORMATION AND FINANCE |

Extracts from Study 12
Competence and resource mobilization

The focus of this study is the articulation and development of competences which enable the mobilization and use of resources by organizations in ongoing value creation, and how this can be managed effectively. The mobilization and use of resources to create value is a central purpose and an enduring concern of organizations – even though how it is managed has varied across time, and across organizations, institutions and cultures. Management accounting is characterized as an integral and distinctive part of the management process of organizations, which adds value by continuously probing whether resources are used effectively in creating value for shareholders, customers and other stakeholders.

The way that Study 12 defines competency and relates it to the issue of resource mobilization is indicated in the extract below.

Extract from Study 12

Competency is used to refer to the successful negotiation of *performance* in a *context* through the use of appropriate *capacities*. *Capability* refers to the *potentiality* to successfully accomplish other performances of the same type in other contexts. Where specific criteria are established to define what successful negotiation of a performance is to mean, these *criteria* become *Competency Standards*. Hence, Competency Standards for Management Accounting will provide *criteria* for assessing the competency of practice *and* practitioners in management accounting.

Four criteria are advanced for assessing *Competent Practice* in management accounting, and four criteria are advanced for assessing *Competent Practitioners* taking various management accounting roles. The structure of the *Competency Standards for Management Accounting* is explained and elaborated in relation to *Competent Practice*. The Competency Standards for Management Accounting are articulated with IMAPS1, and define the attributes of a *Competent Management Accounting Function* in terms of:

- A Function Value Proposition
- Performance Outcomes
- Function Capabilities
- Best Practice

354 | Practices, profession and pedagogy in accounting

These attributes serve as *criteria* for assessments of Competent Practice. It is noted that the criteria are *necessary, but not sufficient* for the determination of Competent Practice; they need to be harnessed to appropriate forms of assessment, and some guidance is provided in this regard.

The structure of the *Competency Standards for Management Accounting* is explained and elaborated in relation to *Competent Practitioners*. This application is an extension of that applying to Competent Practice. Five roles are identified within a Competent Management Accounting Function, structured hierarchically (in terms of responsibility and authority) and in terms of levels of expertise: Novice Practitioner, Assistant Practitioner, Competent Practitioner, Proficient Practitioner, and Expert Practitioner.

Management accounting and the management process

The management process thus involves:

- Establishing organizational directions in terms of objectives and strategies
- Aligning organizational structures, processes and systems to support established directions
- Securing the commitment at a requisite level of those contributing essential skills and effort
- Instituting controls that will guide an organization's progress towards the realization of its strategies and objectives.

The level of contextual change facing organizations, however, requires management to be involved in an ongoing *redirection* of objectives and strategies, and thus in an ongoing *change* of structures, patterns of commitment and controls.

The success of management in securing the vitality and endurance of an organization is likely to be dependent on the effectiveness with which it deploys and redeploys resources:

- The mobilization or development of requisite capabilities for the pursuit of organizational objectives and strategies requires the effective deployment of resources
- Resources are deployed in structures and controls, and in securing commitments to create the capabilities necessary for organizational success

- As requisite organizational capabilities are redefined through ongoing organizational redirection, it is likely that resource deployments will need to alter.

The management of resourcing and resource use is integral both to strategy realization and organizational change. Moreover, without effective resource deployment and use requisite capabilities are unlikely to be developed, and resources are likely to be wasted in ineffective structures, controls and commitments.

It is important to recognize that 'resources' encompass more than those available in financial or physical forms; they include all resources made available, created or used as a result of financial expenditures – work processes, systems, trained personnel, innovative capacities, morale, flexible cultures, committed customers and suppliers, and community support. And, in an increasingly competitive and fast changing world, information and knowledge are likely to be critical resources for organizations, along with the capacity to sustain focus whilst negotiating ambiguity.

Categories or configurations of resources that need to be managed for competitive success and organizational viability are being developed under the labels of intellectual capital, core competences and strategic capabilities. And resources that previously were treated as 'externalities' to an organization's functioning, even though they are critical, are now being 'internalized' and recognized as *organizational resources*. Thus, the environment (natural capital) and social capital (in the form of human capabilities and social infrastructures) are being recognized as resources that organizations should sustain and not waste. Indeed the sustenance or enhancement of economic capital, social capital and environmental capital are being seen as a 'triple-line agenda' for organizations, in equating resource use and value creation.

The management accounting function refers to that part of the management process that is concerned with effective resource use over time. As an integral and distinctive part of the management process, management accounting adds value by continuously probing whether resources are used effectively by organizations – in creating value for shareholders, customers or other stakeholders.

While each functional component of the management process can be isolated analytically, it needs to be emphasized that they are intertwined in practice: each component part will be in interaction with the others, as organizational survival or success is pursued. Hence, management accounting – with its distinctive focus and perspective on resourcing and resource use as one key dimension of organizational activity – needs to 'stand beside' other key dimensions of organizational activity – direction setting, structuring, securing commitment, control, and change. The study goes on to expand on managing the management accounting function, conceptual framework for management accounting, management accounting practice and practitioners.

Competence and performance

Extract from Study 12

The notion of competency

Competency refers to the successful negotiation of performance in a context through the use of appropriate capacities. Thus, in a relational notion: it refers to a relationship (successful negotiation) between performance outcomes (as defined) and appropriate (or requisite) capacities. Neither appropriate capacities nor (contextualized) performances constitute competency – it is the relationship between them that does. Competency cannot be observed directly – it can only be inferred from performance (in context) or capacities manifested, or both.

As a practitioner I want to see performance in relation to competency and the chart on performance expectations demonstrates this (see table 1). For each Element of Competency, the performance expectations associated with a work role are indicated by an appropriate *verb* in active form (indicating the type of action to be taken), a *noun* indicating either the subject or outcome of the action, and a *qualitative term* (adjective or adverb) where appropriate. No attempt was made to pre-specify how such expressions would be used in developing the Competency Standards. However, it is apparent that particular expressions tend to be associated with some key roles and not others, thus providing a further way of distinguishing key work roles from one another at a general level. Table 1 is illustrative.

Table 1: Performance expectations.

Novice practitioner	Assistant practitioner	Competent practitioner	Proficient practitioner	Expert practitioner
• Assist	• Assist	• Perform	• Perform	• Initiate
• Participate	• Participate	• Contribute	• Direct	• Institute
• Display	• Liaise	• Collaborate	• Collaborate	• Approve
		• Liaise	• Propose/ advise	• Review
		• Monitor	• Liaise	• Secure
		• Respond	• Negotiate	• Liaise
		• Report	• Represent	• Negotiate
		• Develop	• Consult	• Represent
		• Manage	• Develop	• Contribute
			• Establish	• Build
			• Manage	• Realize
			• Lead	• Sustain
				• Manage
				• Lead

Competence and key roles

I then jump another 50 pages in the study to an example of performance in operating the management accounting function. There are another 25 pages of examples to help the practitioner. The following extract from Study 12 outlines the key roles involved in operating the management accounting function.

Extract from Study 12

Novice Practitioners

- Participate as a member of the Management Accounting Function in setting (own) personal Performance Indicators.
- Display an appreciation of the need for the Management Accounting Function to 'add value' to the organization.
- Display a willingness to develop personal skills and capabilities, with appropriate guidance.

Assistant Practitioners

- Demonstrate an awareness of processes involved in providing leadership to, and developing and deploying the capabilities of the Management Accounting Function for maximum organizational effect.
- Participate as a member of the Management Accounting Function in setting personal and Function related Performance Indicators.
- At the organizational unit or work group level, exemplify the vision of the management accounting Function by
  - a drive towards business support
  - a focus on adding value
  - offering (unique) skill/technology contributions
  - assisting in flexibly deploying skills and effort in support of needs/priorities.
- Plan and gain approval for the continuing development of personal skills and capabilities, in line with emerging competency profiles of the Management Accounting Function.

Competent Practitioners

- Demonstrate an understanding of processes involved in providing leadership to, and developing and deploying the capabilities of the Management Accounting Function for maximum organizational effect.
- Contribute as a member of the Management Accounting Function in setting personal and function related Performance Indicators.
- At the organizational unit or work group level, exemplify the vision of the Management Accounting Function by
  - a drive towards business support

- a focus on adding value
- offering (unique) skill/technology contributions
- flexibly deploying skills and effort in support of needs/priorities.
- Plan and effect the continuing development of personal skills and capabilities, in line with emerging competency profiles of the Management Accounting Function.

Proficient Practitioners

- Build the long-term vision for the Function into its work processes and developmental initiatives.
- Lead staff of the Function in establishing competency/capability profiles consistent with the vision, and defining associated resource requirements; report to leadership of the Function on the outcomes.
- Work to realize the competency/capability profiles sought for the Function, through recruitment, training, on-the-job coaching, work rotation, appraisal and reward processes.
- Lead processes to benchmark best practice in areas of management accounting work; report progressively on the outcomes to leadership of the Function.
- Contribute to planning the developmental paths of the Function.
- Assign work responsibilities (and associated resource support) within the Function, and monitor performance.
- Lead processes to assess the performance and progress of the Function, in terms of appreciation of its capabilities, productivity and contributions by organizational units/participants served; report on the outcomes to leadership of the Function.

Expert Practitioners

- Establish a coherent long term vision of the role and contribution of the Management Accounting Function
- Use this vision to set directions for the Function, and guide present decisions which might have developmental impacts
- Establish competency/capability profiles for the Function which reflect its vision

- Negotiate the developmental vision of the Function within the organization, and secure resource arrangements necessary for its implementation
- Institute processes to benchmark best practice in management accounting work; use the outcomes in establishing developmental paths for the Function
- Plan the developmental path of the Function, in concrete terms
- Overview (advise on/approve) arrangements for assigning work responsibilities and allocating resources within the Function; assess likely present/future organizational impacts/contributions that might/should result
- Review the performance and progress of the Function in terms of appreciation/recognition/respect from organizational units/participants served; acknowledge/reward accomplishments.

Competences and work roles

The study then goes on to give a work role development profile across the various levels of competency for a management accounting function.

Extract from Study 12

The five key work roles associated with the Management Accounting Function are represented here as 'composites'.

Composite work roles express 'the fullness' of roles in relation to the Management Accounting Function overall, in contrast to the manifestation of roles in relation to each Element of Competency.

Composite work roles are derived from their manifestations in Elements of Competency through a process of 'interpretive aggregation'; each component of a composite role is cross-referenced to its source in an Element of Competency.

Each composite work role embodies:

a) forms of hierarchy, representing 'responsibilities and authority'; and

b) forms of performance expected in relation to management accounting work or organizational engagement.

Table 2: Work role developmental profiles.

Development Profiles	NP	AP	CP	PP	EP
Research Work	✓	✓	✓		
Research Management				✓	
Observer/Learner Participation	✓				
Relationship and Network Building	✓				
Attitudinal Displays	✓				
Work Team Involvement		✓			
Management Accounting Work					
• Strategy Formation				✓	✓
• Project Appraisal				✓	✓
• Business Planning				✓	✓
• Budgeting	✓	✓	✓	✓	✓
• Change Implementation/Management	✓	✓	✓	✓	✓
• Organizational Design/Development		✓	✓	✓	✓
• Performance Measurement	✓	✓	✓	✓	✓
• Organizational Control Systems	✓	✓	✓	✓	✓
Work Team Management					
• Team Focus/Purpose				✓	
• Supervision/Direction				✓	
• Team Building/Development				✓	
• Performance Monitoring/Evaluation				✓	
• Accountability/Representation				✓	
Project Management					
• Administrative Work	✓	✓	✓		
• Time Management	✓	✓	✓		

Development Profiles	NP	AP	CP	PP	EP
• Objective Setting				✓	
Development Profiles	**NP**	**AP**	**CP**	**PP**	**EP**
• Assignment of Responsibilities				✓	
• Performance measurement/monitoring				✓	
• Discourse Management				✓	
Process Management					
• Objective Setting				✓	
• Culture Creation				✓	
• Training/Development		✓	✓	✓	
• Performance Management/Improvement			✓	✓	
Function Management					
• Objective Setting				✓	✓
• Function Structures				✓	✓
• Performance Management/Improvement			✓	✓	✓
• Resource Management				✓	✓
• Discourse Management		✓	✓	✓	✓
• Benchmarking			✓	✓	✓
• Quality Control/Assurance				✓	✓
• Culture Creation			✓	✓	✓
• Context Monitoring/Assessment		✓	✓	✓	✓
• Context Adaptation/Change			✓	✓	✓
Organizational Management					
• Organizational Directional Setting					✓
• Resource Management					✓
• Change Management				✓	✓
• Organizational Structuring					✓
• Performance Management					✓

The outline of the five composite work roles is prefaced by a table (see table 2 above) which illustrates the developmental progression embedded in the role structure associated with the management accounting function. The categories used in this table are derived from the headings and sub-headings used in constructing the composite work roles. Summative assessments may be made of role performance relative to the criteria established through work role composites; these are likely to draw from extended assessments over time of role performance in relation to particular elements of competency.

This demonstrates the completeness of Bill Birkett's work, as well as a need to integrate theory into practice to provide comprehensive profiles. He goes on in the next 35 pages to describe and give examples for each work profile. Further analysis is by individual attributes and I prefer to show the example of the expert practitioner.

Extract from Study 12

Individual attributes partitioned by work role composites

Expert practitioner

COGNITIVE SKILLS

Analytical/Design Skills

- taking a strategic perspective on complex organizational problems
- promote innovation/development of planning technologies
- handling diversity/complexity and a wide range of interacting factors

Appreciative Skills

- having a deep understanding of organizational processes
- having a global, strategic perspective
- taking an overall perspective on an organization
- identifying risks/opportunities in all situations
- making intuitive assessments
- quickly understand a business
- deploying innovative approaches in complex situations
- welcome and use complexity

- imposing the strategic in the midst of complexity

BEHAVIOURAL SKILLS

Interpersonal Skills

- build the right teams
- negotiation/arbitration (between teams)

Organizational Skills

- drive innovation/entrepreneurship
- manipulate systems/networks to get message across
- market 'deals' that are attractive to many people
- manage projects strategically
- focus/organize Function to provide service
- institute/establish the culture of the Function
- develop Function infrastructure
- establish Function capabilities
- focus managerial effort within the Function on entrepreneurship, innovation and securing commitment
- expand the purview of the Function
- negotiate Function objectives/strategies
- establish/negotiate Function boundaries and priorities
- put the 'right' Functional team together
- create/build the Function around this team
- implant Function objectives/strategies/Performance Indicators
- unblock organizations
- negotiate different values in organizational choices/change
- bridge cultures within organization
- use power strategically to effect change
- manipulate systems/networks to effect change
- negotiate structures/cultures/diversity in effecting change
- institute global / multi-national perspectives

- focus managerial effort in organizations on entrepreneurship, innovation and securing commitment
- establish/negotiate organization's resourcing strategies.

Assessment of competency

This study is full of Bill Birkett's 'mind maps' and the diagrams demonstrate his thought processes in every section. I have chosen the following as one of his most typical. The following extract from Study 12 focus on assessment systems for the evaluation of management accounting competences.

Extract from Study 12

Assessment systems

The relationship between criteria, evidence, methodologies, and judgement will be structured by the *system* of assessment used (implicitly or explicitly). The system of assessment binds the process of assessment and those performing the assessment (the assessors) together, 'as a system'. The following diagram is illustrative:

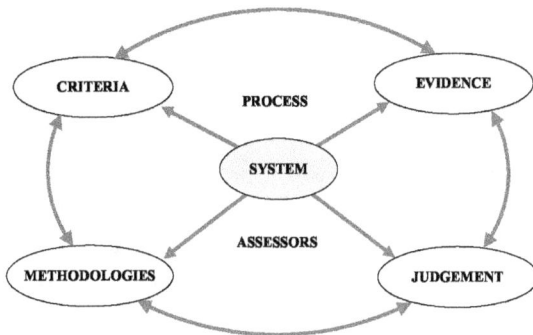

CRITERIA

PROCESS

EVIDENCE

SYSTEM

ASSESSORS

METHODOLOGIES

JUDGEMENT

As part of an assessment system, the *process* of assessment customarily involves attention being given to issues of design, implementation, reporting and review.

Assessors are the other part of assessment systems, and in this area attention customarily is given to issues of assessor selection, support, involvement in the process, and management in relation to the process.

Assessment systems may be of varying quality, with consequent effects on assessment outcomes (see Phillip D. Rutherford *Competency Based Assessment: A Guide to Implementation* Pitman, 1995). The following criteria might be used in seeking to ascertain such effects:

- *Appropriateness* – is the system and the way in which it is exercised appropriate to the type of assessment being made (in terms of criteria, evidence and methodologies to be used, and judgements called for)?

- *Expertise* – is sufficient expertise (both substantively and in relation to the exercise of assessment itself) embodied in assessment systems?

- *Independence* – is freedom from bias and a 'capacity for distancing' built into assessment systems (as attributes of assessors, and the way in which they are managed collectively)?

- *Consistency* – are assessment structures, including assessment systems, such that they can be applied consistently across time and circumstance?

Assessment Structures

Assessment structures refer to the relationship between criteria, evidence, methodologies, judgment and assessment systems.

Profiling management accounting practice

This part of the study addresses the management accounting function. This adopts a similar approach to judging individual competency, but instead focusing on the individual practitioner it applies to the management accounting function. Again the comprehensive approach by Bill Birkett comes through. It may look like an academic approach, but by going through the functional capabilities it identifies where there is a competency gap (the 'no answers') and refers you to the competency that needs to be improved.

In reaching the assessment outcomes, evidence is to be gathered from: first, ongoing performance reviews within the management accounting function where developmental targets are in focus; second, periodic reviews focused on capability issues; and, third, occasional quality reviews which take a comparative or holistic perspective on the capability of the function. Judgment will need to be exercised in reaching the assessment outcome 'competent' or 'non-competent'.

Extract from Study 12

Overall capability of management accounting function

PERFORMANCE CRITERIA	ASSESSMENT OUTCOMES
Function Capabilities	Competency?
• Is the Function guided by a coherent long-term *vision?*	YES/NO
• Is this vision adapted to the contingencies and exigencies faced by the organization?	YES/NO
• Do the *objectives* of the Function involve the provision of value adding support for business initiatives and processes?	YES/NO
• Do the *strategies* of the Function	YES/NO
- entail the blending of long-term perspective with real-time interactions	
- secure the conditions necessary for the effective conduct of management accounting work?	
- provide for proactive or advantageous treatment of contextual change affecting the work of the Function?	
• Is the *structure* of the Function designed to secure its operational flexibility?	YES/NO
• Is the *culture* of the Function highly responsive to business imperatives and organizational needs?	YES/NO
• Does the Function provide continuous, seamless inputs to *business processes?*	YES/NO
• Is the *competence/resource mix* within the Function sufficient to continue to provide highly skilled, cost-effective business support?	YES/NO

PERFORMANCE CRITERIA	ASSESSMENT OUTCOMES
Function Capabilities	Competency?
• Can the Function maintain a capacity to interact effectively in *key relationships*?	YES/NO
• Are *changes* affecting the work of the Function managed	
- proactively	YES/NO
- in relevant/necessary timeframes	YES/NO
- opportunistically	YES/NO
- efficaciously?	YES/NO
• Is the *performance* of the Function acknowledged as necessary and valuable within the organization?	YES/NO
• Is the *leadership* of the Function competent?	YES/NO
OVERALL FUNCTION CAPABILITY	Competent / Not Competent

When the answers to the questions posed above are *negative,* then the competency standards can be used as a *resource* for addressing the relevant issue, along the following lines:

- Go from the negative answer to the statement of function capabilities
- Review the performance criteria associated with the issue
- Move to the element of competency referenced by these performance criteria
- Review (a) the assessment cues associated with the performance criteria (b) the processes associated with the element of competency, and (c) the role structure utilized in constituting the performances entailed by the element of competency
- Use the outcome of these reviews to focus improvements in (a) processes (b) role specifications and (c) performance requirements related

to the elements of competency that have been assessed against the competency standards.

Using the competency standards

The competency standards for management accounting provide a common point of reference for users in organizational domains, educational domains, professional (association) domains and the international domain. The diagram from Study 12 (see figure 4) is illustrative. Within and across these domains the competency standards can be used as:

- a benchmark for development
- a development resource
- a framework for education and training
- a beacon for facilitating understanding.

Figure 4: Using competency standards.

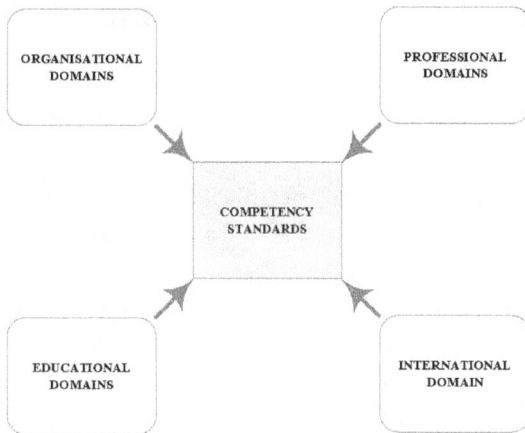

The BOC competency framework for finance management

There is often confusion between the use of the word 'skills' and the word 'competencies'. In BOC the finance function used three categories in career development – skills, business experience, and competencies. Skills were broadly based on professional accounting qualification supplemented by additional accounting skills required for a specialized job, e.g., an understanding of accounting standards if the practitioner was working in a reporting role. Business experience related to experience in working with various aspects of the business, such as operations, marketing or planning. Experience in a business environment or working in an international role were also considered. The notion of competencies was based on the Hay McBer[1] process and focused on management/behavioural characteristics. This was particularly pertinent when referring to the context of the finance function 'Beyond 2000' (refer to figure 3) which characterizes the core competency as innovation and leadership, in comparison to the 1980s when the core competency of the finance function was portrayed as technical in nature (refer to figure 2).

In recruiting graduates into a trainee finance management training program, the main emphasis in interviews was on competencies (as described by the Hay McBer process). Skills and experience would be essential as part of a structured training program, but competencies were regarded as critical for their development. Each trainee then had an appraisal discussion based on their competencies with a mentor twice a year for the duration of the three-year program.

The competency framework (refer to table 3) developed for finance management was an integral part of personal development and succession planning.

The threshold competencies, that is, analytical thinking, self confidence and conceptual thinking, were 'must haves'. This was followed by a group of personal characteristics where achievement motivation was regarded as the most critical. In the group of competencies that address working with others, organizational awareness was the most critical. In the final group entitled 'making it happen', impact and influencing/impact and persuasion were the

---

1 See www.haygroup.com/tl/default.aspx

most critical. By focusing on these competencies in the appraisal process, action plans could be developed where improvements were required.

Table 3: Competency framework of BOC.

Personal characteristics	Working with others	Making it happen
• Flexibility • Information sharing • Achievement motivation • Concern for order and quality	• Teamwork and coordination • Organizational awareness • Developing others • Talent development	• Impact and influencing/ impact and persuasion • Initiative • Team leadership

In conclusion, competencies are critical to the success of the individual management accounting practitioner and of accounting and finance function. Core competencies reflect the requirements of the strategic positioning of the firm and its goals. Skills need to be improved as we aim for the competencies of an expert practitioner, and this can be achieved, in most cases, by training. Competencies, however, as identified above may be those that individual management accountants have naturally, whilst others are achieved by personal development programs and experience.

Postscript[2]

There are a few people that you meet in life who are memorable either as a friend or a work colleague. Bill Birkett was one of those people and for me he sits in both categories.

I first met Bill seven years ago as we both attended an IFAC (International Federation of Accountants) meeting in Peru. He was well established as one of the prime movers in the committee and I was the new boy. His thinking influenced me then and still does today as I move into my second

---

2 Adapted from Mladenovic and Poullaos (with Barbera and Connell) 2005, pp115–16.

term as chair of the Professional Accountants in Business Committee of IFAC.

I often wonder why he is such an influence and now recognize that with the combination of his academic skills and my practical experience, we were two people with the same view of the future wanting to learn more from each other.

Indeed it was Bill's vision of the future that prompted the committee (then called the Financial and Management Accounting Committee, FMAC), to produce the publication, *A profession transforming from accounting to management* in March 2001. The next work to follow was *Competency profiles for management accounting practice and practitioners* in January 2002. This work was led again by Bill. It was not surprising therefore, that when Bill's term as the Australian technical adviser on PAIB came to an end in September 2003 that he was presented with the first award for an outstanding contribution to management accounting.

My tribute to Bill would only be in part if I then did not explain his friendship. Both Bill and Phillipa, his wife, welcomed all of the committee to a barbeque at his home when we visited Australia. When we met, which was only twice or three times a year, it was as if it was only yesterday – a good indication of true friendship. Bill moved to Townsville as executive dean at James Cook University and suggested his 'mate' should come and run a risk workshop for them with its strategy as its content. I readily agreed, but made it clear that my wife Teresa's birthday was not one of the days I wanted to work. Bill not only organized the workshops, but also a memorable day on the Great Barrier Reef followed by a candlelight dinner in the open. Despite his heavy workload, he organized it with the same attention to detail that he gave his academic life.

During the visit Bill and I spent some time discussing the future of management accounting, as we often returned to this topic, and we agreed that strategic direction and value at risk were the new themes. I will miss Bill's wise council as we develop these in our work, but it was our last discussion that I regret will not be fulfilled. Returning to our combination of Bill's academic skills and my practical experience we had decided to jointly write a book on value at risk. We scoped out the content, but it was not to be.

Bill will be sadly missed by many and it is my privilege to add my thoughts to this tribute.

Bill Connell

Chair Professional Accountants in Business Committee, IFAC (2000–06).

References

International Federation of Accountants (Financial and Management Accounting Committee) (1998). *Management accounting concepts (IMAPS1).* New York: IFAC.

International Federation of Accountants (Financial and Management Accounting Committee) (2001). *A profession transforming: from accounting to management (Study 11).* New York: IFAC.

International Federation of Accountants (Financial and Management Accounting Committee) (2002). *Competency profiles for management accounting practice and practitioners (Study 12).* New York: IFAC.

Mladenovic R, Poullaos C with Barbera M & Connell W (2005). Obituary – Professor W.P. (Bill) Birkett (1940–2004). *Accounting Education: An International Journal,* 14(1): 113–17.

14

Competency frameworks: a way forward for internal audit and practice

Peter J Roebuck (UNSW) and Maria R Barbera (formerly UNSW)

Abstract

This chapter outlines the work of Bill Birkett in the development of a common body of knowledge and in particular the competency framework for the internal auditing profession.

This competency framework continues to this day to have significant impact on competency based assessment throughout the accounting profession. The framework was the first of a truly international attempt to explore the internal auditing profession, and involved twenty one countries from a variety of global regions.

The project raised four questions:

- What is to be understood by internal auditing in the future?

- What are the attributes of a competent internal auditing function?

- What capabilities are required by competent internal auditing role takers?

- How are the competencies of an internal auditing function best assessed?

Five individual projects, as summarized in the chapter, were undertaken to address these questions, i.e.:

- Internal auditing: the global landscape

- Internal auditing knowledge: global perspectives

- Assessing competence in internal auditing: structures and methodologies

- Competency: best practices and competent practitioners

- The future of internal auditing: a Delphi study

Competencies form a basis for determining performance and outcomes in many professions. Bill Birkett pioneered the process of establishing competency frameworks for the accounting profession in Australia, South Africa and New Zealand in the late 1990s. Many consider his major contribution to the profession was the project initiated by the Internal Auditors Research Foundation to establish a 'global competency framework'. The following chapter is an overview of this framework. Much of the text is taken directly from the five studies which comprise the outcome of the research (see Birkett et al. 1999a, 1999b, 1999c, 1999d, 1999e). This work was considered the path forward for internal auditing which, until that time, was not globally unified in either thought or context.

The major outcome of the study was a new definition of internal auditing, centred on improved organizational performance being related directly to the management of risks. The following current definition, included in the 2006 Common Body of Knowledge (CBOK), owes much to the earlier work of Birkett et al.

> Internal auditing is an independent, objective assurance and consulting activity designed to add value and improve an organization's operations. It helps an organization accomplish its objectives by bringing a systematic, disciplined approach to evaluate and improve the effectiveness of risk management, control, and governance processes (Burnaby et al. 1999 p3).

Prior to this risk-based definition, most considered the internal audit function to centre around a relatively narrow concept of control. Much of that control was financial control, and consequently much of the work activity of internal auditors was compliance driven only in the financial area. The enlightened works of Birkett et al. expanded the notion of control through the incorporation of risk as the prime focus of control systems. This control was seen as a method of managing risk. The best practice internal audit functions of today clearly focus on risk management, and have an expanded role embracing consulting activities and value added services for evaluation and improvement of the effectiveness of the risk management and governance processes as indicated in the 2006 CBOK study.

Common body of knowledge (CBOK) and the competency framework for internal auditing (CFIA)

The Institute of Internal Auditors Inc (IIA) has a long history in the development of CBOK, which is aimed at providing internal auditors with current thought on issues relating to internal auditing knowledge and competency (Macintosh 1999). The first version was developed in 1972 within the US only. Other subsequent studies attempted to move outside the US to a more global perspective. However it wasn't until 1996 that a global perspective was attempted by the Birkett team. Although this study was originally intended to be the third iteration it evolved into a comprehensive study that documented and defined internal auditing and its competencies on a global scale. The study included 20 countries from a variety of geographic regions. These are outlined in table 1.

Within those countries various affiliates, along with over 200 practitioners and 60 associations, provided wide representation from the profession. The studies conducted by Birkett et al. commenced in 1996 and were published in 1999 (refer to bibliography for details).

An overview of the studies

The Institute of Internal Auditors Research Foundation initiated a project to establish a global competency framework for internal auditing in early 1996, when the project raised four questions about the future of internal auditing:

1. What is to be *understood* by internal auditing in the future – from a global perspective?
2. What are the attributes of a *competent* internal auditing function within organizations from the perspective of best practice globally?
3. What *capabilities* are required of those taking key roles in a competent internal auditing function?
4. How are the competencies of an internal auditing function and the capabilities of those taking key roles *best assessed?*

The unique contribution of this project as a whole was the provision of a resource or point of reference that was previously not available – a global perspective on best practice in internal auditing.

Table 1: Geographical representation.

Region	Country
Africa	Ethiopia
	Ghana
North America	Canada
	United States of America
South America	Bolivia
	Peru
Asian Region	China
	Japan
Australasia	Australia
	New Zealand
India	India (Mumbai)
	India (Delhi)
Scandinavia	Norway
	Denmark
Europe	France
	Germany
	Italy
	Netherlands
	Spain
	United Kingdom
Middle East	United Arab Emirates

Individually, each of the studies contributed to the whole by addressing a different perspective of internal auditing, drawing input from different sources and utilizing a different methodology to probe aspects of internal auditing and the changing environments in which it makes its contribution.

The first study, *Internal auditing: the global landscape*, probed the perspectives of national associations of internal auditors regarding the practice of internal auditing, the competency of internal auditors and its assessment, and the qualifications (academic and professional) required of internal auditors. Information about the activities undertaken by the associations, as well as issues and changes that were current and potentially able to have an effect on the profession and/or work of internal auditing in various countries, was incorporated into the study.

A demographic survey was completed by associations representing 20 countries in Africa, North and South America, Asia, Australasia, India, Scandinavia, the United Kingdom, Western Europe and the Middle East. Further information describing features of internal auditing practice was supplied by 12 of those associations. A vignette was produced for each country from those sources.

Variations were evident in the scope of internal auditing work across nations. Financial auditing, internal control review and fraud detection were major areas of work in most nations, although activity in operational auditing was becoming more significant. Generally, internal auditors spent little time in auditing areas such as environmental management, product and service safety and quality assurance. Variations between countries in the scope of internal auditing work may have been caused by differences in national cultural beliefs, attitudes and values (which influenced business imperatives and sensibilities), differences in organizational managements' views of the role and value of internal auditing, and external events and influences which differentially impacted on the role of internal auditors in those countries.

A great deal of uncertainty existed about the total population of practising internal auditors. National associations lacked reliable information about numbers and work locations, and probably had different definitions of an *internal auditor* and the boundaries of internal auditing work.

Employers of internal auditors assessed applications for internal auditing positions at the time of recruitment and subsequently. At recruitment, having an academic degree was considered to be more important than having a professional qualification; and, in the majority of countries, managerial experiences, a complex and diverse range of knowledge requirements, and a broad range of cognitive and behavioural skills were desired. While assessment of performance on the job was thought critical and widespread, no information was available about the basis, process or methods employed.

Most countries offered, or intended to offer, the Certified Internal Auditor (CIA) qualification, although some reservations were expressed about its syllabus and examination. Despite its accessibility, less than 20% of the worldwide membership of IIA had this designation. Five countries had developed their own national internal auditing qualifications, and in four of those cases, they were offered in competition with the CIA.

Professional education and training was available in most countries through associations of internal auditors, public accounting firms, professional accounting institutes, commercial training organizations, and conference organizers. In all countries, maintenance of the CIA designation required undertaking a specified number of hours of continuing professional education. Australia was the only country among those surveyed where continuing professional education requirements applied to the maintenance of IIA membership.

The profession of internal auditing was seen to have significant strengths and weaknesses, opportunities and threats. The strengths related to the many associations affiliated with the IIA and, in some cases, the European Confederation of Institutes of Internal Auditors (ECIIA), and to the global qualification (the CIA). The weaknesses consisted of a generally unclear or weak image of the profession, a seeming inability to lift managements' expectations about the value of internal auditing services, the lack of resources in some chapters and institutes, and reservation about the syllabus and examination for the CIA qualification. Opportunities arose from the increased interest of regulators and organizations in corporate governance issues, and the necessity in organizations not only for ever-increasing operational efficiency and effectiveness but also for the effective management of a diverse array of risks. There seemed to be a central role for internal auditing from both those directions. The major threats identified were increasing competition from other specialists for the performance of internal auditing tasks in organizations, and the inability of the profession to reserve these tasks to itself.

Legislation and regulations requiring organizations to have internal auditing as part of the corporate governance process were considered likely to contribute to the growth of internal audit *activities*. However, they would only contribute to the growth of the *profession* if the qualifications/ experience required was legislated to be coincident with membership of an internal auditing association (as suggested by ECIIA).

Changes in societal views, national objectives, and organizational imperatives, while varying in their impact across countries, were affecting internal
auditing work in terms of areas of application and the need to add value.

The second study, *Internal auditing knowledge: global perspectives*, sought
answers to the four questions raised by the research were sought from two
sets of authoritative sources. First, answers were sought from a number of
authoritative and interrelated publications by the IIA: *Standards for the professional practice of internal auditing (1998); A common body of knowledge for
the practice of internal auditing (1992);* a number of documents relating to
the CIA examination process; and the *Business-focused quality assurance
review manual (1996)*. Second, answers were sought from a range of publications from around the world which either addressed internal auditing
directly or indirectly by referencing areas and contexts in which it might be
applied under one name or another.

In both cases, an attempt was made to illuminate the relations between
internal auditing practice and its contexts of practice. In essence, the study
probed for changes in the value proposition linking internal auditing to the
organizational context in which it was practised from a global perspective.
The study concluded that the capabilities of key role-takers in a competent
internal auditing function were:

- The knowledge/understanding necessary to sustain the full range of
  performance associated with a role.
- The set of cognitive and behavioural skills that might be displayed selectively in different contexts to bring off the range of performances
  expected for a role.

Attention was then turned to models available for use in assessing the competency of an internal auditing function and the capabilities of key role-
takers. Competency requirements of the function and the capabilities required of key role-takers provided the criteria used in each type of
assessment. Drawing from the full range of courses reviewed in the study, it
was possible then to characterize best practice assessment processes and the
criteria that might be used in evaluating the quality of assessments undertaken (as a type of meta-assessment). While it was apparent that the issues

canvassed in the study had received extensive attention over a long period, this had tended to occur in a piecemeal way. Rarely was a set of issues seen or approached as an integrated whole. The advantage of using the competency framework for internal auditing in this study was that the range of issues were framed together to be seen as mutually related and understood as an integrated whole – from a global perspective.

The third study, *Assessing competency in internal auditing: structures and methodologies*, sought answers to the following questions:

- How is the competency of an internal auditing function within organizations *best assessed?*
- How are the capabilities of those taking key roles in a competent internal auditing function *best assessed?*

Answers were sought from submissions by experts, nominated by institutes or chapters of internal auditors around the world, as representative organizations or educational institutions with a reputation for exemplary or best practice in relation to internal auditing. The questions posed by the study raised a number of issues, which were addressed throughout the report:

- How are the criteria and processes used in judging the quality of an organization's internal auditing function related to the *performance management* strategies of the organization?
- How are the criteria and processes of assessment used to guide and evaluate the development or performance of internal auditing personnel at key role levels and career stages related to an organization's *human resource policies?*
- What relations might hold between *best practice* in internal auditing, the *competency* of an internal auditing function, and the *capabilities* of key role takers in a competent internal auditing function?
- How are the notions of *competency* and *capability* related and defined?
- What relations hold between *assessment* and *learning?*
- What might be meant by *competency standards* in relation to internal auditing, and how might they be used in assessment?

- How can professional associations *add value* to workplace organizations and educational institutions through their approach to assessment?

The following definitions are sustained throughout the report:

- *Capacity* – the qualities needed to sustain or produce performance in context.
- *Competency* – the successful accomplishment of performance in context, through the judicious use of requisite capacities.
- *Capability* – the potentiality to successfully accomplish other performances in other contexts, involving the judicious use of the same or other capacities and an underlying knowledgeability.

The *nature of assessment*, focused on competency or capability and how it might be applied to internal auditing, was considered in some detail. Processes of assessment, assessment structures, and principles governing assessment outcomes were identified and illustrated. The way in which these processes, structures and principles are applied in assessments of the competency of an internal auditing function was outlined as a best practice composite drawn from respondent submissions.

The *role structures* applying to competent internal auditing functions were outlined, along with the attributes of key roles in the structure. Three key roles were identified – entering internal auditor, competent internal auditing, and internal audit manager. Assessments related to these roles were reviewed in three domains of assessment – the workplace domain, the educational domain, and the professional domain. In each case, the application of processes, structures, and principles of assessment was outlined as a best practice composite drawn from respondent submissions.

Often assessments related to internal auditing role-takers in one domain referenced or relied on assessments made in other domains. How *inter-domain assessments* are structured was considered, highlighting the practicalities and principles involved. Internal auditing role-takers were found to be embedded in an extended and elaborate mosaic of assessment.

The study elevated and illuminated assessment as a central concern for both organizations and internal auditing practice, to the point where it is now seen as equal to substantive concerns in the never-ending drive for learning and development.

Competency: best practices and competent practitioners, the fourth study and centrepiece of the series, focused on the development of competency standards for internal auditing that would be applicable globally. It was concluded that the nature of the value proposition linking internal auditing to the organizations it serves had shifted significantly. The focus was on the provision of assurance within organizations, but in a context where a premium is placed on learning in the midst of dynamic change. Organizations appeared to be consolidating the diverse areas in which they sought assurance around the notion of risk exposures and management. If the label 'internal auditing' was to be given to the outcome of such consolidations, then its new mandate would be to add value to organizations by providing proactive, real-time assurance that risk exposures faced were understood and managed appropriately in the midst of dynamic change.

Given such a reconfiguration of the nature of internal auditing it was possible to establish the defining points of reference for a competent internal auditing function as:

- The value added to the organization
- Performance at the level of best practice
- The capabilities necessary to sustain these qualities.

As a dimension of the capability profile of a competent internal auditing function, it was possible to establish possible role structures and the requirements of key roles. These requirements were categorized in terms of, first, responsibilities and authority and, second, performance expectations/criteria. The use of a distinctive research methodology, together with a range of input from 200 expert practitioners around the world justified the claim that the competency standards developed represented 'best practice' globally.

The competency standards established and elaborated a new definition of internal auditing:

> Internal auditing is a process by which an organization gains assurance that the risk exposures it faces are understood and managed appropriately in dynamically changing contexts (Birkett et al. 1999d, pix).

With this point of reference, the competency standards then established:

- The attributes of a competent internal auditing function, in the light of global 'best practice'
- The capabilities required of key role-takers in a competent internal auditing function.

In the project, 'competency' refers to a relational notion – the way in which individual attributes (knowledge, skills, attitudes) are drawn on in performing tasks in particular work contexts. Competency is realized in performance. Hence, it can be defined by reference to particular types of contextual task performance, in terms of what is to be performed, and how well a performance is to be constituted. The performances thus defined became referred to as competency standards. Competency standards established an appropriate linkage between (cf. figure 1):

- Tasks to be performed
- The contexts in which tasks are to be performed
- Specified performance criteria
- Individual attributes entailed by the performance.

Figure 1: Competency standards and linkages.

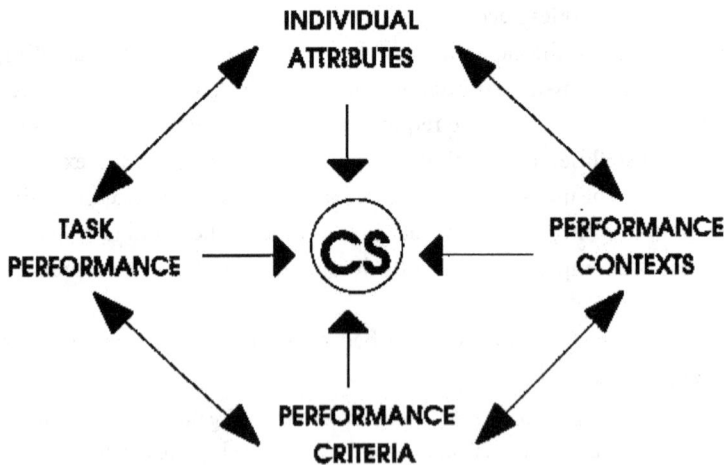

When developing the competency standards, reference was made to a particular language for describing and structuring the components of competency. Thus, internal auditing was delineated as a field of practice in terms of the function it serves within organizations. 'Units of competency' was the label given to the set of tasks whose performance was both necessary and sufficient to meet the functional requirements of the field of practice. 'Elements of competency' was the label given to refer to coherent and sensible clusters of sub-tasks whose performance were necessary and sufficient to meet the outcomes entailed by particular units of competency. 'Performance criteria' referred to aspects of professional performance that were indicative of whether an element of competency was performed competently or not.

Units of competency and elements of competency were established for internal auditing as a field of practice, and performance criteria were defined for each element of competence (along with 'cues' to guide the assessment of performance against them). The 'individual attributes' associated with the field of practice were also identified, using special taxonomy of cognitive and behavioral skills (both skills were seen as necessary to secure competent performance of internal auditing work).

As a result it was possible to define competency standards relating to competent practice in internal auditing by referencing both performance outcomes and the individual attributes drawn on selectively to produce such outcomes (see figure 2).

In the study, a distinction was made between competent practice as an outcome secured through teamwork (for example, through the joint work of the entire staff of an internal auditing function) and the differentiated roles taken by individuals as part of the team. Thus, a distinction was drawn between competent practice as a team-produced outcome, and competent practitioners taking key roles in relation to the outcome.

Roles were defined in terms of the assignment of responsibilities and commensurate authority, and in terms of (mutual) expectations about performance. Also implicit in the specification of roles were expectations about the substantive understandings (knowledge) necessary for effective role performance.

Figure 2: Competency standards and competent practice.

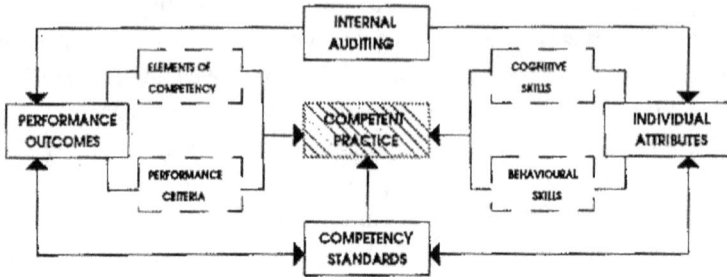

Three key work roles were delineated in relation to an internal auditing function: entering internal auditor; competent internal auditor; and internal auditing management. A competent internal auditing function was seen to be constituted through the interaction of these key roles. The three roles were specified in relation to each element of competency and as composites relating to the internal auditing function overall. (In developing composite roles the substantive understandings were drawn out separately to enhance their visibility and their accessibility for assessment purposes.)

Finally, the individual attributes associated with the function overall were partitioned in terms of key work roles. As a result, the competency standards for internal auditing could be elaborated to incorporate the task displays and individual attribute clusters associated with key work roles. This is illustrated in the figure 3.

In developing the competency standards for internal auditing, the 'bottom line' was always the practical sensibility of the outcomes. The research design, the methods used to validate the outcomes, and the involvement of close to 200 experts in the process were all directed to ensure that the outcome was sensible to practitioners, useful in practice, and representative of best practice.

The competency standards for internal auditing stand as an independently produced global point of reference or benchmark. Hence they can be used in various ways by a range of interested parties. Users (clients/consumers) of internal auditing services may use them to understand the nature of the service they are receiving and to evaluate its quality. Internal auditing managers may use them in assessing the structures, capabilities, and functioning of their own functions, and in the developmental needs of their functions and their personal development. Internal auditing practitioners may use them to assess the contributions they could make to the work of the function and their own developmental needs. Professional associations (or other groups or authorities) may use them as a basis for peer/quality assurance reviews, and as a basis for admission to membership, certification of competence and definition of continuing education needs or requirements.

Figure 3: Development of competency standards.

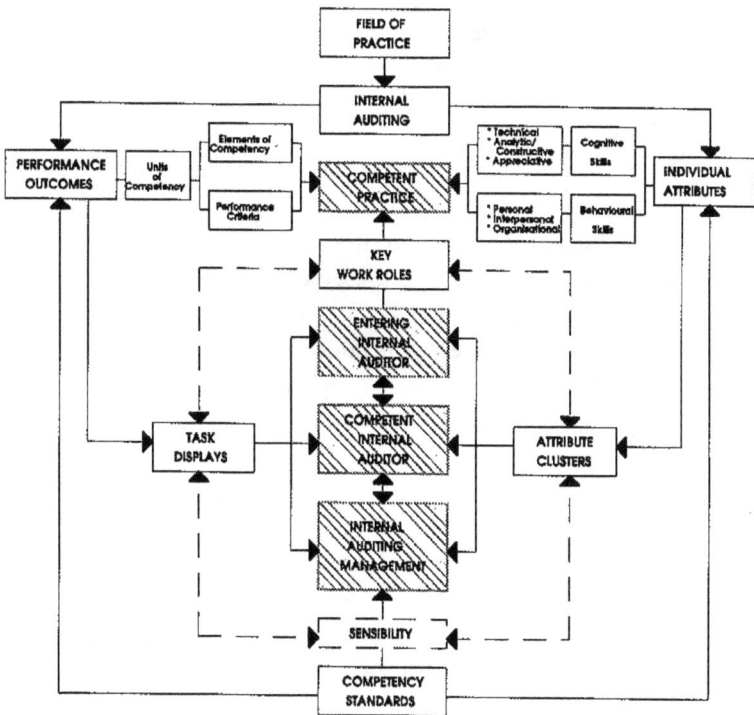

While the competency standards for internal auditing suit the field of practice generally, they still need to be suited to the circumstances of particular users (applications, organizations, industries, sectors, countries). Thus, they serve both as an independent point of reference and as a resource that is adaptable for various uses.

Finally, *The future of internal auditing: a Delphi study*, contributed to the research questions by eliciting and consolidating the opinions of 134 internal auditing experts from around the world regarding:

- The nature of internal auditing in organizations in the future
- The key tasks performed in the name of internal auditing now and in the future
- The drivers of change in these tasks producing the future
- The skills required to perform these tasks in the future
- The sets of knowledge required to perform these tasks in the future
- Ways in which task performance, skills, and knowledge requirements might be assessed as components of competent practice in internal auditing
- Other issues related to the practice of internal auditing in the future and on the path to the future.

A high level of consensus was gained from participants about the shape of internal auditing in the future, despite a level of ambivalence or uncertainty in particular areas. Significant differences in responses between various groupings of participants were also identified in the midst of the overall level of agreement. Thus, it was apparent that different countries, regions, or economic sectors would be entering the future from different starting positions and with different trajectories.

The Delphi study predicted that future internal auditing would be embodied within, or will come to refer to, processes within organizations established to provide assurance that the full set of risk exposures entailed by their functioning are understood and under control.

The provision of such assurance is to be set against a backdrop of dynamic change constantly affecting the interface between an organization and its environments. In this setting, those charged with governing or managing organizations will have to meet twin agendas in securing their organization's success or survival – value creation and risk management. Organizations will be 'under control' when these agendas are managed successfully. Thus, assurance processes in organizations will need to address the realities posed by the dynamics of change, where risk exposures alter continuously and organizations are always on the verge of becoming out of control.

In this context, assurance involves positivity – that risk exposures are under control, or that action is underway to that end. Such assurance cannot be provided if risk exposures are not understood, if risk management systems are inappropriate or ineffective, or if ongoing change undermines existing controls or requires revised forms of control. Assurance will be built on a platform of understanding and learning about risk and control within an organization, and will be built through improvements to risk management and control systems and ongoing adaptation to change.

Assurance processes, thus characterized, become the emerging organizational domain of internal auditing. In this domain, the relationship between internal auditing and organizations can be expressed in terms of a new, distinctive value proposition – here labelled the *internal auditing value proposition*. The proposition expresses a new vision of a compact between internal auditing and organizations to be negotiated in particular settings and institutionalized generally.

Within the framework of this new proposition, it is possible to redefine the tasks and the capabilities involved in providing internal auditing services. Together, the substantive and qualitative requirements of the value proposition, efficient and effective task performance, and the possession of requisite capabilities are taken to constitute the attributes of a competent internal auditing function.

Against this background it is possible to specify the capacities required of internal auditing specialists as they take roles in the flexible teams through which future internal auditing work will be conducted. These capacities can be expressed, in part, in terms of knowledge, cognitive and behavioral skill requirements.

The attributes of a competent internal auditing function and the capacities required of internal auditing specialists provide criteria for assessing the competency of the function and the capabilities of key role-takers respectively. The issues of how and where assessment against these criteria can be conducted are then addressed, along with the criteria that might be used to evaluate the quality of such assessment.

Shifts in the nature of internal auditing and in the role requirements of internal auditing specialists are likely to have an effect on internal auditing as an occupation and on its professional organizations. Against this background, advantage was seen in the global profession of internal auditing, though the benefits were seen to fall differentially and the notion was embraced by participants with varying levels of enthusiasm.

The emergent distinctiveness of internal auditing globally, as a form of work within organizations and as an occupation, is captured and characterized by a global competency framework for internal auditing. The framework provides a distinctive language for communication about internal auditing as it evolves; a distinctive way of thinking about the issues involved; and a different (if not new) way of understanding the outcomes.

The study illustrated the global framework for internal auditing in action in a research setting. But it can be used otherwise – in guiding the renewal of internal auditing as an occupation, or in focusing the development of internal auditing practice in the multitude of work contexts around the world.

A continuing influence

The Birkett et al. (1999) studies have continued to have significant global impact on the profession of internal auditing, with much of Birkett's foresight becoming accepted practice. For the first time, the understanding that the practice of internal auditing should be integrated into the management of organizational risks was proposed. Today this new definition and work practice forms the basis of global 'best practice' internal audit functions. The work of Birkett et al. (1999) formed the foundation of the Institute of Internal Auditors Research Foundation's 2006 study, achieving a global participation of 91 countries and affiliates, resulting in 9,366 usable responses, with questionnaires translated into 16 languages.

It is apparent that assurance services and consulting engagements in the area of risk management, governance and controls continue to expand, with the 2006 CBOK study showing a growth in these areas of over 60%. The 1999 study of Birkett et al. clearly foreshadowed the need for change and the way forward for a profession that continues to expand. As stated in the 2006 CBOK study:

> Who would have thought that internal auditors would be described by the media as rock stars? With the internal auditing activity now becoming a necessary or mandatory activity in organizations around the world (Burnaby et al. 2007).

References

Birkett WP, Barbera MR, Leithhead BS, Lower M & Roebuck PJ (1999a). *Internal auditing: the global landscape*. Florida: The Institute of Internal Auditors Research Foundation.

Birkett WP, Barbera MR, Leithhead BS, Lower M & Roebuck PJ (1999b). *Internal auditing knowledge: global perspectives*. Florida: The Institute of Internal Auditors Research Foundation.

Birkett WP, Barbera MR, Leithhead BS, Lower M & Roebuck PJ (1999c). *Assessing competency in internal auditing, structures and methodologies*. Florida: The Institute of Internal Auditors Research Foundation.

Birkett WP, Barbera MR, Leithhead BS, Lower M & Roebuck PJ (1999d). *Competency: best practices and competent practitioners*. Florida: The Institute of Internal Auditors Research Foundation.

Birkett WP, Barbera MR, Leithhead BS, Lower M & Roebuck PJ (1999e). *The future of internal auditing: a Delphi study*. Florida: The Institute of Internal Auditors Research Foundation.

Burnaby PA, Abdolmohammadi MJ & Hass S (2007). *A global summary of the common body of knowledge 2006*. Florida: The Institute of Internal Auditors Research Foundation.

McIntosh ER (1999). *Competency framework for internal auditing in an overview*. Florida: The Institute of Internal Auditors Research Foundation.

15

Monitoring accounting education in higher education institutions by the professional accounting bodies in Australia 1944–1988

Elaine Evans (Macquarie University)

Abstract

In Australia, the professional accounting bodies monitor accounting education in higher education institutions through a system currently referred to as course accreditation. This paper addresses the question of why this monitoring mechanism was developed over a 40-year period and how it failed as a quality control and quality improvement system for the professional accounting bodies. It concludes that, despite the evidence that the monitoring system was ineffective, professional bodies became 'locked in' to accreditation during the period 1944–88. However, the creation of alternate entry pathways by the professional bodies over the past year or two may signal a reconsideration by them of the efficacy of accreditation.

In Australia, the professional accounting bodies monitor accounting education in higher[1] education institutions through a system currently referred to as 'course accreditation'. These higher education institutions are publicly funded and therefore subject to changes in Commonwealth Government education policy which in turn impacts on accounting education in these

---

1 The terms 'tertiary' and 'higher' in relation to education and educational institutions can be used interchangeably where 'higher education' replaced 'tertiary education' in the late 1970s. However for consistency, this paper uses the term higher education.

institutions. This paper addresses the question of why a monitoring mechanism was developed over a 40-year period from 1944 to 1988, and how and why the professional accounting bodies maintained the system throughout periods of massive shifts in Commonwealth Government education policies despite strong evidence that it failed as a quality assurance mechanism. 'Inside' stories about the development of this monitoring mechanism are constructed from the minutes of meetings of the accounting bodies, their annual reports and professional journals. Other sources include reports of Commonwealth Government inquiries and surveys into accounting education in Australia.

Unlike the UK where professional accountancy training and academic accounting programs remain separate, and where the Institute of Chartered Accountants in England and Wales (ICAEW) does not accredit courses, accounting education in Australia since the 1970s has been more closely aligned to the US system which emphasizes university-based education in preparation for entry to the accounting profession. However, in the US accreditation of higher education courses is undertaken on a peer review basis through the Association of American Collegiate Schools of Business (AACSB).

In Australia, initial educational preparation for the accounting profession is now predominantly undertaken in Commonwealth Government funded higher education institutions. This has resulted in a mutually dependent relationship between the education institutions as providers of accounting education and the professional accounting bodies as monitors of accounting education. This interdependency was problematic for both providers and monitors as power relations shifted, in different eras, in response to changes in Commonwealth Government education policy, in particular changes in funding and structures of higher education. This chapter asks the question, why and how did the professional accounting bodies in Australia accredit accounting courses in higher education institutions?

In seeking an answer, it traces the professional accounting bodies' monitoring mechanisms of *recognition*, *approval* and *accreditation* and the actions and reactions of higher education institutions, following significant shifts in Commonwealth Government policy, and identifies patterns that persisted over 40 years. Of interest is the fact that these monitoring mechanisms have received little outside scrutiny yet throughout this time they were an important sign of both professional power for the professional accounting bodies and legitimization of accounting programs in higher education institutions.

Theorizing accreditation

In generic terms, 'accreditation' is the recognition given to an institution, faculty, school and/or course/program when it meets some minimum set of criteria set by the accrediting body. It is the establishment or restatement of the status, legitimacy or appropriateness of an institution, course etc. Further, it is a set of procedures designed to gather evidence that enables an accreditation decision to be made. The onus is on potential accreditees to demonstrate their suitability; that they meet minimum criteria.

Harvey (2004) argues that its main function is to control a sector and its components, yet as a mechanism of quality control and quality improvement accreditation has limited effect. It is a signal that the 'accredited' institution, course (etc.) is credible and those who are associated with the institution, course (etc.) as a member or graduate have met those minimum standards. The procedures associated with accreditation have clearly defined processes that usually involve substantial documentation and site visits which include interrogation of parties associated with the institution, course (etc.).

Houston and Harman (1978, p49) state that accreditation offers protection to particular groups: institutions against other poorer quality institutions; students against poorer quality institutions and courses; employers against employees with sub-standard qualifications; members of professional bodies against an erosion of the reputation of the credential; and finally professional bodies who want to ensure that only graduates with certified knowledge and skills can enter the profession. Harvey (2004) contends that accreditation processes in higher education institutions represent a power struggle between academics and the accrediting body and tend to result in a diminution of academic freedom, while at the same time imposing a bureaucratic burden on those academics. Further, he states that:

Accreditation can also act as a restraint on innovation and run counter to pedagogic improvement processes. There is a taken-for-granted underlying myth of an abstract authorising power, which legitimates the accreditation activity. This myth of benign guidance is perpetuated by the powerful as a control on those who provide the education and represents a shift in power from educators to bureaucrats (Harvey 2004, p207).

Whilst accreditation is linked to accountability for educational results, in academic institutions, its cost and value for education is disputed by many academics who see it as the most expensive and least value-added processes that universities are required to engage in. Malandra (2008) describes accreditation as schizophrenic because it is focuses simultaneously on compliance and on quality assurance and improvement. Harvey (2004) argues that accreditation can act as a constraint on innovation and in fact run counter to pedagogic improvement processes.

In analysing the accreditation mechanisms of the AACSB International, Lowrie (2008, p358) notes an emphasis on the severity of the accreditation review process and its connection with elitism: the appeal to an exclusive club with a discrediting of those that are not accredited. Yet inclusion on the approved list of a nationally (and internationally) recognized accrediting organization is generally accepted as a significant indication of quality (Houston & Harman 1978) and this quality seal of approval is worth the investment by institutions seeking accreditation.

In summary, accreditation is a sign of quality and accountability determined by an accrediting body through the evaluation of an institution, faculty, school and/or course/program. The credibility of the sign is contestable, the validity of the processes is problematic, and the evaluation and measurement of the (learning) outcomes is imprecise. Yet its connection with privilege is too tempting for institutions, faculties, schools and/or courses/programs to refrain from seeking it.

Through the lens of accreditation[2] as an important legitimising sign of professional power for the professional accounting bodies and a legitimizing process for accounting programs in higher education institutions in Australia, this paper investigates relations between these professional accounting bodies and higher education institutions and asks why accreditation in its several guises survived when the evidence was clear that its association with quality control and quality improvement of accounting education was illusionary at best and non-existent at worst.

From mid-1940s to early 1950s – *recognition*

In the mid-1940s there were five accountancy institutes: the Association of Accountants of Australia (AAA); Australasian Institute of Cost Accountants (AICA); Commonwealth Institute of Accountants (CIA); Federal Institute of Accountants (FIA); and the Institute of Chartered Accountants in Australia (ICAA). The ICAA, FIA and AAA were perceived as representing the interest of public accountants whilst the other institutes represented commercial accountants.

Although there were established courses at universities before World War II, for the most part candidates for the various accountancy institutes were prepared for their examinations by private coaching colleges,[3] correspondence schools and private tutors. Some technical colleges taught accounting subjects but their certificates and diplomas were not recognized by the accountancy institutes. All this changed with the advent of the Commonwealth Reconstruction Training Scheme (CRTS) which was inaugurated in February 1944. The Commonwealth Government embarked on a plan to recruit into training 'for the professions and posts of leadership' (Anderson & Eaton 1982a, p6), returned servicemen who would contribute to social and eco-

---

2 Here accreditation is being used in a generic sense whereas the professional accounting bodies used it in a more specific sense. Later in the chapter the word is italicised to denote its specific use by those bodies.
3 Examples include Hemingway Robertson Institute, Australian Accountancy College, Metropolitan Accountancy College and AE Speck Commercial College.

nomic postwar reconstruction. At this time, universities and technical colleges came under the mantle of Commonwealth Government (financial) support with the provision of full-time training in degree, diploma and certificate courses for returned servicemen. The Commonwealth Government funded places in universities and technical colleges as well as granting subsidies directly to students (Spaull 1982). As noted by Waddington et al. (1950), part-time students who were employed received the full award wages from their employers while the government paid the difference between the employee's assessed earning capacity and the award rate. These financial schemes made accounting education in government funded institutions very attractive, and made the accountancy institutes very vigilant about whether or not the subjects offered at these institutions would be equivalent to subjects in the professional examinations for which the majority of candidates had been prepared previously by the private coaching colleges. These private colleges specifically tutored for the accountancy institutes examinations, however because of the CRTS these institutes needed to establish formal relations with the universities and technical colleges to ensure alignment with their syllabi and examinations. Potential candidates would be supported by Commonwealth Government funding to attend either universities or technical colleges to study accountancy.[4] The benefits of the CRTS to the accountancy institutes were twofold: the Commonwealth Government was now prepared to pay a higher proportion of the cost of training accountants than previously; and the institutes and their members (as employers) were able to access degree and diploma holders.

One of the institutes, the CIA,[5] responded to these changes by declaring that 'no further steps are to be taken to secure correspondence tuition in commercial subjects through private institutions' (Report of the CIA Education Committee, 25 May 1944). The CIA established monitoring and quality

---

4 For a full discussion of the CRTS and its effect on accounting education see Birkett and Evans (2005).
5 At this time, the CIA was the largest and most influential of the four accountancy institutes (excluding the ICAA).

assurance mechanisms for technical colleges in each of the states through a joint board of examiners and granted exemptions from their own examinations for individual subjects passed in courses offered at these technical colleges. At the same time the CIA negotiated agreements to recognize university examinations and in some cases gained membership of university advisory committees. As for the ICAA, it granted exemption from the intermediate examination for holders by examination of a diploma or degree in commerce or economics from an Australian university (GCM 1947: 3821). In addition it granted exemptions from subjects in the Intermediate Examination to graduates of some technical colleges where representatives of the ICAA participated in the setting and marking of relevant examination papers (GCM 1951: 4264). The ICAA did not grant exemptions from the Final Examination. It was certainly in the best interests of the universities and technical colleges to maximize the exemptions granted for their subjects in the professional examinations and a number of universities and technical colleges were 'willing to make the necessary changes in the course to meet the requirements [of the accountancy institutes]' (Report of the CIA Education Committee to General Council, August 1945). Accounting teachers and academics were engaged in establishing the appropriateness of their subjects for professional recognition.

When the Australian Congress on Accounting was held in Sydney in 1949, the status of the accountant and its link to education were discussed. A paper presented by Young[6] (1949) urged accountancy institutes to abandon the conduct of examinations and look to the universities and technical colleges to provide the required instruction and examinations. Yorston (1949), principal of the Australian Accountancy College at the time, argued that accounting had already reached 'professional status' (because of the 'chartered accountant' designation) and that universities and technical colleges should be the medium for postgraduate study. Fitzgerald (1949) advocated closer association between the universities and the accountancy institutes while Smyth (1949) wanted to see a common educational policy between all

---

6 Sir Norman Smith Young was an influential chartered accountant at the time.

the accountancy institutes. Finally Braddock[7] (1949, p270) expressed his disappointment that the profession had failed to convince universities that "there was sufficient breadth and depth of knowledge to warrant the subject being elevated to a degree". Accounting education was a long way from establishing its legitimate place in universities and the need for it to be closely aligned with the accounting profession was contested by some of the accountancy institutes who wanted to control the syllabus because universities paid too much attention to economics and other social sciences.

In the late 1940s and early 1950s there were contending views about the value of higher education in relation to accounting. Sir Harold Howitt (1952, p543), a member of the ICAEW, argued that university graduates did not necessarily make the best accountants. The stance of the ICAA was that its Royal Charter conferred professional privileges and the status of profession was determined from the standing of the institute (Young 1949). However, at the time the ICAA was entering into cooperative relations with universities and technical colleges for recognition of individual subjects as equivalent to ICAA Intermediate Examination subjects and the CIA was active in its pursuit of university education because it deemed this cooperation to be intrinsically linked to accounting's claim to the status of profession (Fitzgerald 1952b, pp417–18).

This period was the beginning of accounting education being 'locked in' to higher education with 'strong bindings' of joint boards of examiners at technical colleges (i.e., on which the professional bodies were represented), who closely scrutinized syllabi, examinations and membership of university advisory boards where appropriate, thus assuring quality control. At this time, it was possible for candidates to meet the educational requirements of the CIA with equivalent subjects at technical colleges and universities where arrangements had been negotiated based on ensuring that minimum criteria were met. But for the ICAA there was always the final examination, irrespective of whether there were full or partial exemptions from intermediate

7 LA Braddock was at the South Australian School of Mines and on the CIA Council. By the mid-1940s the School of Mines had been offering accounting instruction for some time.

examinations. The providers (of accounting education) and monitors (of accounting education) appeared to be in a mutually beneficial and supportive interdependent relationship and recognition as the precursor of accreditation was a signal that technical colleges were credible institutions where accounting education met minimum professional standards.

From early 1950s to mid-1960s – from *recognition* to *approval*

Continuing changes in the educational policies of the accountancy institutes in the 1950s resulted in the entry standard for candidates being raised to matriculation level. This allowed accounting courses to develop both at universities and technical colleges with degrees being introduced in the former, and diplomas (rather than certificates) introduced in the latter (CIA Annual Report 1951). The winds of change were blowing for the accountancy institutes. The South Australian division of the Australian Chartered Accountants Research Society (1952, p504) argued that "Australian industry was growing rapidly and her economy daily becoming more complex, necessitating a greater need for the business executive to have a wide experience of accounting problems". GE Fitzgerald suggested that the role and perception of the accountant and accountancy was changing and that the accountant was a guide to management rather than 'a routine man of numbers' (1952a, p158). Further, he argued that the accountancy institutes needed to maintain the closest possible association with all educational institutions where accountancy was taught for the purpose of extending [professional] knowledge. The accountancy institutes sought to establish 'education for the profession' within universities (Forster 1952, p204). What was acknowledged was that changes to accounting work required broader skills and knowledge than the institutes were providing in their education programs. What was not acknowledged was the impending shift in power relations as the universities in particular sought to broaden education for the profession beyond technical training and narrow confines of the syllabi of the professional bodies. As accounting became established in universities, their dependency on the professional bodies for curriculum development would create tensions between the academics and the accrediting bodies as academics perceived a diminution of their ability to contribute independently to curriculum development.

At the same time as the accountancy institutes were recognising the importance of higher education for the 'profession', the Commonwealth Government identified the need to devise a long-term policy in relation to university funding and how universities could contribute to long-term national economic development. In 1956, Sir Keith Murray, who had been the Chairman of the University Grants Committee in Britain, was asked to chair an inquiry into universities in Australia (Davies 1989, p9). In 1957, the Committee on Australian Universities (the Murray Committee) was set up, and established new shared funding arrangements with the states as well as the Australian Universities Commission (AUC). Sir Leslie Martin from the University of Melbourne was appointed as its chair.

The late 1950s and early 1960s mark the second phase of postwar expansion of higher education in Australia. The expansion took place both in existing and new institutions as a massive injection of Commonwealth and state money flowed into university development. It was a fundamental plank in Commonwealth Government policy that "it must be responsible for ensuring that the nation has a provision of universities to train graduates in the numbers and kinds which the country's situation demands" (The Parliament of the Commonwealth of Australia 1958, p328). As a result the number of accounting courses increased and the (now) two accounting bodies[8] started to change their processes of recognition from individual subjects in technical colleges and universities to recognition of courses. During this time chairs in accounting were established and full-time accounting lecturers engaged at universities. Joint boards of examiners and representation on university advisory boards, as quality assurance mechanisms, were prerequisites for this *recognition*. The ICAA did distinguish between technical college and university graduates by exempting the former from intermediate group 1

---

8 In 1953 the Australian Society of Accountants, the antecedent body to CPA Australia, was formed through the amalgamation of the CIA, AAA and the FIA, whilst the AICA joined in 1966.

examinations only, whilst exempting the latter from groups 1 and 2.[9] The (now) Australian Society of Accountants (ASA) was willing to give full status to technical college and university examinations.

Even though increasing numbers of candidates were satisfying ASA educational requirements by completing university and technical college examinations, the great majority was still sitting for ASA examinations (Meredith 1974a, 1974b, 1974c, 1974d, 1974e). However, the General Council of the ASA was concerned about the standard of its qualification; in particular there had been criticism from overseas bodies when the ASA sought to negotiate mutual recognition. In 1960, the ASA Executive Committee recommended a comprehensive survey of accountancy education in Australia, but it required the cooperation of the ICAA because the Ford and other US foundations who were approached for funding insisted on a joint project. However, the ICAA was looking at a survey of its own educational standards and examination system (Minutes of ICAA General Council 16 May 1960: 5609c, g). This survey would be undertaken by a panel comprised of university professors and ICAA members whereas the ASA envisaged a survey undertaken by an overseas accounting scholar and with wide business community representation on the survey committee. After a series of negotiations, both bodies decided to cooperate in the *Survey of accountancy education in Australia* (the Vatter Survey 1964), undertaken by William J. Vatter, Professor of Business Administration, University of California at Berkeley.

Simultaneously, the Commonwealth Government commissioned a committee to undertake a comprehensive review of Australia's provision of, and requirements for, higher education. The appointment of the Martin Committee in 1961 was a direct outcome of the dramatic increase in funding for universities, which the AUC had won in its first round of negotiations with state and Commonwealth governments. The Martin Committee in Australia

---

9 Intermediate group 1 examinations comprised accounting, auditing and commercial law. Intermediate group 2 examinations comprised company law, banking and exchange, bankruptcy law and miscellaneous law.

was far more limited in scope than the Robbins Committee in the UK; and it had no independent status (Encel 1963). It was a committee of the AUC with Sir Leslie Martin as the chair. The Martin Report (Australian Universities Commission 1964) concluded that the existing system of higher education in Australia was restricted too closely to traditional forms of university education and there were many who needed opportunities for other kinds of higher education. It was critical of the quality of the non-university sector and commented negatively on the influence the accounting bodies had on both universities and technical colleges. In particular, the Martin Report argued that detailed bookkeeping techniques, routine auditing procedures and business practices lacked analytical content and had no place in a university course. The report also suggested that the granting of exemptions from the professional bodies' own examinations had not always had a beneficial effect on educational standards due to the fact that the professional bodies tended to grant exemptions only in respect of courses in which the broad pattern of syllabi corresponded to their own (Australian Universities Commission 1964: 10.35). Recognition processes had robbed many universities, in particular, of an ability to develop the curriculum along the lines advocated by Young, Fitzgerald, Smyth and Braddock in the early 1950s; that is, education for the profession beyond the narrow confines of the professional bodies curriculum.

The recommendations of the 1964 Martin Report spawned Colleges of Advanced Education (CAEs)/Institutes of Technology which would be practically oriented to the needs of industry and commerce, flexible in their teaching methods and admission arrangements and essentially diploma-granting institutions. The Martin Report criticized the universities as being excessively professional or vocational in character, with too many students in pass degrees and with staff who had heavy teaching loads with no time for research. This binary policy demanded a dual system of institutions that were 'equal but different'; i.e. comparable in standards but different in function (Davies 1989, p135).

The binary system would impact on the structure of accounting education as old 'actors' (technical colleges and private colleges) exited the stage and new 'actors' (CAEs/Institutes of Technology) entered at the beginning of

1967. Commonwealth Government policy would require universities to focus on research and accounting education needed to legitimize its identity as an academic discipline if it was to grow and create a stable platform for professional education in universities. This would leave the newly created CAEs/Institutes of Technology to concentrate on professional training to cater for part-time students who hoped to be employed in some type of accounting work. A knowledge base or mode of education delivery that suited one form of higher education system might not suit or be sufficient for another. Yet the professional accounting bodies would have to approve different courses in different higher education institutions, while at the same time be cognisant of those institutions dependence on Commonwealth and state funding, and reliance for establishment and growth on state-based accreditation mechanisms in the form of higher education boards. Monitoring mechanisms would continue to impose a bureaucratic burden on academics as they sought to satisfy the requirements of both the state and the profession.

From mid-1960s to early 1970s – refining *approval*

In the mid-1960s, the ICAA and the ASA had two reports before them as they contemplated the nature of accounting education and its place in the CAEs, many of which were 'upgraded technical colleges'. Both Martin and Vatter had recommended a qualifying examination. The ICAA's final examination was in fact a qualifying examination but the ASA needed to consider introducing such an examination because it did not have an equivalent. Both bodies reconsidered the nature of courses in universities and CAEs/Institutes of Technology that would lead into their different qualifying examinations. In 1966, the deliberations of the ASA included consideration of courses that majored in accounting, interpreted as the equivalent of a full accounting subject in each year of the course,[10] for the purpose of entering the proposed qualifying examination. The course would also include cognate disciplines such as economics, law, mathematics and statistics.

---

10 At this time subjects were run on a yearly basis.

Approval of a major in accounting would depend on discussions with professorial staff with regard to the nature and content of the universities' syllabi and teaching staff at a CAE/Institute of Technology rather than on the basis of a published syllabus (Report of ASA Education Committee to General Council 18 April 1966). This added a layer of complexity to the relationship between higher education institutions and the ASA because either the qualifying examination would have to be constructed in accordance with the curriculum of approved courses or the higher education institutions would construct their examinations in accordance with the requirements of the qualifying examination. A further complexity was the relative independence of the higher education institutions in constructing their accounting curriculum in the absence of any agreement on the core content of accountancy. In general the universities could afford to be less compliant while the CAEs/Institutes of Technology would be more compliant, because many of the latter were commencing new courses from 1967 and might have had to construct their curriculum under the influence of the professional bodies.

Later, when Houston and Harman reflected on the development of professional courses in universities and CAEs/Institutes of Technology, they questioned whether professional bodies had too much power in courses at both universities and CAEs/ Institutes of Technology and if this influence on curricula was desirable (1978, p51). Harvey (2004) contends that the outcome of such a power struggle between academics and accrediting bodies is a diminution of academic freedom demonstrated here in a narrowly based curriculum that would prepare candidates for professional examinations.

The ICAA had also changed its basis of recognition from individual subjects at universities to approved courses at tertiary level (including CAEs and Institutes of Technology). The approved courses included a major in accounting (still unspecified) with commercial law including company law and taxation. Because of its concern about standards at the newly emerging higher education institutions, the ICAA looked to ways of strengthening its final (qualifying) examination (Minutes of ICAA General Council 8 May 1967: 7001). However, this task was stalled by unity talks between the ASA and the ICAA because of an anticipated support for a jointly administered qualifying examination. By the end of 1969 the unity proposals had failed. The ICAA introduced a new final examination to commence in 1972 named the professional year (PY) of study which addressed its concern about the standard of accounting education in the new higher education institutions. Now both bodies would have an examination to act as the arbiter of acceptable standards in higher education institutions. Yet the professional bodies had not reached agreement with academics on the vital question of a common body of knowledge for accountants (Andersen 1968, p144).

The approval of accounting courses involved a complicated system administered separately by the professional bodies. However, the growth in accounting courses as a result of Commonwealth Government policy, differences in course content and the quality of students and staff, necessitated a close association between the two professional accounting bodies and the CAEs/Institutes of Technology. The 'locking in' mechanism was approval of courses required because of a shift to mass education for national development. The system of approval was an untested mechanism of quality control and quality improvement in these newly emerging institutions. Rather than viewing the approval processes as a burden, many academics in the CAEs/Institutes of Technology would appreciate the protection offered to them from the criticisms of academics in established universities[11] that resulted from the Martin and Vatter reports putting universities and other higher education institutions on an equal footing.

From early 1970s to early 1980s – disintegration of *approval*

The 1970s witnessed turbulent times for the higher education sector, and the professional accounting bodies. The Whitlam Labor government came to power in 1972 and in 1974 it abolished tuition fees for higher education, establishing the Tertiary Education Assistance Scheme (TEAS) to provide living allowances for all students (subject to a means test) who were accepted

---

11 When academics in CAEs/Institutes of Technology first sought membership of the Australian Association of University Teachers of Accounting (AAUTA), they were refused (Goldberg 1987).

to study at an approved higher education institution. Commonwealth Government policy meant that the states were no longer responsible for funding higher education. According to Davies (1989) a legacy of the Whitlam era was tightened federal government control of higher education but more generous funding at least in the early 1970s. In 1975, the Fraser Liberal-Country Party government came to power on a platform of cutting central government expenditure and bureaucracy, at a time when there was public disenchantment with higher education. Perhaps as a result of the Whitlam excesses, the new government's education policies implied more rigorous measures of evaluation and accountability of education programs and expenditures. From 1976, under its 'New Federalism' the Fraser government attempted to disengage from some of its acquired responsibilities for higher education.

Anderson and Eaton (1982b, p103) see the late 1970s as being characterized by 'accountability and decline' of higher education. The establishment of the Commonwealth Tertiary Education Commission (CTEC) in 1977 mandated no further growth in university and CAE/Institutes of Technology enrolments. In 1976, the Committee of Inquiry into Education and Training was appointed to consider the provision of educational facilities and services and the relationship between the educational system and the labour market. The Williams Report notes that

> in Australia the power of professional and para-professional associations to act alone on educational requirements is limited by their dependence on publicly financed universities and colleges of advanced education (Education, Training and Employment 1979: 9.28).

King (1978) argues that the higher education sector was not ready to cope with contraction and that there was a growing disenchantment among academics about the direction of Commonwealth Government education policy. West (1978) observed that university education in Australia was no longer demand driven.

Because accounting education in Australia was now 'locked in' to higher education, and subject to variances in Commonwealth agendas for 'manpower planning', the changing education policies of the professional bodies appeared to be piecemeal changes. Many of the changes suggested that expedience, or the feeling of having to do something different here and now, had exercised a greater influence than prolonged reflection on what was necessary or desirable from the general viewpoint of the profession (Chambers 1956, pp73–80). In the Whitlam era when Commonwealth Government funding of higher education was expanding, the qualifying examination, the ASA's monitoring mechanism to control the entry point into that professional body (first held in 1970 because of the increase in the number of accounting courses and the failure of approval as a quality assurance mechanism) was proving problematic. By 1973, the ASA had all but abandoned that examination because so many exemptions were granted on the basis of approved courses at universities and CAEs/Institutes of Technology, even though the appropriateness of these courses as preparation for professional work and life was contestable. In the end, the ASA simply reserved the right, where special circumstances applied, to require some candidates to sit for a qualifying examination. Professor Ray Chambers criticized the accounting bodies for a lack of consensus as to the core of accounting knowledge and its relationship to practice and argued that unless the accounting bodies were satisfied that

> the universities and colleges of advanced education acquainted their students with that common core [as yet not agreed upon] and its relationship to practice, there was a need for a national examination of prospective members of the professional body (Report of ASA Education Committee to General Council May 1971).

But, under the circumstances, what exactly would they examine?

With no clear resolution to the problem of a agreed common core of accounting knowledge and the need for a professional qualifying examination (as argued by some), the ASA turned its attention to the implementation of a new membership structure (Minutes of ASA General Council 17–18 May 1973). The new structure had two levels: the 'provisional member' who required a major study in accounting; and the 'associate' who required additional knowledge of commercial law, taxation law and auditing. A new professional orientation program (POP) would be the means by which provisional members could progress to associate. In May 1974, the General

Council (G15/74) set out the purpose of POP: to cultivate an awareness of the work situation; to inculcate a professional outlook; to create an awareness of the ASA's objectives; and to engender a desire to participate in professional development. The ASA wanted to reconnect accounting education and accounting work because the old qualifying examination did not provide "a test of the candidate's fitness to enter into professional life as an accountant". By inference, neither did the approved courses at universities and CAEs/Institutes of Technology. However, the introduction of the POP was delayed until 1977 when several CAEs were evaluated, with a view to obtaining assistance from them because of their experience in course design. This assistance would eventually facilitate the evolution of a more rigorous program that would rival the ICAA's PY.

However, the PY was not without its troubles. An ICAA Education Policy Committee appointed in 1977 to review the PY initially reported that unrealistic assumptions had been made about the level of academic knowledge attained by the candidates, and that the 200 hours of study recommended by Professor Athol Carrington had developed nearer to 600 hours. The committee believed candidates required these longer hours because of the deficiencies with, and inadequacies of, their basic accounting degree. Clearly, approval processes had failed to ensure quality and accountability in meeting minimum criteria for direct entry to professional examinations. Further, the ICAA considered that the problems could be overcome if the basic educational qualifications for entry to the PY were expanded to include an admission test which not only showed aptitude for clear and systematic thought but also accounting and auditing knowledge. Discussion of the matter ensued over a number of years and finally a trial achievement test was first administered in 1983 with a further test in 1984. All 1984/85 PY candidates were required to sit for the test in 1984 and candidates who received a score below 50 were contacted and advised to consider remedial studies, seek counselling or delay their entry to the PY. However, because so few candidates were affected it was decided not to continue the test after 1986. The ICAA then looked again to strengthen the PY itself as the final arbiter of fitness for the accounting profession because of the wide variation in the standard of students and (approved) courses at higher education institutions (Minutes of ICAA National Council 2 June 1980, NLC 716).

In brief, the higher education institutions were not clear as to what was adequate accounting knowledge; there was no consensus as to a common core of accounting knowledge; and graduates were perceived as being inadequately prepared for the accounting profession. As a result, the accounting bodies strengthened their own examinations, thus signalling that higher education courses were not sufficient professional preparation for candidates. Approval processes monitored by the professional accounting bodies had failed to protect higher education institutions against other poorer quality institutions; students against poorer quality institutions and courses; employers against employees with sub-standard qualifications and importantly the professional bodies themselves against candidates who were deemed to be ill-prepared for professional life.

The 1980s – from *approval* to *accreditation*

Harman (1981, 1982) states that the extensive, dramatic and sudden cutback in Commonwealth government functions and pruning of government agencies undertaken by the Committee of Review of Commonwealth Functions (the 'Razor Gang') in 1981, has no peer in Australian history. Prime Minister Fraser was committed to pushing back some Commonwealth Government functions to the states and education was lacking public support. According to Harman (1981) media and other interest groups complained that universities and CAEs/Institutes of Technology had expanded their enrolments to an unnecessary extent; that public money had been wasted and there should be more emphasis on the Technical and Further Education (TAFE) sector. In addition, the government wanted amalgamations of some CAEs/Institutes of Technology. Cutbacks in funds forced higher education institutions to reduce expenditure and many were unable to fund academic staff to support new developments. An example of the impact of reduced funding for university accounting departments is the University of Tasmania, where there were four senior staff vacancies in 1986. It was possible that two subjects required for the course to be accredited would not be offered, thus jeopardising approval of the accounting course (Minutes of ICAA Education/Examination Committee 1 December 1986, ED 976).

If higher education institutions were hard hit by these decisions, then commerce departments suffered more than other departments. Henderson (1982) bemoaned the poor share of resources that commerce received, claiming that it reflected its low status in universities. The major issue in relation to accounting education was the problem of the quality of education provided in under-resourced accounting departments and the impact this had on relations with the accounting bodies.

So concerned was the ICAA that its National Council decided to tell members that when recruiting new graduates, they should be aware of the significant variations in the course content, quality of teaching staff, and the entry and exit standards of higher education institutions, and to remind them of their responsibility to provide appropriate training for PY candidates (Minutes of ICAA National Council 24 November 1980: NLC. 750). In addition, the ICAA Education Policy Committee blamed the proliferation of business courses for the perception that candidates for the PY had neither the aptitude nor interest in becoming professional accountants. At no point in time did the ICAA blame its own monitoring processes as being inadequate to ensure: quality control and quality improvement in accounting courses; protection for employees against sub-standard graduates; and members against erosion of the credential. The committee thought the problem could be solved by either introducing an admission test like the graduate management admission test (GMAT) from the Graduate Management Admission Council at Princeton University, or a general admission test or even a 'College of Accounting' similar to the College of Law.

The resolution came in the form of a 'statement of knowledge' expected of a candidate entering the PY. In 1982 a representative from the ICAA met with department heads from universities and CAEs/Institutes of Technology who protested about another layer of monitoring by the ICAA. The past experiences of recognition/approval by the professional body had only ensured superficial formal compliance and not credibility of educational standards. The further imposition of more bureaucratic processes would not necessarily ensure higher quality graduates. However, these protests were to no avail and the *Accreditation requirements for tertiary courses* were issued, based on a prescriptive statement of knowledge. The language of monitoring had shifted from approve to accredit and power had shifted from the academics to the bureaucrats.

The accounting bodies were now discussing 'joint' accreditation, however many of the recommendations made by ASA's National Education and Membership Advisory Committee (NEMAC) were not acceptable to the ICAA, in particular a full disclosure of the ICAA's PY results. The ASA claimed that this could be used to indicate variations in academic standards achieved by graduates at the various higher education institutions and, therefore, in the quality of accounting education across universities. The ICAA did not want the ASA to have access to the pass/fail rates of those sitting the PY. This was a point of tension between the two bodies and a potential barrier to joint accreditation procedures. However, when the *Taskforce for accounting education in Australia report* (1988) was released, joint administration of accreditation procedures was introduced. In agreeing to joint administration, both bodies ensured that the procedures 'did not impinge on policy issues and differences between the two bodies' (Minutes of NEMAC 2 May 1988, ED 6/88).

In 1983 there was a change of government at the Commonwealth level. The Hawke Labor government came to power with yet another 'full-blown national reform of higher education' (Bessant 2002, p87) in mind. It could not come quickly enough for accounting academics like Professor Peter Standish (1983) who, at the time, was the President of the Association of Accounting Academics of Australia and New Zealand (AAANZ). In his address at the 1983 AAANZ Conference, he reported on a member survey undertaken. The results showed that:

- accounting education was funded at a level 40% less than the average
- there was little collaboration between academic and professional practice
- a three-year degree structure was too short for a professional degree.

At this time supply of graduate accountants had increased at 5% per annum with demand outstripping supply at around 7%, and membership of the two accounting bodies was levelling out with a predicted decline after 1987 (Wallace 1987). These issues, combined with declining funding of accounting education in higher education institutions brought together AAANZ, the ASA and the ICAA in the Task Force for Accounting Education in Australia, which met between 1985 and 1987, and issued its report in 1988. It targeted the following issues:

- the common core of accounting knowledge
- future professional entry requirements because of changes to accounting work and their effects on educational processes
- accreditation of accounting degrees
- accounting conversion courses.

Tippett (1992, p103) depicts the report's most important recommendations as greater flexibility of undergraduate degrees and later specialization at postgraduate level in a fourth-year part-time program (never realized) and increased funding for accounting departments through a fairer resource allocation (never achieved).

As was the case with the Vatter Survey in 1964, when the release of the Martin Report overshadowed some of the recommendations and constrained reform because of the structure of accounting education in publicly funded educational institutions, the Task Force operated in the shadow of the release of the Dawkins *Green* and *White papers* in 1987 and 1988 respectively. The implications of the *White paper* were that the binary system of 19 universities and 47 CAEs/Institutes of Technology would be reduced to a unitary system of 35 universities. In many cases a painful merger of institutions coming from contrasting traditions in higher education was required (Mahony 1994). Any recommendations from the Task Force would be tempered by Commonwealth Government reforms.

Whilst the recommendations of the Task Force were being considered and accounting education was seen as being in crisis, the ICAA again looked to the PY to overcome the problems of credible accounting education in higher education institutions.[12] However, there was growing discontent with the PY and criticisms included: poor quality group leaders who did not have the necessary knowledge, experience and interest to be effective; the heavy workload of group leaders in marking the case studies; candidates' lack of contribution to the workshops and their lack of commitment to the course as a whole; and poor quality course material. At this time the ICAA turned to the higher education institutions to rescue the PY and transform it into a postgraduate qualification. As opinions were canvassed around Australia a polarization of views became apparent. The academics expressed the view that most universities would resist if the ICAA wanted to exert too much control over curriculum, staffing and examinations, and besides, resources were strained already (Minutes of Education/Examination Committee 3 May 1988, ED 1096). The ICAA expressed concern over the ability of the academics who might just add an additional year of theory (that is exercise their academic freedom and develop accounting as an academic subject) with non-ICAA members training graduates rather than chartered accountants training chartered accountants. The notion of moving the PY into higher education institutions in the foreseeable future was dropped in 1988. However, the long-term ideal that the PY's educational components be delivered through higher education institutions as part of a fee-paying, part-time two-year course of postgraduate accounting education remained and was realized in 2001.[13]

In the late 1970s and early 1980s, the ASA was exploring ways to overcome its dependency on the higher education system whose graduates were deemed unable to enter directly into the profession, despite obtaining approved degrees. The POP had been implemented in 1977 as a discriminator between members at provisional level and those who wanted to move to

---

12 A separate PY Task Force met while the ICAA was participating in the Task Force for Accounting Education in Australia and recommended that the PY be transferred to the tertiary sector.

13 The ICAA did not pursue its plan to deliver the PY as a postgraduate university course. Instead, in 2001 it was successful in securing recognition for itself as a private education provider, and gaining postgraduate diploma for its CA Program (the successor of the PY).

associate level. It was agreed that candidates would not be formally examined but they would be expected to attend an induction program. In spite of a subcommittee being set up in 1978 and a national task force being established in 1980 to investigate reforming the program, the ASA confirmed in 1982 that there was no need for a single stand alone qualifying examination before full membership. The emphasis would be on the development of a professional program for the orientation and development of graduates during their first few years in the profession (Minutes of ASA National Council 14–15 February 1982, NC 23.2/82; Dickens 1983) and not on examining them.[14] However, at this time there were persistent complaints from employers who claimed that graduates (with accredited degrees) were illiterate and technically incompetent (Henderson 1982) and NEMAC was asked to review education policy. Reflecting, and perhaps exacerbating, the lack of consensus on the core of accounting it failed to define the term 'accountant' to the satisfaction of the National Executive Committee (Minutes of ASA National Council 2 June 1986, NC 2.6/86). NEMAC then turned its attention to establishing criteria for recognizing an institution, approving a course of study and monitoring those courses to ensure their relevance to the profession and their continuing quality. When Professor Carrick Martin was appointed Chairman of NEMAC, he proposed a revision of the professional schedule whereby a provisional associate was a graduate having a major study in accounting and introductory studies in information systems while an associate was a graduate with an additional coherent group or sequence of subjects in taxation, business associations law and auditing or finance or management accounting or information technology or other approved combinations (Minutes of NEMAC 16 February 1987, ED 5/87). At the same time it was decided that entry requirements for graduates where the first award did not include a major in accounting, would be a postgraduate course from a uni-

---

14 Minutes of NEMAC meetings suggest that the committee had become distracted by debates over the definition of an accountant. They could not devise a uniform exam because of a lack of agreement on accounting work and because of variations in higher education courses which were accredited as suitable entry to the professional examinations.

versity that included prescribed subjects. These were to be known as 'conversion courses' and were considered by the Task Force as a way of meeting the future requirements of the profession by encouraging graduates with 'non-relevant'[15] degrees to undertake postgraduate study.

The decline in funding for higher education institutions resulted in major issues for the accounting bodies and impacted on the ability of the institutions to provide accounting education at an appropriate level. The joint administration of accreditation of higher education courses failed to stem the criticism of accounting education, as had its previous incarnations as approval and recognition. Yet it continued to be 'locked in' as the monitoring mechanism for the accounting bodies.

Conclusion: why and how and where to from here?

The accounting education environment in Australia between 1944 and 1988 consisted of three key players; the Commonwealth and state governments as funders of higher education institutions; the providers of accounting education; and the professional accounting bodies as monitors of accounting education outside the profession. The power relations between these key players were destabilized by changes to Commonwealth Government education policy, including changes to funding. There was a growing dependence on higher education institutions to 'produce' professional accountants but the accounting bodies expressed dissatisfaction with the 'products' of the higher education institutions. As a monitoring mechanism, the accounting bodies recognized subjects and then approved/accredited accounting courses as being of sufficient quality and quantity to prepare candidates for their own professional examinations or professional levels of membership. When the accredited courses were found wanting, the accrediting bodies strengthened

---

15 'Non-relevant' is the term used for degrees that do not have an accounting major and therefore not accredited by the accounting bodies as a suitable entry qualification to the professional examinations.

their own professional examinations. This pattern was identified over a 40-year period.[16]

In short, the pattern of recognition/approval/accreditation constitutes the continuation of a monitoring and quality control process notwithstanding its endemic 'failure'. So why did the professional accounting bodies persevere with it up until the late 1980s? By the 1970s, entry to the two professional accounting bodies via private college tuition and technical colleges had been abandoned, along with the main corpus of their own examination systems, and graduate entry had become firmly established. Even though the professional bodies were unhappy with the standard of accounting education in higher education institutions, they were locked into accreditation as a monitoring mechanism. It was easier, apparently, to try to overcome its defects with further tinkering than it was for those bodies to re-institute their previously-abandoned examination arrangements. Furthermore, the establishment of joint administration of accreditation in 1988 after a national review of accounting education (by which time the Commonwealth Government had long been established as a, if not the, major driver of professional education change), meant that the political costs to the professional bodies of unilaterally reversing policies that had been developed over a number of decades would, most likely, be too high for them to bear – particularly as they had the option of strengthening their postgraduate entry programs to overcome the perceived deficiencies of university accounting courses.

Recently, however, these bodies have begun (potentially) to unlock accreditation as a monitoring mechanism by turning to alternate entry pathways that do not necessarily require joint accreditation. In 2007, the ICAA introduced the Graduate Certificate (GradCert) in Chartered Accountancy as a pathway for non-relevant (therefore non-accredited) degree

---

16 Indeed, the ICAA's recent addition of a 'new' entry pathway whilst toughening up the PY may be seen as an intensification of this pattern in a context where it wished to expand the quantum of accounting labour available to its members and respond to their concerns about the technical skills of accounting graduates (Poullaos & Evans 2008). As argued below, this move may evolve into a reassessment of accreditation per se.

holders. It has also itself become a provider of postgraduate training in accounting. In 2009, CPA Australia announced the introduction of a foundation program where candidates without a degree will be able to sit foundation examinations or enrol in CPA segments. Neither of these programs is jointly accredited. Both bodies have thereby embarked on a course of action that reduces their reliance on accounting departments/schools for new members/accounting labour. This move is likely to prove troublesome for the higher education institutions where accreditation has provided a safety net of professional legitimation during a period in which they were developing and establishing their accounting curriculum. The 'unlocking' of accreditation would arguably allow academic accountants to be more adventurous in the design of accounting programs. Weaning Australian governments off monitoring university accounting programs by the professional bodies may take a little longer.

References

Primary sources

Australian Society of Accountants (1970). Annual Report.

Australian Society of Accountants (1973; 1974). Minutes of General Council.

Australian Society of Accountants (1982; 1986). Minutes of National Council.

Australian Society of Accountants (1987; 1988). Minutes of National Education and Membership Advisory Committee (NEMAC).

Australian Society of Accountants (1966; 1971). Report of the Education Committee to General Council.

Australian Universities Commission (1964). *Report of the Committee on the Future of Tertiary Education in Australia.* Melbourne: Government Printers.

Commonwealth Institute of Accountants (1944; 1945). Report of the CIA Education Committee.

Commonwealth Institute of Accountants (1951). Annual Report.

Education, Training and Employment (1979). *Report of the Committee of Inquiry into Education and Training*, 3. Canberra: AGPS.

Institute of Chartered Accountants in Australia (1947; 1951; 1960; 1967). General Council Minutes.

Institute of Chartered Accountants in Australia (1986). Minutes of Education/Examination Committee.

Institute of Chartered Accountants in Australia (1980). National Council Minutes.

Taskforce for Accounting Education in Australia (1988). Report. ICAA, ASA & AAANZ.

The Parliament of the Commonwealth of Australia (1958). Report of the Committee on Australian Universities, September 1957.

Vatter WJ (1964). Survey of Accountancy Education in Australia. ASA, ICAA & AICA.

Secondary sources

Anderson CW (1968). The functions of accounting societies. *The Australian Accountant*, March: 133–44.

Anderson DS & Eaton E (1982a). Australian higher education research society. Part I: Post-war reconstruction and expansion 1940–1965. *Higher Education Research and Development*, 1(1): 5–32.

Anderson DS & Eaton E (1982b). Australian higher education research society. Part II: Equality of opportunity and accountability 1966–1982. *Higher Education Research and Development*, 1(2): 89–128.

Bessant J (2002). 'Dawkins' higher education reforms and how metaphors work in policy making. *Journal of Higher Education Policy and Management*, 24(1): 87–99.

Birkett WP & Evans E (2005). Control of accounting education within Australian universities and technical colleges 1944–51: a unidimensional consideration of professionalism. *Accounting, Business & Financial History*, 15(2): 121–43.

Braddock LA (1949). The status of the accountant in Australia. *Proceedings of the Australian Congress on Accounting*, (p270). Sydney: Australian Congress on Accounting, Sydney.

Carrington AS (1970). Education for the profession. *New Zealand Society of Accountant's Convention*, Auckland, March.

Chambers RJ (1956). Educational policy: a suggestion. *The Australian Accountant*, February: 73–80.

Creaney E (1984). *The history of the IAA*. An address by the National Secretary, Perth, WA, July.

Davies S (1989). *The Martin Committee and the binary policy of higher education in Australia*. Melbourne: Ashwood House.

Dickens C (1983). Professional programme. *The Australian Accountant*, March: 19–22.

Encel S (1963). The Robbins report. *Vestes*, VI(4): 247–50.

Fitzgerald GE (1949). The status of the accountant in Australia. *Proceedings of the Australian Congress on Accounting*, (pp265–67). Australian Congress on Accounting, Sydney.

Fitzgerald GE (1952a). The institute. *The Australian Accountant*, May: 158.

Fitzgerald GE (1952b). Valedictory. *The Australian Accountant*, December: 417–18.

Forster A (1952). The profession and the university. *The Chartered Accountant in Australia*, September: 204–05.

Goldberg L (1987). *Dynamics of an entity*. Accounting Association of Australia and New Zealand.

Harman G (1981). The 'razor gang' decisions, the guidelines to the commissions and commonwealth education policy. *Vestes*, 24(2): 28–40.

Harman G (1982). The 'razor gang' moves, the 1981 guidelines and the uncertain future. In G Harman & D Smart (Eds), *Federal intervention in Australian education past, present and future*, (pp163–80). Melbourne: George House.

Harvey L (2004). The power of accreditation: views of academics. *Journal of Higher Education Policy and Management*, 26(2): 207–23.

Henderson MS (1982). The graduate entry scheme. *The Australian Accountant*, June: 300–03.

Houston HS & Harman GS (1978). Course accreditation in Australian colleges of advanced education. *The South Pacific Journal of Teacher Education*, 6(1): 48–68.

Howitt H (1952). Training for accountancy. *The Chartered Accountant in Australia*, March: 539–48.

King RC (1978). Institutional reactions. In T Hore, RD Linke & LHT West (Eds), *The future of higher education in Australia*. Higher Education and Advisory and Research Unit, Monash University.

Lowrie A (2008). The relevance of aggress and the aggression of relevance: The rise of the accreditation machine. *International Journal of Educational Management*, 22(4): 352–64.

Mahony D (1994). A comparison of the Australian and British post binary higher education systems. *Higher Education Research and Development*, 13(1): 71–84.

Malandra GH (2008). Accountability and learning assessment in the future of higher education. *On the Horizon*, 16(2): 57–71.

Meredith GG (1974a). Membership survey 1973: part 1. *The Australian Accountant*, February: 26–34.

Meredith GG (1974b). Membership survey 1973: part 2. *The Australian Accountant*, March: 115–22.

Meredith GG (1974c). Membership survey 1973: part 3. *The Australian Accountant*, April: 168–72.

Meredith GG (1974d). Membership survey 1973: part 4. *The Australian Accountant*, May: 214–17.

Meredith GG (1974e). Membership survey 1973: part 5. *The Australian Accountant*, June: 305–08.

Poullaos C & Evans E (2008). The ICAA pathways project – issues and options for accounting education in Australia. Paper presented to the Sydney University Pacioli Society, 28 November.

Smyth EB (1949). The status of the accountant in Australia. *Proceedings of the Australian Congress on Accounting*, (pp268–69). Australian Congress on Accounting, Sydney.

South Australian Division of the Australian Chartered Accountants Research Society (1952). Is public accounting worthy of a degree? *The Chartered Accountant in Australia*, February: 497–509.

Spaull A (1982). Australian education in the Second World War. St Lucia: University of Queensland Press.

Standish PEM (1983). Accounting education in Australia: 1982–83. *Accounting and Finance*, November: 1–30.

Tippett M (1992). The plight of accounting education in Australia: a review article. *Accounting Education*, 1(2): 99–127.

Waddington DM, Radford WC & Keats JA (1950). *Review of education in Australia 1940–1948*. Carlton: Melbourne University Press.

Wallace M (1987). The supply and demand for accounting graduates in Australia. *Australian Accountant*, June: 46–53.

West LHT (1978). Demand for higher education. In JP Powell (Ed), *Higher education in a steady state*, (pp19–25). HERDSA.

Yorston RK (1949). The status of the accountant in Australia. *Proceedings of the Australian Congress on Accounting*, (pp263–65). Australian Congress on Accounting, Sydney.

Young NS (1949). The status of the accountant in Australia. *Proceedings of the Australian Congress on Accounting*, (pp245–60). Australian Congress on Accounting, Sydney.

16

The study process questionnaire: theoretical and empirical issues for accounting education research

William Birkett and Rosina Mladenovic (University of Sydney)

*Abstract**

For more than two decades there have been an increasing number of calls for greater application of the approaches to learning paradigm in advancing research in accounting education (Williams et al. 1988, Kember & Gow 1989, Lucas 1996, Beattie et al. 1997, Sharma 1998, Booth et al. 1999, Mladenovic 2000). In response, there have been numerous papers published in the area providing many valuable insights into the learning approaches of accounting students and accounting educational contexts. A popular way to measure students' approaches to learning is Biggs' (1987a, b) study process questionnaire (SPQ). Based on a critical evaluation of the SPQ, this chapter identifies a number of issues surrounding the application of the questionnaire in accounting education research and brings into question the interpretations of prior research findings, suggesting that accounting students tend to be 'sur-

* This chapter is a revised and updated version of a paper originally written by Bill and myself after I completed my PhD under his brilliant supervision. The paper was presented at two conferences in 2002. The findings are still relevant today and the original paper has been cited in a number of publications since 2002. While the paper has been updated to incorporate the current literature in this chapter, in the main, the ideas remain the same as we developed together in 2002. Bill was a man way ahead of his time and accounting education is still catching up. It was a pleasure and an honour to work with him and it is wonderful to finally publish this paper in his memory.

424 | Practices, profession and pedagogy in accounting

face learners' or that accounting education contexts tend to impede quality learning. Areas for further research are suggested.

For over two decades concerns have been expressed about the quality of accounting education. Policy makers, the accounting profession, employers and educators require accounting education to be personally liberating, provide suitable professional preparation, address relevant and emergent societal issues, support the development of a broad portfolio of skills and help students become lifelong learners (e.g. Williams, Tiller, Herring & Scheiner 1988; Accounting Education Change Commission (AECC) 1990, 1992; Institute of Chartered Accountants (ICAA) 1996; International Federation of Accountants (IFAC) 1996; Kelly, Davey & Haigh 1999; Albrecht & Sack 2000; Cecez-Kecmanovic, Juchau, Kay & Wright 2002).

In 1997, Beattie, Collins and McInnes claimed that the calls for accounting education reform shared one fundamental common feature – the need to support students to move away from procedural or surface learning and to engage more with a conceptual or deep form of learning. They called for "a program of research in accounting which investigates empirically the role of learning approaches within the accounting discipline" (p10). Others supported this call (e.g. Williams et al. 1988; Kember & Gow 1989; Lucas 1996; Sharma 1998; Booth, Luckett & Mladenovic 1999; Mladenovic 2000), and in response, a large body of published research has emerged. There are currently three published reviews of the research arising from the approaches to learning paradigm, namely, Lucas and Mladenovic (2004), Lucas and Mladenovic (2006a) and Duff and McKinstry (2007).

Research arising from the approaches to learning paradigm employs both qualitative and quantitative research methods. The qualitative methods include phenomenography (mainly interview research) and the quantitative research involves the use of self-report questionnaires and inventories. While qualitative research provides a rich and detailed source of data about variation between students, inventories and questionnaires provide data on a larger number of students which can be used to provide statistical support for the qualitative variation identified. A number of inventories and questionnaires have been employed including:

- approaches to studying inventory (ASI) (Entwistle & Ramsden 1983)
- study processes questionnaire (SPQ) (Biggs 1987a, b) and the revised two-factor study process questionnaire (R-SPQ-2F) (Biggs, Kember & Leung 2001)
- approaches to study questionnaire (Richardson 1990)
- revised ASI (RASI), ASSIST (Tait, Entwistle & McCune 1998)
- reflections on learning inventory (RoLI) (Meyer & Boulton-Lewis 1999, Meyer 2004).[1]

While the Approaches to Learning Paradigm has provided valuable insights for accounting educators to date, Lucas and Mladenovic (2004, p399) and others suggest that there are still many fruitful avenues of further research.

> Research within this framework has added to theory, developed research tools and provided empirical evidence to support changes in teaching ... [however,] there still remain many unresolved issues and there exist tantalising indications that there may be numerous productive lines of research yet to be developed (Gibbs, 2003; Richardson, 2000). In particular, a review of the literature indicates that there is a clear need for further research to be conducted within specific disciplinary settings.

This chapter provides further insights into students' approaches to learning from within the disciplinary context of accounting. Specifically, this chapter focuses on the applicability of the SPQ, one of the most commonly employed instruments, to measure accounting students' approaches to learning. The first research paper employing the Biggs (1987a, b) SPQ in an accounting setting was published in 1989 and since then numerous papers employing this method have been published (Chan, Leung, Gow & Hu 1989; Kember & Gow 1989; Booth et al. 1999; Ramburuth 2001; Davidson 2002; Eley 1992; Cooper 2004; English, Luckett & Mladenovic 2004; Hall, Ramsay & Raven 2004; Ramburuth & Mladenovic 2004; Jackling 2005 a, b). More recently,

---

1 The number and variety of questionnaires and inventories creates difficulties in relation to comparing findings across inventories and questionnaires. For reviews of inventories and questionnaires see Richardson (2000), Duff (2004) and Duff and McKinstry (2007).

Biggs et al. (2001) revised SPQ, the R-SPQ-2F, has been employed in accounting studies (see, for example, De Lange & Mavondo 2004).[2] However, it is important to note that even though the SPQ was *not* developed from within the discipline of accounting, it has been employed without a critical analysis of its applicability.

This chapter provides a critical review of the applicability of the use of the SPQ within accounting education research. A number of theoretical issues relating to the use of this paradigm are discussed. Prior research is reviewed and reinterpreted both in the light of the theoretical issues, and with respect to the factors that are unique to the discipline of accounting. The repeated claims that accounting students are 'surface learners' or that accounting education contexts tend to 'impede quality learning' are brought into question as a result.

The chapter is structured as follows: the first section provides a brief review of the early literature on approaches to learning and summarizes the findings. Section two identifies the differences between the theoretical constructs and the empirical measures relating to the use of the SPQ. Section three reviews and reinterprets the early research on approaches to learning in accounting in the light of the issues identified in section two and the unique disciplinary context of accounting. The fourth section provides a review of recent studies. Future directions for research are suggested in the final section.

---

2 This paper focuses on the SPQ. However, given the main difference between the SPQ and the revised SPQ is that the achieving approach has been dropped, the discussion in this chapter on the deep and surface approach scores is also applicable to the R-SPQ-2F. Given the author is only aware of one accounting study that uses the revised R-SPQ-2F questionnaire – see de Lange and Mavondo (2004) which is summarized in a later section of the chapter for completeness, for ease of reading, only the SPQ will be referred to throughout the chapter.

Accounting education research using the SPQ: early work 1989–2001

Commonly reported findings arising from early research on approaches to learning, including those employing the SPQ, were that accounting courses attracted 'surface learners' and accounting educational contexts were inappropriately designed as students employed surface approaches to learning – thus producing less than satisfactory learning outcomes (a focus on facts rather than arguments, and memorization of information and procedures) (Chan et al. 1989; Gow, Kember & Cooper 1994; Beattie et al. 1997). These criticisms were supported by empirical research which was *interpreted* to show that accounting students tended to adopt a predominantly surface approach to learning (Chan et al. 1989, Eley 1992, Gow et al. 1994, Booth et al. 1999). This was also supported anecdotally by the claims made by teachers in an Australian accounting course, quoted in Ramsden (1992, p32). For example:

> In the final exam, students are weak on conceptual points, such as the matching principle. It is possible to pass without being competent in handling Debit and Credit, or accruals. Students can't write; this may be because they don't understand the concepts. So they concentrate on number-crunching in order to pass.

In Hong Kong, Chan et al. (1989, p189) found that "(a)ccountancy students have a tendency to focus on the bare fundamentals and reproduce them through rote learning rather than to organize their time and follow up all suggested readings". Gow and colleagues (1994, p118) reported that students' use of a deep approach to learning declined from the first to the second year of the course and they interpreted these results as indicating that the "enthusiasm and use of meaningful approaches to study tasks declined as students progressed through their first year". They also found that the average scores relating to a deep approach to learning rose again through the second and third years, but still remained *below* the first-year level. A potential explanation for these results was seen to be a number of factors in the context of learning which promote a surface approach to learning, such as an "excessive workload, surface assessment demands, lack of intrinsic motivation, a didactic teaching style, high staff/student ratios" (Gow et al. 1994, p118).

Booth et al. (1999) collected SPQ scores from accounting students at two large Australian universities and compared them with Biggs' (1987b) SPQ scores for university students' approaches to learning in education, arts and science courses. The scores for accounting students were significantly higher in terms of surface motive, strategy and approach than the scores for arts, education and science students. Arts, education and science students were significantly higher on deep motive, strategy and approach scores (with the exceptions that science students scored similarly on deep motive and male science students scored similarly on deep approach scores).

Ramburuth (2001) surveyed 719 local students and 248 international undergraduate students in the Faculty of Commerce and Economics at a major Australian university to investigate whether international students (mainly from Asia and South East Asia) differed in their *orientation* to learning from local (Australian) students (students were surveyed prior to commencement of their formal studies). A modified version of the Biggs' (1987a, b) SPQ was employed (data were collected for the deep and surface approaches only). The findings showed no significant differences between the two cohorts of students in their orientation to a deep approach to learning. However, the SPQ scores of international students were significantly higher on all dimensions of the surface approach – motive, strategy and overall.

Mladenovic (2001) explored the effects of the learning context created in a second-year management accounting course on students' approaches to learning. The course was designed so that its objectives (in terms of learning outcomes sought) were aligned with teaching methods, curriculum and assessments used. The course also incorporated the portfolio of desired learning outcomes sought in accounting students, as outlined in the introduction of this chapter. The underlying pedagogy included problem-based, case-based and experiential learning philosophies, effectively seeking to support deep learning approaches. Students' approaches to learning were examined before they experienced the course, and then again after, to investigate the effects of alignment in the learning context on students' approaches to learning. The aim was to reduce students' use of a surface approach and increase their use of a deep approach.

The study produced unexpected results. There was no change in students' approaches to learning from first year to second year, despite the aligned second-year learning context; and there was no relationship (with the exception of the deep and achieving approaches) between final grades attained (in cognitively demanding assessments) and the approaches to learning used.

To summarize, early empirical research on accounting students' approaches to learning using the SPQ reported consistent concerning findings that accounting students tend to adopt a surface approach to learning; accounting learning contexts support a surface approach; and thus produce lower quality student learning outcomes. However, the unexpected findings in Mladenovic (2001) prompted further inquiry into the measurement instrument and the interpretations arising from the findings – the results of which were written up in Birkett and Mladenovic (2002). The first part of their inquiry was to examine more closely the nature of the theoretical constructs and empirical measures of deep and surface approaches to learning.

Deep and surface approaches to learning: theoretical constructs and empirical measurements of the SPQ

An approach to learning is made up of a cognitive aspect (strategy) and an affective aspect (motive). While the focus of this review is on the cognitive or strategy aspect of an approach, the affective is mentioned when it is relevant for the discussion, or when it is included as a significant finding in the research papers reviewed within this chapter.

Figure 1 depicts the nature of the *theoretical* constructs and *empirical* measures of deep and surface approaches to learning. In figure 1, the cognitive aspect of the theoretical construct labelled 'deep approach to learning' describes a learning situation where verbs across the entire range from the lowest cognitive levels to the highest levels could be used by a student (to varying degrees, dependent on the nature of the task) and a 'surface approach to learning' describes verbs that could be used which are at the lower cognitive levels only.

Figure 1: Comparing the theoretical constructs for deep and surface approaches with the measurement instrument (SPQ). Adapted from Biggs (2001, p89).

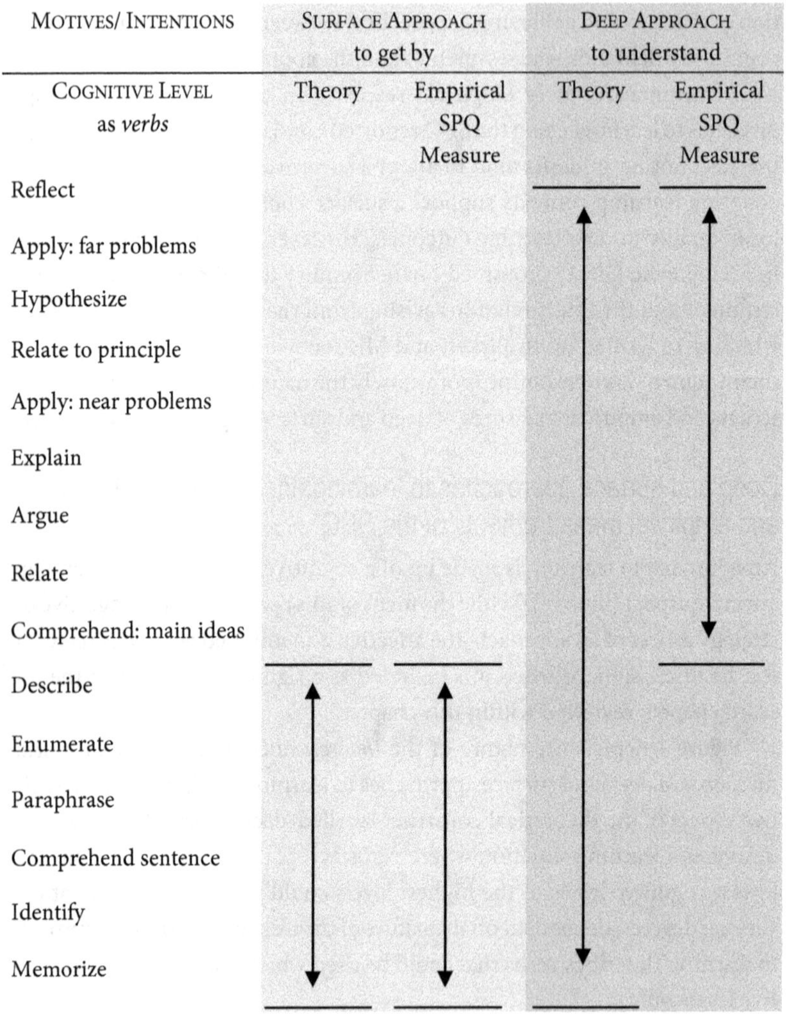

MOTIVES/ INTENTIONS	SURFACE APPROACH to get by		DEEP APPROACH to understand	
COGNITIVE LEVEL as *verbs*	Theory	Empirical SPQ Measure	Theory	Empirical SPQ Measure
Reflect				
Apply: far problems				
Hypothesize				
Relate to principle				
Apply: near problems				
Explain				
Argue				
Relate				
Comprehend: main ideas				
Describe				
Enumerate				
Paraphrase				
Comprehend sentence				
Identify				
Memorize				

Hence according to the theory, a student employing a surface strategy for learning could be seen to memorize, identify, comprehend a sentence, paraphrase, enumerate and at best, describe the phenomena being studied. On the other hand, according to the theory, a student employing a deep strategy could be seen to be performing all of the same lower-level cognitive activities as those employing a surface approach, however, in addition we would be able to observe higher-order cognitive activities such as being able to comprehend main ideas, relate, argue, explain, apply, relate to principle and reflect.

Thus, while the theoretical description of a deep strategy as part of a deep approach to learning includes both higher- and lower-order cognitive activities, the quantitative measure of the cognitive aspect of a deep approach to learning, using the SPQ, only measures the higher-level cognitive strategies from 'comprehend main ideas' to 'reflect'; the lower cognitive levels are measured by the surface approach score in the SPQ.[3] The SPQ treats low-level (surface) and high level (deep) cognitive activities as *dichotomous*, whereas the theory describes them as *continuum*.

The implication of this inconsistency between the theoretical description and the empirical measure, is that when the questionnaires are employed to

---

3 For those unfamiliar with the quantitative measure, that is the SPQ questionnaire, it consists of 42 items which include six independent sets of seven items. Three of the six sets of seven items independently measure the three affective aspects of an approach (i.e. surface motive, deep motive and achieving motive) and the other three sets of seven items independently measure the three cognitive aspects of an approach (i.e. surface strategy, deep strategy and achieving strategy). The students' responses to the seven motive items and corresponding seven strategy items are summed for each of the deep, surface and achieving approaches. The items in the SPQ that elicit the surface strategy (cognitive aspect) score focus on verbs listed in the lower half of figure 1 such as 'memorize'. On the other hand, the items exploring a deep strategy (cognitive aspect) focus on verbs in the upper portion of figure 1, for example, 'relate'. However, if we were to measure a deep strategy in the same way it is represented in 'theory' we would actually sum both the surface and deep strategy scores. As this is not how it is measured in the SPQ there is a discrepancy between the theoretical definition of the cognitive aspect of a deep approach and its empirical measure using the SPQ.

explore students' approaches to learning, the strategy aspect which is measured using the lower-level cognitive activities *may actually be part of a student adopting a deep approach to learning* however, it will be 'captured' in the surface approach score in the SPQ. That is, the theoretical definition of a deep approach to learning and its quantitative measure differ. The importance of this distinction becomes evident when interpreting what the SPQ scores indicate about students' approaches to learning as discussed in the next section as part of the review of the accounting literature employing the SPQ.

Re-interpreting early research findings on accounting students' approaches to learning

An examination of the deep and surface theoretical constructs and empirical measurements underlying the SPQ, highlights the need to re-examine the way research findings have been interpreted. This examination brings into question whether the interpretations arising from the early research using the SPQ that accounting students are 'surface learners' or that they tend to adopt surface approaches to learning in accounting educational contexts are in fact supported by the research findings.

To explain, SPQ profiles (the scores arising from the SPQ questionnaire) tend to show that accounting students generally have higher scores for the surface approach to learning than the deep approach to learning; this has been interpreted as suggesting either they rely on surface approaches to learning or they are surface learners. For example, Chan et al. (1989, p189) claim that the "[a]nalysis of the SPQ data indicates that the accountancy students' motive in studying drift in one direction, to meet course requirements minimally … students have a tendency to focus on the bare fundamentals and reproduce them through rote learning". Beattie et al. (1997, p10) assert that it "is widely believed that accounting attracts a relatively high proportion of reproducing and achieving students". However, this interpretation may be misguided for a number of reasons: first, SPQ measures of the cognitive aspect of the surface approach (such as, memorize or enumerate) may be part of a deep approach to learning and second, it tends to locate approaches to learning as a disposition or characteristic of students, rather than as a response to perceived tasks in learning contexts experienced. These reasons are explored further below.

Memorization and the surface and deep approach to learning

Memorization is measured by the surface strategy component of the SPQ. In this way it can be incorrectly interpreted as 'inappropriate' or part of a 'surface approach to learning'. However, SPQ measures of the cognitive aspect of the surface approach (such as, memorize or enumerate) may, in fact, be an indissoluble part of a deep approach to learning. Biggs (1989) suggests that memorising or rote learning may be appropriate for certain tasks. For example, the use of rote learning to facilitate the recall of formulae and definitions may be an appropriate strategy as part of a deep approach to learning. Biggs (1987a, p61) also illustrates this view in relation to science students when he claims:

> sciences need *both* surface- and deep-related approaches; surface to focus on the fact and detail of formulae and procedures, and deep to understand them (Biggs & Kirkby 1983).

Hence, the use of memorization and rote learning as part of a deep approach should be differentiated from the situation where a student consistently relies on memory to replicate information without understanding. The SPQ in its current form (or in its revised R-SPQ-2F form) is not able to capture this distinction. It appears then, that memorization and rote learning may be appropriate and successful ways to learn in certain contexts and hence the development of more suitable measurement processes requires further investigation. An alternative measurement process is discussed under future research in the final section of the chapter.

Approach to learning: inherent characteristic or contextual response?

Approaches to learning are often incorrectly interpreted as a characteristic or trait of students, rather than as being seen as students' responses to tasks in educational contexts. As Biggs (2001, p75) explains:

> [i]t is misleading to describe deep and surface approaches as learning 'styles' that inhere in an individual (Schmeck 1988), because like a marriage rela-

tionship an approach to learning can only exist in the presence of both parties, the learner and what is being learned, not the learner alone.[4]

This is best illustrated by the results of Eley (1992). In this study he examined a cohort of students who were enrolled simultaneously in both an accounting and a business law course. SPQ scores were collected from these students in relation to each of their courses (see table 1).

Table 1: Sample means for SPQ scores. (Extract from Eley 1992, p247, table 9).

Course	Surface Approach	Deep Approach
Accounting	52.17	34.26
Business Law	49.65	41.43

The SPQ scores reported by the *same* students in relation to different courses were significantly different (p<0.05) on both the deep and surface approaches.

This is an important finding, as it indicates that accounting students' scores for surface and deep approaches vary in different learning contexts – suggesting that students adapt to the requirements of the contexts of learning with a mix of surface, deep and achieving motives and strategies. This brings into question the idea of discipline norms.

Booth et al. (1999) collected SPQ scores from accounting students at two large Australian universities in order to compare them with SPQ scores from

---

4 While approaches to learning are not considered to be inherent traits or learning styles, Biggs (2001) describes students' orientations as preferences or predispositions to use a particular approach. Ramsden (1992, p51) explains the concept further by suggesting that "(a)lthough it is abundantly clear that the same student uses different approaches on different occasions it is also true that general tendencies to adopt particular approaches, related to the different demands of course and previous educational experiences, do exist. Variability in approaches thus coexists with consistency".

students in arts, education and science. In comparing accounting students' SPQ scores with scores from other disciplines, they found that accounting students had higher surface and lower deep approach SPQ scores than the norms for Australian arts, education and science students. Based on these findings, Booth et al. (1999, p296) conclude that

> [t]his finding is of particular relevance to accounting educators as it provides some empirical evidence of widely-expressed concerns that students adopt a predominantly surface learning approach in accounting.

Eley (1992) also reported deep and surface approach SPQ scores for Australian accounting students at Monash University. These scores were compared with those for biochemistry, chemistry and English literature students at the same university. He found that the accounting students exhibited significantly higher scores for a surface approach and lower scores for a deep approach to learning. While Eley's study was based on a small sample (63 accounting students) at only one institution, in the main, his findings are consistent with Booth et al. (1999).

Generally, research using the SPQ suggests that accounting students report relatively higher surface approach scores than do students in other disciplines, and relatively lower deep approach scores. In some cases, these results have been interpreted as meaning (a) accounting learning contexts support surface approaches to learning, or (b) that accounting students are surface learners, consistent with Beattie and et al. (1997) assertion that accounting students tend to adopt a predominantly surface approach to learning.

The appropriateness of this form of inter-disciplinary comparison in the absence of an analysis of the differences in learning context, however, is questionable. Approaches to learning theory emphasizes the importance of the context in influencing students' approaches to learning. Different contexts, as might be expected in different disciplines, are likely to lead to different approaches to learning, and these will be reflected in different patterns or profiles in SPQ scores. It could be argued that, if students correctly perceive what is required in a course and are capable and motivated to adjust their approaches to learning to achieve the desired outcomes, then SPQ scores should reflect the appropriate profile or mix between deep and surface scores for the specific course (or for a specific task). Ramsden (1979) "showed that students switch strategies to suit students' perceptions of course demands" (as quoted in Biggs & Rihn 1984, p281). Thus, learning is context driven – this is the very foundation upon which the approaches to learning paradigm is built.

Comparison of students' SPQ scores across disciplines *only* provides evidence that the approaches to learning used *vary* across contexts. This can be interpreted as students' adaptations to the particular learning contexts faced. If adaptations are grounded in experience, and experiences in a discipline tend to be relatively consistent, it is possible that profiles of surface, deep and achieving SPQ scores from different disciplines reflect appropriate, if different, adaptations. Thus, accounting, science, education, and arts students may score differently on the SPQ because they are appropriately adapted in terms of approaches to learning to their respective disciplines. Of course, this leaves open the issue of whether each discipline is appropriately focused in terms of learning outcomes sought and appropriately configured in terms of the learning context used. This finding is supported by Meyer and Eley (1999, p198) who argue that:

> individual students might well adopt differentiated patterns of learning behaviours that are attributable to the learning contexts shaped by different subjects. That is, perceptions and experiences of learning contexts might be shaped also by the epistemology of a discipline and they might therefore vary considerably from one discipline to another.

It follows that it may be inappropriate to compare SPQ scores across disciplines, as the nature of the context of learning may be quite different; so different in fact that one would expect different patterns of SPQ scores. Thus, SPQ scores in any discipline may provide an inappropriate benchmark for others, and criticisms of accounting students or accounting education based on relative SPQ scores between disciplines may be quite misguided.

To summarize, the above discussion suggests that the early research using the SPQ may have incorrectly interpreted the findings as suggesting that accounting students rely on surface approaches to learning or that they are surface learners, and that accounting educational contexts support surface approaches to learning.

Review of the recent studies using the SPQ 2002–09

Unlike the early research which claimed that accounting students were 'surface learners' and that accounting education contexts 'encourage' students to adopt a surface approach to learning, the recent research using the SPQ published between 2002 and 2009, does not make broad sweeping negative interpretations about the research data.

Recent research arising from the approaches to learning paradigm has instead explored a number of themes including: the relationship between the nature of assessment tasks and students' approaches to learning; the effects of gender; the effects of the learning environment on approaches and changes in approaches over time. The results and the interpretations of those findings in relation to each of these themes are briefly summarized below.

Nature of the assessment task and students' approaches to learning

Davidson (2002) investigated the relationship between accounting students' approach to learning and their exam performance by distinguishing between different types of examination questions. Examination questions were classified into two groups – those requiring more complex answers and those requiring less complex answers. He found that no significant relationships occurred between the use of a deep approach and performance on questions that were less complex, or between the use of a surface approach and any examination questions. However the results showed a significant positive relationship between students' performance on complex examination questions and the use of a deep approach.

The results of Davidson's research suggest that students who adopt a deep approach will do better on complex examination questions, while for less complex questions, it will make no difference if the student adopts a deep or surface approach. Hence this research identifies the importance of classifying the nature of each assessment item (simple/complex) when looking at the relationship between students' performance and approach to learning rather than making generalized negative claims about accounting students.

Like Davidson (2002), Ramburuth and Mladenovic (2004) also investigated 'relationships' with the SPQ. They looked at the relationship between students' orientations to learning (measured using the SPQ), students' level of cognitive engagement in a comprehension task (measured using Biggs & Collis 1982 SOLO Taxonomy) and subsequent academic performance. Performance was measured using the students' final grades in their two first-year accounting units. Students' SOLO scores were determined by analysing a comprehension task students completed upon entry to university. The relationship between these initial SOLO levels was compared with academic performance in subsequent introductory accounting units. The findings revealed a significant positive relationship between SOLO levels at the beginning of the course and students' subsequent academic performance in both units. The students had lower SOLO levels upon entry to university achieved lower academic grades than those students who scored high on the SOLO scale upon entry. While SOLO scores were related to subsequent performance, in contrast with Davidson, there was no positive relationship between a deep orientation to learning and academic performance. However, there was a significant negative relationship between surface orientation and final grade. Perhaps these mixed results can be explained by classifying the assessment tasks as complex or less complex and re-examining the relationships. Further, it is again interesting to note that no broad negative interpretations about accounting students being 'surface learners' are made based on the SPQ scores in either of these studies. This is a marked change from the earlier research.

Gender and approach to learning

De Lange and Mavondo (2004) explored gender differences and their relationship to approaches to learning for business students studying via Open Learning Australia. They employed the Biggs et al. (2001) R-SPQ-2F (a two-factor model exploring surface and deep approaches). They reported significant gender differences in the relationship between approaches to learning and study motivation. They suggested these differences may be due to the different ways female and male students understood the questionnaire and conceptualized the constructs of deep and surface approaches. This is consistent with other research (see, for example, Lucas & Mladenovic 2006b).

Effects of the learning environment on approaches to learning

English et al. (2004) and Hall et al. (2004) investigated the effects of interventions in the learning environment on accounting students' approaches to learning. English et al. (2004) explored the effects of an intervention in an introductory accounting course designed to encourage a deep approach to learning by developing students' written communication skills. Using the SPQ, the effectiveness of the intervention was measured by comparing the students' approaches to learning with those at another Australian university offering a more 'traditional' approach to teaching accounting. At the beginning of the course there were no differences in students' approaches to learning between the institutions. By the end of the course, students studying at the institution where the intervention had been introduced scored significantly higher on the deep approach and significantly lower on the surface approach score than the students at the traditional university. However, while there were significant differences between institutions, the results also revealed that there were no significant changes in students' surface approach to learning scores and a small decrease in deep approach scores as a result of the intervention. Hence English et al. (2004) claimed that the findings only *broadly* confirm the effectiveness of the intervention in encouraging students to employ a deep approach to learning.

Hall et al. (2004) introduced group learning activities designed to improve the quality of students' learning outcomes by encouraging students to adopt a deep approach to learning. Using the SPQ to measure students' approaches to learning before and after the interventions, they found that students exhibited a small, but statistically significant, increase in their deep learning approach and a small, but statistically significant, reduction in their surface learning approach. However, when they looked at students' strategies, while students increased their use of deep strategies they did not decrease their use of the surface strategies. Hall et al. (2004, p502) commented that

> the results appear consistent with the arguments of Birkett and Mladenovic
> (2002), as students do not need to reduce their use of lower-level strategies

(for example, rote learning, paraphrasing) when adopting a deep approach. Further in some learning contexts, lower level strategies as measured by the surface strategy score in the SPQ are required in order to progress to higher levels of understanding. In accounting students must first learn terminology, basic concepts and procedures before being able to apply knowledge to novel problems and reflect/evaluate on the appropriateness of various treatments and methods.

Hence recent studies have re-interpreted the SPQ findings not with broad sweeping negative statements that accounting students are 'surface learners', but rather have looked at the context of learning in accounting and what strategies students employ to successfully learn the subject matter. What was previously interpreted as 'inappropriate' in the early SPQ research is now interpreted as fundamental in the learning process. This interpretation is consistent with the theoretical description of a deep approach to learning.

Jackling (2005a) explored the effects of students' perceptions of the learning environment, on their approach to learning, and on the learning outcomes achieved. She employed a phenomenological research approach to report students' descriptions of their motives and strategies in studying accounting. The sample consisted of 12 second-year commerce students who were selected from a larger study of 121 students who had completed the Biggs' (1987a,b) SPQ. Jackling's results indicated that most students, regardless of their motives, use a variety of learning strategies in preparing for exams, including memorising, re-doing tutorial exercises, reading (for understanding or to memorize) and making notes. However, common patterns also could be identified – students with a deep motive mainly used achieving and deep strategies in their studies. Students with an achieving motive used a similar range of strategies to the students who had deep motives. Students with surface motives more frequently used surface strategies (such as memorising notes and placing less emphasis on doing or re-doing practical questions).

Jackling also examined whether students' perceptions of the teaching/learning environment (in particular, the importance placed on memory) were related to the strategies they used in their study, as a way of testing the premise that perceptions of the learning outcomes required in the course influenced the learning strategies employed by students. The results revealed that students' perceptions that the course required the use of good memory were associated with the use of surface strategies in studying; where the use of a good memory was not perceived as important, deep and achieving approaches were used. A number of students perceived that memory was an important strategy in financial accounting. Jackling (2005a, p283) argued that:

> the importance of memorising as a strategy may be partly attributable to the nature of the course content, given that the course of study was perceived by students to have a procedural orientation, together with a sequential processing of data. These characteristics were similar to course content described by Umpathy (1984, p142) and Birkett and Mladenovic (2002).

It is interesting to note that both Hall et al. (2004) and Jackling (2005a) cite Birkett and Mladenovic (2002) to explain their research findings on students' approaches to learning in accounting. The arguments in Birkett and Mladenovic (2002) could also be applied to Jackling (2005b).

Approaches to learning over time

Jackling (2005b, p606) explores accounting students' approaches to learning over three years longitudinally and cross-sectionally using the SPQ. The cross-sectional and the longitudinal data revealed that accounting students

> increased their use of aspects of deep approaches to learning as they progressed through their undergraduate course. At the same time students ... maintained consistency in surface approaches.

This finding might also be explained, as suggested in Birkett and Mladenovic (2002), as accounting by its very nature, may require some memorization at all levels (introductory to senior accounting units), and hence Jackling (2005b) reported no change in students' surface approach scores over three years. However, in later years students have the capacity to also engage in higher order cognitive tasks as measured by the deep approach to learning. In this way, the surface scores stay the same while the deep scores increase, as memorization may be an indissoluble part of a deep approach.

Memorization

The issue of memorization is also important when we consider the Chinese learner. Using the SPQ, Cooper (2004) investigated the approaches to learning of Chinese and Australian accounting students to explore the 'enigma' of the Chinese learner. They found that while mechanical rote learning can be associated to a surface approach to learning, the Chinese tradition of memorization through repetition can deepen understanding and result in high academic achievement.

The proposition that memorization requires further investigation and further partitioning has arisen a number of times throughout this chapter. This is also recognized by other researchers (Meyer 2000, Lucas & Meyer 2005). Meyer (2000) identified both deep and surface forms of memorising which provide further insights into understanding students' approaches to learning, particularly as memorization relates to the accounting discipline. It may be that the measure of a surface approach using the SPQ, particularly linked with memorization and rote learning, is an over-simplification of the learning approaches adopted by accounting students.

Meyer (2000), as part of the reflections on learning inventory (RoLI) research, discovered three different forms of memorization: memorising before understanding (MBU); memorising after understanding (MAU) and memorising as rehearsal (MAR). MAR is a form of rote learning and this was associated with ineffective learning approaches, MBU was associated with a surface approach to learning, and MAU with a deep approach to learning. This is an important development from the one main type of memorization of *rote learning* as measured by the SPQ.

In summary, recent research on approaches to learning suggests that: it is not sufficient to simply look at the relationships between learning approach and performance, as assessment tasks require careful evaluation in order to establish what type of learning outcome is being assessed; that gender is another factor that must be considered when conducting research measuring approaches to learning; accounting students tend to persistently report high scores on the surface approach to learning as measured by the SPQ and that the arguments in Birkett and Mladenovic (2002) may be used to explain these findings rather than broad sweeping statements that accounting students are surface learners. Finally, memorization as measured by the SPQ needs to be looked at more closely and further examined in relation to the different types of memorization as identified by Meyer (2000).

Discussion, conclusions and future research

Since the first study using the SPQ in accounting setting was published in 1989 there have been numerous papers providing many valuable insights into the learning approaches of accounting students and accounting educational contexts. Early empirical research (1989–2001) reported consistent concerning findings that accounting students tended to adopt a surface approach to learning and that accounting learning contexts supported a surface approach and thus produced lower quality student learning outcomes. However, a critical review of one of the popular ways to measure students' approaches to learning, namely Biggs' (1987a, b) study process questionnaire (SPQ), reveals a number of issues surrounding the application of the questionnaire in accounting education research and brings into question the interpretations of prior research findings suggesting that accounting students tend to be 'surface learners' or that accounting education contexts tend to impede quality learning.

These concerning interpretations may be misguided as the SPQ measure of the cognitive aspect of the surface approach (such as, memorize or enumerate) may be part of a deep approach to learning and second, it tends to locate approaches to learning as a disposition or characteristic of students, rather than as a response to perceived tasks in learning contexts experienced. Hence we need further research that explores what constitutes a deep approach to learning within the discipline of accounting.

Later research (2002–2009) does not tend to make these concerning claims and instead provides insights into a number of themes including the relationships between learning approaches and gender, and learning approaches and student performance on different types of assessment tasks. Further, in some studies (Hall et al. 2004, Jackling 2005a) the high surface approach scores reported are explained by the findings reported in Birkett and Mladenovic (2002) which suggests that the very nature of accounting requires the use of some lower-level cognitive strategies, such as memorize and enumerate, as part of the process of engaging deeply with the subject matter. Given this chapter provides a critical investigation of the usefulness of the SPQ in accounting education research, the findings thus far suggest that accounting education researchers should seriously consider whether it is at all fruitful to continue to employ the SPQ in future accounting education research.

Potential areas for future research include re-examining the singular notion of memorization (rote learning) as measured by the SPQ, by exploring the different types of memorization as identified by Meyer (2000) using the RoLI. Preliminary research has already been undertaken in accounting yielding fruitful results (Lucas & Meyer 2005, Lucas & Mladenovic 2006b). Lucas and Meyer (2005) reported on how students' conceptions of the subject of accounting were linked with deep, surface, and ineffective learning processes. In contrast to the SPQ, this research is insightful as it not only distinguishes between the different forms of memorization and their relationship to surface and deep approaches to learning, but it also supports the identification of students' preconceptions which should be addressed when developing teaching interventions to support learning (Mladenovic 2000).

In their research using the RoLI and a discipline-specific accounting inventory, Lucas and Mladenovic (2006b) were able to identify students at risk of achieving poor results within an introductory undergraduate course. Certain groups, namely males, non-majors and those with English as a second language, appeared to be at higher risk of academic failure. The value of this research is that understanding more about *how* students approach their learning and the nature of their *prior knowledge* provides the foundation for developing teaching interventions to support students at academic risk of failure.

Further research exploring the nature of the cognitive activities (both the lower level associated with the surface approach and the higher level associated with the deep approach) that are most effective in learning accounting would be fruitful. This would provide us with insights in the nature of learning within the discipline and hence inform the educational interventions to improve students' learning outcomes.

Threshold concepts offer another promising direction for progressing our understanding of accounting students' approaches to learning. In order to determine what constitutes a deep approach to learning in accounting, it is necessary to determine *what* it is we wish students to understand and *how* students can then develop that understanding. Lucas and Mladenovic (2007) explain the potential for threshold concepts to become an emerging framework for educational research and practice and Lucas and Mladenovic (2006c, 2009) demonstrate the benefits of its application in an accounting setting.

It appears then, as outlined in the introduction to this chapter, that while research based in the approaches to learning paradigm has provided many insights into, and added to, our understanding of students' approaches to learning and accounting educational contexts, it is perhaps time to move beyond the use of the SPQ to other methods as there are still many unresolved issues and numerous productive lines of research yet to be explored in relation to improving student learning processes and outcomes.

References

Accounting Education Change Commission (AECC) (1990). Objectives of education for accountants, position statement no. 1. *Issues in Accounting Education*, 5(2): 307–12.

Accounting Education Change Commission (AECC) (1992). The first course in accounting: position statement no. 2. *Issues in Accounting Education*, 7(2): 249–51.

Albrecht S & Sack J (2000). *Accounting education: charting the course through a perilous future. Accounting education series 16.* Sarisota, Florida: American Accounting Association (AAA).

Beattie V, Collins B & McInnes B (1997). Deep and surface learning: a simple or simplistic dichotomy? *Accounting Education*, 6(1): 1–12.

Biggs J (1987a). *Student approaches to learning and studying.* Hawthorn, Victoria: Australian Council for Educational Research.

Biggs J (1987b). *Study process questionnaire manual.* Hawthorn, Victoria: Australian Council for Educational Research.

Biggs J (1989). Approaches to the enhancement of tertiary teaching. *Higher Education Research and Development,* 8(1): 7–25.

Biggs J (2001). Enhancing learning: a matter of style or approach? In R Sternberg & L Zhang (Eds), *Perspectives on thinking, learning and cognitive styles.* Mahwah, NJ: Lawrence Erlbaum.

Biggs J and Collis K (1982). *Evaluating the quality of learning: the SOLO taxonomy (Structure of the Observed Learning Outcome).* New York: Academic Press.

Biggs J & Kirkby J (1983). Approaches to learning in universities and CAEs. *Vestes,* 27(2): 3–9.

Biggs J & Rihn B (1984). The effects of intervention on deep and surface approaches to learning. In J Kirby (Ed), *Cognitive strategies and educational performance,* (pp279–94). New York: Academic Press.

Biggs J, Kember D & Leung D (2001). The revised two-factor study process questionnaire: R-SPQ-2F. *British Journal of Educational Psychology,* 71: 133–48.

Birkett B & Mladenovic R (2002). The approaches to learning paradigm: theoretical and empirical issues for accounting education research. Paper presented at the *Accounting and Finance Association of Australia and New Zealand (AFAANZ) Annual Conference,* Perth, Australia, July; and at the *International Association for Accounting Education and Research 9th World Congress of Accounting Educators,* Hong Kong, November.

Booth P, Luckett P & Mladenovic R (1999). The quality of learning in accounting education: the impact of approaches to learning on academic performance. *Accounting Education: An International Journal,* 8(4): 277–300.

Chan D, Leung R, Gow L & Hu S (1989). Approaches to learning of accountancy students: some additional evidence. *Proceedings of the ASAIHL Seminar on University Education in the 1990s,* (pp186–93). Kuala Lumpur.

Cecez-Kecmanovic D, Juchau M, Kay R & Wright S (2002). *Australian business education study: enhancing the quality of Australian business education*. Canberra: Australian Government Publishing Service.

Cooper B (2004). The enigma of the Chinese learner. *Accounting Education: An International Journal*, 13(3): 289–310.

Davidson R (2002). Relationship of study approach and exam performance. *Journal of Accounting Education*, 20: 29–44.

De Lange P & Mavondo F (2004). Gender and motivational differences in approaches to learning by a cohort of open learning students. *Accounting Education: An International Journal*, 13(4): 431–48.

Duff A & McKinstry S (2007). Students' approaches to learning. *Issues in Accounting Education*, 22(2): 183–214.

Eley M (1992). Differential adoption of study approaches within individual students. *Higher Education*, 23: 231–54.

English L, Luckett P & Mladenovic R (2004). Encouraging a deep approach through curriculum design. *Accounting Education: An International Journal*, 13(4): 461–88.

Entwistle N & Ramsden P (1983). *Understanding student learning*. London: Croomhelm.

Gibbs G (2003). Ten years of improving student learning. In C Rust (Ed), *Improving student learning theory and practice – 10 years on*, (pp9–26). Oxford: OCSLD.

Gow L, Kember D & Cooper B (1994). The teaching context and approaches to study of accountancy students. *Issues in Accounting Education*, 9(1): 118–30.

Hall M, Ramsay A & Raven J (2004). Changing the learning environment to promote deep learning approaches in first-year accounting students. *Accounting Education: an International Journal*, 13(4): 489–506.

Institute of Chartered Accountants in Australia (ICAA) (1996). *Guidelines for joint administration of accreditation of tertiary courses by the professional accounting bodies*. Sydney: ICAA.

International Federation of Accountants (IFA) (1996). Prequalification education, assessment of professional competence and experience requirements of professional accountants. In *IFAC Handbook 1999 Technical Pronouncements*, (pp606–22). New York: IFA.

Jackling B (2005a). Perceptions of the learning context and learning approaches: implications for quality learning outcomes in accounting. *Accounting Education: An International Journal*, 14(3): 271–91.

Jackling B (2005b). Analysis of the learning context, perceptions of the learning environment and approaches to learning accounting: a longitudinal study. *Accounting and Finance*, 45: 597–612.

Kelly M, Davey H & Haigh N (1999). Contemporary accounting education and society. *Journal of Accounting Education*, 8(4): 321–40.

Kember D & Gow L (1989). A model of student approaches to learning encompassing ways to influence and change approaches. *Instructional Science*, 18: 263–88.

Lucas U (1996). Student approaches to learning – a literature guide. *Accounting Education: An International Journal*, 5(1): 87–98.

Lucas U & Meyer J (2005). 'Towards a mapping of the student world': the indentification of variation in students' conceptions of, and motivations to learn, introductory accounting. *The Britsh Accounting Review*, 37: 177–204.

Lucas U & Mladenovic R (2004). Editorial – approaches to learning in accounting education. *Accounting Education: An International Journal*, 13(4): 399–407.

Lucas U & Mladenovic R (2006a). Reflections on accounting education research: how accounting education research on approaches to learning has contributed to educational practice. In L Murphy Smith (Ed), *Reflections on accounting education research*, (pp46–56). Sarisota, Florida: American Accounting Association (AAA).

Lucas U & Mladenovic R (2006b). Developing an accounting specific learning inventory for use as a diagnostic tool within teaching. *Accounting and Finance Association of Australia and New Zealand (AFAANZ) Annual Conference*, Wellington, New Zealand, 4th July.

Lucas U & Mladenovic R (2006c). Developing new 'world views': threshold concepts in introductory accounting. In J Meyer & R Land (Eds),

Overcoming barriers to student understanding: threshold concepts and troublesome knowledge, (pp148–59). London: Routledge.

Lucas U & Mladenovic R (2007). The potential of threshold concepts: an emerging framework for educational research and practice. *London Review of Education*, 5(3): 237–48.

Lucas U & Mladenovic R (2009). The identification of variation in students' understandings of disciplinary concepts: the application of the SOLO taxonomy within introductory accounting. *Higher Education*, 58(2): 257–83.

Meyer J (2000). Variation in contrasting forms of 'memorising' and associated variables. *British Journal of Educational Psychology*, 70: 163–76.

Meyer J (2004). The Domain of the RoLI and recent extensions to it. Paper presented to the 2nd RoLI Symposium, Imperial College, London, February.

Meyer J & Boulton-Lewis G (1999). On the operationalisation of conceptions of learning in higher education and their association with students' knowledge and experiences of learning. *Higher Education Research and Development*, 18(3): 289–302.

Meyer J & Eley M (1999). The development of affective subscales to reflect variation in students' experiences of studying mathematics in higher education. *Higher Education*, 37: 197–216.

Mladenovic R (2001). The effects of alignment in the learning context on students' perceptions and learning approaches in accounting. Unpublished doctoral dissertation. Sydney: University of New South Wales.

Mladenovic R (2000). An investigation into ways of challenging introductory accounting students' negative perceptions of accounting. *Accounting Education: An International Journal*, 9(4): 135–55.

Ramburuth P (2001). Cross cultural learning behaviour in higher education: perceptions versus practice. *ultiBASE, the Electronic Journal*, May.

Ramburuth P & Mladenovic R (2004). Exploring the relationship between students' orientations to learning, the structure of students' learning outcomes and subsequent academic performance. *Accounting Education: An International Journal*, 13(4): 507–28.

Ramsden P (1979). Student learning and perceptions of the academic environment. *Higher Education*, 8: 411–27.

Ramsden P (1992). *Learning to teach in higher education*. London: Routledge.

Richardson J (1990). Reliability and replicability of the approaches to studying questionnaire. *Studies in Higher Education*, 15(2): 155–68.

Richardson J (2000). *Researching student learning – approaches to studying in campus-based and distance education*. Buckingham: Society for Research into Higher Education and Open University Press.

Schmeck R (1988). *Learning strategies and learning styles*. New York: Plenum.

Sharma D (1998). Addressing the student quality problem: some directions for accounting education research. *Asian Review of Accounting*, 6(1): 1–29.

Tait H, Entwistle N & McCune V (1998). ASSIST: a reconceptualisation of the approaches to studying inventory. In C Rust (Ed), *Improving student learning: improving students as learners*, (pp262–71). Oxford: Oxford Centre for Staff Development.

Umpathy S (1984). Algorithm-based accounting education: opportunities and risks. *Issues in Accounting Education*: 136–43.

Williams J, Tiller M, Herring H & Scheiner J (1988). *A framework for the development of accounting education research*. Sarasota, Florida: American Accounting Association.

17

Diversity and the student experience in business education

Prem Ramburuth (UNSW)

*Abstract**

Higher education institutions continue to undergo fundamental change as a result of the impact of globalization. An immediate impact is the increasing student diversity and 'cultural mix' at the learning and teaching interface, evident in higher education institutions in Australia. This chapter provides insights into the academic and socio-cultural adaptation experiences of students from diverse backgrounds, as they navigate their way through new learning and cultural environments in Australia. It reports on a qualitative study involving interviews, focus groups and classroom observations that sought to capture the student experience, and provide insights into factors impacting on students' learning and sociocultural adaptation.

Higher education institutions continue to undergo fundamental change as a result of the impact of globalization (Twigg 2005). An immediate and notable

---

* This paper is dedicated to the late Professor Bill Birkett. It presents a study that he commissioned (but did not publish) in his role as Associate Dean, Development. It is an example of his ongoing search to gain insight into the student experience, to understand issues of language, learning and cultural diversity, their impact on student learning and implications for teaching. He sought to capture the student experience across dimensions both academic and socio-cultural, including issues relating to adaptation to new learning environments, personal and professional aspirations, expectations of educational institutions and levels of satisfaction. His aim was to ensure that students from all backgrounds experienced quality learning and teaching in the faculty and in business education.

impact is the increasing diversity and 'cultural mix' of student populations at the learning and teaching interface, which is clearly evident in the higher education institutions of Australia. Researchers (for example, Grace & Gravestock 2009, Humfrey 1999, Ramburuth & Welch 2005) contend that the rich diversity and intermingling of students in the higher education learning environment should bring advantages of global knowledge building, cross cultural learning and the broadening of intellectual horizons. Others, (for example, Kingston & Forland 2008; Smart, Volet & Ang 2000), point to the 'missed opportunities' for such learning, and the failure to take advantage of the diversity, with students choosing, instead, to remain within the safety of their 'same culture' groups and comfort zones, as they navigate their way through their new learning environments.

The processes of sociocultural and academic adaptation are both complex and are not easily achieved. In his early research in this area, Oberg (1960, p177) created the term 'culture shock' to capture the psychological challenges people face when making the transition from familiar cultural environments to foreign ones. He and more recent researchers (Kingston & Forland 2009, Marx 2001) highlight the frequently experienced symptoms that people display in confronting 'culture shock', including loneliness, powerlessness, vulnerability, feelings of inadequacy, loss of confidence and focus, inability to concentrate, and developing stereotypes about the new culture. In recommending strategies for managing cultural transitions, Berry and Sam (1997, p278) stress the need to develop "a new behavioural repertoire that is appropriate for the new cultural context". There are clear implications for students in making the transition to new learning environments that impact on their learning.

Other researchers and practitioners in student learning (Burke 2001, Kingston & Forland 2008, Marx 2001) focus on the challenges in the academic acculturation process, sometimes referred to as 'study shock' or 'academic shock' (Twigg 2005). The concept reflects the response of students in confronting differences in approaches to learning and teaching from prior learning, and the realization that they may have to change or modify learning behaviours to perform successfully in their new education environment. Burns (1991) outlines the levels of stress and anxiety that accompany the transitional learning process and advocates taking these factors into consideration when dealing with students from diverse backgrounds. The note of caution becomes even more important when evidence suggests that the extent to which students manage their learning depends on the extent to which they make their 'behavioural shifts' to their new learning contexts (Berry & Sam 1997).

The increasing diversity in Australian higher education institutions warrants greater understanding of the issues and ongoing research, if we are to provide quality education for all students. The chapter reports on a qualitative study that explored issues of academic and sociocultural adaptation experienced by students in the former Faculty of Commerce and Economics (now the Australian School of Business) at UNSW. The faculty is one of the most diverse at UNSW, and indeed, in Australia, with approximately 35% international students, from 80 different countries, speaking 85 different languages, and 60% with a language other than English at home. The study sought to explore the student experience through semi-structured interviews in individual and focus group settings, and in classroom observations in informal learning contexts, particularly in Peer Assisted Student Support (PASS)[1] and mentoring programs linked to the core disciplines of accounting, economics and business statistics.

Motivational factors and student expectations

Many factors motivate and influence students in their decision making about their learning destinations and pathways. Of particular relevance to this chapter are the factors relevant to students from diverse cultural backgrounds (including international students). In their study, Willis and Kennedy (2004) identified credible institutional sources as strong influencers – these include websites and institutional literature, as well as effective marketing strategies and communication. Ahmed (2006) draws the link between

---

1 PASS is a learning support program that is based on 'supplemental instruction', an international program that uses outstanding students as leaders to provide learning assistance in courses where students are encountering difficulties.

effective marketing and the development of 'realistic' expectations amongst potential students, which generally leads to higher levels of student satisfaction. She, therefore, cautions against creating 'unrealistic' expectations. East (2001) further alludes to vigorous marketing campaigns and strategies that Australian universities use with promises of 'quality of service' (p1), and emphasizes the need for the 'delivery' of quality for reputation building and sustainability. Her study, however, revealed gaps in what students from diverse backgrounds sought (that is, quality in teaching, improvement in English language, experience of Australian culture, and interaction with local students) and what they believed they had received. Similar findings were reported in a much larger study by Sovic (2008) at the University of the Arts, London, with students emphasizing the dissatisfaction and levels of stress that the gap between expectations and reality created. In the Australian context, both the reputation of the institution and the attractiveness of the country as a study destination are strong drawcards, which Mazzarol and Soutar (2002) and government reports (such as the Victorian Department of Innovation, Industry and Regional Development 2008) refer to as 'pull' factors that attract students.

Mazzarol and Soutar (2002) also identify economic and social forces that 'push' students abroad to pursue their education. Social factors include motivation offered by family, friends, peers, as well as the desire to broaden horizons and seek freedom from the 'ties that bind', which could include cultural, traditional and educational expectations deemed to be restrictive. Twigg (2005, p94) found strong evidence of such responses in a study at her Higher Education institution in the UK:

> I enjoy life here. I sometimes like the individual life. If you live on your own, you will be mature. I feel more independent, which is quite a problem when I go back (Thai student).

The impact of family (particularly parents) as influencers in seeking an international education is of particular significance in some cultures (Kim, Markham & Cangelosi 2002), for example, in students from Asian backgrounds. The reasons for encouragement include perceptions of a better education, higher regard for foreign qualifications, potential of higher status on return to the home country, and improved employment and professional prospects (Soutar & Turner 2002).

Learning and academic adaptation

In making the transition to new learning environments, evidence suggests that many students are unprepared for differences in learning and teaching styles they may encounter, leading to elements of 'study shock' (Burke 2001). In an Australian study, for example, Chalmers and Volet (1997, p95) identified the extent of the learning adjustment that may be required of students from diverse backgrounds:

> Before we came we were subject to a different education system and we were asked to change our way of learning into what the Aussie's, or rather the Higher Education's way of learning is. (It is) totally different, so we have to have a very dramatic change in our way of learning.

Researchers such as Phillips (1990), Niles (1995), Ramburuth and McCormick (2001), Wong (2004) and others identified differences in learning and teaching styles between Asian and Western cultures (with the caveat that the generalizations offered may not always apply, because of differences between countries and cultures in Asia). In offering comparative analyses, Phillips (1990) drew attention to non-reflective and 'surface' approaches to learning observed in some Asian education systems, in contrast to the reflective, discursive and analytic approaches required in Australian education institutions, with implications for students studying across cultures. In a more recent study in the United Kingdom, Sovic (2008, p13) noted students' lack of understanding of learning differences they may encounter:

> What is not coming across to these international students is the specific pedagogical approach in the UK: (there is not) an emphasis on teaching skills that are associated with what is known as the 'surface' approach to learning and a transmission approach to teaching. There is more likely to be an emphasis on the conceptual development of the person and a creative and explorative approach to practice.

Similar observations are made in studies in Australia (Ballard & Clanchy 1991, Niles 1995, Volet & Ang 1998).

Language and communication competence

Language permeates all aspects of learning across the disciplines including the numeracy-based disciplines (which generally form the core in business education), and is also identified as a major factor impacting on the learning and confidence of students, especially those from diverse backgrounds who may have English as a second language (Brislin & Yoshida 1994, Hirsch 2007, Sovic 2008). Wierzbicka (1991, p453) emphasizes this point in the comment that, in addition to being "a tool for communication, it is also a tool of human interaction", and it is through language that we convey our thoughts, feelings and intentions, as well as relate to other people. In addition, students new to the disciplines in business education will have to learn the 'language of the disciplines' in their programs of study (for example, the 'language of accounting'). This is essential for shared understanding and shared meaning in the learning and teaching discourse in the courses undertaken. Where there are gaps, institutional support and skills development initiatives to bridge the gaps in required levels of language and learning competence must be provided. In her study, Twigg (2005, pp103–04) provides evidence of the initial language and communication difficulties experienced by students, and the patience required in the learning process:

> If you don't understand you can ask again, but it depends on your confidence. When I first started meeting people in a group, I didn't understand jokes or slang words which aren't used in Pakistan, but you learn over time. It is all in the process of learning.

Sociocultural adaptation

Most students on campus expect to interact socially on campus, forging long- and short-term relationships. Students from diverse backgrounds expect to engage in social interactions with local students, and gain exposure to Australian culture, participate in cross-cultural communication, and enhance English language communication. Bruch and Barty (1998) view the opportunities for cultural exchange as being one of the most beneficial outcomes of the process of globalization. They and others (for example, Smart et al. 2000) contend that forging new friendships, developing new networks, communicating with native speakers of English, participating in local events, all assist in facilitating the process of social acculturation. However, studies involving diverse-background students in the United Kingdom (Kingston & Forland 2008), the United States (Tartar 2005) and in Australia (Smart et al. 2000, Volet & Ang 1998), have found that students experience great difficulty in bridging the 'cultural divide'. In an Australian study that examined issues relating to social cohesion between international and local students, Smart et al. (2000) found instances of difficulties and disappointments:

> When I first came, I had the expectation to meet many Australians but did not. Only 'hi-bye' friends, not close friends ... We do not have much interaction with the locals. We would like to mix more. We are the shy sort but there are no opportunities to mix.

They identified factors that inhibit intercultural interactions on campuses as being cultural differences, lifestyle differences, negative stereotyping and ethnocentrism. Ti (1997) identified lifestyle factors such as the drinking and partying culture of some Australian students as a strong inhibitor to sociocultural interactions. Reluctance by students from diverse cultural backgrounds to participate in these types of social activities, has led to negative stereotyping as indicated in the local student comment below (Smart et al. 2000, p28):

> The Australian attitude is that they have tried to include the Asians in the past, and they have now given up on including them – they expect a negative response ... Some people won't interact because they are solely here to get a degree and go back home. They aren't concerned with a social life.

Volet and Ang (1998, pp10–11) also found that a large percentage of students from diverse cultural backgrounds preferred to remain within their comfort zones, and interact only with people of "the same wavelength", and "stick to our own culture and friends". To counter such practices, Bruch and Barty (1998) advocate the establishment of formal institutional structures to foster sociocultural interactions on campus, or risk losing potential benefits of interacting across cultures.

Research approach

The purpose of this study was to investigate the academic and sociocultural adaptation experiences of students from cross-cultural backgrounds in a large and diverse faculty, the Australian School of Business (formerly the Faculty of Commerce and Economics). The study adopted a qualitative approach to data collection (Yin 2003) and involved a combination of face-to-face interviews, focus groups and classroom observations to gather data on the student experience. Qualitative data analysis was deemed to be more appropriate to both identify trends in the data and probe into students' experiences (Miles & Huberman 1994). The sample comprised 10 focus groups of five students per group (total 50 students); 10 face-to-face interviews with undergraduate students and nine interviews with postgraduate students, to probe issues identified in the focus groups (total 19 interviews); and classroom observations in the PASS mentoring program in the core disciplines of Accounting, Economics and Business Statistics (five classes of approximately 22 students per class and a total of 120 students). A semi-structured interview schedule was devised to guide the interview process, provide a consistent framework for data collection, and, at the same time, enable the use of open-ended questions to provide opportunities for extended interviewee responses and individual narratives (Denzin & Lincoln 2003). The interviews, focus groups and classroom observations were between one to two hours in length. The data were collected by two interviewers to ensure objectivity in the data gathering process and recorded in the form of field notes. It was then transcribed and analyzed for content trends and themes relating to the student experience.

Discussion and insights

Responses gathered in the focus groups and interviews, and observations gathered from class visits, provide valuable insights into the student experience in the faculty, and reflect many of the issues raised in the literature. They highlight the more specific experiences of students from diverse backgrounds as they pursue their studies and seek to find stability, academic success and friendships in their new learning and sociocultural environments. The limitation of the study is that the discussion and comments reflect only some of the experiences of students, and do not present a full picture. Nevertheless, the findings do provide valuable insights and understanding.

Cultural adaptation and making the transition

Almost all students interviewed in this study experienced culture shock of some kind, whether at the more general level of "missing home and the family" or having "to travel in Sydney on my own and I got lost all the time". But some expressed stronger feelings of displacement than others:

> I arrived here alone and I had to arrange everything by myself. It was quite difficult for me because I couldn't adjust myself with living, speaking and listening in English ... So, I was quite lonely and homesick. It was quite scary when you felt that you had no family or friends to help or care for you because they are so far away (Thai postgraduate student).

For others, the loss of confidence and identity, and the confusion accompanying 'culture shock' concerned them the most:

> This is not who I am. I know myself very well. I am a kind of person who is always positive and talkative, and has a sense of humor. I was, if anything, the person who took the initiative among the students in class in Japan. Since the life in Sydney was started, my confusion about myself has been growing bigger. Every day I feel as if I saw myself as another different person, who is dependent, timid, and vulnerable, and somehow who is always staying away from discussions in the class (Japanese postgraduate student).

Most students indicated that they had some knowledge of what to expect in Australia, gathered from institutional brochures and from friends already studying or living in Australia, knowledge which they thought would be sufficient in acculturation. However, they also acknowledged that they had not been fully prepared for the extent of cultural differences, and how to live and function in a foreign environment, with one suggestion being "someone should prepare us". The loss of their familiar frames of reference and the anxiety experienced is evident:

> I cannot use my measure (frame of reference) here, which I used to use in Japan. Almost all of my own assumptions and expectations are completely

useless here. Of course, I have got some rough information of a western culture before I came and I had some friends from western countries, so I believed that it would be not so difficult to live in Australia ... However, from a tiny matter to a serious situation, I cannot use my measure or frame which has been cultivated in Japan, so I end up being at a loss, thinking "how should I behave? (Japanese postgraduate student).

However, what is encouraging is that many of these students also reported that, after a few months, and after developing strategies to overcome their difficulties, they were able to gradually acculturate to varying degrees. Most felt it was a challenge to settle down but it was not impossible. An interesting observation was the difference between the undergraduate and postgraduate student responses, with the undergraduate group expressing some concern but less anxiety about coping with their new learning and sociocultural environment. Common themes among the undergraduate students included security and safety, good accommodation (lifestyle was important), and discrimination, with some of the factors impacting on the acculturation process identified in these sample comments:

It's a very bad experience to go to a country and they discriminate against you because of some factor you can't change, not because of your personality, not because you do something to them, but just because of your appearance. It's really unbelievable because I come from a multi-cultural country, Hong Kong, as well.

What helped me was attitude of the people ... Generally I found Australians to be very nice and very willing to help people. They aren't so aggressive to get up, to get profit. They do need money but they're not so aggressive to get money and forget everything else. That's quite nice, quite good. This is different from my country.

The theme of friendship and trust in facilitating the acculturation process was a recurring one, which students identified as important in enhancing the quality of their experience on campus, as was the theme of wanting greater interaction with local and other students:

I have enjoyed the people I have met ... For example, when queuing up for food in the cafeteria is it easy to talk to someone, whereas back home, if you started to talk to someone, they would think that you have some ulterior motives. People here trust others more, and they are more friendly, so I didn't have difficulties getting to know them. But I did have difficulty finding adequate and sufficient opportunities to interact deeply enough so that you understand them.

Motivational factors and expectations

In exploring motivational factors, it was interesting to note the emphasis on 'push' factors (Mazzarol & Soutar 2002), that is, social drivers for students from diverse backgrounds seeking education abroad and in a business faculty, with parents being the strongest influencers. It could be that the sample comprised a large representation of students from Asian backgrounds (reflecting the profile of the student mix in the faculty), thereby presenting culture-specific perspectives. Nevertheless, parents seem to play a key role (albeit in different ways), as reflected in themes stressing the importance of the family, parents wanting to avoid poor experiences they may have had, parents wanting to replicate their success attained through education, and parents attributing status, respect and good job prospects to university education. The comments provide an indication of the responses (from undergraduate students). In the case of Student A, her father's struggle to attain education and social status had a profound influence on the way he raised his children, imposing strict regimes of educational discipline:

> Yes, he sort of felt that he didn't want us out of his care, that he didn't want us to go through the pain ... He didn't want us to regret anything, to make mistakes. So basically we had a lot of impositions on us, like what we should do, how we should live our lives.

Another perspective to parental expectations to succeed is presented by Student B, who did not want to disappoint her mother who sacrificed a great deal so that her daughter could be successful:

> I can't fail because it would break my mother's heart. Sometimes I feel really alone. I don't have any social life with friends, I just study. I only have my mother and she works in two jobs so she can support me here. I really miss her and I realise coming here how much she has sacrificed for me.

For some students studying at an Australian university meant escape from rigid and high pressured education systems in their home country, as indicated by Student C:

> It's very high powered there. They expect us to do compulsory extra curricular activities on top of our studies, and study from 7.30am ... class finishes at 5pm and if we have extra curricular activities it will be on Saturdays ... Back there it's too competitive, it's about who is above you and who is below you ... Here, they appreciate me for what I am and I appreciate them for what they are.

For others, it was not only an escape from rigid educational systems, but also the commencement of a journey of self discovery, as indicated by Student D:

> Basically I have more time to explore, about people, about my self ... time to push that human part forward. Back there (Singapore), everyone is so competitive. When I come here I realised that there is this other side and basically it taught me to be more understanding of people. Now I've got time to garden.

And finally, there is the traditional expectation, consistent with findings in the literature (for example, Soutar & Turner 2002) of improved job prospects: "If you go back home you have a higher chance of good job and a better chance than the domestic students".

Learning and academic acculturation

Students' responses to issues of learning and academic acculturation can be divided into four distinct, but interrelated, themes: levels of awareness and readiness to learn in their new Higher Education context; perceptions of quality in teaching and expectations of teaching staff; language and communication, and learning support which provided opportunities to enhance learning and academic performance.

Awareness of learning differences

Consistent with findings in the literature, (Burke 2001, Twigg 2005) there were students who experienced aspects of 'study shock' and were unprepared for the differences in approaches to learning that would be required of them when transitioning from high school to a higher education context, as is evident in the comments of these undergraduate students:

> It was a very big shock because I didn't know what to expect. I expected it to be a lot easier but it's not ... suddenly you have this huge pile of books to read before your next lecture or tutorial. You really have to push your limits yourself.

> I was overwhelmed by it all, there's lots of freedom in this place. Coming from high school, obviously there was a lot of discipline there, teachers guiding you in different directions. I spent a lot of first session being undisciplined in my work.

Similar finding were made with students transitioning from diverse backgrounds to their new learning environments, for example, international students, who found themselves 'lost' in the transition process:

> It's a very different way to do things ... International students don't know how to start or where to start, and what are the expectations ... They (lecturers) should understand we have no experience in this way ... We want to learn the correct way so we can do well ... But how can we, if we don't know? (postgraduate student).

Then were also students who experienced difficulties making the transition from undergraduate studies to postgraduate studies, and engaging in more independent approaches to learning:

> It was very difficult to adjust my study attitude in the beginning. It was very different from being an undergraduate to being a postgraduate student. In the postgraduate degree you are required to do more self study and there are a lot of assignments which involve a lot of research ... It's been a problem accessing the right material.

Most students, however, do find their way as they progress through their programs of study, and begin to recognize the skills that will be required of them in an Australian university, with positive and rewarding outcomes as evidenced in this comment:

> The most important and valuable thing that I've learnt is how to think critically, which is very good. This skill was kind of learnt in one of my lectures, when the lecturer told us that theory is not always right. You have to apply them and find the controversies and sort of compare them, so there is a twi-

light zone in which you can never see things clearly which is really good. I learnt that skill early on in the session so I've been applying that to all of my subjects (postgraduate student).

Similar to findings in the study by Twigg (2005), some students from diverse backgrounds were able to make a complete switch in their approaches to learning, once they overcame initial difficulties, as is evidenced by these comments:

> I prefer the Australian way now ... In Korea we don't have much opportunity to give a presentation in the class and we don't have an opportunity to discuss the issues, so it's just like lectures. In the Australian way, I think the lecturers and the system make the students study. If you don't study they will fail you ... in Korea it is easy to graduate once you get in, they don't fail many people. Compared to the lecturers in Korea, the lecturers in Australia are more friendly and more willing to help students with their study.

Feedback on teaching

In general, most students interviewed expressed satisfaction with the quality of the teaching they experienced. They found their lecturers 'friendly', 'easy to talk to', 'well prepared', 'entertaining', and 'very knowledgeable in their disciplines'. There were, however, perceptions that the communication styles of some lecturers were ineffective and the presentation of course content and course information was sometimes unclear (to students already disadvantaged by language problems):

> The first thing for teachers, especially Australian teachers, is that they should understand the difficulty that an international student has ... especially our language our problems ... They should speak and explain more clearly ... They are really good lecturers, but they don't understand our difficulties. They speak very fast with an accent ... and use some words ... and slang we don't understand (postgraduate student).

> Sometimes they (lecturers and tutors) speak so fast and they expect you to know the language, so sometimes we would skip points when taking notes. I feel very bad to ask them to repeat what they said. This is not fair and so you feel no good if you keep going and asking (undergraduate student).

Many students also recognized that part of the problem with being unable to understand their lecturers was their own difficulties with the English language. The greatest fear expressed was the fear of troubling the teaching staff with their language problems. Some students found the quality of their tutorials 'uneven', that is, not consistently good, while others were quick to recognize the outstanding quality of their tutorials and the impact on their learning:

> I found our tutorials really excellent. There are a lot of contributions from everyone, and it's a lot more relaxed in a way. The atmosphere is good, because we can speak whenever we want to, and everyone is kind of people-oriented. There's no one who doesn't have an opinion and doesn't share it (undergraduate student).

Language and communication

In both their academic and sociocultural interactions, students from diverse backgrounds found that language played a key role in their accomplishments. There was a general feeling that, whilst learning in itself could present challenges they could 'catch up' on the content and knowledge in the disciplines, but language learning was a much slower process, especially in learning to manage the nuances of the English language. Some were prepared to invest the time and effort as is evident in the following comment:

> I attended every tutorial and spoke all the time … The more I spoke the more I learned how to use the language … even if you make a mistake while you speak in English, the audience will understand. I know that the Australians are most forgiving.

This student's response also highlighted the link between language, communication and confidence building as referred to in the literature (see Brislin & Yoshida 1994, Hirsch 2007, Sovic 2008), and in the student's comment that "My confidence has built up. If you have confidence you are able to succeed in whatever you want to do in life." But not all students experienced this level of achievement in the English language. Some did try, but were frustrated at the slow pace of competence acquisition, and even more frustrated with the intricacies of the English language, as noted here:

> I always hoped, before I came here, that it (English language) would be learned within a year. There's never an end to it … there's so much to language than just words. Some of the things said, you have no way of knowing

what is meant. Sometimes when people say 'catch twenty two', it takes a long time to understand and people have to explain it to me.

Seeking clarification of meaning is not easy for students from diverse backgrounds, when asked "why not seek help?", a frequent response was that "we feel stupid asking the same question". Insight to how students perceive the language issues confronting them is summed up in this postgraduate student's observation:

> The main reason why students are reluctant to ask for help is because of their non-English speaking background. They are not able to present their problems or they are just afraid to present their problems and risk someone having to ask them again and again. This would be very embarrassing for the students. So the root cause of their problem is their inability to express their problems in English.

However, many were proactive in seeking help from the support services provided by the faculty and its Education Development Unit (EDU),[2] recognizing that they need to take responsibility for their language learning:

> Presently the learning facilities in the business faculty are great. It has to be a two way thing. The students have to do their work, come up with the problems and ask for help from the learning advisers, instead of at first not doing any work and expecting the learning advisor or the peer assistant just to explain and just give them another lecture.

Others devised more innovative strategies to cope with the interrelated task of listening, comprehending and note taking in lectures, all at the same time (challenging for students with English as a second language). They used an approach they referred to as the 'secretarial method', that is, one student tries to understand the material by simply listening to the lecture, while another takes notes which they will use for future reference. Others were more reflective and philosophical about their language learning:

---

2 EDU was established in the faculty in 1998 to provide support for students to enhance the quality of their learning, and to address the needs of staff in supporting their students' learning. The courses focused on language and communication skills development, strategies for learning across cultures, preparing for assessment and exams and numeracy skills development. The courses were attended mainly by students from diverse backgrounds.

In my memory, I remember when I was about seven and I first learned to ride a bicycle. I had this ride in the countryside and I can always remember when I looked up and saw so many stars, so many. Then I knew what the word 'countless' meant, that's how you learn words.

Supporting students in their learning

Much has been written about institutional responsibility in bridging the gap between the learning and language capabilities between students from diverse backgrounds and their counterparts on campus (for example, Bruch & Barty 1998, Ballard & Clanchy 1991, Grace & Gravestock 2009, Sovic 2008). They highlight the need for inclusive approaches to learning and teaching, and the provision of appropriate support strategies, not only to bridge learning and language 'gaps' (regarded as a 'deficit' model), but to maximize the learning potential of students. Analyses of student responses indicated that those who took advantage of the support initiatives and informal learning programs offered by the EDU benefited, whilst those who did not still struggled, much to the frustration of some students who wanted to see their peers succeed:

> In my opinion there is a lot of assistance around and I think there are a lot of confused students out there too, but the thing to do is to bridge these two and bring them together ... I agree, in the Business Faculty, we have one of the best support systems at UNSW. We need to enlighten students as to what services are offered and make them aware that if they have problems to not be afraid to seek help.

Students who did participate in the learning support initiatives were very specific about the skills they gained, and, equally important, seemed to gain new levels of confidence. They recognized and valued the support available, as indicated in this comment by a postgraduate student:

> The assistance I got from the EDU with my writing assignments was helpful ... I've written so many essays and assignments in my life but still after a few years you forget and need to be taught how to do it properly and correctly. So I found the assistance very helpful with how to structure my essays. Paragraphing etc. have a different structure in my culture. Overall, I feel I have been very lucky with these programs and the unit which helps me with my written assignments. I'm happy with the way things are.

Essential to learning and succeeding in a business faculty is the requirement for strong numeracy skills. Many students from diverse background found a mismatch in the levels of skill required for successful study and skills sets they possessed. The faculty, therefore, set up PASS mentoring programs in the core courses of accounting and financial management, macro and micro-economics and quantitative methods. In this initiative, outstanding students act as leaders to enhance the quality of student learning, especially amongst first-year students. Many of the PASS leaders are students from diverse back-grounds and are able to empathize with the learning difficulties of fellow students. Observations of the PASS classes provided in-depth information of their impact in developing numeracy skills, creating learning contexts where students could ask questions freely without fear of embarrassment, and a friendly atmosphere where students felt supported. To many the latter was more important than the actual numeracy skills development, and they viewed the classes as a 'safety net for learning' and 'a place for making friends'. These students also interpreted the PASS initiative as an indication of the faculty caring for its students, and developed a respect for the PASS leaders:

> They (PASS leaders) were helpful ... they got me through a lot of things be-cause they explain the concepts very well and some of them went to the trouble of doing a follow up after the PASS class, like emails and the sort of thing, so that I can ask more questions that I come across.

> The class ... it's basically a one-to-one approach. They sort of give the actual feel of what they experience, what they've come across and they being the top students ... They sort of give you an idea of how to learn and the kind of an-swers they would come up with. In this way, so you have rough idea of the top notch work the Faculty expects from students.

The learning gained through in specific disciplinary areas is also evident:

> With Accounting I found that the PASS group is useful because they [PASS leaders] do the work and they explain everything, and we do the asking about some key terms, some important information. I didn't study accounting be-fore, but if I do all this work in PASS, I find it's really helpful. The system really works and it's really worth it to do.

Social cohesion

Lack of 'social cohesion' on campuses, despite the rich diversity that has emerged with the globalization of higher education, was evident in the findings and generally consistent with those reported earlier in the literature (see Bruch & Barty 1990, Burke 1990, Smart et al. 2000, Volet & Ang 1998). Perspectives were gained from students who were regarded as being local Australian (English speaking), local Australian (from diverse backgrounds), and international students. It was the latter group that felt the most isolated, expressing disappointment at not being able to the intermingle with Australian students as they had expected:

> Basically there should be more interaction between overseas and local students. If they really want this university to be an international university they should foster more interaction ... After coming here students become quite disappointed because they immerse themselves in an Asian community, which isn't' good in the long-term.

> It is so hard to make local friends, especially for the group project ... their English is better, and I think that if we group with them, we'll do much better. They seem not to like to group with us. They like to group with their own culture people ... But even if we can group with them, they might criticise us ... I don't know ... But I still like to look for local friends. I would like to talk to them directly, and invite them to be a member in my group ... I could learn a lot.

But, despite the disappointment in not be able to find Australian friends or learning partners, some students were still able to make the best of their intercultural experiences on campus, even though limited:

> It has been a good experience overall, even though it has been a bit different from what I expected. I thought Australia would be a place where there would be a lot of Australians and that I would have a chance to mingle with a lot of Australians, but I have found that, especially the course which I am studying, commerce, is quite Asian dominated. So, most of the time I am meeting Asians, apart from the Aussie lecturers ... But I've has great fun knowing some Australians and a lot of Asians from different countries.

In contrast, some local Australian (English speaking) students held the view that students from diverse backgrounds did not understand their 'many commitments off campus', and tended to 'concentrate more on their studies only and did not participate in extra-curricular activities', making it difficult to find the time or occasion to interact. They also commented on the generally 'poor language and communication skills as a major problem in group assignments'. At the same time, Australian students were positive about the 'exposure to many different cultures and the learning of new things', and admired 'the persistence' of students from diverse backgrounds in pursuing their studies and achieving academic success despite the many hardships encountered.

Discussion and conclusion

The globalization of higher education has brought a 'cultural mix' of students and levels of diversity that have not been experienced in our classrooms before. Diversity brings together a rich milieu of cultures, a multiplicity of ideas, new ways of thinking, and new skills, norms and values. It also presents challenges by drawing attention to cultural differences and creating new expectations. This study sought to capture the experiences of students from diverse backgrounds, and provide insights into factors that facilitate and/or hinder their academic and sociocultural adaptation.

More specifically, it identifies transitional factors such as 'culture shock' and 'study shock' that many students have to contend with in the process of adapting to their new living and learning environments respectively. These factors are bound to impact on students' wellbeing and their learning, and therefore need to be taken into consideration when managing students from diverse backgrounds. Researchers and practitioners (for example, Burke 1990, Smart et al. 2000), stress the importance of appropriate preparation for entry into new and foreign cultures, and recommend the establishment of effective acculturation programs, both at the stages of pre-departure and arrival, as well as ongoing strategies to cater for needs that may arise.

Students arriving in the faculty seek a quality educational experience and move out of familiar learning environments in pursuit of this education. The study identifies and confirms factors that hinder student learning, including differences in learning and teaching styles experienced in prior learning backgrounds, the lack of preparation for coping with these differences, lack of graduate attributes such as critical and analytical thinking, and independent and research-oriented approaches to learning. However, what many of these students do bring with them is the enthusiasm for and commitment to learning. It is important that the faculty captures this commitment and continues to offer and expand strategies to facilitate transition and bridge learning differences. Students acknowledged academic staff commitment to teaching and knowledge about their disciplines. Nevertheless, academic development programs should also be offered to ensure that teaching staff are also supported in understanding, managing and teaching to the diversity inherent in their classrooms. The academic development initiatives could include strategies for facilitating inclusive teaching and intercultural interactions between students from diverse backgrounds and local students, an issue that is not easy to resolve, as indicated in the literature (see Grace & Gravestock 2009, Kingston & Forland 2008, Smart et al. 2000, Tartar 2005).

The evidence suggests that the faculty's support programs have been effective in assisting students in their learning and language development, the latter being of particular concern. Indications are that those students who access support programs benefit in both the quality of their learning and in confidence. However, just how effective the programs are in assisting the wider student population, beyond the group interviewed, is not known and requires further investigation. At the same time, students from diverse backgrounds must also take responsibility for their learning and cultural adaptation. They need to ensure that they are well prepared for entry into their new learning environments, have appropriate prior knowledge and skills in the disciplinary area in which they choose to study, and develop competence in English language and the language of their discipline. Clearly, those who make the effort to continuously improve their language competence, using some of the strategies revealed in this study, benefit in both the quality of their work and in their sense of self. Both are important.

The faculty (and Australian higher education, in general) continues to attract high levels of students from diverse backgrounds. Investigation into the student experience in this area, therefore, must continue to ensure understanding of factors that impact on their learning and the highest level of student satisfaction.

References

Ahmad S (2006). International student expectations: the voice of Indian students. *Australian International Education Conference.*

Australian Education International (2000). *Overseas students statistics 2000.* Canberra: Australian Government Publishing Service.

Ballard B & Clanchy J (1991). *Teaching students from overseas: a brief guide for lecturers and supervisors.* Melbourne: Longman Cheshire.

Berry JW & Sam DL (1997). Acculturation and adaptation. In JW Berry, MH Segall & C Kagiticibasi (Eds), *Handbook of cross-cultural psychology: social behavior and applications,* 3, (pp191–326). Boston, MA: Allyn and Bacon.

Biggs J (1990). Asian students approaches to learning: implications for teaching and learning. Keynote discussion paper, *8th Australasian Tertiary Learning Skills and Language Conference,* Queensland University of Technology, 11–13 July.

Bruch T & Barty A (1998). Internationalizing British higher education. In P Scott (Ed), *The globalization of higher education,* (pp18–31). Buckingham: The Society for Research into Higher Education.

Burke B (2001). Adjusting to a new culture and learning system: double trouble for international students. Paper presented at the IDP Seminar, Bangkok, March.

Burns B (1990). The adjustment of overseas students: a study of the academic, cultural, social and personal problems of overseas first year students at an Australian university. In M Innes-Brown & P Hedges (Eds), *Proceedings of the Internationalisation of Industry, Government and Education in Western Australia Conference,* Curtin University of Technology, Perth.

Chalmers D & Volet S (1997). Misconceptions about students from South-East Asia studying in Australia. *Higher Education Research and Development,* 16(1): 1–11.

Cullingford C & Gunn S (Eds) (2005). *Globalisation, education and culture shock*. England: Ashgate.

Denzin NK & Lincoln YS (1998). Entering the field of qualitative research. In Denzin NK & Lincoln YS (Eds), *The landscape of qualitative research: theories and issues*. Thousand Oaks, CA: Sage.

East J (2001). International students identified as customers: their expectations and perceptions. *Changing Identities: Language and Academic Skills Conference*, University of Wollongong.

Grace S & Gravestock P (2009). *Inclusion and diversity*. New York: Routledge.

Harris R (1997). Overseas students in the United Kingdom university system. *Higher Education*, 29: 77–92.

Hirsch D (2007). English language, academic support and academic outcomes: a discussion paper. *TESOL*, 2(2): 193–211.

Hofstede G (2001). *Culture's consequences: comparing values, behaviours, institutions and organizations across nations*. Thousand Oaks, CA: Sage.

Humfrey C (1999). *Managing international students*. Buckingham: Open University Press.

Kember D & Gow L (1991). A challenge to the anecdotal stereotype of the Asian student. *Studies in Higher Education*, 16(2): 117–28.

Kim D, Markham FS & Cangelosi JD (2002). Why students pursue the business degree: a comparison of business majors across universities. *Journal of Education for Business*, September–October: 28–32.

Kingston E & Forland H (2008). Bridging the gap in expectations between international students and academic staff. *Journal of Studies in International Education*, 12(2): 204–21.

Marton F, Dall'Alba G & Tse KL (1993). The paradox of the Chinese learner, occasional paper 93.1. Educational Research and Development Unit, Royal Melbourne Institute of Technology, Victoria.

Marx E (2001). *Breaking through culture shock*. London: Nicholas Brealey Publishing.

Mazzarol T & Soutar G (2002). 'Push-pull' factors influencing student destination choice. *International Journal of Educational Management*, 16(2): 82–90.

Miles MB & Huberman AM (1994). *Qualitative data analysis*. London: Sage.

Niles S (1995). Cultural differences in learning motivation and learning strategies: a comparison of overseas and Australian students at an Australian university. *International Journal of Intercultural Relations*, 19(3): 369–85.

Oberg K (1960). Culture shock: adjustments to new cultural environments. *Practical Anthropology*, 7: 177–82.

Phillips DJ (1990). Overseas students and their impact on the changing face of professional education in universities. Paper presented at the *Australian Association for Research in Education Annual Conference: the Changing Face of Professional Education*, Sydney University.

Ramburuth P & McCormick J (2001). Learning diversity in higher education: a comparative study of Asian international and Australian students. *Higher Education*, 42: 333–50.

Ramburuth P & Welch C (2005). Educating the global manager: the role of cultural diversity in international business education. *Journal of Teaching in International Business*, 16(3):5–27.

Smart D, Volet S & Ang G (2000). *Fostering social cohesion in universities: bridging the cultural divide*. Canberra: Australian Education Foundation, Department of Education, Training and Youth Affairs.

Soutar GN & Turner JP (2002). Students' preferences for university: a conjoint analysis. *International Journal of Education Management*, 16(1): 40–45.

Sovic S (2008). Lost in transition? The international students' experience project. London: Creating Learning in Practice, Center for Excellence in Teaching and Learning, University of the Arts.

Twigg C (2005). Overseas students in higher education. In C Cullingford & S Gunn (Eds), *Globalisation, education and culture shock*. London: Ashgate.

Volet SE & Ang G (1998). Culturally mixed groups on international campuses: an opportunity for inter-cultural learning. *Higher Education Research and Development*, 17(1): 5–23.

Wierzbicka A (1991). *Cross-cultural pragmatics: the semantics of human interaction*. New York: Mouton de Gruyter.

Willis MK & Kennedy RE (2004). An evaluation of how student expectations are formed in a higher education context: the case of Hong Kong. *Journal of Marketing for Higher Education*, 14(1): 1–21.

Wong JK (2004). Are the learning styles of Asian international students culturally or contextually based? *International Education Journal*, 4(4): 154–66.

Yin RK (2003), *Case study research: design and methods*. Thousand Oaks, CA: Sage.

Index